ALAN AYCKBOURN

Plays One

A Chorus of Disapproval

A Small Family Business

Henceforward . . .

Man of the Moment

Introduced by
the Author

faber and faber

LONDON · BOSTON

This collection first published in 1995 by Faber and Faber Limited
3 Queen Square London WC1N 3AU

Photoset by Parker Typesetting Service, Leicester
Printed in England by Clays Ltd, St Ives plc

All rights whatsoever in these plays are strictly reserved and application for
permission to perform them must be made in advance, before rehearsals
begin, to Casarotto Ramsay Ltd, National House, 60–66 Wardour Street,
London W1Z 3HP

A CIP record for this book
is available from the British Library

ISBN 0–571–17680–1

2 4 6 8 10 9 7 5 3 1

Alan Ayckbourn

'If people want to know about life in England in the Sixties, Seventies and Eighties, they will need to study Ayckbourn's plays. He is a profoundly moral writer and I think he has reached a new synthesis between the comic and the serious – the painfully funny . . . We are a fortunate age to have had our own Molière.' Sir Peter Hall

Born in London in 1939, Alan Ayckbourn spent most of his childhood in Sussex and was educated at Haileybury. Leaving there one Friday at the age of seventeen, he went into the theatre the following Monday and has been working in it ever since as, variously, a stage manager, sound technician, lighting technician, scene painter, prop-maker, actor, writer and director. These talents developed thanks to his mentor, Stephen Joseph, whom he first met in 1958 upon joining the newly formed Library Theatre in Scarborough. He was a BBC Radio Drama Producer from 1965 to 1970, returning to Scarborough to take up the post of Artistic Director of the Theatre in the Round, left vacant after Stephen Joseph's death in 1967. He has premièred over forty of his plays at this Yorkshire theatre where he spends the greater part of the year directing other people's work. Some thirty of his plays have subsequently been produced either in the West End, at the Royal National Theatre or the Royal Shakespeare Company. They have been translated into forty languages and have been performed throughout the world, receiving many national and international awards.

Contents

Introduction

I suppose what immediately links these plays is that they were written within a four-year period (1984–87) and could be loosely described as belonging to my 'social' period.

That is to say, they all deal with Society, capital S, in contrast to some of my earlier domestic pieces where human activity tended to revolve around the sexual tensions of the dining table or the three-piece suite. Even *Henceforward* . . . in its claustrophobic way is light years apart from the family familiarity of, say, *The Norman Conquests*.

A Chorus of Disapproval had a curious start. I wanted to write a play about an operatic society, heaven knows why. My first idea was to pen something for a large cast, using professional principals and a supporting cast of dozens of amateur singers. The latter would be seated in the auditorium, to all appearance like members of the audience, but they would from time to time during the action stand up and sing some linking comment or other like an operatic Greek chorus. I planned to base the play around a presumed production of *The Vagabond King*. I had read the libretto and I confess it amused me no end, particularly its choreographic stage directions.

Several things conspired to thwart the original idea. The Rudolph Friml Estate, fearing for their play, refused to release the rights. For which I didn't blame them one bit. Simultaneously, those members of the local Scarborough Operatic Society whom I had approached seemed reluctant to accept anything but leading roles, for which I didn't blame them either; and finally Equity, the Professional

Actors' Trade Union, declared the whole idea of including amateurs in this way unacceptable. Which forced me into swift solutions, all of them, it transpired, blessings in disguise.

First I decided to work with an entirely professional company and thus with a much smaller cast; sensible and far more economic. Secondly, to avoid further copyright problems, I found an author who had been dead so long that he and his relatives no longer cared. Which led me to a musical play I greatly admired and had always wanted to produce, Gay's *The Beggar's Opera*. Which in turn provided the missing piece to the whole venture. Gay's play had a plot which echoed almost perfectly the one I intended to write and provided the perfect mirror image on which to build my own dramatic structure.

Moral: always work with something you admire and not with something which you only set out to make fun of. That way you might even manage to raise your game rather than lower it.

A Small Family Business, written in 1986, was unusual in that it was the first play for over twenty years which I had to submit and await someone else's verdict as to whether it merited production.

Sir Peter Hall, who had introduced me to the National Theatre in 1977 with *Bedroom Farce*, had been an occasional producer of my plays on the South Bank ever since (including *A Chorus of Disapproval*). In 1985, Peter asked me if I'd like to take a break from Scarborough and come and run my own company at the National. My brief was to direct three plays over a two-year period, one in the conventional proscenium-arched Lyttelton, another in the large open-staged Olivier and a third on the smaller-scale, flexible Cottesloe stage. The only condition was that the one in the Olivier must be a new one of my own. I would have choice of the other two plays and be able to hand-pick my own acting company of twenty. The prospect of playing with such large toys proved irresistible.

I knew the Olivier of old. Not the friendliest of spaces for those purveyors of modern low-key naturalistic drama. 'For love scenes you stand six feet apart and shout at each other,' Michael Bryant, that most experienced of Olivier performers once advised me. 'All other scenes you stand twenty feet apart and yell.'

In the end, the solution I came up with was a variation of the one I first used with my first play in the Lyttelton, *Bedroom Farce*. Namely, if you can't find anything big enough to fill the space, then divide the space. With *A Small Family Business* I found the perfect excuse to put on stage something that had always been till then beyond my wildest budget, namely a two-storey house complete with working kitchen and bathroom. The biggest dolls' house in the world. Peter described the piece as a modern morality play. He said it reminded him of Ben Jonson. I later read some Ben Jonson but I must confess I didn't understand much of it. Still, I was very flattered.

While I was waiting a year to direct that (the National always need things so far in advance) I wrote *Henceforward* . . . This combined two or three of my interests at the time. It's a play about the creative process: always difficult to portray on stage and rarely that convincing. Actors sitting pretending to be novelists, scratching away fiercely with quill pens whilst declaiming their prose aloud at twice the speed they are supposedly writing – *Wuthering Heights* in five days. It never makes good theatre. Nor do classical composers humming or painters holding up one thumb and squinting, and as for poets . . . But a modern composer, that was a different matter, especially one who worked entirely electronically with pre-sampled and generated sound. The result there could be, with only the smallest dramatic licence, quite immediate.

Henceforward . . . is on the surface a comedy but it

does present a gloomy prediction of a possible future world where society, maybe as a direct result of the behaviour portrayed in *A Small Family Business*, has all but collapsed. And I suppose any play in which the hero allows his wife and daughter to die whilst he finishes writing his latest composition can't be considered all funny. (I wonder where I got this reputation for being a comic dramatist.)

Jerome, the composer, was based on someone whom I met briefly one Christmas: an art historian who chose to live, or rather to remain living, in one of the bleaker of our Northern inner-city no-go zones. Alone on the top floor of his vandalized and abandoned tower block he sat writing, surrounded by the sounds, the images and the beauty of Renaissance music and art. 'Why do you stay there?' I asked him. His answer was quite chilling. 'I feel', he said, 'that if I go, then the light might finally go out completely.' The idea that each of us has a duty to provide illumination, as it were, in order that others might see more clearly is an image that has remained with me.

Henceforward . . . also provided me with the opportunity to indulge my love of robots. In particular the British (sorry-about-that-mate-we're-still-waiting-for-the-part) sort of robot: totally eccentric, idiosyncratic, unserviceable and unreliable.

Finally, in *Man of the Moment*, written in 1988, I turned my attention to the nature of celebrity and fame, particularly with regard to television. Based on the unoriginal but eternally true observation that good news is no news and bad news is good news, I reflected on the question of why it is that the camera can often make the really good appear dull whilst transforming villains into instant sources of fascination and attraction. The answer is, of course, that whereas it doesn't tell flat lies, the camera often tells less than the whole truth. And to make it work for us we master techniques and tricks, all those skills which come naturally to the manipulators, the dissemblers and the con men but which are often beyond the capability of the earnest, the decent and the sincerely honest.

Driving each day to the National whilst rehearsing *Man of the Moment*, I passed posters for the film *Buster*, celebrating the life and crimes of one of the Great Train Robbers. It occurred to me then that the forgotten man in that media-celebrated event was the train driver himself who subsequently died of his injuries. Who would make the film about him? It was a small journey from there to the staged reunion between Douglas Beechey, the have-a-go bank clerk and the successful media star and reformed bank robber, Vic Parks. Once again, and by no means for the last time, I brought light and darkness face to face on stage, clear cut and identifiable.

Would that the choice was always that easy.

Alan Ayckbourn
March 1995

A CHORUS OF DISAPPROVAL

Characters

Guy Jones
Dafydd Ap Llewellyn
Hannah Llewellyn
Ian Hubbard
Fay Hubbard
Jarvis Huntley-Pike
Rebecca Huntley-Pike
Ted Washbrook
Enid Washbrook
Linda Washbrook, *their daughter*
Bridget Baines
Crispin Usher
Mr Ames
Raymond
Stage Managers (non-speaking)

The action occurs between the first rehearsal
and first performance of an amateur production of
Gay's *The Beggar's Opera* (February–May).
It takes place in and around
a small provincial theatre.

A Chorus of Disapproval was first presented at the Stephen Joseph Theatre, Scarborough, on 2 May 1984 with the following cast:

Guy Jones Lennox Greaves
Dafydd Ap Llewellyn Russell Dixon
Hannah Llewellyn Alwyne Taylor
Bridget Baines Jane Hollowood
Mr Ames Paul Todd
Enid Washbrook Dorcas Jones
Rebecca Huntley-Pike Heather Stoney
Fay Hubbard Lesley Meade
Ian Hubbard Mark Jax
Jarvis Huntley-Pike Alan Thompson
Ted Washbrook Robert Cotton
Crispin Usher Daniel Flynn
Linda Washbrook Caroline Webster

and subsequently at the Olivier Theatre, London, on 1 August 1985 with the following cast:

Guy Jones Bob Peck
Dafydd Ap Llewellyn Michael Gambon
Hannah Llewellyn Imelda Staunton
Bridget Baines Jenny Galloway
Mr Ames Paul Todd
Enid Washbrook Jane Wenham
Rebecca Huntley-Pike Moira Redmond
Fay Hubbard Gemma Craven
Ian Hubbard Paul Bentall
Jarvis Huntley-Pike David Ryall
Ted Washbrook James Hayes
Crispin Usher Daniel Flynn
Linda Washbrook Kelly Hunter

Directed by Alan Ayckbourn
Settings by Alan Tagg
Musical Direction by Paul Todd

Act One

The lights come up abruptly on a stage filled with people and we are suddenly and unexpectedly into the final moments of a first performance of an amateur production of Gay's The Beggar's Opera. *The performance by PALOS (The Pendon Amateur Light Operatic Society) is filled with gusto and enthusiasm. What it lacks in polish (in some quarters) it makes up for in flourish. Among the performers are centre, on a small raised platform,* **Guy Jones** (*Macheath*).

He is surrounded by his 'doxies'. Amongst these are **Hannah Llewellyn** (*Polly Peachum*), **Linda Washbrook** (*Lucy Lockit*), **Rebecca Huntley-Pike** (*Mrs Vixen*), **Fay Hubbard** (*Dolly Trull*), **Bridget Baines** (*Jenny Diver*) *and others. Also present are* **Ted** *and* **Enid Washbrook** (*Mr and Mrs Peachum*), **Ian Hubbard** (*Matt of the Mint*), **Crispin Usher** (*Filch*), **Jarvis Huntley-Pike** (*Lockit*) *and others. At the piano,* **Mr Ames** (*The Beggar*).

Guy (*as Macheath*)
Thus I stand like the Turk, with his Doxies around;
From all sides their Glances his Passion confound;
For black, brown and fair, his Inconstancy burns,
And the different Beauties subdue him by turns:
Each calls forth her Charms to provoke his Desires:
Though willing to all; with but one he retires.
But think of this Maxim, and put off your Sorrow,
The Wretch of To-day, may be happy To-morrow.

All
Each calls forth her Charms and provokes his Desires:

7

Though willing to all; with but one he retires.
But think of this Maxim, and put off your Sorrow,
The Wretch of To-day, may be happy To-morrow (*etc.*)

*The dance that accompanies the final chorus finally
finishes with a triumphant tableau. The lights dim
slightly to indicate the curtain has fallen. The company
shuffles quickly into fresh positions. Muffled applause is
heard. The lights brighten as the curtain goes up and the
applause becomes louder and clearer. The company is
all smiles at once. Several of these pre-rehearsed variants
follow with finally Guy as Macheath taking a solo call
and being applauded by his fellow artistes. Graciously,
he presents his two leading ladies, Hannah (Polly) and
Linda (Lucy). Both, in turn, are presented with
bouquets. Next, the company turns in the direction of
Mr Ames (The Beggar) at the piano who rises and
makes a sheepish acknowledgement. The general bow
follows and, at this point, with a sort of reluctant
alacrity, the producer, Dafydd Llewellyn, springs on to
the stage from the auditorium. The cast, in turn,
applauds him. Looking somewhat incongruous in his
modern clothes, he bows modestly and finally raises his
hands for silence. The applause ceases.*

Dafydd Ladies and gentlemen, thank you all for that
wonderful, wonderful reception. There are a million
people I ought to thank. There are a million people I'd like
to thank and there are a million people I'm afraid I'm not
going to thank, at least by name or you'll be sitting here
till tomorrow morning.

He laughs. The cast smiles with relief.

I will, if I may, restrict myself to saying this. Thank you,
wonderful cast. Thank you, wonderful, wonderful Stage
Management. Thank you, marvellous audience. But thank
you most of all to one individual without whom none of

8

this could have happened. He joined PALOS but a few weeks ago. The emergency occurred and the man rose to the occasion. What more can I say? – He's been . . . Well, your reception said it all. Ladies and gentlemen, our very special Macheath, Mr Guy Jones.

Dafydd turns and presents Guy who acknowledges fresh applause. Again, the cast joins in. The curtain falls finally. The lights again dim to indicate this and the applause becomes muffled, finally dying out. The cast starts to disperse, chattering and laughing and moving towards the dressing room. Guy, quite suddenly, is all alone. No one, once the curtain has fallen, speaks to or even acknowledges him. He stands for a moment before starting to remove his costume, beginning with his wig and hat, then jacket and cravat. Stage managers begin to move round him re-setting and striking props, including the raised platform. In time, the remaining stage lights go out and are replaced by harsh working lights. Similarly the stage reverts from a performance to a rehearsal state. Hannah, still in her basic Polly costume, comes on carrying Guy's clothes. She watches him for a second.

Hannah (*softly*) Well done.

Guy Mmm?

Hannah Well done.

Guy (*dully*) Thank you.

Hannah (*indicating his clothes*) Here are your . . .

Guy makes no move.

I'll leave them here . . .

Hannah puts the clothes gently on a table and makes to leave.

Guy Thanks.

Hannah (*turning as she goes*) I – (*changing her mind*) Right. I must . . . Goodbye.

Guy Yes. Goodbye.

Hannah goes. Guy finishes changing, finally putting on his mac. He seems about to leave but turns in the doorway and surveys the darkened stage. We hear the distant sound of the piano playing 'Youth's the Season made for Joys'. It's a fragment, a wistful echo of his memory. It is now three to four months earlier. February and very cold. Voices and laughter are heard from a distance in the dressing rooms offstage. Guy, having entered from the street, stands uncertainly wondering whether to proceed further. Bridget, in a coat, hat and boots, enters with a small rehearsal table which she bangs down rather noisily. At first appearance she is a rather graceless, galumphing girl who has long ago dispensed with social niceties and conventional sexual role-playing. She gives no sign of having seen Guy but continues on her way. Guy makes a little gurgling sound in his throat.

Bridget (*turning back at the last minute*) Did you want somebody?

Guy Mr Jones.

Bridget Mr Jones?

Guy Yes.

Bridget No.

Guy No?

Bridget No. No Mr Jones here.

Guy No, no . . .

Bridget This is the Operatic Society.

Guy Yes, yes.

Bridget We haven't any Mr Jones.

Guy No. You won't have.

Bridget No?

Guy Well, you might have but . . . No, I'm Mr Jones.

Bridget You're Mr Jones?

Guy Yes. (*Slight pause.*) Sorry.

Bridget We'll start again, shall we?

Guy Yes.

Bridget I've just come in. Right?

Guy Right.

Bridget OK. So. Who do you want?

Guy Mr Llewellyn. Mr – (*looking at an envelope he has taken from his pocket*) – Mr D. Ap Llewellyn.

Bridget Is he expecting you?

Guy Yes, I think so. He said round about this time.

Bridget Wait there, then. Mr Jones, yes?

Guy Yes.

> *Bridget goes.*

> *Guy hops around a little. Half because of nerves, half because of the cold. He spies a piano in the corner and moves to it. From the envelope he is holding he produces a small piece of music, obviously torn from a book. With an inexperienced finger, he taps out the odd note and attempts to match them with his voice.*

Whatever he plays appears to be outside his range. He clears his throat but it's quite obvious that his voice has packed up completely. With sudden determination, Guy screws up the piece of music, stuffs it into his pocket and marches towards the door. Before he can leave, there is a burst of chatter from off and Dafydd enters. He is a busy, slightly overweight, energetic man in his late thirties. A live-wire. The mainspring of the society. Never using one word where three will do, never walking when he can hurry. Whatever the temperature, Dafydd always appears to find it a little on the warm side.

Dafydd (*seeing Guy*) My dear chap, I'm so sorry. I'm deeply sorry. I knew you were coming. I wrote down you were coming. It slipped my mind. How do you do? Dafydd ap Llewellyn. Good of you to come along. We're on our first stages of rehearsal. Just getting started. Broken for tea for ten minutes.

Guy Ah. Yes.

Dafydd (*calling*) Mr Ames? I'll just fetch Mr Ames in and he can play for you. Brought something along to sing, have you?

Guy Well, I had sort of –

Dafydd (*calling*) Mr Ames? Otherwise we've got plenty of bits and pieces lying around, you know. And of course, Mr Ames, he's encyclopaedic. He's played practically every musical comedy you could name. Choose a key, choose a tune, choose a tempo, he's away – where the bloody hell is he? Excuse me. (*He moves to the door, calling.*) Mr Ames? – ah, there you are. This is Mr Ames.

Mr Ames enters. He is a small, intensely shy man whose silent, unobtrusive personality is in direct contrast to that of Dafydd.

Dafydd Mr Ames, this is Mr – God, I'm afraid I don't even know your name – Mr . . . ?

Guy Jones.

Dafydd Mr Jones – not Welsh, are you?

Guy No. No. 'Fraid not. From Leeds.

Dafydd (*dubiously*) Leeds?

Guy Originally.

Dafydd Originally from Leeds. Right. This is our Mr Ames. Mr Ames, Mr Jones is going to sing for us. Give us an idea of his range. And intonation. Which is a polite way of saying can he sing in tune? (*He laughs.*) If not, welcome to the club. What are you, tenor, are you?

Guy I think I'm a sort of light baritone. I think.

Dafydd Oh yes? Light baritone, eh? Yes, we've got plenty of those lurking in the back row, haven't we, Mr Ames? They're what we call our down the octave brigade.

Guy (*laughing*) Yes, yes . . .

Dafydd Come on then. Let's have a listen. Did you say you had some music? Or shall we ask Mr Ames to rifle through his golden treasure chest of memories?

Guy (*fumbling for his music*) No, I've brought . . . (*unable to find it and rummaging through his pockets*) Just a second . . .

Dafydd Bit of *Merry Widow*? Fancy that?

Guy (*somewhat panic-stricken at the thought*) No, no, please . . .

Dafydd *West Side Story*? *Oklahoma*? *The King and I*?

Mr Ames plays a bar of this last.

Guy (*finding his music at last*) No. Here we are. Found it. Here. (*He holds up the crumpled piece of music.*)

Dafydd Is that it?

Guy Sorry.

Dafydd You shouldn't have splashed out like that, you know. Not just for an audition. (*He laughs again, and takes the scrap of music from Guy and gives it to Mr Ames.*) Here we are, Mr Ames. Second Act of *Tannhäuser*, by the look of it. (*He laughs.*) No, I'm sorry, Mr Jones. We're only having a little joke. Don't mind us, you'll get used to it. Possibly. (*briskly*) Right. Seriously for a moment. Be serious, Llewellyn, boy. What have we got here? (*putting on his reading glasses*) My word, my word. You still claim you're not Welsh? What does that say there, Mr Ames? What does it say to you? 'All Through the Night'. '*Ar hyd y nos*'.

Guy Yes. Coincidence.

Dafydd (*mock serious*) Well. I don't know. Should we allow a man from Leeds to sing this, Mr Ames? Eh? What do you think?

Guy It was just the only song I happen to . . .

Dafydd Well. Seeing your name is Jones. Maybe. Special dispensation, eh?

Guy (*gamely trying to keep up with the joke*) Thank you very much . . .

Dafydd Just this once.

Guy It was the only song I knew in the piano stool. My mother used to sing it. Years ago.

Dafydd Your mother's Welsh, then?

Guy No.

Dafydd But she sings?

Guy No, she . . .

Dafydd Bring her down. Bring her down next time with you.

Guy No, she's dead.

Dafydd (*sadly*) Ah. Well. Too late then. Too late. Sad. Can you play that, do you think, Mr Ames?

Mr Ames Yes, yes . . . (*He plays a chord or two, peering at the music.*)

> Enid Washbrook appears in the doorway during this. Behind Enid, her daughter Linda cranes round her to catch a glimpse of the newcomer.

Enid Are we starting again, Dafydd?

Dafydd In just one moment, Enid, just one moment. We'll give you a call. We're just going to hear this gentleman sing . . .

Enid Oh, right. Excuse us, won't you . . .

Dafydd We'll give you a call.

Enid (*to Guy, as they go*) Good luck.

Guy Thank you.

> Enid and Linda go out.

Dafydd Now, Mr Jones, the million dollar question. Are you going to sing this in Welsh or in English?

Guy Well, I'm sorry, in English if that's all right . . .

Dafydd (*hopping about in mock pain*) Oh, oh, oh, oh . . . Like 'Pomp and Circumstance' in Japanese . . . If you must, if you must . . . Right. When you're ready, Mr Ames. Take it away . . .

Mr Ames plays the introduction. Dafydd moves away slightly. Guy opens his mouth to sing. Before he can do so, Dafydd is there before him sounding off in a full Welsh tenor.

Dafydd
Holl amrantau'r ser ddywedant, Ar hyd y nos,
Dyma'r ffordd i fro gogon-iant, Ar hyd y nos;
Go-lau a-rall yw tywyll-wch, I arddangos gwir
  brydferthwch,
Teulu'r nefoedd mewn ta-welwch, Ar hyd y nos.

Dafydd stops singing. Mr Ames stops playing. There is a respectful silence.

Sorry. I'm sorry. I sincerely beg your pardon, Mr Jones. Every time I hear . . . (*He breaks off, too moved to continue. Then, clapping Guy on the shoulder*) It's all yours. Take it away, boy.

Guy (*horrified*) Right.

Mr Ames re-starts the introduction. Dafydd moves away to the far reaches of the auditorium. Guy, by now very nervous, misses the introduction first time round but manages on the second.

(*nervously*)
While the moon her watch is keeping,
All through the night,
While the we–

Dafydd (*calling from the darkness*) Mr Jones, sorry to interrupt you just as you were getting underway. That's lovely. Very pleasant. A little tip. Just try facing out this way a bit more, would you? You're not in need of the music, are you?

Guy (*straining to see Dafydd*) No, no.

Dafydd No, it didn't appear you were reading it. (*waving Guy away from the safety of the piano*) Now. Just try placing your weight equally on both your feet. Legs slightly apart. That's it. A bit more. Now, can you feel yourself balanced, can you?

Guy Yes, yes.

Dafydd Singing is a great deal to do with balance, Mr Jones. Balance, you see. You can't sing on one leg now, can you? You'd feel unbalanced.

Guy Yes, yes.

Dafydd Good. Shoulders back, then. Shoulders right back, man.

Guy Yes.

Dafydd That's better. That's better. Now, before you start this time, Mr Jones, I want you for a moment to breathe, if you would. Like this. (*Dafydd demonstrates noisily from the darkness.*) In through the nose, you see, out through the mouth. That's it. And again. Deep as you can, that's it.

    Guy sways and staggers.

No, no. There's no need to hyperventilate. Breathe normally, that's all. Now, Mr Jones, can you feel all that air, can you? In your passages? Can you feel it rushing along your passages?

Guy Yes, yes.

Dafydd Blowing the cobwebs from your passages?

Guy (*coughing slightly*) Yes.

    From this point, people begin to assemble, unseen by Guy, to listen to him. First to appear are Jarvis Huntley-Pike and Ted Washbrook. Jarvis is a man in his late fifties – the epitome of a 'Knowing Northerner'. Ted, ten years younger, is a mild, pleasant, abstracted, ineffectual man.

Dafydd Now you look like a real singer, Mr Jones. From the top, please, Mr Ames. From the top.

Mr Ames starts again.

(*over the introduction*) Let it flow out of you, Mr Jones. Let it flow. It's a song that sings itself, you see. Like a river. (*singing*) Holl amrantau'r . . . You see?

Guy Yes, yes. (*He waits for the introduction to come round again.*)

Fay Hubbard and Enid Washbrook enter and stand watching. Fay is an extremely attractive woman in her thirties. One of the local younger married jet-set. Enid, a little older, is a careworn sort of woman, even less effectual than her husband, Ted.

(*singing*)
While the moon her watch is keeping,
All through the night,
While the weary world is sleeping,
All through the night.

Dafydd (*over this, as he sings*) Good, good. Don't hunch. Don't hunch. You can't sing if you're hunched, Mr Jones. Good. (*joining in with him, singing*) All through the night.

Linda Washbrook and Crispin Usher have meantime entered. Linda is the nicely brought-up, rather petulant daughter of her over-anxious parents, Ted and Enid. Crispin, her currently unsuitable boyfriend, is a tough, hostile young man very much at odds with his present environment and with most of the Society.

Guy
O'er my bosom gently stealing,

Visions of delight revealing,
Breathes a pure and holy feeling
All through the night.

As Guy reaches the final stages of the song, Ian Hubbard and Rebecca Huntley-Pike appear. They are followed by Bridget. Ian, Fay's husband, is almost her male counterpart. An ambitious young man with a cultivated laid-back cool designed to make money and charm women, in that order. Rebecca, Jarvis's wife, is younger than him by a few years. She has that dignified appearance of one who has just had several stiff drinks. Maybe she has. Guy finishes.

Dafydd (*applauding*) Bravo. Bravo.

The rest of the company joins in his applause. Guy jumps in alarm, unaware that such a large audience has gathered.

Ah, here they all are. Ladies and gentlemen, may I present a new member of our Society. Mr Jones, who has just passed with flying colours.

A burst of general chatter and greeting.

(*through this*) Now, these are – these are a lot of different people who are going to have to introduce themselves. I can't be doing with that.

The following section overlaps.

Rebecca Hallo, welcome. Is he playing Matt the Mint?

Dafydd Ah, well. Maybe, maybe.

Rebecca We need a Matt the Mint. He'd be wonderful. Lovely voice.

Guy (*smiling gratefully*) Thank you.

Rebecca Isn't it? A lovely voice. Most unusual.

Fay Yes.

Rebecca Mr Jones, is it?

Guy Guy.

Rebecca Guy. Oh, that's a nice name. I like the name, Guy, don't you? It's very masculine.

Enid Manly, yes. Manly.

Fay Frightfully, yes.

Ian Are we going on or going home? I'm for going home.

Jarvis I don't care what we do. Five past ten, I'm in the pub. I tell you.

Dafydd Everybody, could I have your attention? Please. Just a second, everybody.

Bridget (*shouting*) Shut up!

Rebecca I do wish she wouldn't shout like that.

Dafydd Now, everybody, I must apolo–

Rebecca Why can't she just ask people to be quiet?

Dafydd I must apologize, ladies and gentlemen, for making much, much slower progress than I anticipated. So, apologies for calling you all in and for keeping you hanging around. Mind you, I must say this evening has not been wasted. We've done some good solid groundwork and that's surely going to pay off later. So what I'd like to do just before we call it a night, is a quick recap from the top. OK? All right, Ted?

Ted From the top?

Dafydd If you'd be so kind. OK, Mr Ames?

Rebecca Oh, good. We can watch.

Ted (*to Mr Ames*) We're going from the top, apparently.

Mr Ames Right.

Jarvis What's the time, then?

Ian We've got half an hour yet.

Fay (*to Rebecca*) Do you want to go over now?

Rebecca Not on your life. We've all been sitting back there in the cold for two and a half hours. Let's see what they've been up to, for heaven's sake.

Dafydd So. The house lights dim. Blackout. Mr Ames in position. Ted in position. And then the soft glow of lamp light very gently – and – cue.

Mr Ames (*reading as The Beggar*) If Poverty be a Title to Poetry, I am sure Nobody can dispute mine. I own myself of the Company of Beggars; and I make one at their Weekly Festivals at St Giles. I have a small Yearly Salary for my Catches, and am welcome to Dinner there whenever I please, which is more than most Poets can say.

Ted (*reading as Player*) As we believe by the Muses, 'tis but Gratitude in us to encourage Poetical Merit wherever we find it. Be the Author who he will, we push his Play as far as it will go. So (though you are in want) I wish you Success heartily. But I see 'tis time for us to withdraw; the Actors are preparing to begin. Play away the Overture.

> *Ted exits with a flourish. Then reappears somewhat sheepishly having evidently gone off the wrong way. He tiptoes across to the correct exit, and, with an apologetic look at Dafydd, goes. A silence.*

Dafydd (*choosing to ignore Ted's mistake*) Splendid, splendid. Well done.

Rebecca Is that it?

Dafydd Yes, yes. So far.

Rebecca That's all you've done?

Dafydd Yes.

Rebecca My God. We're not on till page 30. When do you want us? Next June?

Dafydd All right, all right.

Ted (*anxiously*) Was that OK?

Dafydd Marvellous, Ted, marvellous.

Rebecca Riveting. Can't wait to find out who done it. Right, let's have that drink, then.

A general move to the door. Chatter.

Jarvis (*confidentially to Dafydd*) Just looking at that scene, I think you'll find it might benefit from a bit of gesture, you know . . .

Dafydd (*gathering up his things*) Yes, yes, thank you, Jarvis. I'm sure it would . . .

Jarvis It's just in those days they used their arms a lot, you know. Great deal of gesture.

Dafydd Yes, well, I'll be stuffing it full of gestures at a later stage, Jarvis. Be patient. You won't see the stage for arm movements . . .

Jarvis You don't mind me saying . . . ?

Dafydd Not at all. It's just, you know with Ted you can't go too fast. It takes a month or two just to get him pointing the right way . . . You know old Ted. (*He laughs.*)

Jarvis (*going out*) You don't mind me coming up with the odd idea, do you, now and again?

Dafydd Not at all, Jarvis, any time . . . feel free . . .

Jarvis goes out.

(*calling*) You really must do a production yourself some time. (*muttering*) And I'll come and bugger yours up, you interfering old fascist . . . (*seeing Guy is still there*) Ah, Mr Jones, you're still here. Splendid. Fancy a quick pint? We usually go across the road to The Fleece. He's a cantankerous old bastard, the chap who runs it, but it's the best pint for 30 miles . . .

Guy Righto. Splendid. Lead on.

Bridget comes from backstage.

Dafydd Ah, Bridget. You'll switch off, will you?

Bridget Yes.

Dafydd Bridget's our stage manager. Also playing Jenny Diver. We couldn't function at all without Bridget. She's the one who keeps us all sane, Mr Jones.

Guy Good for you.

He smiles at Bridget. Bridget doesn't react. Dafydd gathers together his papers. Guy perseveres cheerily.

I'm just going over the road to brave this cantankerous old publican. See you over there, perhaps?

Dafydd You certainly will. Bridget's his daughter.

Guy Ah.

Bridget Are we picking it up tomorrow from where we stopped?

Dafydd Yes, we'll carry straight on, my love.

Bridget Right. From the bottom of page 1, then.

Dafydd Oh, now please, please. Don't you start, there's a 'dear. (*to Guy*) Fit then, are you, Mr Jones? Right. Away we go.

> *The scene changes to the pub. A crowded saloon bar containing most of the Society. Dafydd and Guy jostle their way in.*

Dafydd (*shouting above the din*) Tends to get a bit crowded but it's worth it for the beer.

Ian (*calling across*) Pint, Daf?

Dafydd Oh, bless you, my love. Though I think it's my shout.

Ian It's all right, I'm getting them.

Dafydd Pint for you, Mr Jones?

Guy Would it be all right to have a gin and tonic?

Dafydd Gin and tonic? That's what they're drinking in Leeds, is it? Right. (*calling*) Ian? Can you get this fellow a gin and tonic?

Ian Gin and tonic. Is he coming in here a lot, is he?

Dafydd (*laughing, to Guy*) You mustn't mind him. He's got a great sense of humour. Ian and his brother, they're in partnership together. The brother does the work. Ian spends the money. (*He laughs.*)

Rebecca (*her voice ringing across the pub, to Guy*) We've all voted for you to play Matt the Mint. We think you're lovely.

Guy Thank you.

Dafydd Mrs Huntley-Pike. Another singer we put well to the back. In her case preferably in the car park.

Guy Like me, you mean? (*He laughs.*)

Dafydd God, no. You haven't heard her. If she sang in the dairy she'd make cheese. I tell you. Married, of course, to old Councillor Huntley-Potty-Pike. One of the whiz-kids on our Council. Which explains why this town's in the state it is.

Ian (*arriving with the drinks*) There you go.

Dafydd Ah, thank you, Ian. Bless you.

Ian Gin and tonic.

Guy Thank you very much.

Ian Hope you don't want ice because he hasn't got any.

Dafydd He's got ice, the miserable old sod. He just hides it. You can't charge for it, don't put it out. That's his maxim. His beer mats are screwed to the bar. Cheers.

Ian Cheers.

Guy Here's to the – production.

Dafydd Yes, why not? Here's to it. *The Beggar's Opera*. (*waving his glass in the direction of the women's table*) To *The Beggar's Opera*.

Fay (*echoing*) Yes. *The Beggar's Opera*.

Rebecca Hear, hear. *The Beggar's Opera*.

Guy When do we – when does it – start? Open?

A phone rings faintly from behind the bar.

Dafydd Oh, not till May. We've got three and a half months yet. Still, with dear old Ted there, I think we're going to need it. Mind you, we've got used to him now, haven't we, Ian? We had him one time in, what was it, *Sound of Music*, was it? –

Bridget has appeared the other side of the bar and is

now calling and waving in an attempt to attract Dafydd's attention.

Bridget (*calling*) Dafydd. Dafydd.

Ian (*seeing her, to Dafydd*) Dafydd, I think she wants you.

Dafydd (*turning*) Hallo. Yes, my love?

Bridget (*miming*) Phone. Phone.

Dafydd Ah. Telephone. Do excuse me, won't you? (*to Guy, handing him his pint*) Hang on to that a second, would you mind?

Guy (*taking it*) Certainly.

Dafydd (*moving away*) I trust you.

Bridget It's Hannah for you.

Dafydd What the hell's she want . . .

Dafydd goes to a corner of the bar, takes the receiver, sticks a finger in his ear and starts a conversation which we cannot hear. With the departure of Dafydd, the small talk between Ian and Guy seems thin on the ground.

Ian Cheers.

Guy Cheers.

Pause. Guy, rather nervously, takes a swig of beer.

Ian Get on well with Dafydd, do you?

Guy Well, yes, I think –

Ian I hope so, because you're drinking his beer.

Guy Oh, God, yes. Sorry. Do you know that's something that I'm always . . . well, not always – but occasionally –

Fay approaches them and interrupts.

Fay Darling, have you got a light? They're all dreary non-smokers over there. (*smiling at Guy, her reason for joining them*) Hallo, I'm Fay. I'm this thing's wife. How do you do.

Guy Hallo.

Fay You don't know what a pleasure it is to see a new man in the Society. It's mostly filled with us boring women. Dreadful.

Guy (*gallantly*) Dreadful for some, perhaps.

Fay (*throwing her head back with a tinkling laugh*) Yes. Depends on your point of view.

Ian (*not quite to himself*) Jesus . . . (*He moves away to put his glass on the bar.*)

Fay (*after him*) Where are you off to?

Ian Going to bring the car round. Why?

Fay Heavens and not yet closing time. What's come over him? (*She smiles at Guy again.*) Hallo.

Guy (*a fraction uneasily*) Hallo. Well, I suppose I must be making a move, too.

Fay You got a car? Only otherwise we could drop you.

Guy No, thanks. I'm mobile . . .

Jarvis (*who is heading towards them with some empty glasses*) I say, I say.

Fay (*under her breath*) Oh, no. Quick, hide, take cover.

Jarvis (*reaching them*) I say. Yes. You. You're a Scotchman, aren't you?

Guy No, no.

Jarvis They're the only people who do that, you know. The Scotties. That's the way you tell 'em.

Fay Tell what?

Jarvis Look, look, look. Look, you see. Glass in each hand. Whisky, beer. Whisky, beer. That's the way they do it. Scotty, right?

Guy No.

Jarvis Always tell 'em. Always tell 'em. (*He moves away.*)

Guy I didn't understand that at all.

Fay (*laughing*) Don't worry. He's completely mad.

Guy Ah.

Fay Quite harmless, though.

Guy Glad to hear it.

Fay No, it's her you've got to watch. (*She nods towards Rebecca.*) Hallo. (*She smiles again at Guy.*)

   Ian returns from the bar en route to the door. He drags Fay out with him.

(*as she's whisked away*) I think this means we're going. Goodnight, then.

Guy Goodnight.

Ian 'Night.

Fay Do excuse us. Some nights he can hardly contain himself.

   Fay and Ian go out.

Jarvis (*from the bar calling to Guy*) Hey! I say, you, Jimmy . . . Jimmy.

Guy (*mystified*) Me?

Jarvis You want another wee dram in there . . . ?

Guy No thank you, this is gin . . .

Jarvis (*to Bridget*) And a wee one for our friend from over the border.

Guy Oh, Lord . . .

Over in the other corner of the bar, Mr Ames begins playing the piano. Shortly, Ted starts singing and is then joined by most of the others.

Ted (*singing*)
Fill ev'ry Glass, for Wine inspires us,
    And fires us
With Courage, Love and Joy.

All
Fill ev'ry Glass, for Wine inspires us,
    And fires us
With Courage, Love and Joy.

Ted
Women and Wine should Life employ.
Is there ought else on earth desirous?
Fill ev'ry Glass, for Wine inspires us,
    And fires us
With Courage, Love and Joy.

All
Women and Wine should Life employ (*etc.*)

Guy stands bemusedly as this starts. His bemusement slightly increases as Jarvis passes him and pours a large scotch into his gin glass. Jarvis moves to the piano and joins the singers. Dafydd, having finished on the phone, rejoins Guy.

Dafydd (*over the singing*) Good old Ted. Get him near a piano, he's away. Marvellous music, isn't it? All traditional tunes, you know. All the tunes Gay used were traditional.

Guy Really?

Dafydd Still as fresh as they ever were . . .

Bridget, from the other side of the bar, appears, ringing a large bell. The singing stops.

Bridget My dad says he's not licensed for music and dancing and would you please stop that bloody row . . .

A chorus of booing and catcalls.

Only he didn't say please, like I did.

Crispin Why's he got a piano for, then?

Bridget That's reserved for private functions . . .

Rebecca This is a private function . . .

Crispin Yes. Bugger off . . .

Bridget Hey, you. Watch your language, you. You're not in the gutter now, you know . . .

Jarvis (*to Mr Ames*) Play a Highland Fling for the Scotty over there . . .

Bridget Sorry. Those are the rules of the house. Thank you very much. And last orders, please . . .

Crispin You want to get rid of that piano if people can't use it . . .

Bridget (*ignoring this*) Last orders, please.

Linda It's a filthy place, anyhow.

Bridget You know where to go if you don't like it, don't you? Sitting there drinking half of shandy for three hours. We can do without you for a kick off . . .

Linda What's it got to do with you what I drink? What on earth business is it of yours, may I ask . . .

Bridget (*mimicking her*) What on earth business is it of yours, may I ask?

Dafydd All right, girls, that's enough now . . . Call a truce.

Linda Snotty little barmaid . . .

Ted Now, now, Linda . . .

Bridget (*looking dangerous*) Hey . . . hey . . . You watch yourself.

Enid Now come on, Linda, we're off home now . . .

Dafydd That's enough . . .

Ted Now, now, now . . . Linda . . .

Crispin plays a provocative chord on the piano.

Bridget Hey, you. Did you play that? You touch that piano again, you're out that door, all right . . .

Crispin Yes, miss . . . Wasn't me, miss . . .

Linda plonks out several notes on the piano.

Enid Linda! Oh, she is a naughty girl . . .

Ted Now, now, now, Linda. Now, now . . .

Bridget (*coming round the bar like a tornado*) All right, you. I've had it up to here with you . . .

Dafydd Bridget. Easy, Bridget girl. (*to Guy*) God, she doesn't want to get her roused. That girl set up *Carousel* single handed . . .

Bridget approaches Linda.

Bridget Come on. Out I said.

Linda Really? You try and make me leave.

Bridget (*shoving her*) Out. Out . . .

Rebecca Peace, children . . .

Enid (*with her*) Stop them somebody. Someone stop them . . .

Ted (*with them*) Now, now, Linda. Now, now . . .

Dafydd (*with them*) I think we've all had our bit of fun and high spirits, people . . .

Crispin, during this last, steps between the two women and confronts Bridget.

Crispin Hey . . . Who you pushing around, then?

Bridget Anyone who gets in my way. Want to make something of it?

Crispin Haven't you ever heard that the customer's always right? Haven't you ever heard that, then?

Bridget Not in this pub they aren't. Now sod off . . .

Crispin Language, language . . .

He pats her under the chin. Bridget really goes wild, launching herself at Crispin with an initial knee to the groin which he narrowly avoids. She follows this with a huge swinging punch, which again he narrowly avoids and which – had it connected – would certainly have laid him out cold. Under this barrage of kicks and punches, Crispin beats a somewhat undignified retreat towards the door. Linda watches appalled. The others respond with a mixture of amusement and alarm.

Bridget (*as this happens*) Go on . . . get out, out, out, out, OUT!

Crispin (*half amused at this onslaught*) All right, all right, all right. I'm going, I'm going.

They both disappear into the street momentarily. Then

Bridget returns triumphantly. She gets a cheer. Linda stalks with dignity to the door. Bridget with mock politeness holds open the door for her.

Enid (*apprehensively*) Linda . . .

Linda (*coolly*) Good night.

Bridget Good nate.

Linda goes out.

And it is now time, please, so can I have your glasses? Thank you.

Mutters and groans of complaint.

Jarvis (*calling to Guy*) Hey! Scotty. Remind you of Glasgow, eh? Home from home. (*He laughs.*)

Dafydd (*gloomily*) Whenever you're in here you just have to keep saying over to yourself, 'I know it's hell but the beer is good.' That my glass, is it?

Guy (*handing him the totally depleted glass.*) Yes. Sorry.

Dafydd Oh, well. Bang goes another reason for living. (*He shrugs.*) I hope Bridget hasn't offended that lad. We need him for the show.

Guy What's he playing?

Dafydd Macheath. Well, maybe he wasn't the most ideal choice for the leading role. Temperamentally, anyway. But we had no real choice. Not with Tommy Binns' cartilage problem.

Rebecca and Jarvis pass them on their way out. Rebecca moving with extreme, sedate caution.

Goodnight, both.

Rebecca Goodnight. (*with a glassily charming smile to*

Guy) See you tomorrow.

Guy Yes, indeed . . .

Jarvis See you the noo. Eh? See you the noo . . . (*He laughs.*)

Guy (*laughing*) Yes, yes . . .

Rebecca (*as they go out*) Are you sure he's Scottish . . . ?

  Rebecca and Jarvis leave.

Dafydd See you where, did he say?

Guy The noo.

Dafydd It's just round the back. (*He roars with laughter and slaps Guy on the shoulder.*) Sorry, Guy, you'll have to bear with my coarse Welsh rugby player's humour . . . Beg your pardon.

Guy Are you a rugger player?

Dafydd God, no. Can't stand the game. Had to play it for seven years. Total misery. But my Dad was a fanatic. One of those. All his language was in terms of rugby, you know. That man's up-and-under imagery constituted my entire verbal childhood upbringing. Making sure life fed you plenty of good clean ball. Getting women in loose mauls and all that bollocks. God, I was glad to leave home . . .

Guy Your poor mother . . .

Dafydd No, she was all right, she left with me . . .

  Ted and Enid pass them.

Goodnight, Ted. Enid . . .

Enid We're going off in search of Linda, Dafydd . . .

Ted She's only a child you see, Dafydd . . .

Enid (*almost overlapping him*) She's always been mature, you know . . .

Ted (*almost overlapping her, in turn*) . . . physically, you know . . .

Enid . . . physically . . . but emotionally . . .

Ted . . . her emotions are still very far from . . .

Enid . . . for her age . . .

Ted . . . mature, you see.

Enid . . . immature, yes.

Ted And we're not happy with this lad at all, Dafydd. I mean we're not . . .

Enid . . . snobbish at all . . .

Ted . . . class conscious. But he's not right . . .

Enid . . . he's very wrong . . .

Ted . . . he's a very wild lad . . .

Enid . . . oh, very wild . . .

Ted . . . and we've got a feeling we know where he'll finish up, don't we, Enid?

Enid Yes, I'm afraid we do. Only too . . .

Ted . . . too well . . .

Enid . . . too well . . .

Mercifully they both run out of steam. Slight pause.

Dafydd Well. If you find you do have a problem, give me a ring at home.

Ted Thank you, Dafydd . . .

Enid Thank you very much, Dafydd . . .

Dafydd I'll be back there in ten minutes. So. 'Night.

Ted Goodnight.

Enid Goodnight. I hope you sleep well. (*to Guy*) All through the night. (*She laughs.*)

Guy Thank you. Goodnight. (*He laughs.*)

Ted and Enid go out.

Dafydd An effortlessly witty woman is Enid, you'll discover. Listen, we haven't settled this business of casting, have we? Think we ought to settle that now, don't you?

Guy Yes. That would be nice. Give me something to be getting on with. If I know what I'm playing . . .

Bridget (*making a threatening move to come round the bar*) Are you two leaving or do I have to throw you out?

Dafydd (*retreating in haste*) No, no, Bridget. We're going. We're going. Have you got your car, by any chance . . . ?

Guy Yes. Just round the corner . . .

Dafydd Well, look, my place is only a couple of streets away. I could give you a script and a cup of cocoa. That suit you?

Guy Fine. Lead on.

Guy and Dafydd leave the pub. Bridget continues to clear up for a moment. Suddenly, Crispin is in the doorway. He stands menacingly. Bridget sees him and tenses, ready for a scrap. Silence. Crispin advances on her slowly. They stand face to face. With a sudden swift movement he reaches out and grabs her by the back of her head. Their mouths meet in a savage kiss. The scene changes to Dafydd's sitting room. Pleasant and comfortable but small. Certainly too small for Dafydd.

A room shared with children. A large, male, home-made rag doll sits on one of the chairs.

Dafydd (*in a whisper*) Yes . . . As I thought. She'll be in bed. She's not much of a night owl, my wife. Of course the children get her up pretty early . . .

Guy How many do you have?

Dafydd Two. Twin girls.

Guy (*indicating doll*) Is that theirs?

Dafydd Oh yes – let me take your coat – he's what they call their Other Daddy. Whenever I'm away, they bring him out and pretend it's me. I think it's been left there as a hint by someone this evening. I'll put the kettle on. Won't be a second. If you're cold at all, put the fire on. Personally, I think it's pretty warm, don't you? Wait there . . .

He goes out. Guy surveys the room. After a moment, he sits and waits patiently. It's obviously quite chilly. Quite suddenly and unexpectedly, Hannah enters. She is in her night things, her face shiny with cream and she is obviously not expecting company.

Hannah (*speaking as she enters*) Dafydd, if you want anything to – (*seeing Guy*) Oh.

Guy (*rising*) Hallo, I'm –

Hannah Oh, God. Excuse me.

Hannah flees the room. Guy stands a little bemused. The following conversation is heard off.

Hannah Dafydd . . .

Dafydd (*cheerfully*) Hallo, darling. Got a little bit held up. Sorry.

Hannah You told me you weren't bringing anyone home.

Dafydd Yes, I know, I know.

Hannah I mean I phoned especially, Dafydd. I phoned and said would you be bringing any of them home tonight . . .

Dafydd (*under her*) It was a spur of the moment decision . . .

Hannah . . . And you said no, which is why I got ready for bed.

Dafydd You can go to bed. You can go to bed.

Hannah Not if there's someone here I can't.

Dafydd It's all right. This chap doesn't matter.

Hannah Who is he?

Dafydd He's no one. He's no one important. He's a small-part player, that's all.

Hannah I'll get dressed.

Dafydd (*calling after her as she departs*) Don't bother. He's not worth getting dressed for. (*Pause.*) God damn it.

A door slams off. A second later, Dafydd reappears. He is holding a script.

Here we are. Sorry to keep you. (*suddenly aware that Guy must have heard some of that*) Things are just – heating up out there. By the way, I never asked you. Tea, coffee or cocoa?

Guy Tea?

Dafydd No problem. Now – (*he studies the script*) – I – er – hear you ran into the wife.

Guy Well . . .

Dafydd Or rather she ran into you. (*He laughs.*)

Guy That's more like it, yes.

Dafydd (*feeling some explanation is due but unable to think of one*) Yes. She's – you know – women . . .

Guy Yes.

Dafydd Never like being taken by surprise, do they? Unless they know what it is in advance. (*He laughs.*) I'd like to surprise you for your birthday, darling, what would you like? Now then. This casting business. I have a feeling, an instinctive feeling in my bones, you know, and I'm not often wrong – sometimes, not often – that you'd make a pretty good Crook-Finger'd Jack. Fancy that, do you? Having a crack at Crook-Finger'd Jack?

Guy Yes, he sounds pretty interesting . . . yes . . .

Dafydd I'll be honest, it's not a vast – you know *The Beggar's Opera* at all – ?

Guy No. It's one I haven't . . .

Dafydd No, well, it's as I say, it's not a vast part. But he does feature. He features pretty strongly really. I mean for the sort of size of part he is. I mean, he's got – what – in terms of speeches – ? (*He flicks the script vaguely.*) Well, he's got probably just the one line in Act Two but he's the sort of character, you know, at the end of an evening, an audience tend to remember quite graphically . . .

Guy Perhaps that's because of his finger . . .

Dafydd (*failing to see this small joke*) What? No, you see the play's full of these marvellous characters. There are the highwaymen . . . (*savouring the names*) Crook-Finger'd Jack, Jemmy Twitcher, Nimming Ned, Ben Budge, Matt of the Mint . . . (*He reflects.*) Yes, there was the possibility of that character but – my feeling is, as director, that Matt of the Mint could be a little too adventurous for you first time round.

Guy No, fair enough. I wasn't . . .

Dafydd That, of course, is not in any way a reflection on . . .

Guy No, please, please. I'll be guided by you . . .

Dafydd (*relieved*) Well. Good. Good. I'm giving that particular part to Dr Packer who has, to be fair, had a good deal of experience. Still, it'll only be the first of many for you and us. Hopefully.

Guy I hope so, too.

Dafydd Good. (*handing Guy the script*) You want to take this one?

Guy Thank you.

Dafydd You'll find he comes on around page 32. Then he goes off on page 35, I think. And then I'm thinking seriously about bringing him on again in Act Three. But that's to be confirmed.

Guy Splendid. Thank you very much.

Dafydd Quite a departure for PALOS, this, you know . . .

Guy PALOS?

Dafydd Pendon Amateur Light Operatic Society . . .

Guy Oh, yes. Sorry. Of course . . .

Dafydd Makes a change from *The Student Prince*. Not that I don't . . . But it's good to have a change now and then. I had a lot of opposition in committee over this one, I can tell you. Lot of old die-hards there. Original walk-ons in *Chu Chin Chow*. You know the sort . . . But I'm absolutely convinced that this show – first produced when was it – ? 1728 – it's as entertaining and as vital and as relevant as it was then . . . Suky Tawdry . . . Dolly Trull . . . Mrs Vixen . . . Those are the whores and pimps of the town . . . almost see their faces in their names, can't you? Polly Peachum. That tells you all you need to know about her, doesn't it? What an age, eh? What an age. Well, compared to our own.

Guy Yes. Yes. Of course, they didn't have any . . .

Dafydd I mean, look at us today. Sex shops, I ask you. Can you imagine Captain Macheath furtively purchasing marital aids . . . ? What's happening to us, Guy? What's happening to us, eh? (*Slight pause.*) Sorry, I get a little – over-enthusiastic occasionally. So I'm told.

Guy Not at all. Did you ever consider doing the theatre professionally? I mean, it's just that you seem . . .

Dafydd Oh, I was, I was. I was in the profession for some years.

Guy Really?

Dafydd Oh, yes. I've done my bit.

Guy As a producer?

Dafydd No, no. Acting in those days. I was acting. And a little bit of stage management, you know.

Guy Whereabouts?

Dafydd (*vaguely*) Oh, all over. A lot of it in Minehead.

Guy Oh. Yes.

Dafydd Still. That's under the bridge. Respectable solicitor these days. Well, reasonably. What line are you in, then?

Guy Oh, I'm –

Before he can reply, Hannah enters. She has made

41

herself more socially presentable now, pretending the earlier encounter with Guy did not occur. She carries a tray with two mugs of cocoa. Guy rises politely. Dafydd, unused to such niceties in his own home, does so belatedly.

Hannah Hallo . . .

Guy Hallo.

Dafydd Here she is . . . This is my wife, Hannah.

Hannah How do you do?

Guy How do you do?

Dafydd Dearest, this is Mr Jones. Guy Jones.

Hannah Hallo.

Guy Hallo.

Dafydd Let me . . . (*He helps her with the tray.*) . . . On here, shall we?

Hannah Yes, it'll mark it on there . . . (*to Guy*) Do sit down, please . . . Brrr! It's cold in here. Heating's off.

Dafydd Is it? Can't say we'd noticed, had we? Boiling.

Hannah I presumed you both wanted cocoa. I saw the tin was out.

Dafydd Oh, no. Guy wanted tea. Sorry, love . . .

Guy It doesn't matter . . .

Hannah I can make tea . . .

Guy No, please, really . . .

Dafydd Tea's no trouble . . .

Guy No, this is perfect. Please.

Hannah Well. If you're quite sure.

Guy I'm just as happy with this.

Slight pause.

Hannah Well, I'll leave you both to it, then.

Dafydd Don't go, don't go . . .

Hannah If you want to talk business . . .

Dafydd No, we've finished. Sit down for a second.

Guy (*smiling*) Please.

Hannah Well. Only if I'm not in the way. (*She sits.*)

Dafydd Anyway. Hardly call it business, could we?

Hannah Oh?

Dafydd Guy's going to be giving us his Crook-Finger'd Jack.

Hannah Sorry?

Dafydd Our missing brigand. He's just joined us.

Hannah Oh. Wonderful.

Dafydd Think he'll make a good Jack, do you, Hannah? Think he'll make a highwayman?

Hannah Well. Possibly . . .

Dafydd Oh dear, Guy. She doesn't sound too convinced. Doesn't he convince you?

Hannah Yes. I just think he looks a bit handsome for a highwayman. (*She smiles nervously.*)

Dafydd (*roaring with laughter*) Well, I don't know what you say to that, Guy, I really don't. What do you say to that?

Guy I don't really know.

He smiles. Dafydd's laughter subsides. A silence.

Dafydd Maybe we can give him an eyepatch.

Hannah Yes . . .

They laugh. Another silence.

Dafydd Are the girls all right?

Hannah Yes. They're asleep.

Dafydd Gwinny stopped coughing?

Hannah Oh yes, I gave her the linctus.

Dafydd Good. Good. (*Pause.*) Good.

Hannah (*to Guy*) We have twin girls.

Guy Yes . . .

Hannah Gwynneth who's got a cold. And Myfanwy who's just getting over it . . . They just go in circles.

Guy Nice names.

Hannah Yes. Dafydd's mother chose them.

Dafydd With our help.

Guy Ah . . .

Dafydd Everything's Welsh in this house . . .

Hannah Except me, that is.

Dafydd Except her, that is. She was made in Middlesex.

Guy (*rather over-reacting*) Oh, really? Middlesex.

Hannah Yes. Are you from Middlesex, then?

Guy No.

44

Hannah Oh.

Dafydd He's from Leeds. Aren't you?

Guy That's right.

Hannah Oh. Leeds, yes . . . Is your wife local?

Dafydd No, dearest, he hasn't got a wife . . .

Hannah No?

Guy No, she . . . She died, recently.

Hannah Oh, dear.

Dafydd Oh dear, I didn't know that. Accident, was it?

Guy No. Not really, it was . . . (*He searches for words.*)

Dafydd Deliberate. (*He laughs.*)

Hannah (*fiercely*) Dafydd . . .

Dafydd Sorry, sorry. I do beg your pardon. I'm sorry, Guy.

Guy That's quite all right . . .

Hannah He's always doing that.

Guy She was ill for some time, actually . . .

Hannah Oh, dear. How long's she . . . How long's she – been now?

Guy Just over a year . . .

Hannah Ah.

Dafydd Ah . . .

Guy It took me a little time, obviously, to adjust . . .

Hannah . . . yes, it would . . .

Guy Still, eventually I decided it was high time I took a

45

grip on things and got out and about again. Which is why I took the plunge and wrote to David . . .

Dafydd (*correcting him*) Dafydd . . .

Guy (*attempting the correct pronunciation*) Dafydd . . .

Dafydd Nearly. (*spelling it out slowly*) Da–fydd . . .

Guy Da–fydd . . .

Hannah Oh, really. It's near enough.

Dafydd Near enough is not enough . . .

Hannah It's bad enough as it is. How do you fancy standing in the Dry Cleaners trying to pronounce your own surname?

Dafydd (*the full Welsh*) Llewellyn. What could be simpler? Llewellyn . . .

Hannah You work locally, though, do you?

Guy Yes, I'm with BLM, actually.

Dafydd BLM? Over on Western Estate?

Guy That's right . . .

Dafydd The big boys, eh?

Guy Well, they are, I'm not.

Hannah What do they do, BLM? I've always meant to ask.

Guy Well . . .

Dafydd That's a difficult one to answer, eh, Guy?

Guy Just a bit . . .

Hannah I mean, what do they do? Do they make anything?

Dafydd (*laughing*) Vast profits mostly . . . Right?

Guy Right. (*He laughs.*)

Hannah Oh well, don't tell me if you don't want to . . .

Guy We're a multi-national company that's become extremely diversified . . .

Dafydd Diversified, dearest. That means they're into all sorts of different –

Hannah (*tetchily*) Yes, I know, I know . . .

Dafydd All right . . .

Hannah I know what diversify means.

Guy (*a fraction embarrassed*) And so it's a bit difficult to pin down. Certainly it is from my limited viewpoint. In a rather small local branch in a rather obscure department called Alternative Forward Costing. In which I am a very small cog indeed.

Hannah I'm impressed anyway.

Dafydd It's interesting you should be in BLM because –

In the hall the phone rings.

Hannah Who can that be . . . ? (*She starts to rise.*)

Dafydd (*rising*) I'll go, I'll go. It could be Ted . . .

Hannah Oh, is it Linda trouble again?

Dafydd (*as he goes*) Yes, as usual. As usual . . .

Dafydd goes out.

Hannah It's these friends of ours, they have this daughter that they absolutely dote over. And of course she just takes terrible advantage of them all the time . . .

Guy Yes, I met them.

Hannah Did you? Yes. She's a real headache for them. She set fire to all her mother's clothes, you know . . .

Guy Set fire to them?

Hannah Yes. Enid wasn't in them at the time but it was everything she had in the world except what she was standing up in. They both came home from a meeting of the Civic Society and her wardrobe was ablaze.

Guy Heavens.

Hannah Mind you, I can't help thinking, in some ways, they brought it on themselves. I hope ours will turn out all right. Do you have children, Mr – ?

Guy Guy, please. No. My wife wasn't able to have any. She – wasn't very strong . . .

Hannah Shame. Do you miss her a lot?

Guy (*as if considering the question for the first time*) Yes. Yes, I do. Very much.

Hannah That's nice. For her, I mean. Of course not for you. I'd like to think I'd be missed.

Guy You?

Hannah Yes.

Guy Why? (*An awful thought.*) You're not . . . ?

Hannah Oh, no. No, I'm right as rain. I think. So far as I know. It's just I sometimes wonder, I suppose a lot of us do probably, whether if I – you know – died, people would really . . . Silly really, isn't it?

Guy I'm sure you'd be missed.

Hannah Maybe.

Guy By David – Dafydd. And your children.

Hannah Yes, possibly the children would. For a few years more, anyway. I don't know about Dafydd. Now he *is* missed. You see that big doll there? Every time Dafydd's out of the house for more than 20 minutes the girls insist it's brought out. Then all their games revolve round that wretched doll. Tea with Daddy-doll and walks with Daddy-doll and supper with Daddy-doll and bed with Daddy-doll . . . Well, I've stopped them taking it to bed with them now. I did think that was getting too much of a good thing. Of course, Dafydd thinks it's terribly funny. I suppose it is quite flattering for him, really. The trouble is, my family are under the impression that there's a female counterpart to that thing that runs round the house after them. Only it happens to be me. Hooray for Mummy-doll. (*Slight pause.*) Heavens. I haven't talked like this for years. I am sorry. It's very boring of me.

Guy (*gently*) No.

Hannah No?

Guy No.

He smiles at her. Hannah, uncertainly at first and then more warmly, smiles back at Guy. As they gaze at each other, Dafydd returns from the phone to break the spell.

Dafydd (*as he enters*) That was Enid. They got home and found Linda in bed.

Hannah is about to say something.

Yes, that's what I asked. And the answer is no. Fast asleep on her own. So, false alarm. they still have a daughter and more important we still have a Lucy Lockit. What's been going on in here? Anything I should know about?

Hannah I think it's my bedtime, if you'll excuse me . . .

Guy (*looking at his watch*) Oh, Lord, yes. I must be . . .

Dafydd Don't go on my account. I'm a late one myself . . .

Guy No, it really is . . .

Dafydd (*going out briefly*) I'll fetch your coat, then.

Guy (*to Hannah*) Thank you very much for your hospitality . . .

Hannah Not much of that. You didn't even drink your cocoa.

Guy Another time, perhaps.

Dafydd returns and helps Guy into his coat.

Thank you. I hope, in any case, I'll see you again before too long.

Dafydd What her? You're talking about Hannah, you mean? You'll see her tomorrow night.

Guy (*pleased*) Oh, really?

Dafydd Didn't she tell you she's in the show? She's our Polly Peachum, aren't you, love? (*He cuffs her affectionately.*)

Guy Oh, I see. Good Lord.

Hannah (*as she leaves with the tray*) I look better in the mornings. Usually. (*She laughs.*) See you tomorrow.

Guy Goodnight. (*He stares after her somewhat as of a man enchanted.*)

Dafydd (*a man with his mind on more serious things*) Listen, Guy . . . a word before you go . . .

Guy Yes?

Dafydd This coincidence of your working for BLM. It could be quite opportune. The point is, I'm acting for a client at the moment who's involved in purchasing a couple of acres of wasteland. Small stuff. Nothing very exciting. Except for two things. One, the land is actually slap bang adjoining your premises –

Guy Oh, round the back there, you mean?

Dafydd Yes, the old sports field. Used to be a sports field. Second, and this is only hearsay, rumour has it that you boys are shortly planning to expand. Any truth in that, do you know?

Guy No, I don't . . . Not so far as I know . . .

Dafydd Only, of course, if you are, then of course the land in question could suddenly be worth a bit. Do you follow?

Guy Yes, I do see.

Dafydd Depending of course on how many people get to know about it. I mean, putting it in plainer words, if the chap who's selling it doesn't know, whereas we who are buying it do know – then we could be getting a bargain. But you've no definite knowledge yourself?

Guy No, as I say, not that's come to my ears. I could ask . . .

Dafydd Well, tactfully if you do. Don't want to disturb things, do we? Of course, if you could help, there'd – there'd be some arrangement, no doubt . . .

Guy Oh, there'd be no need for . . .

Dafydd Oh, yes, yes. Fair's fair. Fair's fair . . .

Guy Yes. Though I suppose if we were being really fair, we really ought to warn the person who's selling the land.

Dafydd Oh, I don't think that's on.

Guy No?

Dafydd If I did that, I'd be betraying my own client, wouldn't I? Wouldn't be ethical.

Guy I see.

Dafydd No. It's up to this other fellow's solicitor to warn him. Not me. Anyway. Keep your ear to the ground.

He steers Guy towards the front door.

Guy I will certainly.

Dafydd But remember, mum's the word.

Guy Oh, yes, rather. Goodnight then. See you tomorrow.

Dafydd You betcher. Seven o'clock. And we're really going to get cracking, I can tell you. You won't see that stage for dust.

Guy (*moving away*) Right . . .

Dafydd (*calling after him as Guy goes*) Better bring your racing skates . . .

Dafydd stands in the doorway for a second, savouring the night air. A man well pleased with his evening's achievements. As he stands there, lights up on Ted. He is in full evening dress, holding his script.

Ted (*as Peachum, singing*)
A Fox may steal your Hens, Sir,
A Whore your Health and Pence, Sir,
Your Daughter rob your Chest, Sir,
Your Wife may steal your Rest, Sir,
A Thief your Goods and Plate.
But this is all but picking,
With Rest, Pence, Chest and Chicken;
It ever was decreed, Sir,
If Lawyer's Hand is fee'd, Sir,
He steals your whole Estate.

Lights come up on the full rehearsal area. Also on stage now are Dafydd, prowling the auditorium watching Ted. Guy sitting to one side, absorbed and eager to learn. Bridget sitting with the prompt script, slightly bored and restless. And away in another corner Ian, at present reading the evening paper and taking no perceptible interest in proceedings. As the song finishes, Ted consults his script, makes to sit, changes his mind and exits offstage. As he does so Enid, as Mrs Peachum, and Hannah, as Polly, come on, also holding their scripts. Enid is also in evening dress.

Hannah (*reading, as Polly*) 'Twas only Nimming Ned. He brought in a Damask Window-Curtain, a Hoop Petticoat, a Pair of Silver Candlesticks, a Perriwig, and one Silk Stocking, from the Fire that happen'd last Night.

She stops at the end of her speech. Both women look up expecting Ted to reply, but he has gone.

Dafydd (*yelling*) Go on, go on, go on. Don't stop again, for God's sake. We're ten days behind as it is.

Hannah We can't go on.

Dafydd Who's next, Bridget? Keep your eye on the script, girl. Who speaks next?

Bridget Ted.

Dafydd Ted? Well, where the hell is Ted? He's just walked off the stage. Where's he gone to? (*yelling*) Ted!

Ted returns a little apprehensively.

Ted Did you want me, Dafydd?

Dafydd Ted, love, there is no earthly point in leaving the stage when you're in the middle of a scene, now is there?

Ted (*consulting his script*) Oh. Don't I go off? I thought I went off . . .

> *Enid and Hannah go to Ted's rescue, showing him where he is in the script.*

Hannah . . . I don't think you go off till there, Ted . . .

Enid . . . there, dear, you see. Not till there . . .

Ted . . .Oh, I see. There. I thought it was there . . .

Dafydd (*on the move with impatience, as he passes Guy over this last*) Unbelievable this, isn't it? Unbelievable. Ten days we've been at this. Ten days. And where are we – ? Page 15 or something . . .

Hannah (*to Dafydd*) We've got it now. It was a mistake.

Ted My mistake. Sorry, everyone. I shouldn't have gone off . . .

Dafydd Well, I'm sure you were only expressing in actions, Ted, what will by this stage be the heartfelt wish of the entire audience . . .

Ted (*laughing, nervously*) Yes, yes . . .

Dafydd Those that won't already have dozed off, or died of old age . . .

Hannah (*in a warning tone*) Dafydd . . .

Dafydd Why are you dressed like a cinema manager, anyway, Ted?

Hannah It's their dinner dance, Dafydd. They were due there an hour ago. You promised to release them early.

Dafydd Oh, terrific. My whole rehearsal grinds to a halt because of a Co-op staff dance, does it?

Ted No hurry, Dafydd. No hurry. We didn't want the dinner.

Dafydd All right. Let's get on. (*fiercely*) On, on . . .

Hannah (*picking it up again, as Polly*) . . . one silk stocking, from the Fire that happen'd last Night.

Ted (*as Peachum*) This is not a Fellow that is cleverer in his way, and saves more Goods out of the . . .

Bridget That's cut.

Ted Sorry?

Enid I think we cut that, dear . . .

Dafydd (*storming on to the stage*) Ted, that is cut. That was cut two days ago . . .

Ted I'm sorry. I didn't have it . . .

Dafydd You don't have anything, Ted. That's your trouble, man. You don't have any ability, you don't have any intelligence, you don't have one single scrap of artistic sensibility and most important of all you don't even have a bloody pencil.

Hannah Dafydd . . .

Dafydd (*wrenching Ted's script from his hands*) *That* is cut . . . (*stabbing his finger at the page*) *That* is cut and *that* is cut. And the whole – (*wrestling with the script*) – sodding thing is cut. (*He rips Ted's script in several pieces. Breathless*) There! That make it any easier for you? You boneheaded – tortoise . . .

> *Ted stands shattered. He opens his mouth to reply and finds himself unable to do so. He leaves the stage rather swiftly, one suspects on the verge of tears.*

Enid Oh, Dafydd . . . You really are – sometimes. You really are . . . There was no need for that . . .

> *Enid goes off after Ted.*

Dafydd God, it's hot in here, isn't it? Anybody else find it too hot?

Hannah (*in a low voice*) That was unforgivable, Dafydd. To Ted of all people. Absolutely unforgivable . . . (*She picks up the torn script, angrily shouting.*) And these scripts are supposed to go back. I hope you realize that.

   Hannah goes off after Ted and Enid.

Dafydd (*searching for fresh allies*) Dear old Guy. Dear old Guy. You sitting there quietly picking up some tips, are you?

Guy (*smiling*) Yes, yes . . .

Dafydd I'm afraid this is what we term the amateur syndrome, Guy. When the crunch comes, they can't take the pressure, you see. Want to be off to their dinner dances. God, there are times when I come close to wishing I was back at Minehead.

Guy I wondered – if you had a minute – I wondered if I could ask you about Crook-Finger'd Jack . . .

Dafydd Who?

Guy My part. Crook-Finger'd Jack . . .

Dafydd Oh, Crook-Finger'd Jack. Yes. What about him?

Guy It's just that I've been thinking about it over the past few days, you know, and I wondered whether you'd like him with a finger.

Dafydd A what?

Guy A finger. (*He holds up his hand and demonstrates.*) Something like that. (*Pause. Offering Dafydd an alternating choice of hands*) Which do you think?

Dafydd (*snapping out of his reverie*) Yes. Do you think we could leave that for a day or two longer, Guy, old boy? I've one or two rather more pressing matters.

Guy Oh yes, yes. Of course. Sorry.

Bridget I'm going to make some tea. (*She starts to get up slowly.*)

Dafydd Splendid, my love, excellent . . .

Rebecca and Fay come on, followed by Linda. All in their coats. Bridget goes off.

Rebecca Dafydd. We come to you as a deputation. We have been sitting backstage in that ghastly smelly little kitchen for the best part of two weeks . . .

Dafydd All right, all right, all right. Don't you start . . .

Rebecca We're not being unreasonable, Dafydd. All we want to know is, will you be needing us this evening or will you not? If not, fair enough. Only some of us have nice comfy homes we'd prefer to be in . . .

Dafydd Go on, go home. Go home to your nice, comfy little homes. Go on, bugger off, the lot of you.

A glacial moment. Bridget crosses and goes off.

Rebecca Well, I am certainly not staying after that. Not to listen to language like that.

Dafydd Goodbye.

Rebecca And furthermore, I shall be having a word with the Committee about this whole business. Do you realize Mr Washbrook is in tears out there?

Dafydd So am I . . .

Rebecca (*to Fay*) Are you coming, Fay?

Fay No point in staying here, is there?

Rebecca sweeps out. Fay goes to follow.

(*to Ian, indicating Guy*) We're going over the road, all right?

Ian Right. (*He starts to fold up his paper.*)

Fay (*seeing Guy is watching her, brightly, to him*) You coming for a drink?

Guy Probably. In a minute.

Fay Good. See you over there.

Fay goes out after Rebecca. Linda trails after them. Bridget returns with a pint of milk.

Dafydd Linda, is your Crispin around anywhere, do you know?

Linda I don't know where he is. Why should I know?

Dafydd Well, have you seen him?

Linda No, I have not seen him and I have no wish to see him, thank you very much . . . (*at Bridget*) I should ask her.

Dafydd Oh, God. (*to Bridget*) Do you know where he is?

Bridget Where I left him, probably.

Dafydd Where?

Bridget In my bed. Asleep.

Linda glares furiously and goes. Bridget goes out, looking pleased. She passes Ted and Enid, now in their coats, who both cross the stage on their way out. Both are very tearful and snuffling softly. Dafydd watches them.

Dafydd (*rather lamely*) Goodnight . . . folks. Have a great evening, won't you? (*after they've gone, filled with remorse*) Oh, God. (*He sits.*)

Almost immediately, Hannah returns.

Hannah I told the Washbrooks they could go. Phone for you, backstage. Dr Packer. Says it's urgent.

Dafydd More problems . . . more problems . . .

Dafydd goes off. Hannah catches Guy's eye briefly and smiles. Ian intercepts the look. Hannah goes after Dafydd. Ian now also moves to the door.

Ian Right. After that exhausting night's work, I feel like some refreshment. (*to Guy*) You coming?

Guy I was just going to run my line a couple of times. I've got one or two ideas I'd like to try . . .

Ian (*drily*) Well, don't get stale, will you? Two months to go yet. (*He starts to move off.*)

Guy (*calling him back*) I say . . . (*demonstrating his Crook-Finger'd Jack stance again*) Do you think this is too obvious? Crook-Finger'd Jack . . .

Ian Can't be too obvious for Dafydd. Did you see his *Sound of Music*?

Guy No.

Ian He had them all on trampolines.

Guy Heavens.

Ian Bloody hills were alive, I can tell you. So were the front stalls. Once they got in their costumes they couldn't control the bounce, you see. Screaming nuns crashing down on the punters. Three broken legs and one of them concussed on the spot bar. Probably some still up there for all we know . . .

Guy (*not knowing quite whether to believe this*) Yes. I think I'll try it without the finger to start with . . .

Ian By the way . . . ?

Guy Mm?

Ian We'd like to invite you round some evening. To our place.

Guy Oh. That's very nice. Thank you.

Ian I don't know if you've got anyone you'd care to bring. I understand you're not married any more . . .

Guy No, my wife was –

Ian Yes. Well. I dare say you've got a friend. Or someone. Eh?

Guy Yes, I think I could probably find a friend, yes.

Ian (*smiling*) Female, of course.

Guy Oh yes. Of course. Don't want to spoil your numbers.

Ian No, no. (*Pause. Uncertain whether Guy has got the message*) The point is Fay and I, we – well, you've probably gathered by now she's pretty – gregarious.

Guy Yes.

Ian And she likes to meet new people. All the time. And frankly, so do I. So it all tends to work out. If you follow me.

Guy (*who doesn't*) Well, that's splendid. When were you thinking?

Ian Is Friday OK for you?

Guy Friday, yes.

Ian We can have a bit of fun. (*He laughs.*)

Guy Splendid.

Ian Don't forget your friend, though.

Guy I won't.

Ian (*as he leaves*) And I'd like to talk to you about your job sometime. I'm very interested in that.

Ian goes.

Guy (*puzzled*) Really?

Realizing he is alone, he decides to experiment.

(*as Jack*) Where shall we find such another set . . . (*He breaks off.*) No. (*trying again*) Where shall we find such another Set of Practical Philosophers who to a Man are above the Fear of Death? Ha! Ha! Ho. (*He tries again.*)

Jarvis has entered from backstage, on his way home. He watches him. Guy stops, rather embarrassed as he becomes aware of Jarvis.

Jarvis Hey! The noo. That's what I like to see. A man practising his craft. I have a story about that. Will interest you. When I first went into t'firm as an apprentice lad – no matter I were boss's son I started on t'shop floor – the first day there the foreman says – big fellow he was – sweep that floor spotless, lad. Spotless. I want to eat my dinner off that floor. All right? And I sort of half swept it, you know, like you might. And when he comes back he said, what's this then, he says? And he bends down and he picks up this handful of sawdust that I'd missed, like. Under the bench. And he says, you're not expecting me to eat me dinner off this floor then, are you? He says, I'd like to see you try it, my lad, he says. And he tells me, sit down, and he fetches a gummy-bowl and spoon from rack and he makes me eat all that sawdust. Just as it is. Every scrap.

Guy Heavens.

Jarvis Nothing on it. Nor milk nor sugar. Raw sawdust.

And it's the same like that every day for three months. No matter I were t'boss's son. Those lads down in that shop, they taught me the hard way with mouthfuls of sawdust.

Guy Tough life.

Jarvis Oh, aye. Mind you, a while later, me Dad had his stroke and I took over t'firm. I went down that shop, first thing I did, and sacked every bloody one of 'em. But I learnt the trade. I were grateful to 'em for that.

Guy Jolly good.

Jarvis Keep at it. Practise your gestures. They all had gestures, you know . . .

Guy I will, I will.

Jarvis And another thing. Don't put on that fancy voice for it. Use your natural accent. That's what I do. Besides, he could be a Scotty. Couldn't he? A Scotty.

Guy True, only . . .

Jarvis Stick up for thissen then, lad. Stick up for thissen. People won't think the less of you for it, you know.

Guy Yes. Right. Thank you.

Jarvis goes out. Guy briefly tries his role with a thick Scots accent. More for his own amusement than anything.

Wherrr shall we find such anotherrr wee Set o' Practical Phullussupherrs, Jummy. Whoo to a man are above the ferr of dea' . . .

Hannah comes on with two cups of tea. She catches some of his performance.

Hannah I brought you some tea.

Guy Oh, thank you.

Hannah Dafydd's on the phone. Another crisis, I think.

Guy Ah, well.

Hannah You – er – you weren't thinking of playing him like that, were you? With that funny accent?

Guy No, no. That was just an – experiment.

Hannah Oh, good. Only I thought you nearly had it right yesterday. With the limp. The slight one.

Guy Yes. Maybe I'll stick to that. I think it's waiting all this time to rehearse the scene, it makes you – anxious . . .

Hannah Yes. He'll get to you eventually.

Guy Oh, yes, I'm sure.

Hannah (*more to herself*) God knows when, though. (*producing her script*) I wondered if you'd mind awfully hearing my lines again.

Guy No. Not at all. (*He takes her script.*) Where would you . . . ?

Hannah Just from the top of the page.

Guy OK.

Hannah (*as Polly*) And are *you* as fond as ever, my Dear?

Guy (*reading, as Macheath*) Suspect my Honour, my Courage, suspect any thing but my Love. – May my Pistols miss Fire, and my Mare slip her Shoulder while I am pursu'd, if I ever forsake thee!

Hannah (*as Polly*) Nay, my Dear, I have no Reason to doubt you, for I find in the Romance you lent me . . .

She hesitates. Guy nods encouragingly.

. . . you lent me, none of the great Heroes was ever false in Love.

She smiles at Guy. Guy smiles at her. Dafydd enters.
His head is bowed. Hannah and Guy wrench their
attention away from each other. Dafydd solemnly beats
his head against a piece of furniture.

Hannah (*to Dafydd*) Problems?

Dafydd One or two. Dr Packer has just phoned to inform
me that faced as he is with the alternative of either
reorganizing the new hospital rostas entirely or relinquishing
the role of Matt of the Mint, he has reluctantly decided on
the latter course of action. So there you are. Once again, as
my father would put it, we are beaten by the bounce.

Hannah What are you going to do?

Dafydd How the hell should I know?

Hannah (*softly, nodding in Guy's direction*) Guy . . .

Dafydd (*sotto*) What?

Hannah Guy.

Dafydd Guy?

Hannah Yes.

Dafydd You think so?

Hannah Of course.

Dafydd (*turning to Guy, extending a hand*) Guy . . .

Guy Yes?

Dafydd I think you are to be cast in the role of saviour.
Can you do it? Matt of the Mint?

Guy Oh.

Dafydd For me? For us all?

Guy Well. I'll have a go.

Dafydd Thank you. Thank you.

Hannah Super.

Dafydd (*brightening*) Splendid. Well, what do you say? A drink to celebrate?

Guy Well, why not?

Dafydd I'll get them in. I'll get them in. (*moving to the door*) But tomorrow, remember, we work . . .

Guy Er . . .

Dafydd Yes?

Guy What about Crook-Finger'd Jack?

Dafydd What about him?

Guy Only, I'd just learnt him. I wondered if . . .

Dafydd Forget Crook-Finger'd Jack, boy. You're Matt of the Mint. You're a star now. Nearly.

Dafydd goes.

Hannah I'm so thrilled for you. Well done.

Impetuously, she kisses him. As it turns out, it is a far more serious kiss than either of them intended. Guy eventually releases Hannah. He moves to the door, looking back at her. She looks at him. Finally, he leaves without a further word. As this occurs, the introduction is heard to the next song. The lights come up on Enid, whilst also remaining on Hannah.

Enid (*as Mrs Peachum, sings*)
O, Polly you might have toy'd and kiss'd,
By keeping Men off you keep them on.

Hannah (*as Polly, sings*)
But he so teaz'd me,

And he so pleas'd me,
What I did you must have done.

Enid *and* **Hannah** (*together*)
But he so teaz'd thee/me
And he so pleas'd thee/me
What you/I did I/you must have done.

The lights at once crossfade again and we are in Fay's sitting room. She is dressed to kill. Fay holds two exotic drinks.

Fay (*calling*) We're in here . . .

Guy (*off*) Right.

Fay (*calling*) Can you find it all right? Light switch is just inside the door.

She listens. Hears nothing. Assumes all is well. She puts the drinks down on the table and checks her already faultless appearance in the mirror. Guy enters.

Guy Sorry. At last.

Fay (*indicating his drink*) Help yourself.

Guy Thank you. (*He takes his drink.*)

Fay Do tell me if it's too strong, won't you? I can never tell.

Guy (*going to drink*) No, I'm sure this will be absolutely – (*He nearly chokes as he drinks but controls himself.*) That's – perfect, yes.

Fay Ian's just popped out. To get some more tequila. I'm afraid we're hooked on it, these days.

Guy Oh, yes?

Fay Have you been there?

Guy Sorry?

Fay Mexico.

Guy No. No. Not Mexico . . .

Fay Glorious. Parts of it. If you dodge the poverty.

Guy Ah.

Fay So. You're the first.

Guy Yes. (*looking round*) Yes. Looks like it.

Fay I'm all right, then, anyway.

Guy Yes?

Fay I've got you. (*She laughs.*)

Guy Yes, yes. (*Pause.*) I suppose that means I'm all right as well then. (*He laughs.*)

Fay (*laughing with him*) Very true, yes.

    Pause.

Guy (*indicating the walls*) Nice pictures.

Fay (*vaguely*) We find them quite stimulating.

Guy Yes. She's going it a bit, that one up there, isn't she?

Fay Yes. What about him behind you, then?

Guy (*turning in his chair and then with obvious shock*) Oh, good Lord. Yes. (*studying the picture*) Good Lord.

Fay We have to take them down when Ian's mother comes to stay . . .

Guy Yes, I can see she'd probably . . .

Fay Wait till you see what we've got in the bedroom. (*She laughs.*)

Guy (*laughing inordinately*) Yes. Wow. Yes. (*Pause.*) You look very nice.

Fay Thank you. So do you.

Guy (*straightening his tie*) Ah.

Fay Do you want to take that off?

Guy No, no. No. That's OK.

Fay I love men in ties . . .

Guy Oh, yes? (*Pause.*) You'd like it in our office then. It's full of them.

   Pause.

Fay Look. I might as well say this early on. Then we can relax and enjoy ourselves. If there's anything you particularly like or positively dislike, you will say, won't you?

Guy Oh no, no. I'm not at all fussy, never have been. I take just what's put in front of me.

Fay I mean, as far as I'm concerned, don't worry. I'm very easy. I don't think there's anything. Anything at all. Well, I suppose if it was excessively cruel or painful . . . I would draw the line.

Guy Oh, yes, yes. (*He considers.*) You mean like veal, for instance.

Fay Veal.

Guy Veal, you know . . .

Fay No. I don't think I've tried that.

Guy You haven't?

Fay No. Something new. How exciting. I can't wait. Veal. How do you spell it?

Guy Er . . . V–E–A–L . . .

Fay You mean the same as the meat? What's it stand for?

Guy No idea . . .

Fay Very Exciting And Lascivious . . . (*She laughs.*) No? Viciously Energetic And Lingering . . .

They both laugh.

Guy Vomitmaking Especially At Lunchtime . . .

Fay screams with laughter.

Fay (*recovering, glancing at her watch*) Your friend's late . . .

Guy Yes. She is. I'm beginning to get a bit worried. I would have picked her up in the car only she's very independent and she does like to make her own way.

Fay Why not?

Guy Quite.

Fay Has she got far to come?

Guy No, only a bus ride. From Wellfield Flats.

Fay Oh, yes. I know. Near the park?

Guy That's it.

Fay Wellfield Flats. Aren't those for old people?

Guy That's right.

Fay Oh, I see. She works there, does she? As a nurse?

Guy No, no. She lives there.

Fay Lives there?

Guy Yes. Only – well, it's rather tricky. She's a proud old soul and she always hates it when people know she lives at

Wellfield. So, if you could try not to mention it, I'd be grateful. You know what they're like at that age . . .

Fay What age?

Guy Well, she doesn't let on but my guess is early seventies . . .

Fay Seventies?

Guy But you'd never know it. She's up and down flights of stairs like nobody's business. She nursed my wife through a lot of her illness. I've always been grateful to her for . . .

He tails off. Fay is weeping with laughter.

You all right?

Fay Yes, yes . . . (*recovering a fraction*) And she's coming here? Tonight?

Guy Well, I hope so . . .

Fay I can't wait to see Ian's face . . .

Guy Ian?

Fay Dear God, this is wonderful . . . I love you. I love you.

Guy You needn't worry about the pictures. She's very broadminded. She's a game old bird, she really is. You'll like her.

Fay (*re-composing herself*) I'm sure. I'm sure.

Guy (*more dubious*) I hope Ian will get on with her but . . .

This starts Fay laughing again. She lies on the sofa and flails her legs.

(*confused*) Sorry, I'm not quite with all this I'm . . .

Fay sits up suddenly and listens.

Fay Shh. He's back. Listen. Don't tell him about your friend. Keep her as a surprise.

Guy A surprise?

Fay Please . . .

Guy All right. Why?

Ian enters brandishing a tequila bottle.

Ian All over the bloody place. Driven five miles for this – Hiya, Guy – Hallo, doll. You going to fix us one . . . ?

Fay Sure. (*taking the bottle*) Guy? Another one?

Guy Well, if it could be not quite so –

Fay Sure . . . (*She gathers up both their glasses.*)

Ian Well, where's your friend, then?

Guy (*with a glance at Fay*) Oh, she's . . . she's . . . coming shortly.

Fay gives a stifled squeak of laughter.

Ian What's the joke?

Fay Nothing. Nothing . . .

Ian There is someone else coming, I take it?

Fay (*going out*) Oh. Yes. Definitely someone else coming . . .

Fay goes out. Her laughter is heard ringing down the hall.

Ian How many's she had, then?

Guy No idea.

Ian (*settling*) Like the pictures?

Guy Yes, I've been admiring them. Amazing.

Ian (indicating one particular picture) Fay can do that, you know.

Guy (*with disbelief*) Can she really? How incredible.

Ian One of the few women I know who can. You must get her to show you. (*briskly*) Now, just before things start hotting up and getting out of hand – Could I just clear up this little business matter?

Guy Of course, of course.

Ian I won't beat about the bush. My partner and I have this little building firm, as you probably know, and we're contemplating buying a small piece of land which, as it happens, adjoins your factory.

Guy Yes, I know the piece. It so . . .

Ian Good. Well, there is a rumour – (*laughing*) – isn't there always? – that BLM may be intending to develop their existing premises. In which case, of course, the land in question could become a little more expensive. You follow?

Guy Yes. As a matter –

Ian All I'm asking is, is the rumour true?

Guy Well, all I can give you is the same answer I gave Dafydd. I honestly have no idea, but I'll try and find out. I've had no luck so far.

Ian (*slightly sharply*) Dafydd?

Guy Yes. I presume he's acting for you on this.

Ian Yes, yes. Maybe he is. (*Slight pause.*) Don't take this the wrong way but – I could make this worth your while . . . I think I can speak for Fay and say we both could . . .

(*He looks up at the picture and winks.*) OK?

The doorbell rings.

Ah, that'll be your friend. (*yelling*) Doorbell, doll . . . (*To Guy*) The sort that likes to keep you waiting, is she? (*He grins.*)

Guy Well, not if she can help it. She may have fallen over, of course . . .

Ian Fallen over? What is she? On skates?

Fay enters. She carries the drinks.

Where is she then?

Fay You have to answer it.

Ian Why?

Fay Because you have to . . .

Ian Oh, all right. (*He moves to the door.*)

Fay (*giving him a drink*) Here.

Ian (*taking it*) Ta.

Ian goes out.

Fay (*calling after him*) You may need it. (*to Guy*) Quick, quick . . . (*dragging him to the window*) Here. Have a look. Is that your friend? My God, it must be. (*She giggles.*)

Guy Yes. That's Dilys. She looks a bit the worse for wear. Hope she's all right . . .

Fay Come on. Quick . . . (*She drags him again, this time to the door.*) Bring your drink . . .

Guy Why, where . . . ?

Fay Beddy-bys . . .

Guy Sorry?

Fay I'm in desperate need of veal. Now.

Guy (*as she drags him off*) Veal? What, in bed . . .

As they leave, Ian's voice is heard returning along the hall.

Ian (*off*) Yes, well, perhaps you'd like to tidy up in the bathroom. (*entering, speaking back to someone behind him*) The light's just inside the door. Can you manage? That's it . . . Well done . . . (*He stands in the doorway with his drink. Stunned.*) Bloody hellfire. (*He drains his glass.*)

The lights fade on him and come up on a section of moonlit street. Guy, paralytically drunk, staggers into view. He stops under a street lamp.

Guy (*bellowing into the night*) Fear not, good citizens, now abed. Matt of the Mint is here. The highwayman with the hole in the middle. Matt of the Mint. V.E.A.L. Voraciously Enterprising Acrobatic Lover . . .

Guy starts to sing as Matt. Drunkenly unaccompanied at first and then, as the scene changes, as part of the rehearsal, along with the other three men, Mr Ames accompanying. Dafydd paces about watching.

Let us take the Road.
Hark! I hear the sound of Coaches!
The hour of Attack approaches,
To your Arms, brave Boys, and load,
See the Ball I hold!
Let the Chemists toil like Asses,
Our Fire their Fire surpasses,
And turns all our Lead to Gold.
Hoorah! Hoorah! Hoorah!

The song ends triumphantly. Ted, Crispin, Jarvis and Guy clink their papier-mâché tankards with great dash. Bridget is back on the book.

Dafydd Excellent. Bravo. Well done all, thank you. Couple of minutes and we're going on to Macheath and the ladies. Guy, please, could I have a moment?

Ted, Crispin and Jarvis are making their way backstage.

No, no, Crispin, don't go away, boy. I need you in a minute.

Crispin remains behind. Ted and Jarvis go off.

(*to Guy*) He's like an animal, that boy. Only got to mention a coffee break and he's got his trousers round his knees. He's got both those girls on a string, you know. Linda and Bridget. It's not fair on the rest of us, is it . . . ?

He laughs. Guy manages a smile.

Now. Just a word, Guy. Fay's just had a chat with me. And. Well, it's Ian. According to Fay, he doesn't think he's going to be able to do the part after all. So. We are now without a Filch. Which is serious, because it's a very big part indeed. So, I think you know what's coming, Guy. What do you say? Filch. Could you do it?

The women, mustered by Bridget, are beginning to assemble on the other side of the stage. They are Rebecca, Fay, Hannah, Enid and Linda.

Guy Well . . .

Dafydd You know, a month ago I wouldn't even have considered asking you but – lately . . . It's doing you good, these dramatics. You're growing in confidence every day. Can I take it you'll agree?

Guy All right.

Dafydd Good man. (*He shakes Guy's hand.*)

Guy And . . . thank you.

Dafydd Don't thank me. Thank Fay. She suggested you straightaway. Of course, I agreed. (*moving to address the assembly as a whole*) Ladies and gentlemen, I'd like to run the dance, please . . . Take your places. But just before we do, unfortunately I have to announce yet another cast change. Unavoidably, Ian Hubbard has had to withdraw from his featured role as Filch and that part will now be taken by our all-purpose replacement, Mr Guy Jones. (*All the women applaud.*)

Rebecca I said he should have played it in the first place.

Dafydd There is, however, no truth in the rumour that, at his present rate of progress, he will shortly be taking over from yours truly.

He laughs. One or two looks are exchanged.

Thank you, Mr Ames.

A dance. The women parade around Crispin as Macheath.

Women (*singing*) Youth's the Season made for Joys,

Crispin (*singing, as Macheath*) Love is then our Duty,

Women She alone who that employs,

Crispin (*as Macheath*) Well deserves her Beauty.

Women
Let's be gay,
While we may,
Beauty's a Flower, despised in decay.
Youth's the Season (*etc.*)
Let us drink and sport to-day.

Crispin (*as Macheath*) Ours is not tomorrow.

Women Love with Youth flies swift away,

Crispin (*as Macheath*) Age is nought but sorrow

Women
Dance and sing,
Time's on the Wing,
Life never knows the return of Spring.
Let us drink (*etc.*)

Dafydd (*calling encouragement*) Come on, Ladies, give it some body, some body . . . remember these are all pimps and whores. Horizontal women. All of them . . .

Rebecca (*softly but audibly*) Some of us may be . . .

Dafydd Come on, Linda, head up, try and sell it to us. Sell us your body, Linda . . .

Bridget (*with a laugh*) She couldn't give it away . . .

Dafydd Bridget, shut up . . . (*to the dancers*) That's it . . . good . . . better . . . (*as the dance is finishing*) And we all look towards Macheath and curtsy . . .

The women are all turned in Guy's direction except for Enid who, quite correctly, is facing Crispin. Seeing she is the only one doing this she hastens to conform with the others.

(*seizing Enid and shaking her furiously*) No, not at him, at Macheath. Macheath . . . Oh, I give up . . .

The music ends. Crispin goes.

All right. Thank you very much everyone. Fifteen minutes. Thank you.

Dafydd, Mr Ames and Bridget leave. The women follow, discussing as they go the events of the dance and

77

in particular sympathizing, some of them anyway, with the luckless Enid.

Bridget (*as they go*) The kettle's on . . .

Guy is left alone for a moment. He rises to follow the rest of them. He seems to us very pleased with life thus far.

Act Two

The overall scene is very much the same; the time, a little later on into rehearsals. At the start, a light comes up on Crispin as Macheath.

Crispin (*sings, as Macheath*)
If the Heart of a Man is deprest with Cares;
The Mist is dispell'd when a Woman appears;
Like the Notes of a Fiddle, she sweetly, sweetly
Raises the Spirits and charms our Ears.
Roses and Lillies her Cheeks disclose,
But her ripe Lips are more sweet than those.
Press her, caress her, with Blisses her Kisses
Dissolve us in Pleasure, and soft Repose.

> *As the song finishes, we crossfade to a café table. Basically a 'four', at present it contains just Guy and Hannah. Used cups and plates and a cakestand with several cakes still remaining. Hannah is eating one of these. There is a tense air about the scene. Most of the tension, it would appear, being generated by Hannah.*

Hannah (*after a pause*) Well. What are you going to do about it? (*Pause.*) I mean, you can't have both of us, can you? (*Pause.*) You can't have your . . . (*She tails off as she looks at the cakestand.*) You'll just have to make up your mind, Guy. Me or her.

Guy (*muttering unhappily*) It's not – that – easy . . .

Hannah What? What did you say?

Guy (*rather too loudly*) I said it's not that easy . . .

Hannah Sshh! Sshh! All right. Do you want the whole restaurant to hear us? (*Pause.*) I mean, why do you want two of us, anyway?

Guy I don't want two of you –

Hannah Isn't one enough?

Guy I love you both in – different ways –

Hannah I'm glad to hear it. I suppose I'm the one who's good for sewing on buttons and doing your washing. That takes a great deal of arranging, I'll have you know. Using our machine while Dafydd's out of the way. Sorting out socks at midnight. (*A sudden practical thought.*) You don't have any of his pants, do you? He's mislaid a pair.

Guy Sort of Paisley patterned?

Hannah Those are them. If you have them, give me them back, will you?

Guy I think I've got them on, actually.

Hannah Oh, God. Guy. (*Pause.*) Well, it's obvious you don't go to Fay for your washing. Despite all those pale clothes she wears, I always get the feeling that there's something very grubby underneath.

Guy Oh, come on, Hannah. (*Pause.*) Have a cake.

Hannah I've had quite enough cake. And I'm sick to death of us meeting in cafés and pubs and bus shelters . . .

Guy Well, where else can we go?

Hannah Nowhere. It's too small a town. Everybody knows.

Guy Yes, I know.

Hannah Except Dafydd, of course.

Guy No. I honestly don't think he does know. I thought at first he was turning a gigantic blind eye but . . .

Hannah Dafydd doesn't know. He's amazing. Even the twins are suspicious. They've started calling that Daddy-doll of theirs Guy. Fortunately, Dafydd just thinks they're starting early for bonfire night. (*Pause.*) No, he doesn't want me – in that way – any more, so he assumes no one else could possibly – want me. (*Pause.*) I'm not sure anyone does, really. (*She cries. Angry tears.*)

Guy Hannah. Now, Hannah . . .

Hannah (*savagely*) It's just damn lucky for you that Dafydd doesn't know about us, that's all I can say. Otherwise he'd sort you out, he really would. He'd beat you senseless. He'd punch you into a pulp. He'd smash your face in and jump on you and he'd kick you where it really hurt. And I'd laugh. Ha! Ha! He's bloody tough. He was a rugger player, you know . . .

Guy Yes. Yes, he told me.

Hannah sobs.

Please don't, Hannah. Please . . . People are staring. I'll get the bill.

Hannah (*seeing someone behind Guy*) Oh, no . . .

Guy What is it?

Hannah It's her. She followed us here. She's spying on us.

Guy Oh, Lord . . .

Fay comes into view. She has evidently been shopping. She carries several bags.

Fay Hallo, you two.

Hannah ignores her.

Guy Hallo, Fay.

Fay What a funny place to come for tea. A right little clip joint . . .

Hannah Is that why you're here?

Fay (*sitting at the table between them*) May I join you?

Hannah You most certainly may not.

Fay Thank you. Whew! I'm exhausted. You look terrible, Hannah. What is it, darling, hay fever?

Hannah I'm allergic, that's all. To certain smells.

Fay regards Hannah for a moment. A silence.

Guy Look, this is all very awkward. I think it would be better if one of us left, I really do.

Fay It's all right. I'm not stopping . . .

Hannah Good.

Fay I just wanted to give something to Guy.

Hannah What?

Fay produces a paper bag from amongst her shopping.

Fay (*passing it to Guy*) Here . . .

Hannah What is it?

Fay Private.

Hannah (*taking hold of the bag*) What?

Fay Mind your own business . . .

Hannah I demand to know what it is. I demand to know . . .

Fay Get your hands off . . .

Guy (*interceding, mildly*) Now, now. Now then. Come on, girls, people are . . . (*He smiles round the restaurant.*)

Hannah and Fay stay deadlocked.

Fay Then tell her to let go.

Hannah I refuse to allow her to walk in here and start giving you things . . .

Guy Hannah . . .

Hannah How dare she give you secret presents right under my nose . . . She's just trying to humiliate me. That's what she's doing . . .

Fay Let go.

Hannah No.

Guy Look. Let's be adult about this, shall we? (*looking at them in turn*) Girls? Please. Look, let me have it. And I'll open it. And then there'll be no secrets. All right? Hannah? Hannah . . .

Hannah All right. I want to see.

Guy Fay?

Fay (*shrugging*) Fine with me . . .

They release the bag to Guy.

Guy Right. OK. Now then. (*opening the bag and removing the contents*) Let's see what we have in . . . (*He holds a pair of Paisley-patterned pants.*) Oh, God.

Fay They were under the bed. I didn't want you to catch cold. (*She giggles.*)

Hannah (*looking at Fay with extreme loathing*) You total bitch. You total and utter grubby, smutty, grimy, unhygienic little bitch. (*snatching at the pants*) Give me those. Give me those at once . . .

83

Guy (*holding them still*) Hannah . . .

Fay Don't do that . . .

Hannah Give them to me . . .

Fay (*joining in the tussle*) Let go, at once . . .

Guy Now this is silly. Now come on . . .

They tug.

Hannah Give me those pants . . .

Fay Hannah, they are not yours. Now let go. They don't belong to you . . .

Hannah Oh, yes they do . . .

Fay Nonsense . . .

Guy I think they do actually, Fay.

Fay They're hers?

Hannah Yes.

Fay (*letting go*) Darling. I'm terribly sorry . . .

Guy (*also letting go*) I mean, when I say hers I meant –

Fay Hannah, darling, who ever would have guessed? It just goes to show. Behind the most boring exterior . . .

Hannah (*stuffing the pants into her handbag*) How dare you do this? How dare you . . . ?

Fay . . . lurk the weirdest of hang-ups . . .

Guy Fay, please . . .

Hannah (*rising and putting on her coat*) I'm not stopping here . . .

Fay Don't worry, darling, your secret is safe.

Hannah (*to Fay*) You'll be sorry for this. I promise you, you'll be sorry for this . . .

Hannah goes out.

Guy (*rising*) Oh, Fay . . . really. There was no need for that. Really.

Fay Oh. Are you going?

Guy Yes, of course. I've got to . . . (*He indicates Hannah.*)

Fay Help her choose a jock strap . . .

Guy Fay, please, don't keep on. Those are Dafydd's . . .

Fay Dafydd's?

Guy Of course they were . . .

Fay Curiouser and curiouser . . .

Guy A mix-up in the wash. That's all . . .

Fay I shan't enquire further, darling. Don't worry. I'll see you this evening, then. At rehearsal.

Guy Rather.

Fay And I'll be in later, if you want to pop round . . .

Guy (*doubtfully*) Well . . . Not this evening, Fay . . .

Fay By the way, Ian was asking if you'd heard anything yet. About the land.

Guy Oh. No. Sorry.

Fay Only Jarvis is not going to hang on for ever. If we don't buy it somebody else will.

Guy Jarvis? You mean it's Jarvis who owns it?

Fay (*feeling she may have said too much*) Yes. Didn't you know? I thought you did.

Guy No, I didn't realize he owned it.

Fay (*shrugging*) Not that it matters. The point is, have you been asking? Because that was part of our deal, darling, wasn't it?

Guy Deal? How do you mean?

Fay I mean, Ian did give up his role for you, didn't he? Filch.

Guy Oh, Filch. Yes. I didn't ask him to, you know.

Fay No, but you didn't say no, did you? But then you haven't actually said no to anything, have you? Not that I'm complaining. But I suppose Ian might. Eventually. If you don't come up with the goods.

Guy Well, I am . . . I am asking round. Discreetly, of course.

Fay Oh, good. It'd be horrid if it all got nasty, wouldn't it? Bye-bye, darling.

Guy (*rather uneasily*) Bye . . .

Guy goes rather unhappily. Fay sits on at her table for a minute, smiling to herself. A light comes up on Linda.

Linda (*as Lucy, sings*)
Thus when a good Huswife sees a Rat
In her Trap in the Morning taken,
With pleasure her Heart goes pit a pat,
In Revenge for her loss of Bacon.
Then she throws him
To the Dog or Cat,
To be worried, crushed and shaken.

As the song ends, Fay exits. General lights come up on Linda to reveal she is in rehearsal with both Hannah and Crispin, as Polly and Macheath. Also in attendance,

*Bridget with the prompt script, as usual. Dafydd is
prowling the auditorium and, away in one corner
paying little attention, Jarvis sits with a small portable
cassette player clipped to his person and a pair of
lightweight headphones clamped on his ears. He is in a
private world of his own. Guy, who has entered during
the song, also watches the ensuing rehearsal. Crispin
stands holding a freestanding mock-up rehearsal gaol
door, through which he plays the scene.*

Linda (*as Lucy, speaking*) Am I then bilk'd of my Virtue?
Can I have no Reparation? Sure Men were born to lye,
and Women to believe them! O Villain! Villain!

Hannah (*as Polly*) Am I not thy Wife? – Thy Neglect of
me, thy Aversion to me too severely proves it. – Look on
me. – Tell me, am I not thy Wife?

Linda (*as Lucy*) Perfidious Wretch!

Hannah (*as Polly*) Barbarous Husband!

Linda (*as Lucy*) Hadst thou been hang'd five Months ago,
I had been happy.

Hannah (*as Polly*) And I too – if you had been kind to me
'till Death, it would not have vex'd me – And that's no
very unreasonable Request, (though from a Wife) to a
Man who hath not above seven or eight Days to live.

*Under this last exchange, Dafydd seeing Guy has joined
the rehearsal strolls over to him.*

Dafydd (*in a loud whisper*) Sorry. We're running a bit late.
Be with you in a second.

Guy (*sotto*) OK.

Dafydd Bloody hard work it is with these three. This lad –
great voice. But he moves like something out of Austin
Reed's window. And as for this prissy little madam . . .

(*Indicates Linda.*) Look at her. I've seen rougher trade on a health-food counter . . .

The rehearsal continues.

Linda (*as Lucy*) Are thou then married Monster? . . . (*She hesitates.*)

Bridget (*prompting loudly*) Art thou then married to another?

Linda (*as Lucy*) Art thou then married to another? Hast thou –

Bridget (*interrupting her*) Hast thou two Wives, Monster?

Linda All right, all right, I know it . . .

Bridget I was giving you the line . . .

Linda Yes, well, I knew it. I knew it, didn't I?

Hannah wanders away from the exchange. There's evidently been quite a lot of this sort of thing. Crispin remains amusedly detached. Dafydd returns his attention to the rehearsal.

Dafydd All right, all right, girls. Come on, get on with it now.

Linda Every time I pause for breath, she reads out my line. Would you kindly ask her not to, please?

Dafydd Bridget, don't read her lines out unless she asks for them. And Linda, you stop pausing for so much breath.

Linda I have to breathe, don't I?

Bridget (*in an undertone*) Not necessarily . . .

Dafydd You can't take that long breathing onstage. You want to breathe deeply, you breathe offstage in your own time . . . on we go. And Bridget, shut up!

Bridget (*muttering to herself*) I thought the only reason I was here was to prompt. I mean, what's the point of sitting here for three months . . . ?

Dafydd Bridget. Shut up! Go on.

A slight pause. The women look at Crispin.

Crispin Oh, it's my go, is it? Right. (*as Macheath*) If Women's Tongues can cease for an Answer – hear me.

Dafydd whimpers audibly at Crispin's effort.

(*looking out in Dafydd's direction*) I heard that . . .

Linda (*as Lucy*) I won't. – Flesh and Blood can't bear my Usage.

Hannah (*as Polly*) Shall I not claim my own? Justice bids me speak. Sure, my Dear, there ought to be some Preference shown to a Wife! At least she may claim the Appearance of it. (*pointedly in Guy's direction*) He must be distracted with his Misfortunes, or he could not use me thus!

Another silence. Hannah looks at Linda.

Linda (*realizing belatedly that it's her*) Um. Oh. Yes. Um. Oh. Eee. (*She twists herself in knots trying to remember. To Bridget, reluctantly*) What is it, then?

Bridget (*prompting*) Oh . . .

Linda (*repeating her*) Oh . . .

Bridget (*forming the first syllable of 'villain'*) V . . . v . . .

Linda (*with her*) V . . . v . . . vain . . . vish . . . voo . . . ver . . . ver . . .

Dafydd (*screaming from the back*) Look, what the hell is this, twenty bloody questions?

Linda (*wailing*) She won't tell me my line . . .

Dafydd Bridget, for God's sake, tell her her line . . .

Bridget You just told me not to. (*reading rapidly*) Oh villain villain thou hast deceiv'd me I could even inform against thee with pleasure not a prude wishes more heartily to have facts against her intimate acquaintance . . .

Linda starts wailing during this monotone rendition by Bridget.

Dafydd Bridget! That'll do . . .

Bridget stops.

Bridget (*innocently*) What?

Hannah (*comforting Linda*) Now, come on, dear . . .

Linda (*scarcely audible, weeping*) She does that all the time. She keeps doing it. All the time . . .

Dafydd gives a vast groan of impatience.

Hannah Just a minute, Dafydd, just a minute . . .

A very private women's huddle between Linda and Hannah that none of us can hear. Crispin, the root cause of all this, stands looking quite pleased with himself. He pulls faces at Dafydd through the gaol door.

Dafydd (*to Guy*) Look at that smirking oaf. I wish to God they were professionals. Then I could sack them. These bastards, they've got you over a barrel. Unless you say well done all the time they don't turn up. What are those two doing? It's like a loose scrum. (*yelling*) Come on, injury time's over. Give her a slice of lemon, change her shorts, and get her back on the field.

Hannah (*leaving Linda, to Dafydd*) Right. She's all right. (*to Linda*) All right?

Linda nods and resumes her position.

Linda (*as Lucy, in a colourless tone, growing increasingly inaudible*) O Villain, Villain! (*She sniffs.*) Thou has deceiv'd me – (*Sniffs.*) I could even inform against thee with Pleasure. Not a Prude wishes more heartily to have Facts against her intimate Acquaintance, than I now wish to have Facts against thee. I would have her Satisfaction, and they should all out . . . (*She peters out.*)

Dafydd (*who has moved closer and closer to her in an attempt to hear*) And . . . Mr Ames! Don't tell me he's died now. Mr Ames . . .

Mr Ames (*cheerily*) Hallo?

Dafydd Song.

Mr Ames Sorry. (*He starts to play.*)

Hannah (*singing, as Polly*) I'm bubbled.

Linda (*singing, as Lucy*) I'm bubbled.

Hannah Oh how I am troubled!

Linda Bamboozled and bit!

Hannah My Distresses are doubled.

Linda
When you come to the Tree, should the Hangman refuse,
These fingers, with Pleasure, could fasten the Noose.

Hannah I'm bubbled, (*etc.*)

The song ends. The scene resumes without pause.

(*speaking, as Polly*) And hast thou the Heart to persist in disowning me?

Crispin (*as Macheath*) And hast thou the Heart to persist in persuading me that I am married? Why, Polly, dost thou seek to aggravate my Misfortunes?

91

Dafydd groans again at this rendition.

Linda (*as Lucy*) Really, Miss Peachum, you but expose yourself.

Bridget sniggers.

Besides . . . (*crossing to Bridget, furiously*) Will you stop laughing at me? Will you stop laughing?

Dafydd (*from the back*) Hey, hey, hey, hey . . .

Bridget It was funny . . .

Hannah Linda . . .

Linda I'll soon make you stop laughing.

She grabs the unprepared Bridget by her hair and hauls her off her chair and on to the floor.

Bridget (*furious*) OW . . .

Crispin (*with great relish*) Wey-hey!

Linda I'll teach you, I'll teach you . . .

Bridget Now, let go. Let go, I'm warning you . . .

Hannah Oh, dear heavens. That's it. That's it. No more . . .

Dafydd (*ineffectually, trying to part them*) Now come on, girls, come on . . .

Jarvis's attention has been attracted by the scrap onstage.

Jarvis (*to Dafydd, loudly because of his headphones*) Good scrap that. Very convincing. First class.

Dafydd Oh, shut up.

Jarvis does not hear but smiles. The girls are fighting in earnest now. Close-combat stuff, on the floor, rolling over and over, both seeking for an advantage. Bridget's greater strength is matched by Linda's white fury. Mr

Ames, at Crispin's beckoning, starts up another song. During the course of this, the fight continues silently until Guy and Dafydd manage to prise the girls apart. All this in mimed silence, although presumably in reality the din is quite loud.

Crispin (*singing, together with Mr Ames, with unusual relish*)
How happy could I be with either
Were t'other dear Charmer away!
But while you thus teaze me together,
To neither a Word will I say;
But tol de rol, (*etc.*)

As the song finishes, 'normal sound' is resumed. The combatants are panting and exhausted. So are the rescuers. Guy is holding Bridget; Hannah holds Linda. Dafydd stands between them, gasping to regain his breath, before speaking. Jarvis has watched it all from his ringside seat with great enjoyment.

Dafydd (*at length*) All right now . . . listen to me . . . both of you . . .

Bridget attempts to struggle free from Guy. Guy clings on.

Now come along, Bridget. Bridget! Bridget . . .

Dafydd makes to slap Bridget's face. She quietens. He goes to pat her instead. She snaps at his hand and he all but loses his fingers.

Jesus! All right . . .

Linda starts to struggle too.

Hannah I can't hold her much . . .

Dafydd (*to Hannah*) All right, take her backstage. Backstage. Run her under a tap.

Hannah starts to drag Linda off.

(*to Guy*) And her. Outside. (*assisting Guy with Bridget*)
All right, I've got her. Come on. Outside, you. Outside.

*Hannah takes Linda off. Guy and Dafydd take Bridget
out, lifting her between them. Dafydd returns almost
immediately. Guy presumably remains outside in case
Bridget decides to return. Dafydd now turns his
attention to the smirking Crispin.*

Dafydd As for you, you sniggering Herbert. This is all
your fault. You were entirely to blame for that.

Crispin Bollocks. (*He goes to leave.*)

Dafydd (*after him*) I've a good mind to sort you out, boy,
I really have.

Crispin (*turning suddenly, violently*) Right you are.
You're on.

Dafydd (*taken aback somewhat by his change of tone*) What?

Crispin Come on, then . . .

Dafydd No, that's not the way. Violence is no solution.

Crispin I've been longing to have a go at you. Come on.

*Crispin starts to advance slightly on Dafydd. He, in
turn, retreats rather apprehensively.*

You've been getting up my nose for a few weeks now . . .

Dafydd Now come on, boy, be your age. Ah ah. Now,
now. I'm a . . . I'm a middle-aged man, you know. Very
nearly. That wouldn't be fair. Let's be reasonable . . . Now,
don't you . . . don't you try it . . . I'm a lawyer, you know
. . . I could have you for . . . I won't, of course, if you
don't (*nose to nose with Crispin, unable to retreat further,
nervously*) Well, now what? Eh? (*He laughs.*)

Crispin Well . . .

Dafydd Yes?

Crispin How about this for starters?

Crispin brings his knee up sharply and moves back. Dafydd gives a fearful whistling sound and bends double. Hannah and Guy have both returned separately to witness this.

Hannah Dafydd . . .

Guy Hoy . . .

Crispin (*cheerfully*) Bye all . . . (*He strolls out.*)

Dafydd (*in pain*) Oooooorrrggg.

Jarvis (*who was watching this*) No, that wasn't as convincing as the other one . . .

Dafydd (*glaring at Jarvis, his face twisted in malignant pain*) I'll kill him. I'll kill that old bastard . . .

Jarvis (*smiling, unhearing*) You don't mind an opinion, do you?

Guy You OK?

Hannah Is he all right?

Guy Yes, I think he's been hit in the . . .

Hannah (*sympathetically*) Oh, yes. It's very painful there, isn't it?

Dafydd Of course it's bloody painful . . .

Guy Cold water helps . . . I think.

Hannah Right. Well, you . . . (*starting to lead Dafydd away*) You'd better come and sit with Linda. You can have the sink after her . . .

They start going off, Hannah picking up Linda's bag on their way. Dafydd groans.

Carefully, dear. That's it . . .

Hannah and Dafydd go off.

Guy (*to himself*) Oh, well . . .

Jarvis (*removing his headphones and offering them to Guy*) Have a listen to that. Tell me what you think it is.

Guy somewhat reluctantly puts on the headphones. Whatever he hears is very loud and not too pleasant. He hastily takes them off.

Guy God! What is it?

Jarvis Give up? That is an actual recording of an 1812 Boulton and Watt beam engine which is still used to this day for pumping water to the summit of the Kennet and Avon canal.

Guy Good heavens.

Jarvis It lifts one ton of water 40 feet on each stroke of the engine.

Guy Amazing.

Jarvis That's what I've been listening to for the past hour.

Guy A beam engine?

Jarvis Aye.

Guy What, all evening?

Jarvis No, no, no. This is called 'The Vanishing Sounds in Britain'. Issued by the BBC. All vanishing sounds . . .

Guy Well, listening to that, it's probably a good job, isn't it? (*He laughs.*)

Jarvis (*not hearing*) What's that? (*He switches off the recorder.*) No, I gave the record to the wife last Christmas, but she wasn't so keen . . .

Guy Look. May I have a quick word with you? (*looking round to see that they're alone*) It's about a piece of land that apparently belongs to you. Round the back of the BLM factory. Do you know it?

Jarvis I not only know it. I own it.

Guy Yes.

Jarvis I'll tell you a very interesting little tale about that bit of land . . .

Guy (*his heart sinking*) Oh, really . . .

Jarvis That land was purchased by my grandfather, old Joshua Pike, for the benefit of his employees. He were a philanthropist and a deeply religious man – chapel, you see – but his other passion, apart from t'firm, were cricket. Cricket mad. You with me?

Guy Aye. Yes.

Jarvis Well, he bought that land off a widow woman and he had his lads, his workers, levelling and draining and returfing it – in their own time, mind – not his. And, well, when it were finished – well, some said it were the finest strip for a hundred mile or more. Like a billiard pool. And he said to the lads, there you are, lads, go to it. That's my gift to you. That's my bounty.

Guy Wonderful.

Jarvis Only one thing – bearing in mind he were a chapel man – not on Sundays, lads. Never on the sabbath. Well, any road up, year or so later, he's out for a stroll one Sunday afternoon with his children and his grandchildren – taking the air, like – and what should he spy as he's passing the cricket field but a bunch of workers laughing and joking and chucking a ball about like it were Saturday dinner time. And the old man says nowt. Not at the time. But the next day, Monday morning first thing, he sends in his bulldozers and diggers and ploughs and he digs that land up from one end to the other. Then he sets fire to t'pavilion and he puts up a 12-foot wooden fence. Palings. And to this day, not a ball has been thrown on that field. That's the sort of man he was. Me grandfather. Dying breed.

Guy Another vanishing sound of Britain. Yes . . . (*after what he hopes is a respectful pause*) The point is, with regard to this land . . . There is a rumour, unconfirmed I may add, that BLM are contemplating buying it. Possibly. In which case it could be worth a bit. If you were considering selling it.

Jarvis considers this.

So.

Jarvis Say no more.

Guy You follow me.

Jarvis I'm glad of the information. I trust you. You're a Scotty. And I'll see you're looked after, don't worry.

Guy No, I don't need looking after. Really.

Jarvis Then why are you telling me?

Guy Well, I – thought you ought to know – it's just that I wouldn't want people to put one over on you. Friendly.

Jarvis (*laughing sceptically*) Friendly? Oh, aye? That's a good one.

Guy Well, if you don't believe me . . .

Jarvis Don't come the friendly with me, friend. I've a few

98

years to go yet but when I leave this earth, I'll be leaving it fair and square. Same as me father did and me grandfather. I owe nothing to no one. They're all paid off. I've paid off my business. I've paid off my family. There's no claim on me from any quarter. And I don't intend to start making exceptions with you. You see me right. I'll see you right. Right?

Guy Right.

Rebecca comes in from the road. She is in time to catch the end of this conversation. She looks at them a trifle suspiciously.

Rebecca Hello.

Jarvis Aye.

Guy Good evening.

Rebecca Has Dafydd got to us yet?

Guy No. I don't think he's got to very much, actually . . .

Rebecca How unsurprising. Where is he? Back there?

Guy Yes.

Rebecca I'll sort them out then. I've had enough of this . . .

Rebecca goes backstage.

Jarvis I've paid her off and all. My mother's 92. She's paid off.

Guy You paid your mother off?

Jarvis A hundred quid a week tax free and a bungalow in Paignton. She's not complaining. (*as he moves to go backstage*) You'll be paid off. Don't worry . . .

Jarvis goes off. Guy, alone and as keen as ever, decides

to have a quick private rehearsal. He takes up his script. He reads other people's lines but tries to speak his own without looking.

Guy (*reading*) Come hither Filch . . . blurr, blurr, blurr . . . (*He skips.*) Where was your Post last Night, my Boy? (*without the script*) I ply'd at the Opera, Madam; and considering 'twas neither dark nor rainy, so that there was no great Hurry in getting Chairs and Coaches, Made a tolerable on't. These seven Handkerchiefs, Madam.

Guy checks the script and is pleased to see he got it right. He is about to continue when he sees Dafydd has appeared. He is very subdued and is sipping a beaker of tea.

How are you feeling?

Dafydd Oh, pretty good. Like a man who's just spent his wedding night with an electrified steam shovel . . .

Guy nods sympathetically.

Well. Now we are in a hole. If that boy doesn't come back we're over the dead-ball line, I can tell you. Trying to do *The Beggar's Opera* without a Macheath is a bit of a non-starter even for Peter Brook. So. (*Pause.*) Oh, it makes you want to . . . Who cares, anyway? Who cares?

Guy I do.

Dafydd Ah, Guy, Guy. My rock. But nobody really cares. Not in this country. Anything you want to mention's more important than theatre to most of them. Washing their hair, cleaning their cars . . . If this was Bulgaria or somewhere we'd have peasants hammering on the doors. Demanding satisfaction or their money back. This place, you tell them you're interested in the arts, you get messages of sympathy. Get well soon. Well, maybe they're right. Why beat your brains out? Every time I vow I'm just going to have a ball. I'm not going to take any of it seriously. It's just a play, for God's sake . . . And every time it gets like this. Desperate. Life-and-death stuff. Look at me. You'd think to look at me I was in really serious trouble. While all that's happened, in fact, is that a play might not happen. That's all. But of course the irony is that outside these four walls, in the real world out there, I actually am in serious trouble and I couldn't give a stuff. Now that really does raise questions, doesn't it? If I were my psychiatrist I'd be worrried that all was not well. And I'd be right.

Guy (*cautiously*) Any – particular sort of trouble?

Dafydd (*evasively*) Well, apart from being beaten up by a singing Yahoo . . . nothing very original. I don't know. Things, you know. Hannah. Things like that. (*Pause.*) She's a bloody deep-freeze of a woman. That's the trouble. Physically. I mean, she's great in other ways. Wonderful at keeping the home going and things. I mean without her . . . (*He smiles.*) I call her my Swiss Army Wife, you know. No man should be without one. (*He laughs.*) Yes, yes . . . It's just that she's – she's got a blade missing if you know what I mean. Always has had. Isn't her fault of course. Just not in her nature. Right from our wedding night. Ice tongs to lift her nightdress, I'm telling you . . .

Guy You didn't . . . find out – before you were married?

Dafydd Well, not from my part of Wales, boy. Not too hot on sale or return there, you know. Mind you, I assumed she'd thaw. Given a little warmth. And, you know, general encouragement. (*with more passion, suddenly*) God, it's not that I didn't try . . . I really wanted to make it work, I really did. The nights I spent – battering at those damn defences of hers. But nothing. Knock one down she'd build another.

Guy (*trying to lighten it*) Well. You managed to have twins . . .

Dafydd (*darkly*) Yes. Well, we never talk about that. Never.

Guy Ah . . .

Dafydd Sorry, Guy. Bloody bore. I'm sorry. Why should I bore you with me and Hannah? Sorry . . . Don't know what came over me. I think it takes a kick in the crutch to make a man painfully aware of his own mortality . . .

Rebecca returns.

(*irritably*) Yes?

Rebecca Sorry to interrupt. First, I thought you'd like to know that the tannoy's on . . .

Dafydd Oh, God . . .

Rebecca And second, in a vain attempt to prevent Hannah from hearing, we had a meeting . . .

Dafydd Oh, yes. And?

Rebecca Well, what are we going to do? Scrap the production? I mean that boy, from all accounts, doesn't intend to come back, does he? So what do we do?

Dafydd I don't know what we do. You tell me. You're the one who keeps holding bloody meetings. Next time try inviting me. Maybe I can make a few suggestions.

Rebecca Very well, to start with. We need a new Macheath. Agreed?

Dafydd Yes. And where are we going to find him? Eh?

Rebecca Well . . . (*She looks towards Guy.*)

Guy Ah.

Dafydd You mean Guy?

Rebecca He's the natural choice, isn't he? It's either him or Ian Hubbard . . .

Dafydd Oh God, anyone rather than Ian Hubbard . . .

Rebecca (*pointing towards the tannoy mike*) Shh!

Dafydd Sorry. (*in a whisper*) Could you do it?

Guy I –

Rebecca Do it? He'd love it . . .

The lights close down to a single spot on Guy. Rebecca and Dafydd leave.

Guy (*singing, as Macheath*)
Which way shall I turn me – How can I decide!
Wives, the Day of our Death, are as fond as a Bride.
One Wife is too much for most Husbands to hear,
But two at a time there's no Mortal can bear.
This way, and that way, and which way I will,
What would comfort the one, t'other wife would take ill.

At the end of the song, the lights come up on Rebecca's garden. A seat. A garden table. Guy stands looking round.

Rebecca (*hailing him*) Yoo-hoo! Over here, Guy. It's so sweet of you to pop round. Excuse the midges, won't you? Would you like a cup of tea? Shall I ring for some tea?

Guy No. No, thank you. Had my tea at home, just now.

Rebecca Sure? A sherry or something?

Guy No. Thanks all the same. Not with rehearsals in a minute.

Rebecca (*picking up her own glass*) Quite right, quite right. You put the rest of us to shame, Guy. Mind you, I don't think it would matter that much if I drank myself silly. They always manage to hide me behind a piece of scenery anyway . . .

She laughs. Guy laughs politely.

Do sit down. (*proffering a cigarette box*) Do you? No. You are good. None of the vices. Practically. (*She smiles.*) We all think you're going to be an absolutely wonderful Macheath.

Guy Thank you.

Rebecca I take the view that Dafydd's terribly lucky to get you. Whatever the price.

Guy I'm sorry?

Rebecca There's no need to be sorry. You've jollied us up no end, Guy. All of us. In our different ways.

Guy Well . . .

Rebecca Now, what I'm really hoping is that you're going to make my day as well. After all, you've made nearly everybody else's. One way or another. It must be my turn, mustn't it? Surely?

Rebecca smiles at him warmly. Guy shifts a little uncomfortably. They are left thus as a light comes up on Ted, Enid and Jarvis.

Ted, Enid *and* **Jarvis** (*singing*)
In the days of my Youth I could bill like a Dove,
Fa, la, la, (*etc.*)
Like a sparrow at all times was ready for Love,
Fa, la, la, (*etc.*)
The Life of all Mortals in Kissing should pass,
Lip to Lip while we're young – then the Lip to the Glass,
Fa, la, la, (*etc.*)

At the end of the song the lights return to their previous state. Rebecca and Guy have been chattering away.

Rebecca Now. This little favour I wanted to ask . . . (*seeing Guy's expression*) Don't look so terrified. It's not what you're thinking . . .

Guy No, no. I was –

Rebecca God forbid. Six years sharing a mattress with Jarvis cured me of that. No, it's just that I understand you and he were talking the other evening . . .

Guy Yes? Oh, yes. About the –

Rebecca About our little bit of land.

Guy Yes. As a matter of fact I wanted to talk about that too, actually.

Rebecca Good.

Guy (*fumbling in his pocket*) The point is I've – well, it's rather awkward – (*He produces a bulging envelope.*) I got this in the post this morning.

Rebecca Oh, how gorgeous. (*peering*) What is it? I'm sorry, I haven't my glasses.

Guy It's £500.

Rebecca Oh, super.

Guy In notes. Cash.

Rebecca Lucky you. What happened? Someone passed away?

Guy Not – so far as I know. No. I rather thought it came from you.

Rebecca Me?

Guy Well, rather from Jarvis.

Rebecca Jarvis?

Guy I think so.

Rebecca It sounds very unlikely. You'd be the first person who managed to get money out of Jarvis. None of his wives ever could, I can tell you . . . Two of them died trying, poor things.

Guy I'm pretty certain it is from him.

Rebecca What does it say? With love from Jarvis?

Guy Of course not. It's –

Rebecca Then how do you know? Why on earth would my husband send you £500?

Guy Because I – I warned him about this rumour. About the land. I can't at present find any foundation in truth in it, but there's this rumour that –

Rebecca (*slightly impatiently*) Yes, I've heard the rumour.

Guy You have?

Rebecca Oh, yes.

Guy Well. I told Jarvis simply because I was anxious that he shouldn't be taken advantage of. Or you.

Rebecca Well, that's awfully sweet of you. Thank you. Of course, it could work both ways, couldn't it? I mean, supposing this rumour wasn't true but everyone assumed it was, then the price would go up and Jarvis would be laughing. And the joke would be on these very unscrupulous people that you've so kindly been warning us about. Which would be a sort of poetic justice, wouldn't it?

Guy Ah.

Rebecca Of course, the whole thing would be helped

tremendously if someone strategically placed like yourself did nothing to deny the rumour. Even, dare one say it, encouraged it?

Guy Oh, I don't think I could . . .

Rebecca No, no, heaven forbid. That's entirely up to your conscience. Anyway, you've got much too much on your mind already with Macheath. We mustn't worry you. Just remember, though, when they're all clapping and cheering you on the first night, it was me who got you the part. Remember that . . .

Guy Yes. And I'm very grateful. I –

Rebecca (*with the barest glance at her watch*) Now, we must dash, mustn't we? We don't want to keep them waiting. Do you have your car? (*She is moving away as she speaks.*)

Guy Yes, thank you . . . You know, I'd really love to know how this rumour started. It's extraordinary . . .

Rebecca (*looking at him for a second and then realizing the question was without guile*) Well, I suspect that's something we shall never know, shall we? Any of us. Coming?

Guy (*indicating the envelope on the table*) What about – ? What shall I do with this? The money?

Rebecca That's up to you, surely. Have fun with it, I should.

Guy I can't accept it. Possibly.

Rebecca Don't be so absurd.

Guy If I took it, that would be . . . it'd be . . .

Rebecca Well, suit yourself what you do with it. Only for heaven's sake don't leave it there. Or people might get the idea you were giving it to us. And that wouldn't look good at all, would it?

Rebecca goes out. Guy stares at the envelope undecided. He half moves away. He stops. After a second or so he returns to the money. He takes it up and pockets it. As he does so, the lights change and we are back in the rehearsal room. Guy now changes into his basic Macheath costume. He is assisted in this by several of the women in the company who fuss round him. Amongst these are Hannah, Fay, Enid and Linda. All of these are in part, most, or all of their costume. The production is entering its final phase. From here on we are very conscious that the production is 'lit'. While this activity ensues, silently, Bridget, also in costume for her role as Jenny Diver, sings.

Bridget
Before the Barn-door crowing,
The Cock by Hens attended,
His Eyes around him throwing,
Stands for a while suspended,
Then One he singles from the Crew,
And cheers the happy Hen;
With how do you do, and how do you do,
And how do you do again.

The other women sing with her at the chorus. As the song finishes, the lighting rehearsal continues. Guy remains midstage. The women and Mr Ames leave the stage. The rehearsal has apparently been delayed for technical reasons. Dafydd enters from the lighting box.

Dafydd Sorry, Guy. We'll be underway pretty soon now. If nothing else blows up on us. (*indicating the lighting box, confidentially*) He's slow, this electrician, though. Twenty minutes changing a colour. Unbelievable. I mean, why volunteer to light a show if you suffer from vertigo?

He knew there'd be ladders. Man's a half-wit, he
should . . .

Another single light comes up on stage.

(*calling to the box*) Thank you, Raymond, that's – that's
lovely. (*standing in a vivid orange patch of light, to Guy*)
This look like firelight to you?

Guy (*uncertainly*) No. Not a lot.

Dafydd No, nor me. I'll cut it later. Better leave it for
now. It took him three hours to focus . . . (*calling again*)
Yes, we're wild about that, Raymond. We like it very
much. (*consulting his plan*) Could I see your number 18
now, please? That's my number 15, your number 18.
Thank you. (*to Guy*) Haven't even got the same bloody
numbers, these plans . . . (*as a light comes up*) No, that's
number 17, Raymond. That's your number 17. My
number 12. The one I want to see is my number 15, your
number 18.

Raymond (*a distant voice*) That is number 18 . . .

Dafydd What's that? No, that's number 17. My number
12. I don't want number 17. I want number 18. My
number 18, your number 15.

Raymond I haven't got a number 15 . . .

Dafydd No, hang on, as you were. *My* number 15. *Your*
number 18 . . . (*Another lamp comes on.*) No, no, that's
number 56. That shouldn't even be bloody plugged up . . .
Hang on, hang on. For God's sake. I'm coming up,
Raymond. And somebody, please open some doors. It's
sub-tropical in here . . .

*Dafydd goes up to the lighting box. Guy, on his own,
walks about the stage getting the feel of his costume and
feeling slightly sick with nerves. He clears his throat and*

swings his arms. Hannah enters with the jacket of his costume.

Hannah (*handing it to Guy*) Here. That should be better.

Guy Thank you.

Guy puts on the jacket. There is an awkward formality between them.

Hannah Let me know if it's still uncomfortable . . .

Guy No, no. This is perfect.

Dafydd (*emerging briefly in the doorway of the lighting box*) Try circuit 12 plugged into 22. 22, Raymond, 22. My . . . what the hell is it, it's my auxiliary 96. Look, Raymond, next time you re-number the bloody patch field you might tell everybody else about it, will you . . . ? (*He goes inside again.*)

Hannah Guy . . . ?

Guy Yes?

Hannah Why haven't you phoned?

Guy Oh, Hannah . . .

Hannah (*moving to him*) What is it? What have I done?

They stand together, instinctively clear of the lights and thus out of Dafydd's view.

Guy Look, I've been . . . I've had all this on my mind, haven't I? The play . . .

Hannah Is that more important than us?

Guy No, it's . . . We've been together every evening, for God's sake.

Hannah If you call that being together . . .

Guy Well, it's been very difficult, Hannah. I've only had just over a week to learn the thing . . .

A brilliant light strikes them both as Raymond locates another circuit. Instinctively, they both move away.

Dafydd (*emerging*) That's fine. Keep that one, don't lose it. Now 27 and 28 should be paired . . . Let's have a look at those. (*muttering*) Within the next 25 minutes if possible . . . (*He goes in.*)

Guy Look, there's no point in discussing this now. We can't decide anything in the middle of a –

Hannah (*loudly*) Well, when can we?

Two more lights illuminate them suddenly. Hannah and Guy look towards Dafydd.

Dafydd (*emerging*) Sorry, my loves, I'll be with you in a minute. Try not to get impatient . . . (*He goes.*)

Hannah and Guy move out of the lights again.

Guy All right. If you want to talk about it, we will . . . OK. I think it's all got to stop. All right? I think it's been tremendous fun and I think you're wonderful, but it simply has to stop.

Hannah (*stunned*) What are you talking about? Stop?

Dafydd (*emerging*) Perches one and two. Again, they should be paired . . . (*He goes.*)

Hannah Why? Why?

Guy Well. For one thing, Dafydd . . .

Hannah Dafydd?

Guy Yes.

Hannah Who the hell cares about Dafydd?

More lights come up on them again.

Dafydd (*emerging again*) I don't like the look of those two.

Hannah and Guy move again.

Lose them. Give me the other side. Perches 7 and 8, I think. (*He goes.*)

Hannah What's Dafydd got to do with anything?

Guy Hannah, Dafydd has everything to do with everything. He is your husband and he's my friend. And if I felt that I was responsible for your leaving him . . .

Hannah I'm leaving him anyway, whether you stay or not, so that has nothing to do with it . . .

A light, this time illuminating them brilliantly from the knees downwards. Guy and Hannah both jump instinctively.

Guy (*irritably*) Get away . . .

Dafydd (*emerging*) Well, those are no earthly use at all, Raymond. They're lighting his socks. He'd have to be a midget. What do you think we're doing, *Snow White*? FOH 4 then. Let's try that . . . (*He goes.*)

Hannah No, I know exactly what you're doing. You're using Dafydd as an excuse to ditch me, that's all . . .

Guy That just isn't true . . .

More lights come, replacing the others. Guy and Hannah are clear of them.

Hannah Don't try and pretend to me that you'd consider Dafydd for one single moment . . .

Dafydd (*calling*) I say, you two . . .

Hannah . . . if it didn't suit you. It didn't worry you two weeks ago . . .

Dafydd (*calling*) I say, you two –

Guy I think he wants us . . .

Hannah (*angrily*) Yes?

Dafydd (*coming onstage*) Sorry. Were you running lines? Look, just to save time, would you mind standing for me? I just want to check this focus.

He moves Guy and Hannah into the lights.

Just move into that one, that's right . . . Bit further forward, Hannah. Thank you. Just hold it there.

Dafydd moves away into the auditorium to check the effect.

Hannah (*as he goes, muttering*) Feeblest excuse I have ever heard in my life . . .

Dafydd Hannah, dear, be Annie Anderson for a minute, would you? She's a little taller than you – can you just go up on your toes?

Hannah goes up on tiptoe.

Bit more. Thank you.

Hannah (*awkwardly*) I would have preferred it if you'd been honest and said another woman . . .

Dafydd Guy, my love . . .

Hannah Which, of course, it is.

Dafydd Guy, could you go down to Tony Mofitt's size? Would you mind . . . ?

Guy crouches low.

Guy About there?

Dafydd Fine. Just hold it. (*He considers for a second.*) No, that's not going to work, Raymond. Show me something else . . .

During the next, a number of lamps flash on and off the contorted pair, as Raymond offers Dafydd, who is pacing the auditorium, alternative light sources. Dafydd rejects each in turn.

Hannah (*on the verge of tears again, softly*) I was prepared to give up everything for you, you know . . .

A lamp comes on.

Guy (*softly*) I know, I know . . .

Dafydd (*calling*) No.

Hannah (*softly*) My home, my marriage, even my children . . .

The light goes off and another comes on.

Guy (*softly*) I don't think you were, Hannah, not if it came to it.

Dafydd (*calling*) No . . .

Hannah (*softly*) I meant every single thing I said to you . . .

The light goes off and another goes on.

Guy (*softly*) I meant everything I said, too . . .

Dafydd (*calling*) No. Not in a million years . . .

Hannah (*softly*) You were playing around with Fay and – God knows who else. You used me, Guy . . .

The light goes off and another goes on.

Guy (*louder*) That is a lie –

Dafydd (*calling*) Yes! That's it . . . What number's that?

Dafydd rejoins them onstage to check his plan. Hannah lets out an involuntary moan of misery.

(*looking up at them*) Oh sorry, relax, loves. Sorry. Thanks for your help. (*He resumes his task.*)

A sob from Hannah as they relax their positions. During this Mr Ames returns, now in all but full costume.

Guy Hannah . . .

Dafydd What's the matter with her?

Guy Er . . .

Dafydd (*peering at her*) You daft halfpenny, you been staring into lights again, haven't you? How many times do I have to tell you? Shut your eyes, girl . . .

Dafydd cuffs her affectionately. He moves away towards the lighting box.

Guy (*imploring*) Hannah . . .

Hannah (*deeply miserable*) Oh, Guy . . .

Dafydd Now, let me see with that added to it, the state of cue 54 C . . . (*He goes back into the lighting box.*)

Hannah I do love you so much, Guy . . .

Guy I love you, Hannah . . .

Music starts under. As it does a rather romantic light setting comes up. Presumably Cue 54 C.

Hannah (*sings, as Polly*)
O what Pain it is to part!
Can I leave thee, can I leave thee?

O what Pain it is to part!
Can thy Polly ever leave thee?
But lest Death my love should thwart,
And bring thee to the fatal Cart,
Thus I tear thee from my bleeding Heart!
Fly hence, and let me leave thee.

Guy (*sings with her, as Macheath*)
But lest death my love should thwart (*etc.*)

> *As the song is ending, Hannah runs from the stage. Guy is left standing miserably. The last notes cut off as the lights resume a more natural state.*

Dafydd (*re-emerges, calling back behind him*) Save that now, Raymond. Save it and replug for the top of the show. God, I think we're there (*comes down on to the stage*) Sorry, Guy. You've been wonderfully patient. Thank you.

Guy Dafydd . . .

Dafydd Yes, my love . . .

Guy I feel I do have to talk to you about something . . .

Dafydd Oh, yes? (*calling*) Give me the workers, would you, Raymond? And will someone on stage management bring me the A ladders . . . ? Yes. Sorry, Guy. What's the problem?

Guy Well – it's a ridiculous time to say it but . . .

> *The lights switch to working lights.*

Dafydd (*yelling*) Thank you. (*staring up at the spot bar*) I'm going to take this frost out of here, Raymond. I hate it. Passionately. I can't live with a frost up here, I'm sorry . . . (*Aware that Guy is still with him, drawing him aside, quietly*) Guy. Just let me say this. You're going to be sensational, boy. No doubt of it. Just do what you've been doing in rehearsal. The audience are going to lift your game, anyway. You're home and dry . . .

During the last, a couple of the stage management now in costume have brought Dafydd the ladders, which they set up for him.

Guy Dafydd, it's not the show I'm talking about . . .

Dafydd (*indicating the ladders*) Would you steady this, I just want to alter something. Ta.

Dafydd shins up the ladders. Guy steadies them reluctantly.

(*from the top of the ladders*) Now's your chance to get our own back. Tip me off if you want to.

Guy (*wearily*) I don't want to do that, Dafydd.

Guy Ah well, all I can say is, it's a good job it's you down there. There's a whole committee of them back there would do it with pleasure.

Jarvis comes on from backstage with part of his costume on.

Jarvis Hey! Is this right?

Dafydd (*barely glancing*) Great, Jarvis. Knockout.

Jarvis These aren't the right trousers, of course . . . (*He indicates his everyday trousers.*)

Dafydd No, no, obviously. It's burnt out, this. (*He examines the frost he has recently removed from the lamp.*)

Jarvis Nor do they appear to have sent me any boots. The girl's having a look . . .

Dafydd Oh, dear . . .

Jarvis I asked specifically for boots. I wanted some boots. The man's a gaoler, he'd have boots. He'd never have shoes, not in a gaol . . .

Dafydd Don't worry, Jarvis, we'll find you some boots, don't worry . . .

Jarvis Well, I'm not playing him in shoes, that's all. I need to find some boots . . .

Jarvis goes off. Dafydd has come down the ladders.

Dafydd It would help if he found his bloody lines for a kick off. (*yelling*) Finished with the ladders! (*showing Guy the frame*) Warped. Look at that, eh?

He starts to move back towards the lighting box. As Dafydd does so, Ian, dressed in his street clothes, strolls in. He carries the evening paper.

(*as he goes, to Ian*) What time's this, then? What time's this?

Ian (*rather aggressively*) Not on till Act Two, am I?

Dafydd Fair enough. Fair enough.

Ian (*to Guy*) Seen the paper, then?

Guy No. I've not really had time.

Ian All over the front page. I shouldn't think it'd be much of a surprise to you . . . There you are. Closure Shock. (*to Dafydd*) BLM's closing . . .

Dafydd What's that?

Ian (*holding up the paper*) BLM. Closing down . . .

Rebecca has entered and stands listening.

Dafydd Closing down?

Ian That's what it says . . . 500 jobs gone.

Dafydd Oh dear, oh dear . . .

Ian They're relocating 130 . . .

Guy One hundred and twenty-eight actually.

Ian Oh, you did know then?

Guy Oh, yes.

Ian I bet you bloody did. Don't miss a trick, do you?

Rebecca How long have you known this?

Guy Since I found the note on my desk this morning. Along with most of us. (*looking at them*) It's true.

Ian (*moving away*) I believe you, sunshine . . .

Guy It's true . . .

Ian Sure, sure, sure . . . (*He goes.*)

Guy (*angrily after him*) If it makes you feel any better, I don't happen to have been included in the hundred and twenty-eight . . .

Rebecca I'm hardly surprised . . . (*to Dafydd, indicating her costume*) Do you think this is all right, Dafydd? Since I'm bound to be standing behind some huge tree or something it probably doesn't matter, anyway.

Dafydd That's super, Beccy, super . . .

Rebecca You actually like it?

Dafydd It's just right.

Rebecca (*moving off*) Oh, well. It's your production, darling. If you're expecting laughs, you won't be disappointed, will you? (*to someone offstage as she goes*) I told you he would. He likes it . . .

Rebecca goes off.

Dafydd (*yelling*) Come on. Let's get underway. How are you doing, Raymond? Dare I ask? (*He walks into the A ladders.*) I have requested these ladders be moved. Why haven't they? Bridget, somebody. Please.

Dafydd has moved back to Guy who sits very miserable in one corner of the stage. Bridget enters briskly. Dafydd goes to perch on a table to chat to Guy.

Guy, I'm desperately sorry to . . .

Bridget whisks the table from under Dafydd. Dafydd sits wearily beside Guy.

I'm desperately sorry to hear all this, Guy. I really am. Is that what you wanted to tell me, just now? God, I'm sorry. It's just like I said, isn't it? Here we are, playing around with pretty lights and costumes held together with safety pins. Out there it's all happening. (*more positively*) You'll be OK. I know you will. Don't despair, old friend. (*He clasps Guy affectionately round the shoulders.*) Excuse me, I'm going to have to light a few fireworks back there . . .

Dafydd goes off. The stage managers have returned and are moving the ladders off. Fay comes on with Guy's wig and a small mirror.

Fay (*handing these to Guy, coolly*) Here.

Guy Oh, thank you so much . . .

Fay She's done what she can with it . . .

Guy (*busying himself, examining the wig*) This is fine. Absolutely fine.

Fay You must be feeling pretty pleased with yourself.

Guy How do you mean?

Fay You seem to have succeeded in making fools of most people, haven't you?

Guy I don't think I have . . . I didn't intend to.

Fay Calculating little bastard, aren't you? Well, you certainly fooled me. Congratulations. That doesn't often happen. You didn't really convince Ian, I'm afraid. He said you were a shit from the start . . .

Guy (*hurt*) Thanks.

A silence. The cast begins to assemble onstage. First Rebecca. Then Jarvis and then Hannah. All ignore Guy. Jarvis has found some boots from somewhere. He busies himself putting these on. Rebecca hums tunelessly. Bridget comes in to wait. She is followed by Mr Ames.

Bridget He's coming in a second. He's talking to Ian.

Rebecca looks at Fay. The silence continues. Ted and Enid enter. They alone seem blissfully unaware of the atmosphere.

Enid (*as she comes on, loudly*) Oh yes, they're all . . . Oh. (*aware of the silence, in an undertone to Ted*) They're all out here . . . (*Pause. Whispering*) I think we're waiting for Dafydd.

Ted (*whispering*) Yes.

Enid (*indicating Ted's neckware*) Is your bit all right? Do you want me to tie it again?

Ted No, it's perfect now. Perfect. (*Pause.*) These shoes are a bit tight.

Enid Oh, dear.

Ted I was supposed to have some boots but somebody's pinched them . . .

Enid Oh, dear.

Linda comes on.

Oh, that's better, Linda. That's much better. (*to Ted*) She's taken the ribbon off it. It's better.

Ted Much better . . .

Dafydd enters, somewhat subdued.

Dafydd Sorry, everyone, but . . . (*He trails away, his mind obviously elsewhere.*) Right. Sorry. Here we go then. This is a technical run mostly for stage management and lighting and so on. But, none the less, do please feel free to stop if there's anything at all . . . that . . . er . . . is worrying you. At all. So. Yes. Right. Off we go. Good luck.

Everyone begins to disperse in various directions. Guy is one of the last to leave, having first put on his wig.

Bridget (*yelling as she goes*) Act One beginners stand by please . . .

Dafydd and Guy are alone on stage.

Dafydd (*approaching Guy, in an undertone*) Ian's just told me, you bastard. About you and Hannah. I just want you to know, I think you are a total and utter bastard. And my one prayer is that one of these days you'll get what's coming to you. OK? That's all I have to say to you.

Dafydd moves off towards the lighting box. Guy stands.

(*turning as he goes*) Having said that, all the very best of luck for the show and I hope it goes really well for you. Good luck. (*as he goes*) Come on, Raymond. Let's have the opening state, please . . . Come on. Lights and music.

Guy is left onstage. The lights close down to him alone. Prison cell lighting comes up as music starts under. Guy is joined as he speaks by Hannah as Polly and Linda as Lucy. We are gradually into the first performance of the production, near the end of Act Three (Scene XV).

Guy (*as Macheath, speaking*) My dear Lucy – My dear Polly – Whatsoever hath past between us is now at an end. – If you are fond of marrying again, the best Advice I can give you, is to ship yourselves off to the West Indies, where you'll have a fair chance of getting a Husband a-piece; or by good Luck, two or three, as you like best.

Hannah (*as Polly, speaking*) How can I support this Sight!

Linda (*as Lucy, speaking*) There is nothing moves one so much as a great Man in Distress.

(*singing*)
Would I might be hang'd!

Hannah (*singing*)
And I would so too!

Linda To be hang'd with you.

Hannah My Dear, with you.

Guy (*singing*)
O Leave me to Thought! I fear! I doubt!
I tremble! I droop – See, my Courage is out.

Hannah No token of Love?

Guy See, my Courage is out.

Linda No token of Love?

Hannah Adieu.

Linda Farewell.

Guy But hark! I hear the Toll of the Bell . . . (*etc.*)

> *During the song the action has moved to Tyburn. A scaffold has been erected. Essentially this is the platform that was centre stage at the start of the play with the addition of a gallows arm. A hooded Hangman stands waiting there as the rest of the opera is played out.*

Jarvis (*entering as Gaoler*) Four Women more, Captain, with a Child a-piece! See here they come.

He gestures. Rebecca, Bridget, Fay and Enid enter with prop babies, making baby-crying noises as they come.

Guy (*as Macheath*) What – four Wives more! – This is too much. – Here – tell the Sherriff's Officers I am ready.

A long drumroll. The women hurl aside their babies and with a hiss of anticipation join the rest of the company around the scaffold platform. Guy, flanked by two guards (Crispin and a stage manager) approaches. He steps up. The Hangman prepares to place the noose around his neck. The sound of the crowd and the drumroll increase in volume. Guy takes a last look around; at the Hangman, at the noose and, finally, at the company that has now assembled. A faint look of apprehension passes over his face as he notes their eager faces. Suddenly Ted, as the Player, appears, apart from the crowd.

Ted (*as Player, with a cry*) Wait!

Total silence. All on stage, with the exception of Guy, freeze totally. Guy looks slowly around him.
Ted and Mr Ames, after a moment, also unfreeze.

(*to Mr Ames*) Honest Friend, I hope you don't intend that Macheath shall be really executed.

Mr Ames (*as Beggar, at the piano*) Most certainly, Sir – To make the Piece perfect, I was for doing strict poetical Justice. – Macheath is to be hang'd; and for the other Personages of the Drama, the Audience must have suppos'd they were all either hang'd or transported.

Ted Why then, Friend, this is down-right deep Tragedy. The Catastrophe is manifestly wrong, for an Opera must end happily. All this we must do to comply with the Taste of the Town.

Mr Ames Your Objection, Sir, is very just; and is easily remov'd. For you must allow, that in this kind of Drama, 'tis no matter how absurdly things are brought about – So

> *With a snap of his fingers and the gesture of a magician . . .*
> *Ian rushes on in his Matt of the Mint costume, brandishing an official document.*

Ian A reprieve! A reprieve for Macheath!

All (*in an awed murmur*) A reprieve?

> *Ian gives the document to the Hangman who reads it.*

Hangman A reprieve!

All A Reprieve for Macheath!

> *A great deal of cheering. The gallows arm is removed. All push forward to congratulate the prisoner. The Hangman, removing his hood, reveals he is Dafydd. He embraces Guy. A serving wench brings ale for them both.*

Guy (*as Macheath, holding up his hands for silence*) So, it seems, I am not left to my Choice, but must have a Wife at last – Look ye, my Dears, we will have no Controversie now. Let us give this Day to Mirth, and I am sure she who thinks herself my Wife will testifie her Joy by a Dance.

All Come, a Dance – a Dance.

Guy (*sings*)
Thus I stand like a Turk, with his Doxies around;
From all Sides their Glances his Passion confound;
For, black, brown and fair, his Inconstancy burns,
And the different Beauties subdue him by turns:

Each calls forth her Charms, to provoke his Desires:
Though willing to all; with but one he retires.
But think of this Maxim, and Put off your Sorrow,
The Wretch of To-day, may be happy To-morrow.

Chorus But think of this maxim (*etc.*)

This time, as with The Beggar's Opera *itself, the performance ends happily and triumphantly (if a trifle cynically). The actors take their curtain calls. As the curtain falls for the last time they embrace each other, most especially their hero of the night, Guy himself. Relieved and exalted, they return to their dressing rooms.*

A SMALL FAMILY BUSINESS

Characters

Jack McCracken, *a business man*
Poppy, *his wife*
Ken, Ayres, *his father-in-law*
Tina, *his elder daughter*
Roy Ruston, *Tina's husband*
Samantha, *his younger daughter*
Cliff, *his brother*
Anita, *Cliff's wife*
Desmond, *his brother-in-law*
Harriet, *Desmond's wife*
Yvonne Doggett, *Harriet's sister*
Benedict Hough, *a private investigator*
Lotario Rivetti ⎫
Uberto Rivetti ⎪
Orlando Rivetti ⎬ *Italian business men*
Vincenzo Rivetti ⎪
Giorgio Rivetti ⎭

Note: It is the author's intention that the Rivetti Brothers
be played by the same actor.

A Small Family Business takes place in the sitting room,
kitchen, hall, landing, bathroom and bedroom in the
houses of various members of the family over one autumn
week.

A Small Family Business was first performed at the
National Theatre on 5 June 1987. The cast was as follows:

Jack McCracken Michael Gambon
Poppy Polly Adams
Ken Ares Ron Pember
Tina Diane Bull
Roy Ruston Adrian Rawlins
Samantha Suzan Sylvester
Cliff Russell Dixon
Anita Elizabeth Bell
Desmond John Arthur
Harriet Marcia Warren
Yvonne Doggett Barbara Hicks
Benedict Hough Simon Cadell
Lotario Rivetti Michael Simkins
Uberto Rivetti Mischa Melinski
Orlando Rivetti Liam Sheminicks
Vincenzo Rivetti Neil MacSkimish
Giorgio Rivetti Khelim Cassimin

Act One

We appear to be looking at a cross-section of a modern or
recently modernized house, perhaps on an executive-type
estate. Ours is a rear view. Four rooms, two up and two
down. Downstairs, to one side, is the sitting room.
Modern furnishings, fitments with hi-fi, etc., a settee,
armchairs, low tables. Neutral carpeting. It is a fairly large
area, being two rooms knocked into one and then
reseparated by a room divider, forming what we shall refer
to as the 'near sitting room' and the 'far sitting room'.
When people move to the far sitting room they are
partially, sometimes totally, obscured from view. The
doors from both original rooms have been retained and
lead to:

The hallway with stairs up to the first floor. At the far
end is the front door leading to an indeterminate front
path and street beyond.

A further door off the hall leads to the back kitchen,
which is in full view. This is modern and well equipped
and, like the sitting room, sufficiently lacking in detail to
be practically identical to a hundred other kitchens.

There is a fourth door leading off the hall to a front
dining room beyond the kitchen and thus out of view. A
hatchway from the kitchen links these two rooms and,
when open, affords us a glimpse through. At the far end of
the kitchen, there is a back door leading to an
indeterminate yard beyond.

The stairs from the hall lead to the landing above,
similarly shaped and with, again, four doors leading off it.
The two furthest from us lead to rooms (presumably
bedrooms) which we cannot see. Visible to us and situated

*above the sitting room (but only half its depth) is a
bedroom with a double divan bed, modern sliding
cupboards, etc. In style, the room is once again modern
and nondescript. Rather as if the owners had in all cases
settled for a standard range of good, modern, mass-
produced units to satisfy their needs throughout the house.
Which, as we discover, is indeed the case.*

*Finally, across the landing from the bedroom, the
bathroom. Matching modern fitments, bath with shower
curtain, lavatory, basin, etc., all in a matching,
unobtrusive pastel shade.*

*During the course of the play, the various areas will
serve as rooms in the different houses of the family. At
present though they are all as we naturally presume them
to be, i.e. forming a single dwelling, Jack's and Poppy's
house.*

*It is an evening in winter. All the downstairs areas and the
landing above are lit.* **Poppy**, *a woman of 40, is standing
by the front door, her face pressed against one of the small
side windows, looking out into the night.*
*In the sitting room, ten guests are chattering away in
rather subdued tones. They are:* **Ken Ayres**, *Poppy's father,
a man in his seventies, at one time the family's driving
force but now rather eccentric and unpredictable. Also
present is his son,* **Desmond Ayres**, *an overweight,
ineffectual, fussy man of 42;* **Harriet**, *44, Desmond's wife,
a thin, nervous woman with an unfortunate dress sense;
Harriet's older sister* **Yvonne**, *50, who by contrast is
simply, even severely dressed. Calm, impassive and
efficient, she stands near Ken taking care of his needs
silently and efficiently. Also Jack's younger brother* **Cliff**,
*40, who likes to be thought of as an easy-going wheeler-
dealer, though his need to be loved gives him a certain
weakness;* **Cliff's** *wife* **Anita**, *36, an attractive woman,
expensively overdressed, outgoing and shrewd;*

accompanying her, and taking rather too much interest,
Uberto, *an elegant Italian business man of 35.*

*Finally, there are the younger family members. Jack's
and Poppy's elder daughter,* **Tina Ruston**, *is 23 and takes
after her mother. She is strong, capable and has a maturity
that comes with the accepted responsibility of looking
after two small children and coping with her impractical
husband,* **Roy Ruston**, *who is 25 and a hopeless dreamer.
Pleasant enough to meet briefly, he is infuriating to live
with. He's already beginning to regret the family he started
six years ago with such premature abandon.*

Tina's younger sister **Samantha**, *16, completes the
group. Standing a little apart from the others, she seems
aware that she alone, still at school and unattached,
represents a new and different generation. She is at a stage
when life is often a painful, intensely private experience.*

*All have drinks and are waiting for someone to arrive.
We have a second to take in the scene. Then Poppy, at the
hall window, sees someone approaching. She hurries to the
sitting room.*

Poppy Ssssh! Everyone! He's here.

The chatter subdues. One or two 'sssh's'.

Jack's here. His car's just turned into the road. Can we
turn the lights out, please?

*People oblige, switching off the table lamps nearest
them. Poppy extinguishes the overhead with the door
switch.*

Ken What's happening now?

Yvonne Jack's here, Mr Ayres. He's just arrived.

Ken Jack who?

Poppy Everyone! Quiet as you can, please. I'll try and get
him to come straight in here.

Anita (*from the darkness, with a silly giggle*) It's very dark.

Others Sssh!

Poppy (*moving to the kitchen*) Quiet as you can. He'll come in from the garage.

She goes into the kitchen and pretends to busy herself at the sink.

Anita (*from the darkness*) Oooh!

All Sssh!

Anita Who did that? Who was it did that?

Cliff Be quiet.

Anita No, that really hurt, that did. Who did that??

All Sssh!

Tina Quiet! He's here.

A silence. The back door opens. **Jack***, a forceful, energetic man of 45, enters.*

Jack I'm back.

Poppy (*kissing him*) How did it go, then?

Jack All right. You know. Fond farewells. Usual thing. We shall miss you for ever thank God he's gone at last . . .

Poppy (*affectionately*) They never said that.

Jack They were thinking it. Cheering me through the gates, they were. Goodbye, you old bugger, goodbye. (*sensing a slight nervousness in her*) I'm not that late, am I?

Poppy Only a little.

Jack (*looking at her properly for the first time*) You're all dressed up, aren't you?

Poppy No, I've had this for ages.

Jack (*a horrid thought*) We're not meant to be going out?

Poppy No, no.

Jack Thank God for that. I don't want to see anyone else. Not today.

He goes into the hall.

Anita (*softly*) Oh, dear, what a shame.

Tina Sssh!

Poppy Make us both a drink, will you?

Poppy hangs his coat up in the hall.

Jack (*calling back to her as he does so*) I drove back past the factory this evening . . .

Poppy What's that?

Jack On my way home just now I drove back past my new office. Do you know, I suddenly felt very excited.

He has returned to the kitchen doorway.

Poppy I'm glad.

Jack We're going to the stars with this one, darling, we really are. This is going to be the one.

Poppy It will be if you have anything to do with it . . .

Jack (*holding her*) No, no. Not me. Us. You and me.

Poppy (*not really believing this*) Yes.

They kiss.

Jack Come on, what are you dressed up for, then?

Poppy No reason. I just felt like it.

Jack Trying to take my mind off my work, were you? Eh?

Poppy (*coyly aware of her audience next door*) Don't be silly.

Jack Sammy upstairs?

Poppy No, she's out tonight.

Jack Just us, is it?

Poppy Yes. There's nobody here.

Jack I see.

Poppy Go on. Make us a drink.

Jack (*taking her hand and starting to lead her*) First of all, follow me.

Poppy Where are we going?

Jack (*heading for the stairs*) Not far, I promise. Not far.

Poppy (*alarmed*) Jack, no, we can't. Not now.

Jack I fancy it right now, I don't mind saying . . .

Anita (*sotto*) Oh, my God . . .

Poppy No, we can't. Really. Jack.

> *Poppy pulls away from Jack and remains at the foot of the stairs. Jack continues to retreat upstairs.*

Jack Come on.

Poppy No.

Jack (*more firmly*) Come on.

Poppy No. I'm going in here. (*Indicates the sitting room.*) I want a drink.

Jack Poppy . . .

Poppy (*opening the door*) I'll be in here.

Jack Poppy, if I have to come down and fetch you . . .

Poppy Bye-bye.

Poppy goes into the sitting room and closes the door. She crowds in with the rest of her guests.

Jack Poppy!

Poppy (*calling girlishly*) Woo-hoo! (*to the others*) I'm ever so sorry. This is so embarrassing.

Tina (*hissing*) Mum. What are you playing at?

Poppy It's the only way I can get him in here. (*calling*) Woo-hoo!

Jack I'm going to have to come in there and get you, Poppy . . .

Cliff This'll be entertaining.

Anita It's all right, Poppy, we'll shut our eyes.

Poppy Sssshh!

Jack Poppy! If I have to come and fetch you, Poppy . . . You know what that means, don't you? (*starting to take off his jacket*) It means rough trade. Rough. Rough. Poppy. (*Throws his jacket over the banisters and starts to descend, treading heavily.*) Right. Here come the Vikings. You hear him coming, Poppy? (*Takes off his tie and starts to unbutton his shirt.*) It's Erik the Hairy, coming for you.

Anita giggles.

Roy Eric the Who?

Poppy Oh God, I want to die. I really want to die.

Jack (*in a strange Norwegian accent*) Nordsky! Nordsky!

Where she hidey-hole the little Angley-Sexey girl? Here he come, Hairy Erik with his meatey axey –

He opens the sitting room door, slowly reaching round for the light switch as he does so.

(*calling softly*) Angley-Sexey Girl! Come for a little pillage. Look who's here. Look who's here . . . (*switching on the light*) Look who's . . . Oh, for crying out loud!

A roar from everyone.

Poppy Look who's here.

Jack is mortified. Poppy, almost equally embarrassed, hugs him amidst much merriment. The following six speeches overlap.

Jack I don't believe it. I really don't believe it. How long have they been there?

Poppy I'm sorry, Jack, I didn't mean it to happen like that, I promise.

Jack That was without a doubt the most embarrassing moment of my life . . .

Cliff (*simultaneously with this last*) I wish they'd carried on. It was just getting interesting, wasn't it?

Anita Fascinating. What was all this Viking business, that's what I'd like to know?

Uberto Viking? *Per favore, che cos'è un* Viking?

Anita starts to try and explain.

Jack (*singling out Ken and shaking him by the hand*) Hallo, Ken old lad, how are you? What a rotten trick to play on someone.

Ken (*effusively*) Hallo, then. Hallo then, old lad. Good to see you here. (*to Yvonne*) Who is he?

Yvonne This is Jack. You know Jack, Ken.

Ken Of course it's Jack. I know Jack. He's my son-in-law. (*trying to stop the chatter*) Ladies and . . . Ladies and . . .

Poppy Sssh! Everybody!

Desmond Quiet, everyone . . . Quiet a minute –

Silence.

Ken (*to Yvonne*) Who's this, then?

Desmond I'm Desmond, Dad. Everyone, I think – my father would like to say a few words.

Ken I won't talk for long because I know that you know we all know who we're all talking about. We all know that. Our Jack here –

He grasps Desmond by the arm, who gently removes the hand and places it on Jack's arm instead.

– my son-in-law . . . (*worried by Desmond's gesture*) What's that?

Desmond Nothing, Dad.

Ken Well, don't do it. (*resuming*) Jack, my son-in-law, loving husband to my Poppy there, who's coming home to run the business and all I can say is, welcome home, Jack, and not before time . . .

Applause.

That's all I wanted to say.

Applause.

Jack (*starting his reply*) Well, Ken, I'm sorry I –

Ken When I started this firm, I started it with twenty-five pounds, a hand cart and a good woman. Well, over the years the money's devalued, the cart's disintegrated and

Gracie? – well, Gracie, God bless her, has departed. Only her name lives on in the firm, Ayres and Graces. Ayres, that's me. Gracie, that's her. And I know if she was here – which she probably is, since she's never been known to miss a party – she would undoubtedly reiterate me that if there was anyone who can move this firm forward into the twenty-first century, it has to be Poppy's Jack who's the man to do it. He's done wonders for that duff load of frozen-food merchants he's just been with. What the hell's he going to do for a good firm?

Laughter and applause.

Jack (*after checking that Ken has finished*) Thank you, Ken. I'll do my best. I'm bracing myself for the culture shock of jumping from fish fingers to furniture – and I hope you'll have observed that all the fixtures and fittings in this house have come from the right place. Well, a man's got enough problems without in-law trouble as well . . .

Laughter.

Well. I think we're all aware that the business hasn't been as healthy as it might have been, just lately. Demand is sluggish, we know that. Consequently, productivity's also down and generally, I think it's fair to say – so far as I can gather, everyone's lost a bit of heart. Now it's very hard in this country for a business man to say something even halfway idealistic, without people falling over backwards laughing. To them it sounds like a contradiction in terms, anyway. But. Putting it as simply as I can. If I do nothing else, and during the coming months I can assure you I plan to do plenty, but if I succeed in doing nothing else I am determined to introduce one simple concept. And that concept is basic trust.

He pauses for effect.

Ken Basic what did he say?

Yvonne Trust.

Ken Oh, basic trust. Yes.

Jack I'm talking about establishing the understanding that so far as every individual member of that firm is concerned, working there is no longer going to be purely a question of take, take, take . . . whether it's raw materials from the shop floor, an extra fifty quid on our car allowances or paper clips from the office. We're there because we actually believe in what we're producing. Let's try and put across the idea that many of us believe in it so strongly that we are even anxious to put something back in. Effort. Hard work. Faith. Where do you think we'd be if we could do that? I'll tell you, we'd be top of the bloody league, that's where we'd be. We're a small family business. Even today, we're still essentially the same as we always were. There's no them and us about it. When it comes down to it, it's all us. That's all there is. Us. Ken and Des and Roy, there. All the lads we have working for us; all the girls in the office. They're practically family themselves, aren't they? It shouldn't be that difficult to achieve. All I'm saying is – let's start with the paper clips, shall we? Let's start with trust, that's all . . . (*Slight pause.*) Sorry.

A rather startled silence, then applause from everyone.

Ken Great speech, Jack, great speech . . .

Jack Thank you.

Ken I knew I'd got the right man.

Desmond (*confidentially, to Jack*) Just what was needed. Very inspiring.

Jack Thanks.

Roy Fantastic. I couldn't understand a word of it, but fantastic.

Poppy Roy, can you make sure everyone's got a drink?

Roy Wilco.

During the next, Roy and Desmond move into the far half of the sitting room to replenish their drinks. Harriet follows. Poppy stays talking to Ken and Yvonne. Samantha sits herself in a corner with her half-finished glass of Coke and continues reading a hardback book.

Anita (*over this last*) You're a lovey talker, Jack. Beautiful. I could listen to you for hours.

Jack I meant it, Anita.

Anita Jack, I want you to meet Uberto Rivetti. Uberto is a business associate of Cliff's. Visiting from Italy.

Jack How do you do, Mr Rivetti.

Anita This is my brother-in-law – (*to Jack*) – he doesn't speak hardly any English. *Mio cognato.* Jack.

Uberto *Piacere. Grazie per avermi invitato. Che bella casa!*

Jack Thank you. (*to Anita*) What's he saying?

Uberto *E che bella famiglia. Sua moglie e le bambine sono simpaticissime.*

Anita *Grazie.* Uberto said he liked your speech.

Jack Oh, thank you very much. (*to Anita*) How long have you been speaking Italian?

Anita I'm learning. Off a tape. I listen in the mornings when I'm jogging. Trouble is, I speak it better when I'm on the move. Look, Jack, I'm sorry we can't stay, but Uberto has a dinner engagement and I promised I'd look after him . . .

Jack Oh, shame . . .

Anita We wanted to pop in. Just to say congratulations.

Jack Is Cliff going as well, then . . . ?

Anita No. No. Not Cliff.

Jack (*slightly embarrassed*) No. Sorry.

Anita (*kissing him*) See you soon.

Uberto Bye-bye.

Jack Yes. *Ciao!*

Uberto *Cuai! Si!*

Anita and Uberto move off towards the front door. Poppy accompanies them.

Ken (*more confidentially*) Come and talk to me tomorrow, all right? At home.

Jack Sure.

Ken (*moving away*) I'll be there all day. All right?

Jack I will . . . 'Night, then.

Yvonne Goodnight, Jack. I have to get him home . . .

Ken and Yvonne move off to the front door, where Poppy is saying goodbye to Anita and Uberto. Cliff emerges from the front sitting room.

Poppy Oh, are you off as well, Yvonne? Won't you stay for something to eat?

Yvonne No, Ken would like to get home. He never stays up too late . . .

Cliff Get you a drink after all that, Jack?

Jack Ta. I'm just going to freshen up. Scotch. With plenty of water.

Cliff Coming up.

He returns to the drinks.

Tina (*kissing Jack*) Fantastic, Dad. Wonderful . . .

Jack Sorry, I didn't mean to go on quite so much.

Tina No, seriously. I think what you said was absolutely terrific. About time somebody said it.

Jack Oh, thank you. Praise indeed from one's own daughter.

Tina checks round both rooms and gathers up empties and any bowls of snacks that need replenishing. Samantha is now reading while listening to her personal stereo.

(*noticing her*) Hallo, Sammy.

Samantha Hallo, Dad.

Jack Didn't see you there. All right, then?

Samantha Yes, I'm all right.

Jack Right.

They appear to have run out of conversation.

Good.

Jack goes back into the hall. As he does so, Poppy returns from the front door having said goodnight to Ken, Yvonne, Anita and Uberto.

Poppy It's supposed to be a party this, you know, not a party political broadcast.

Jack Sorry, I've already said sorry. I've apologized.

Poppy (*hugging him*) I was so proud of you. Really proud.

Jack Oh, well . . .

Poppy If the whole bloody world was as good as you there'd be no problem, that's all I can say. (*kissing him briefly*) I love you very much.

Jack I love you.

Poppy Only don't make any more speeches or we'll never get anything to eat, all right?

Jack (*smiling*) Promise.

> *Jack starts upstairs. Poppy goes into the sitting room through the far door to check all is well. Simultaneously, Tina comes out through the near door with an empty crisp bowl in her hand.*

Tina Don't make too much noise when you're up there, will you, Dad? Kevin and Michelle are asleep.

Jack (*pleased*) Oh, have you brought the terrible terrors?

Tina We had to. Marianne's gone home to Germany for a fortnight.

Jack Roughing it, are you? Why, in my young day . . .

Tina Times change, Dad. I keep telling you . . .

Jack German nannies! You staying the night?

Tina Yes. Roy and I are in the spare room with Kevin. Michelle's in with Sammy.

Jack Didn't Sammy object?

Tina She didn't have any choice.

Jack It's like Fort Knox trying to get into her room. It's got a combination lock, have you seen it?

Tina Just don't wake them up.

> *Jack goes into the bedroom and, having dumped his jacket and tie on the bed, goes off down the landing and*

into first one and then the other of the far rooms. Tina, meanwhile, goes into the kitchen and starts to search for more crisps in the cupboards. Poppy comes through from the far sitting room.

Poppy (*seeing Samantha sitting alone*) I'm glad you came down for this, Sammy. Your Dad really appreciated it.

Samantha I'm sure he did.

Poppy Anyway, it's good you're here and not sat in your room all evening.

Samantha I can't sit in my room, she's dumped her sodding baby in there, hasn't she?

Poppy Now, Sammy, that'll do.

Samantha It'll be piddling and sicking all over my things.

Poppy No, she won't, she's fast asleep. She's only two. She's a beautiful little thing.

Samantha I hate babies. I hate the smell.

Poppy You won't say that when you've one of your own.

Samantha I'm not having sodding babies.

Poppy Now, Sammy, I'm warning you. Once more and you'll go straight up to your – I'll get your father down to you.

Samantha Great. He might even talk to me.

Poppy Oh, Sammy, why don't you go in there and socialize? They'd all love you to socialize. Go on.

Samantha (*resuming her book*) I don't want to socialize.

Poppy (*sighing*) I don't know, I'm sure. He adores you, your Dad, you know, he really does.

Poppy goes across the hall and into the kitchen. Tina

has been searching in vain for refills for her bowl.

Tina Mum, have you got any more crisps?

Poppy Yes, up the top there in the . . . No, don't give them any more, we're going to eat in a minute.

Tina Want a hand, then?

Poppy Yes – I've done most of it – If you go in there, I'll pass things through to you, OK?

Tina goes into the dining room. Poppy opens the fridge and starts to take out foil-covered plates of food. These, in due course, she uncovers and starts to pass to Tina in the dining room, through the hatchway. Cliff, who is carrying his own drink as well as one for Jack, comes through the sitting room. He has an ice bucket hooked over a spare finger.

Cliff (*to Samantha*) Somebody care to replenish this, would they?

Samantha ignores him, apparently engrossed in her book.

Somebody? Anybody?

Samantha What?

Harriet, who has been witnessing this from another part of the room, now marches in and takes the bucket from him.

Harriet All right, I'll do it.

Cliff Oh, ta.

Harriet Fat lot of use asking that child to do anything.

Cliff Ice is in the freezer.

Harriet (*as she goes*) Heavens! How unusual!

Harriet goes through to the kitchen. Samantha pulls a face at her back. Cliff laughs, unperturbed, and goes upstairs to look for Jack.

(*to Poppy*) I'm just going to fill this.

Poppy Help yourself.

As Poppy passes plates through to the dining room, Harriet takes a full ice tray from the freezer compartment and goes to the sink and runs the tray under the tap to loosen the cubes before refilling the bucket.

(*to Tina, through the hatch*) Move everything up a bit if they won't go on. There should be enough room.

Cliff, now upstairs, is looking for Jack.

Cliff (*calling*) Jack! Jack, I've got your drink here, mate.

Jack comes out of one of the far bedrooms.

Jack Sssh! They're asleep.

Cliff Oh, yeah, right. Here.

Jack Thanks. (*drawing Cliff back along the passage*) Here, come and have a look at this. Have you ever seen anything like this?

They disappear momentarily. In the sitting room, Desmond is talking with Roy who has switched on some music from the hi-fi. Samantha sits, continuing to read. Meanwhile, in the kitchen –

Harriet (*apropos of nothing*) It's all coming to a head, you see.

Poppy (*absorbed in her tasks*) Uh-huh?

Harriet I am no longer welcome in my own home, that's what it comes down to.

Poppy Oh dear.

Harriet I think this is the first time I've had the courage to walk into a kitchen for over a month.

Poppy Lucky you. I wish I was that nervous.

Harriet You can laugh. It's all right for you, Poppy, you've always got a job you can escape to.

Poppy I have to work. We need the money, dear. (*through the hatch to Tina*) Move those side plates round. You should fit that on the end there. By the mousse. (*A muffled reply from Tina in the dining room.*)

> *Jack and Cliff reappear along the landing. Jack goes into the bedroom. Cliff follows him in.*

Jack Incredible to be able to sleep like that, isn't it?

Cliff You can when you're a kid. I used to sleep upside down, do you remember?

Jack Upside down? What, you mean like a bat?

Cliffa No. Down the bedclothes. With my feet on the pillow. Don't you remember?

Jack Oh, yes. I remember your feet . . . (*Jack takes off his shirt and throws it in the clothes basket. He hunts for a new one in a drawer.*)

Harriet I cannot face going into our kitchen these days. I get as far as the door and I cannot even bring myself to go in there to soak a bag of tea.

Poppy (*at the hatch, to Tina*) No, the other side, love. That's it. (*Tina replies once more.*)

Harriet I can hear him in there grilling and stewing till all hours of the night. I can smell it for the rest of the day. It seeps through the house. In the curtains. In my hair. In

Peggy's fur. (*Cliff sits with his drink, watching Jack.*)

Cliff Good speech, just now. I almost believed it myself.

Jack I meant it.

Harriet (*tearfully*) He's in there all weekend making these huge meals. Three or four courses at a time . . .
(*Shudders.*) You know it's reached a point where the smell of food can actually cause me to vomit, do you know that?

Cliff Do you do that sort of thing, then?

Jack What sort of thing?

Cliff You know, all that Hairy Erik and dragging her up to bed by the hair. That what she likes, then?

Jack Well. Only in fun, you know.

Cliff Is that right?

Jack Nothing violent.

Cliff No, really?

Jack Mind your own bloody business . . .

> *Jack goes into the bathroom and washes his face and hands. Cliff follows him and stands watching in the doorway. Roy, downstairs, has similarly come through to this end of the sitting room and is watching Samantha. Desmond is left alone in the other half of the room, eating peanuts.*

Roy (*to Samantha*) Good evening, sister-in-law. Good book, then?

Samantha Brilliant.

Roy Think I'd like it?

Samantha You wouldn't even understand the page numbers, brother-in-law.

Harriet It's all because I dieted. That's the reason this has happened. I should never have dieted. I should have just kept on eating with him. But I can't, you see. I can no longer look a full plate in the eye. That is the truth . . .

Cliff My wife wouldn't go for that.

Jack Wouldn't go for what?

Cliff All that Hairy Erik stuff. Anita doesn't go for that.

Jack Look, give it a rest, Cliff, there's a pal.

Cliff Sorry. No offence.

Jack Just clear out of the bathroom, OK?

Cliff Yes, yes, sure.

Cliff goes out closing the door. He wanders back to Jack's room and sits on the bed.

Harriet Well, he's not going to get rid of me that easily, that's all I can say. He's had years from me, he can pay for them. I'll have him for every penny. He's got thousands salted away. I know he has. Thousands.

Poppy Really? Desmond has? How's he managed that?

Harriet He never spends anything, that's why. He's a mean man. I've never met such a mean man. The only thing he spends money on is food. That's his god, that is. Food is his god. (*Sits, sniffing.*) He used to care about me. Now he won't even look up from his plate.

Poppy Look, I promise you, Harriet, you can come round whenever you like. Any evening. I'll be only too happy to listen, dear. But not just at the moment, my love. I'm sorry.

Harriet I'm sorry.

Poppy (*through hatch*) What's that? Sorry? No, leave

them to do that themselves. Some people may not want it . . .

Harriet (*half to herself*) I'm sorry. (*She seems very near collapse as she stands clasping the empty ice tray.*)

Poppy (*irritably*) Look, sit down for heaven's sake. And give that to me.

> *Poppy takes the ice tray from Harriet's limp grasp and bangs it down by the sink. Harriet sits. Poppy picks up the last two plates of food and goes out to the hall. Roy stands behind Samantha trying to read over her shoulder.*

(*as she goes*) I don't know what we're going to do with you, Harriet, I really don't . . .

Samantha Look, do you want something, or what?

Roy No, I was only being sociable.

Samantha Why?

Roy Well, it's a party, isn't it?

Samantha Go away.

Roy You've got to be sociable.

Samantha All right. (*Closes the book, wearily.*) We'll have a party, then. Got any stuff, have you?

Roy Any what?

Samantha Stuff? Columbian talc? (*spelling it out*) Cocaine?

Roy Oh, that. No, I don't use that.

Samantha Terrific. Great party, then, isn't it?

> *Samantha lays aside her book in the living room, rises and goes towards the hall.*

Roy Where are you going?

Samantha goes into the kitchen and, ignoring Harriet, helps herself to a fresh tin of Coke from the fridge. Roy takes up Samantha's discarded book and studies it. Meanwhile, Jack comes out of the bathroom and into the bedroom. He starts to put on his clean shirt.

Cliff You know something. In my opinion, you've got a really good relationship. You and Poppy.

Jack (*modestly*) Yes. I think we have.

Cliff I reckon she's really crazy about you . . .

Jack You needn't sound so surprised.

Cliff No, but – after, you know – all this marriage. It's quite rare, in my experience.

Roy (*now engrossed in Samantha's book*) Bloody hellfire!

Jack Who's that Italian poncing around with your Anita, then? Who is he?

Cliff (*evasively*) Oh, he's just business. You know.

Jack You and Anita all right?

Cliff Oh, yes. Yes. We're all right. But. Well. Once you've been round the circuit a few times – well, you get to know the hairpins. If you know what I mean.

Jack Getting bored with her, are you?

Cliff No. No. Not at all. She may be getting bored with me, but that's another story, eh? (*Laughs.*) God, she's expensive, though. You've no idea, Jack. I have to sleep in our spare room these days. There's no room for me in our bedroom, it's full of her clothes. Ball gowns to the bloody ceiling, I'm telling you. You're dead lucky with Poppy, mate.

Jack No, Poppy doesn't wear that many ball gowns . . .

Poppy (*sticking her head through the hatch*) Harriet, would you mind . . . (*seeing Samantha is there*) Oh, Sammy love, pass me another tablespoon, will you? From the drawer.

Harriet I'd have done that.

> *Samantha finds a spoon. Jack selects a fresh tie and starts to knot it.*

Samantha (*passing a spoon through*) Here you are.

Poppy Thank you, dear. And, Sammy, take the ice bucket through when you go, will you?

Harriet (*rising angrily*) Well, let me do something, for goodness' sake. I'm not incapable yet, you know.

> *She snatches the ice bucket from Samantha and hurries into the hall.*

Samantha All right, Auntie, all right . . .

> *Poppy sighs and closes the hatch. Samantha looks scornfully after her aunt.*

Desmond (*who is just emerging*) Any chance of any food yet?

Harriet (*snapping*) Trust you to think of food. (*She goes back into the sitting room.*)

Desmond (*lamely*) Just . . . feeling a bit peckish, that's all.

> *Desmond moves hesitantly in the direction of the dining room. Samantha remains in the kitchen drinking Coke. Suddenly there is a tentative knocking at the back door. Samantha turns, startled.*

Samantha Who's that?

More knocking.

(*trying to spot whoever it is through the glass*) Hallo?
Who is it? (*More knocking.*) All right. Hang on.

She unlocks the door and opens it to reveal **Benedict Hough**, *an unimpressive, unmemorable man of indeterminate age – probably in his mid-thirties.*

Benedict Oh, hallo there, Miss McCracken. I have got the right house then, haven't I?

Samantha (*attempting to close the door at once*) Oh no, you haven't. You just get out . . .

She all but closes the door, only Benedict manages to wedge a foot in it.

Benedict (*calling through the crack in the door*) Miss McCracken . . . please, Miss McCracken, this isn't going to help one little bit . . . I can obtain legal assistance if necessary, Miss McCracken, and a warrant if needs be . . .

Samantha (*over this*) You just get out. Get out. You are not coming in. Sod off . . .

The dispute begins to attract attention. Roy looks up from his book and moves to the hall uncertain what to do. Poppy sticks her head through the hatch.

Poppy Sammy? Sammy, what is it?

Samantha (*struggling*) Tell him to go away . . .

Roy Who is it?

Poppy Just a minute, love. Hold on.

Her head disappears. Harriet comes into the hall from the far sitting room. Tina's face replaces Poppy's at the hatchway.

Harriet What's going on? What's happening?

Tina Who is it, Sammy? Who is it?

Samantha (*almost hysterical*) Tell him to just go away. Go away.

Poppy is now at the foot of the stairs.

Poppy (*calling*) Jack! Jack! Will you come down, please? (*seeing Roy*) Roy, go and help her, for God's sake. Someone's trying to break in.

Roy Roger. Wilco.

Roy goes into the kitchen to help Samantha. Jack comes out of the bedroom to the top of the stairs.

Jack What is it? What's wrong?

Poppy Would you come, please, to the kitchen. Sammy needs help.

Jack comes downstairs rapidly and into the kitchen. Desmond comes out of the dining room, guiltily eating something in his fingers. As they do this –

Desmond What's happening?

Poppy Someone's trying to break in the back door – and, Desmond, please leave something for the others to eat, will you?

Roy (*with this last, coming to Samantha's help*) OK, Sammy, let me . . .

Harriet (*alarmed*) Someone's trying to break in the back door . . .

Samantha (*frenziedly*) Just keep him out . . . keep him out –

Roy Who is he . . .

Benedict (*from outside*) Miss McCracken, you really can't behave like this . . . you really can't . . .

Jack (*arriving in the kitchen*) All right, what's going on here? Roy, out of the way.

Roy steps aside. Poppy comes into the kitchen and hovers inside the doorway.

Poppy Careful, Jack. He may be armed.

Jack Sammy, leave it to me.

Samantha (*still clinging grimly to the door trying to close it*) You mustn't let him in, Dad . . .

Jack Sammy, just stand out of the way –

Jack moves Samantha gently but firmly away from the door. As a result Benedict, no longer meeting any opposition, is propelled into the room. Jack grabs him and holds him by the front of his mac. The others gather in and around the kitchen doorway, watching.

(*threateningly*) Right, that's it.

Benedict (*alarmed*) Please, please, please . . .

Jack Close the door, Roy.

Roy closes the door.

Benedict Please, don't do that too much, I –

Jack Who are you? Eh?

Benedict The name is Hough. Benedict Hough. (*finding it hard to breathe*) Might I take it I'm addressing Mr McCracken?

Jack Why?

Benedict (*gurgling*) Harrgh!

Poppy I think you'd better let him breathe, Jack. I don't think he can breathe . . .

Jack Behave yourself, then. (*He releases Benedict.*)

Tina Careful, Dad . . .

Jack Now. What are you doing here?

Benedict It's a personal matter, Mr McCracken. (*looking towards the others*) A delicate personal matter.

Jack Why were you creeping round the back door?

Benedict I wasn't sure if this was the right house.

Jack (*angrily*) What do you mean, the right house? Slinking about in the dark, terrifying the life out of my teenage daughter. What's your game then, sunshine?

Benedict (*agitatedly*) She shouldn't have given me a false address then, should she?

Jack Who gave you a false address?

Benedict Your daughter.

Pause.

Jack Who? Sammy?

Benedict If that is Sammy, then yes.

Samantha Dad, he's a loony . . .

Jack (*pointing to Samantha*) You're talking about her?

Benedict She gave me a false name as well. (*producing a small notebook*) Imogen Gladys Braithwaite. Of 12A, Crab Apple Lane . . .

Jack (*to Samantha*) Is that what you told him?

Samantha What?

Jack Did you tell this man your name was Gladys . . . ?

Samantha Never.

Benedict Oh yes, you did, young woman, don't you try making me out a liar –

Samantha Oh, shut your pukeface.

Jack Hey! Hey! Hey!

Benedict Don't you call me pukeface –

Jack Hoy! Hoy!

Benedict I'm not standing here to be called pukeface.

Poppy Sammy? What's all this about?

Jack Look, would you all like to go into the other room and enjoy yourselves, please? While I sort this out?

Poppy I want to know what Sammy's supposed to have done.

Jack Please, Poppy. It'll be easier on our own. We won't be long.

Poppy (*with a last anxious look at Samantha*) Sammy?

Samantha It's nothing.

Poppy (*reluctantly*) Come on then, Roy.

Roy Check.

> *Everyone leaves and troops silently into the far sitting room, shepherded by Poppy. Roy closes the door.*

Jack Now, what exactly are we talking about?

Benedict We're talking about shoplifting, Mr McCracken.

Jack (*incredulously*) Shoplifting? What, Sammy?

Benedict I regret so.

Jack You're not police, are you?

Benedict No, no. Private security firm. (*Produces card.*)

Mannit Security Services – Benedict Hough.

Jack And my daughter is suspected of shoplifting?

Benedict Your daughter was apprehended whilst in the act of shoplifting.

Jack (*to Samantha*) Is this true?

Samantha No.

Jack Truthfully no? On your word of honour?

Samantha Yes. How many . . . ?

Jack (*satisfied*) All right, Sammy, you don't need to say any more. I know you well enough to tell when you're lying. You have denied this accusation, Sammy, and I believe you. (*with some dignity*) I think you should know, Mr Hough, that traditionally in this family, when we give each other our word we mean it. On the strength of this, I am prepared to believe my daughter rather than you. So where does that leave you, eh?

Benedict That leaves me with, number one, a video recording taken by a security camera of your daughter in the act of removing and concealing goods about her person; two, an eyewitness who also saw her; three, the fact that, subsequently, having furnished me with a false name and address she physically assaulted my colleague, Mrs Clegg, and made off, discarding the stolen goods as she went, in front of two further independent witnesses. That's where it leaves me, Mr McCracken.

Jack (*after a slight pause*) What goods are we talking about?

Benedict A family-sized bottle of Clearalene medicated shampoo and a stick of Little Miss Ritz waterproof eye-liner. Total value, one pound eighty-seven p.

Jack (*incredulous*) One pound eighty-seven p?

Benedict Correct.

Jack You are harrying my daughter for one pound eighty-seven p?

Benedict I think 'harrying' is a rather emotive term, Mr McCracken.

Jack It must have cost you a quid to get out here . . .

Benedict That's hardly the point . . .

Jack One pound eighty-seven p?

Benedict If you want to put it in perspective, Mr McCracken, perhaps you'd care to multiply that sum by several thousand similar cases and you'll appreciate how much that firm expects to lose in a year. And as to whether it's several hundred pounds' worth of photographic equipment or merely a handful of – hairgrips is hardly the point, is it? Theft is theft is theft, Mr McCracken.

Pause. Jack considers this.

Jack (*turning to Samantha*) What have you got to say, then?

Samantha shrugs.

Is this true? Well, obviously it's true, he's got a film of you, hasn't he?

Benedict A video recording.

Jack How much more have you taken?

Samantha Nothing.

Jack (*getting angry*) A bottle of shampoo? The bloody bathroom's swimming in it. And what else? Eye-liner, was it? For crying out loud, Sammy . . .

Samantha (*moving to the kitchen door*) Oh, Jesus . . .

Jack Come here, I'm talking to you –

Samantha I'm not staying for this –

She opens the door.

Jack (*too late to intercept her*) Sammy!

Samantha Don't believe me, I don't care . . .

Samantha rushes off upstairs. Jack comes out into the hall after her.

Jack (*roaring*) Sammy! Samantha, come down here.

Poppy comes rushing out of the sitting room. Samantha rushes into the bathroom and locks the door. Jack stops on the stairs.

Poppy Jack?

Jack (*controlling himself*) All right. No panic.

Poppy Where's Sammy?

Jack She's in the bathroom, I think.

Poppy Who is that man?

Jack Sammy's been caught shoplifting –

Poppy Oh, my God . . .

Jack Don't worry. I'll sort it out.

Poppy She'd no need to do that, had she? She'd no need.

Jack Can you get rid of people, love? I think this party's sort of over . . .

Poppy (*stunned*) She'd no need. No need to . . .

Jack (*gently*) Poppy . . .

Poppy Yes, all right.

Jack I'll – talk to this man . . . Make him see reason.

Poppy Yes, you talk to him, Jack. Tell him she couldn't have done it. I'll get rid of them. (*Turns back to the sitting room.*) Tell him she had no need.

Poppy goes into the living room again. Tina and Harriet have just started to emerge, their curiosity proving too much for them. Jack goes into the kitchen where Benedict has been inspecting the fitments. Jack closes the door again.

Jack Sorry to keep you.

Benedict This is a very well-appointed kitchen. I wouldn't mind taking a small bet as to the manufacturer. Ayres and Graces. Am I right?

Jack Absolutely.

Benedict Best to keep in with the father-in-law, eh? Hardly right for you to be seen with a Poggenpohl, would it? (*He laughs.*)

Jack Yes, all right. Now –

Benedict By the way, congratulations.

Jack What?

Benedict On your appointment. As the new managing director. Many congratulations.

During this next, Poppy quietly sees off their guests, Harriet, Cliff and Desmond. She stands just outside the front door talking to them. Roy sits in the sitting room and continues with the book. Tina goes upstairs, tries the bathroom door briefly and then goes along to check on her children. Samantha sits miserably in the bathroom, able to cry now she's alone.

Jack How did you know that?

Benedict Ah. Never reveal your sources. First rule of the private investigator, that is.

Jack I thought you were a store detective.

Benedict I am – we are by way of freelance. We'll tackle most jobs if asked. We were approached by Pollocks the Chemists to see if we could help stem their losses. I am pleased to say we've achieved that objective. We finish on Saturday.

Jack And how many 16-year-olds have you managed to trap in the process?

Benedict Schoolchildren are some of the worst offenders, Mr McCracken. Catch them early, that's my belief.

Jack You're going to prosecute my daughter, then?

Benedict I can't see I've much option, have I? I can't very well let her go, when we're already proceeding with a dozen similar cases.

Jack Now, look . . . Sammy gave you the wrong name, didn't she? For all anyone knows, you could still be looking for this Gladys –

Benedict Imogen Gladys Braithwaite . . .

Jack Who's to say you ever found her?

Benedict Oh, quite so.

Jack So. It's in your hands then, isn't it?

Benedict I suppose it is.

Jack Well.

Slight pause. They look at each other.

Benedict I'm pleased you aren't attempting to coerce me, Mr McCracken . . .

Jack You mean bribe you?

Benedict I'm overjoyed that you're not going to try that.

Jack No, I don't do that sort of thing.

Benedict I'm delighted.

Jack I'd never do that. Never.

Benedict Good.

Pause.

Good. Splendid.

Pause.

Well, I think I can perhaps overlook your daughter's – momentary lapse . . .

Jack If you felt you could, I'd be delighted –

Benedict Yes. I'm sure I could feel I could . . .

Jack Well, then. What more can I say, Mr – ?

Benedict Hough.

Jack Hough. I'm sorry I can't offer you a drink but we do have company this evening . . .

Benedict I fully understand.

Jack We'll use the front door this time, shall we?

Benedict Yes, that would probably be more convenient.

Jack is about to open the kitchen door. Poppy has closed the front door on her guests and returned to the sitting room.

Mr McCracken. On another matter . . .

Jack Yes?

Benedict I have, again via my sources, heard that your firm – your father-in-law's firm . . . is experiencing one or two troubles . . .

Jack Really? You do hear a lot, don't you? What troubles are these?

Benedict I feel it would be improper of me to elaborate –

Jack Well, then, that's that, isn't it?

Benedict I'll leave your father-in-law to tell you the details . . .

Jack Be honest, Mr Hough. You are talking through the seat of your trousers, aren't you?

Benedict I think you should listen to your father-in-law first, Mr McCracken. As his new managing director, he will be expecting you to make certain investigational arrangements. And when it comes to the choice of investigator, it would obviously be in your gift just as much as . . . this other affair is in mine – (*noticing a rather dangerous look in Jack's eye*) Now that is not bribery, Mr McCracken. No tainted money will have passed hands. That is a *bona fide* business proposal which is something quite other. A man in your position will appreciate that distinction, I'm sure. (*Smiles at Jack.*) I'm sure you do. Yes. (*Slight pause.*) Terrible thing, all this shoplifting. Can't blame the kids sometimes. The temptation must be insuperable. Trouble is, it's usually just the beginning. Before you know it, they're setting about senior citizens. (*with a certain relish*) You know what my solution would be? Corporal punishment. You take my advice, Mr McCracken, you give it a try. She's not too old for it, you know. The bigger they are . . .

Jack (*quietly*) Goodnight, Mr Hough. (*opening the kitchen door*) I think I must ask you to leave now before I do you some damage. All right?

Benedict nervously retreats through the door. During the next, Poppy and Roy emerge from the sitting room through various doors and Tina hurries along the landing and halfway downstairs to investigate. Samantha listens at the bathroom door.

Benedict (*hurriedly going through to the hall*) Be careful, Mr McCracken, be careful. All right then, all right. Forget what I said. Forget every word. I'm doing you no favours at all then, Mr McCracken. Forget it. Forget I spoke . . .

Jack (*calmly*) Just as you like . . . It's up to you.

Poppy (*alarmed*) Jack . . . ?

Benedict You don't get anything for nothing in this world, Mr McCracken, just you remember that. I'll see your daughter has the book thrown at her. I'll see she . . .

Jack (*with a terrible roar*) GET OUT OF MY HOUSE!!

Benedict retreats out the front door. Jack slams it after him and stands, trying to compose himself. Poppy hurries to him.

Poppy Jack? Are you all right?

Jack (*breathless*) Oh, I was that near to – I was very near to violence then . . .

Roy Want me to go out and do him over?

Jack No, I do not, thank you, Roy. You would no doubt get lost between here and the garden gate.

Roy (*unoffended*) Roger. Fair enough.

Poppy Tina, try and coax Sammy down, will you? She'll listen to you.

During the next, Tina goes upstairs again as far as the bathroom door.

(*to Jack*) Easy, love. Steady the Vikings. You're shaking. Roy, get him a drink.

Roy Right.

Jack Scotch and water with plenty of water.

Poppy Come on, sit down a moment.

Solicitously, she leads Jack into the near sitting room. Roy goes to the drinks.

Tina (*knocking gently on the bathroom door*) Sammy . . . it's only me. It's Tina. Sammy? He's gone now, it's all right. Dad threw him out.

Poppy I take it you couldn't come to any agreement?

Jack Hardly.

Tina Sammy . . . let me in, please . . .

Poppy Ah, well. I'm sure you did what you could. We'll just have to make sure we stand by her, won't we? All of us. The family. She'll have to face the consequences. But we'll face them with her.

Jack (*impressed by this*) You're a good person, Poppy.

Under the next, Samantha opens the bathroom door. Tina takes her gently by the arm and, talking softly to her, brings her downstairs. Roy arrives with Jack's drink.

(*taking glass*) Thanks, Roy.

After a moment, Roy sits and resumes reading his book.

Poppy We must all talk it over. Tina's fetching Sammy down. She always listens to Tina.

Jack She never listens to me . . .

Poppy Nonsense. She worships you.

Jack She hardly talks to me these days at all. Hardly get five words out of her.

Poppy Maybe she's a little nervous of you . . .

Jack Nervous of me? What's she got to be nervous about?

Poppy Well. You're a lot to live up to sometimes, Jack. You set very high standards for yourself and you expect them from other people. I mean, fair enough but –

Jack (*amazed*) What are you talking about?

Poppy (*who has said enough*) Nothing.

Jack I don't know what you're talking about.

Poppy What's that you're reading, Roy?

Roy It's Sammy's book. Very naughty.

Poppy (*shrugging*) Oh. Well . . .

Roy Price is a bit naughty, too. Twelve quid. Imagine spending twelve quid on a book. I mean, how does Sammy manage to spend twelve quid on books, that's what I want to know . . .

A silence.

Ah.

Jack Stand on your head for a minute, Roy, there's a good lad. Take the weight off your brain.

Tina (*arriving in the doorway*) Here she is.

Poppy (*to Samantha*) All right, Sammy? Come and sit down. Are you all right, dear?

Samantha Yes.

Jack Hallo, Sammy.

Samantha 'lo.

Poppy We've been saying, Samy, that whatever the outcome of all this, darling, we're going to stand by you. We're a family.

Samantha You all coming to prison with me, are you?

Poppy You're not going to prison. Is she, Jack? Sammy's not going to prison?

Jack Course you're not.

Poppy Your Dad did what he could to persuade the man but –

Samantha Yes, I heard him.

Jack Why, Sammy? That's what I don't understand. For less than two quids' worth of goods.

Poppy Is that all it was? What made you do it?

Samantha I don't know.

Jack (*sharper*) You must know . . .

Poppy All right, Jack.

Jack No, I want to know. Why?

Samantha Something to do, wasn't it?

Jack Something to do?

Samantha Yes.

Jack Bloody hell.

Samantha Everybody does.

Jack Everybody does what? Would you speak up, Sammy, I can't hear you?

Samantha (*louder*) Everybody steals things.

Jack Oh, do they? I see. That's the reason. We all steal things. Tina steals things. Your Mum steals things, does she? Are you saying I steal things?

Samantha No. You don't.

Jack Of course I don't. Neither does Tina. Nor does your Mum. You're on your own, Sammy. You're the only one that steals round here, I'm afraid.

Samantha Mum does.

Jack What?

Samantha Steals.

Poppy I do not.

Samantha You do.

Poppy When?

Samantha From where you work. You nick things from your office. You're always bringing things home.

Poppy Oh, come on, Sammy, that's hardly the same, is it?

Nobody answers.

Well, it isn't. I mean, all I take is the odd pencil or paper . . . clip . . .

Slight pause.

Well, it's not the same thing at all, is it?

Jack (*to Tina*) Do you steal things?

Tina No. Of course I don't. No. (*Pause.*) Not really. (*looking at Samantha*) Not like I used to.

Jack Oh, you used to?

Tina No – just the odd . . . thing. Jar of jam. Tin of sardines. Nothing. They never missed it. Only when Roy and I were starting out. When we were hard up.

Jack You were never hard up.

Tina We have been, you don't know . . .

Jack Yes, I do know. Because I made very sure you never were . . .

Tina You may have thought you did –

Jack As soon as you told us you were expecting Kevin, I paid for your wedding, I set you up in a flat and I got Ken to give Roy a job. And I gave you a cash sum as well. Not that we could afford it –

Poppy True.

Jack So don't try that one.

Tina It still wasn't enough.

Jack So you were reduced to stealing things, is that it? You were so poor . . .

Tina Yes, we were. (*Slight pause.*) Also I resented paying for them.

Jack Ah, well. Now that's something quite different, isn't it?

Poppy Come on now . . .

Tina I resented the vast profits all these firms were making off basic necessities of life we couldn't do without even if we wanted to . . .

Jack Bloody hell, let's all sing 'The Red Flag', shall we?

Tina Look, don't you make fun – Roy, stand up for me, will you?

Roy Everybody steals a bit, don't they?

Jack Look, what's the matter with you lot? You're just sitting there thinking up reasons for taking things that don't belong to you. That's all you're doing. Am I the only person here who actually thinks it's wrong? It can't be just me, can it? Am I the only one left with any moral values at all?

Poppy Come on, Jack. We're changing the subject.

Jack Well, that's one down, isn't it? Nine to go. Next! Thou shalt not kill. What about that then? Let's have a crack at that one next, shall we?

Tina Dad . . .

Jack Anybody here object to killing people? No. Right. Good. Carried.

Poppy Jack, for God's sake, don't get so excited. You just fly off at things. You'll have a heart attack or something. He did this with that man just now. Shouted at him and threatened him. If he'd just kept a bit calmer he might have been more co-operative . . .

Jack Calmer? Do you know what that man was trying to do? I'll tell you. He was attempting to blackmail me.

Tina Blackmail?

Samantha Yes. Employ me and I won't prosecute. Can you believe that? I mean, if I reported that to the authorities he'd be the one in gaol, not Sammy.

Poppy Wait a minute. He said he'd let Sammy off if you gave him a job?

Jack Unbelievable, isn't it?

Poppy So what did you say?

Jack You heard what I said.

Silence.

What's wrong?

Poppy You'd rather Sammy went to court than give him what he wanted . . . ?

Jack No, that's twisting it . . .

Tina No, it isn't.

Jack Do you realize if I'd given in to him . . .

Poppy Sammy wouldn't be prosecuted.

Jack You can't give in to a man like that.

Poppy Why not?

Jack Because. Where does it end, for one thing? Anyway, I don't want him working for me. I don't even want him in the same town.

Tina So, Sammy has to go to court . . .

Jack You cannot simply buy your way out of things by giving into blackmail and threats –

Tina Dad, we're talking about Sammy's future –

Jack Look, to hell with Sammy, there's a principle at stake here. (*Slight pause. Trying to retract*) No, I didn't mean that.

Samantha turns and runs upstairs again. This time she goes into one of the far rooms, presumably her own. The door slams.

Tina (*going after Samantha*) Oh, terrific. That's amazing, that is, absolutely amazing. My own father. Why don't you put the handcuffs on her while you're about it?

Tina goes upstairs after Samantha. She stands at the end of the landing and talks to her sister softly through the door, as before. After a minute or two, Samantha lets her in.

Jack Now come on, come on. No need for everyone to start getting over-excited. I've said I didn't mean that, I'm sorry.

Poppy is staring at him incredulously. Roy has dived deeper into his book.

I don't know what we're all getting so excited about, I'm sure.

Poppy picks up a couple of glasses and starts for the kitchen.

Poppy (*as she goes*) I never would have believed it of you.

Jack (*following her*) What?

Poppy That you'd do that. To your own daughter.

Jack Do what?

Poppy You had a chance to save her and you refused it.

Poppy enters the kitchen and puts the glasses on the draining board. She makes for the sitting room again.

Jack (*following her as he speaks*) Rubbish. All I did was stand up to blackmail and insist she face the consequences of her own actions. She knew what she was doing –

Poppy (*entering the near sitting room*) Oh, well, let them cut off her hands then, why not?

Jack (*still following her*) It's a good job they don't, isn't it? Or else there'd be very few left in this house with any limbs at all –

Roy Short-handed, eh? (*He laughs.*)

Jack (*savagely*) You, shut up!

Poppy takes up a tray of dirty glasses and returns to the kitchen.

Poppy (*more calmly*) In spite of what you might think, Jack, none of us are hardened criminals –

Jack (*trailing after her*) I never said you were . . .

Poppy But let me tell you that there have been times when I could have become one without the slightest difficulty. And I have been tempted. God, I have been tempted at times . . .

Jack Rubbish.

Poppy puts the tray of glasses down on the table, transfers them to the sink and, during the course of the next, washes them up. Jack, by reflex, in turn dries them and puts them back on the tray.

Poppy (*handing him a tea-towel*) Jack, you are the nicest, most honest, upright, undevious man I have ever met. And I love you for that. I always have done. I've admired you. And I've tried to live up to you, I promise. But I am here to tell you that at times it has not been easy.

Jack What, living with me?

Poppy No, trying to make ends meet . . .

Jack We're comfortable enough . . .

Poppy Only because I budget down to the last penny, we are . . .

Jack We manage perfectly well . . .

Poppy Jack, you don't shop. When was the last time you went shopping? I mean serious shopping. Not just for hi-fi . . .

Jack You make it sound as if we're on the bread line. We're both earning, aren't we?

Poppy Do you think I like going to work?

Jack I assumed you did –

Poppy Well, you've assumed a hell of a lot, it seems to me . . .

Jack Why else are you working?

Poppy Because otherwise we couldn't manage. Oh, we'd live. We'd still live a bloody sight better than most people, but we wouldn't live in the style to which you and the kids have gradually grown accustomed.

Jack (*calculating*) Listen, there's my salary plus your salary, which amounts to what, per annum . . . ?

Poppy Gross, an awful lot. Net, not much. I can assure you.

Jack Ah, well. That's the same the world over, isn't –

Poppy No, it is not the same. That's what I'm trying to tell you. Because everybody else works little fiddles. That's what the system's designed for. That's what it allows for. Everybody – everybody but us, that is – everybody else bends it a little; just a little bit here and there; and they don't quite declare that; and they tell a little lie about that. Not dishonest, Jack, just a little bit fuzzy round the edges sometimes . . .

They have finished washing and drying and Poppy has taken up the tray of clean glasses and started for the near sitting room.

Jack (*following as before*) Rubbish. You're making out that everybody . . .

Poppy (*entering the near sitting room*) Everybody does.

Roy True.

Poppy You just shut up!

During the next, Roy, injured, gathers up his book and retreats to the dining room. Poppy starts a furious tidying of the near sitting room.

How do you think Harriet manages three holidays a year because of her nerves? And Cliff drives that damn great Porsche? And Anita never wears the same outfit twice? God, I'd kill for some of her clothes –

Jack Well, don't tell me Desmond's doing better than us. They're not well off, him and Harriet.

Poppy Only because Des is salting it all away somewhere.

Jack Rubbish. I don't believe that.

Poppy Even him – (*indicating the departed Roy*) – even that – oaf – he's doing better than we are . . . Here I am married to a very successful man, and we're living like failures. It's not fair.

Poppy bursts into tears, rushes out of the room and upstairs, crying as she goes. Jack follows bewildered.

(*from the landing*) Jack, I admire you and I will defend you and your principles with my dying breath, but do you always have to be quite so unbelievably *honest*? (*A pause.*)

Jack I see. So, if Sammy breaks the rules and then I bend the rules, two wrongs will make a right? Is that it?

Poppy It has been known.

Jack Well, well . . . Can't trust anyone these days, can you? Even God got it wrong. Poor old soul.

Jack heads towards the front door.

Poppy Jack . . . Jack? Where are you going?

Jack reaches the front door.

Jack I'm going down to the King's Head. I'm sure, once I'm pissed, I'll see it all much, much more clearly.

Jack goes out and closes the door. Tina comes out of Samantha's room and along the landing to the top of the stairs.

Tina Has he gone out?

Poppy Yes. Gone for a drink.

Tina Has he – ?

Poppy Oh yes. He'll come round to it. He'll come round. You know what your Dad's like with his principles. (*as she goes along the landing*) Sammy. It's going to be all right, love . . .

Poppy and Tina go into Samantha's room.

A light change to indicate that the location (if not the setting) has changed. It is late afternoon. The front doorbell rings. In a moment, Yvonne comes from the dining room. She is apparently in the midst of domestic tasks. She opens the front door to admit Jack. He has on his car coat.

Yvonne Hallo, Jack. Ken's expecting you.

Jack Sorry, been a busy afternoon. Trying to get to grips with everything all at once.

Yvonne First day at work. What do you expect? (*indicating her appearance*) Excuse all this, I've been . . .

Jack You haven't given up looking after him, I see.

Yvonne Force of habit, I suppose. Been nursing him for thirty years at work. Hard to give it up.

Jack You shouldn't need to clean his house for him, though. He can afford someone for that, can't he?

Yvonne Oh yes, she comes in most mornings. That's no problem. I'm just sorting things out a bit. There's stuff here that hasn't been moved since Grace died. Her clothes are still in the bedroom; her wheelchair's parked in the middle of the sitting room; and there's a jigsaw puzzle on the dining-room table she was doing the day she was taken ill. They've been dusting round it for four years –

Jack Ah, that's sad, isn't it? Gracie never finished it, then?

Yvonne He's upstairs, I think. Want to go up?

Jack (*as he moves to the stairs*) If you ever fancy coming back to work, Yvonne . . . I can always use a good secretary. I don't think much to the one I've inherited . . .

Yvonne Edith's all right.

Jack She's too tall. She frightens me. (*turning to look upstairs*) How is he today?

Yvonne Fine.

Jack Comes and goes a bit these days, doesn't he? I mean, last night he seemed a lot worse.

Yvonne That's because there were too many people. He's never good when there are too many people.

Jack (*starting upstairs*) I'll see what he wants then.

From the dining room, a grandfather clock chimes the half hour.

Yvonne Jack.

Jack (*turning*) Yes?

Yvonne Don't – underestimate him entirely, will you? He still knows what's what better than most of us.

Jack Believe me, I have never underestimated Ken.

Ken comes from one of the far bedrooms and along the landing.

Ken Who's that there? Is that Des, is it?

Jack No, it's me, Ken. It's Jack.

Ken Course it is. Course it's Jack. Did she let you in? (*shouting vaguely in the direction of the stairs*) Did you let him in, Yvonne?

Yvonne (*calling as she returns to the dining room*) Yes, Ken.

Ken Good. (*winking at Jack, confidentially*) She doesn't let people in unless I tell her to.

Jack Really? (*looking around*) Well, where do you want us to – ?

Ken In here.

Jack What?

Ken Sssh! In here. Not a word.

Ken opens the bathroom door and, pushing Jack inside, closes and bolts the door after them. He then reaches in behind the shower curtain, switches on the shower, flushes the lavatory and turns on the washbasin taps.

Jack What the hell are you doing?

Ken (*above the noise of water*) They have microphones now that can pick up a pin dropping on Venus . . .

Jack (*raising his voice slightly*) On what?

Ken Venus. The big one these days, Jack, is security. No use having the good ideas if they're not secure. Some of those yellow men, they've got them rolling off their production lines before you've had a chance to finish your meeting.

Jack I think it's the other way round these days, Ken.

Ken I know what I'm saying. I fought them, boy. (*picking up a bathroom stool*) Here. Look at this. See?

Jack One of ours, isn't it?

Ken A Princess Wilhelmina bathroom stool second series, modified. Am I right?

Jack Right.

Ken You're wrong.

He upturns the stool and shows Jack the trademark on the underside.

Jack (*reading*) 'Donizetti. Made in Italy.' Italy?

Ken Right down to the same paint, Jack.

Jack You sure?

Ken I had it analysed. It's a rip off. Even the glue.

Jack What they retailing these at, then?

Ken Roughly 20 per cent above what we are.

Jack *Above?* Then what are we worrying about?

Ken Because the bastards are crowding us out of the market.

Jack How come?

Ken Look at that label, Jack, look at that label. Italian. They'll pay twenty quid more just for that. You know this country. Stick an 'i' on the end of your trademark, they'll mortgage their testicles for it. Custom-made designer stools fashioned by Mediterranean craftsmen. All that cobblers. Time was, whatever you bought in this country, you looked for just one word. Birmingham. And you bought it, no questions.

Jack How widespread's this?

Ken Every line we've got, Jack, including the new ones – (*indicating lavatory*) – flush that again, will you? – I tell you, Jack, they are releasing our new lines almost simultaneous with us. That new three-drawer vanity unit, Miss Felicity, we'd hardly got them out of the drying shop . . . I've tried tracing their end but it's a maze, Jack. It's a ball of string that disappears up some Swiss banker's back passage. We'll have to catch it this end, if we're going to catch it at all. It's an inside job. Someone's selling us short from inside the firm, that's a fact. Industrial espionage. Which is a fancy name for daylight robbery.

Jack Right.

Ken You'll need to take someone aboard. Someone you can trust. Someone sharp who can nose it out. I'll have to leave it to you to choose. Things aren't so easy for me since Gracie went, you know.

Jack I'll deal with it, Ken.

Ken I get the odd blank patch, you know –

Jack Yes.

Ken Funny, it just sort of drops away. It's like one minute it's someone you know, the next you can't even remember meeting them before . . . You see them looking at you and you know they're thinking who the bloody hell does he think I am? And you yourself haven't a notion . . . Mind you, they say it's when you start looking in the mirror and you're puzzled, that's the time you need to worry. Seventy-five next week, you know.

Jack We hadn't forgotten, Ken.

Ken I can leave this with you then, can I?

Jack I'll get moving on it.

Ken Not a word though. That we're arranging to get someone in. Just you and me.

Jack Only us, is that it?

Ken Only us.

Jack Not Yvonne?

Ken (*rather vaguely*) Well, yes, I might have told her. Well, she's my right arm, like. Wonderful girl. Rock solid. Bloody sight more use than her sister, anyway. I wish Des had married her and not the other one.

Jack I hear him and Harriet have got problems, yes.

Ken I warned him when he married her. I said, whatever you do, son, keep clear of thin women. They're trouble. They're for magazine covers only. No use for nothing else. And look at her now. Death warmed up. Don't mention this to Des, either.

Jack No?

Ken I know he's your partner but he's no head for the business. Never has had, more's the pity. My own son. Should have been a cook in a girls' school, that's more his line. The truth is, he's more than halfway to nancy, if you ask me.

Jack Oh, I don't know, Ken . . .

Ken You know my Gracie, she was thirteen and a half stone when she died and we never had a cross word. God, she could laugh. Remember her laugh?

Jack Nobody could forget her, Ken. (*Slight pause.*) Well,

I'll get going then.

Ken Yes, you get off. Want to make use of the facilities, before you go?

Jack No, thanks all the same.

Ken opens the door to let Jack out.

Ken You'll manage to find someone, will you? For this job?

Jack Yes – I . . . I think I've got someone who'll do.

Ken Make sure he's a good man. We need a good man.

Jack Sure. Cheerio.

Ken Cheerio, son.

Jack goes downstairs quite thoughtfully. As he does so, from the dining room, the grandfather clock strikes six. Ken remains in the bathroom. He is about to leave when he catches sight of himself in the bathroom mirror. He stops and stares, looking slightly puzzled as he examines his own reflection. Jack stands in the hall, looking for Yvonne.

Jack (*calling quite softly*) Yvonne?

Yvonne comes hurriedly and a little guiltily out of the dining room. She has on an attractive (and expensive) brooch which she wasn't wearing earlier.

Yvonne Oh, hallo. Are you off?

Jack Yes.

Yvonne Had your talk?

Jack Yes. I gather you know about . . .

Yvonne Oh yes. It was me who advised him to get someone in.

Jack Well. We are.

Yvonne Good. I hope you find out something.

Jack I expect we will. See you soon. (*as he goes, noticing her brooch*) That's nice. Your brooch.

Yvonne Oh, yes. It's . . . not mine. It was Grace's. I was just seeing how it looked. On me.

Jack Lovely.

Yvonne Yes, isn't it? Bye.

Jack Bye.

Jack goes out of the front door. Yvonne closes it and goes back slowly to the dining room, fingering the brooch. Ken has now left the bathroom and has gone off again into one of the far bedrooms.

The location changes again. It is evening now, a couple of days later. A rumble of thunder and rain. Poppy dashes in through the back door with an armful of washing. She closes the door and regains her breath. She is wearing a rather smart, up-to-the-minute outfit, slightly but not radically different from her usual clothes.

Samantha, meanwhile, is coming downstairs. She is wearing a dress and appears, somewhat reluctantly, to have made an effort.

Poppy (*to herself*) I knew I'd forget these . . . I knew I would . . .

Samantha comes into the kitchen.

There you are. You didn't remind me and I forgot them. See?

Samantha I don't know why you still hang the washing out. Why don't you get a drier? Everybody else has a drier.

Poppy (*starting to fold the clothes*) I'm not wasting money on driers when there's good fresh air . . .

Samantha Good fresh rain . . .

Poppy (*surveying Samantha*) Oh, that's better. You look really nice now.

Samantha I feel stupid.

Poppy Lovely.

Samantha I hate dresses. They're all draughty.

Poppy Well, once you've said thank you to your Dad, then you can change into what you like.

Samantha Getting dressed up just for that.

Poppy Thank your lucky stars you're not in prison. You'd have to wear a dress in prison.

Samantha No, I wouldn't.

Poppy You would if they told you to. If they told you to put a dress on you'd soon jump to it. (*examining her own attire for a moment*) This doesn't look too young for me, does it?

Samantha (*ignoring her*) I'm not seeing that man if he comes, anyway. I'm not talking to him.

Poppy We'll see.

> *She has finished sorting the washing. She hands a pile of Jack's underwear to Samantha.*

Here. Take these up and put them in the airing cupboard.

Samantha (*recoiling in revulsion*) Yurrr! Yurrr!

Poppy Sammy, don't be so silly, for heaven's sake.

Samantha Yurrr!

Poppy It's perfectly clean. (*Handing it to her.*) Now go on and don't be so stupid.

Samantha reluctantly accepts the load.

Samantha Yurrk.

As she is about to go, Jack comes in the back door hurriedly running from the rain.

Poppy Here he is.

Jack (*shutting the door*) Hey, what a downpour, eh?

Poppy (*kissing him*) Hallo dear. (*helping him off with his coat*) You must be tired.

Jack Just a bit.

Poppy You're not going to have to work every Saturday, are you?

Jack I sincerely hope not.

Poppy (*taking coat to the hall*) I'll hang this up for you.

Jack (*noticing her outfit*) Is that new, is it?

Poppy (*feigning surprise*) Oh, yes. I got it this afternoon. Anita came round and we both went shopping. She helped me choose it.

Jack Oh.

Poppy You don't think it's too young for me, do you?

Jack No, it's fine.

Poppy (*convinced now it's wrong*) Yes. It was Anita, she kept on and on . . . (*giving up*) Anyway. (*indicating Samantha*) Look who's here to say hallo to you.

Poppy goes into the hall. She hangs up the coat in a cupboard and then goes into the far sitting room, anxious not to intrude.

Jack Hallo, Sammy. All right, are you?

Samantha I'm all right . . .

Jack Right.

Pause.

Samantha (*rather as if she's been rehearsed in this*) Thank you for what you did in getting me out of trouble and I promise I won't do it again and I am very sorry for bringing shame on the family.

Jack (*a little taken aback*) Yes. Good. I'm sorry if I've – er . . . I'm sorry. I don't know if I have done anything but if I have, then I'm sorry.

Samantha You haven't.

Jack Good. Fine. Right. Well. Go and sit down, shall we? Till this bloke arrives? Not that I intend to make him very welcome. I would like it known he is here under sufferance.

He moves off into the hall. Samantha follows Jack across the hall to the sitting room. As she does so, the front doorbell rings. Poppy immediately comes back into the hall.

Poppy That'll be Mr Hough. Just stay down a second, Sammy, and say hallo.

Samantha I am sodding not . . .

She rushes upstairs.

Poppy (*half-heartedly*) Sammy . . . She keeps saying that word lately.

Jack For once, I'm inclined to agree with her.

*Samantha goes into her bedroom and closes the door.
Doorbell.*

Poppy Now, Jack . . .

*Poppy opens the front door to admit Benedict. A clap of
thunder.*

Benedict Good evening, Mrs McCracken.

Poppy Good evening, Mr Hough. Do come in. Let me
take your . . .

She helps him with his mac.

Benedict Thank you. Good evening, Mr McCracken. Not
the nicest of weather.

Poppy No, terrible. Do come through.

Benedict Thank you.

*Poppy leads him through to the sitting room. Jack hangs
up his coat and follows.*

What a beautiful house this is.

Poppy Thank you. Do sit down.

Benedict Thank you.

*They sit. Jack joins them. He remains hostile to
Benedict.*

May I say how delighted I am that things have worked
out.

Poppy Yes, it's good they have, isn't it?

Slight pause.

Benedict (*with a look at Poppy*) Do you want me to . . . ?

Jack You carry on, Mr Hough. I keep no secrets from my
wife. She's an equal part of the team.

Benedict And a very decorative one, too, if I may say so. (*Favours Poppy with a leer.*) Well. As soon as I received your telephone call last Thursday confirming my appointment to investigate this matter, I set certain inquiries in motion.

Poppy That's quick work. I'd no idea you'd already started.

Benedict Oh, I haven't. Not officially. I don't officially start till next Monday. That was the earliest I could without it looking –

Jack Pre-arranged.

Poppy I see.

Benedict I'm itching to go through those files, though. That's where we'll find him, Mr McCracken. Our man's in there somewhere. He's had access to all the information at the right time, in the right department. He'll have left his thumb print somewhere.

Jack I hope you're right.

Benedict However, what I have been able to do, in the meantime, is a little inquiring regarding the other end of the chain . . .

Jack Donizetti?

Benedict Precisely. It seemed to me, you see, that if we failed to catch our fly in your ointment at this end, we might be able to trace him back at the other. It's a longer shot, but . . .

Jack And?

Benedict I'm getting warmer. Donizetti is a subsidiary of a company registered in Holland, W.K.P. Limited. W.K.P. is, in turn, owned by Lorelei International who are Spanish based but probably part Libyan, part Brazilian owned. Lorelei, in turn, are little more than an offshoot of a company based somewhere near Milan and trading under the name of Rivetti. That's as far as I've got, so far.

Jack (*thoughtfully*) Rivetti?

Poppy We could sue them, couldn't we? If we're sure it's them?

Benedict Well, you could try.

Jack (*trying to remember*) Rivetti . . .

Benedict But from my experience of international law, that could take the rest of your life.

Poppy Oh? Have you had experience of international law?

Benedict Only indirectly.

Poppy Oh.

Jack (*realizing*) Rivetti!

Poppy Jack?

Jack What?

Poppy Anything wrong?

Jack What? No. Nothing at all. Well, thank you so much then, Mr Hough.

He grabs the bewildered Benedict by the arm and starts to propel him towards the front door. Poppy follows, mystified.

Benedict (*startled*) Oh, right . . .

Poppy Jack, what are you . . . ?

Jack Good night, Mr Hough – Poppy, get his coat –

You've been a great help. Thank you so much. I look forward to renewing our acquaintance on Monday.

Benedict Yes, I don't . . . I don't . . . I don't . . . I don't quite see –

Poppy (*handing Jack the coat*) Here you are.

Jack Ta. Sorry to rush you away, Mr Hough. I'm expecting a phone call any minute.

He thrusts Benedict and his coat through the front door.

Benedict Yes, right-ho. Goodbye . . .

Poppy Bye . . .

Jack slams the front door and now gets his own coat out of the cupboard.

Jack, what on earth are you . . . ?

Jack I've got to be wrong. Please God I'm wrong. Tell me I'm wrong . . .

Poppy Where are you going now?

Jack is halfway across the hall and entering the kitchen.

Jack I'll be back as soon as I can . . .

Poppy Won't you tell me where you're going?

Jack To see one of Mr Rivetti's business associates . . .

Jack goes out of the back door, leaving it open. Poppy follows him to close it, puzzled.

Poppy Mr Rivetti . . . ? Mr . . . ? (*realizing*) Oh, my God, Mr Rivetti!

Poppy changes her mind and hurries out after Jack, closing the back door behind her.

Jack. Wait a minute. You'd better be sure.

As the door closes, the lights change to indicate another location. The hall and landing lights are on but the rest of the house is in darkness. The doorbell rings insistently. After a moment, the far bedroom door opens and a figure appears on the landing jumping, trying to get into a rather tight pair of designer jeans. It is **Giorgio Rivetti**, *the strikingly similar younger brother of Uberto whom we met earlier. Giorgio is 25, a freshfaced, attractive, rich young Italian. Like his brother, Uberto, he speaks little English. The doorbell rings again. Giorgio mutters agitatedly to himself. Another figure appears on the landing, naked except for a sheet wrapped round her. It is Anita. In her free hand she holds Giorgio's discarded shirt. He snatches it from her.*

Giorgio *Mio Dio, dovevamo andare in albergo.*

Anita It's all right, Giorgio. It's not my husband –

Giorgio *Te l'avevo detto che era meglio andare in albergo. Adesso tuo marito è tornato e mi spara.*

Anita – it can't be. You're quite safe. Cliff has got his own key. (*with difficulty*) *Non è mio marito.*

Doorbell rings again. Giorgio yelps in panic.

Look, for God's sake, Giorgio, wait there while I get rid of them . . . *Aspetta qui!*

Anita starts downstairs. Giorgio hovers on the landing, nervously.

Giorgio *Aspetta qui, già . . . Avremmo dovuto andare al Savoy.*

The doorbell rings again.

Anita Wait!

Anita reaches the front door, Giorgio goes back into the

*far bedroom and re-emerges on to the landing with his
shoes and socks which he endeavours to put on while
listening to what's happening below.*

(*talking through the front door*) Who is that, please?

Jack It's Jack, Anita . . .

Anita Oh hallo, Jack, how are you?

Jack Let me in please.

Anita Jack it's not very convenient at the moment. I
wonder if you could come back . . .

Jack Anita, open this door or I'll kick it in.

Anita (*doing so*) Look, Cliff's not here at the moment,
Jack, he –

Jack bursts in, pushing her aside.

Careful!

Jack Where is he? Where is that brother of mine?

Anita I've said, he's not here.

Jack (*moving first to the kitchen and switching on the
lights*) Cliff! (*Seeing the room is empty, he crosses to the
sitting room and does the same.*) Cliff!

Anita How many more times, he's not here. He's down
the pub. I promise you, he is. He's got some darts
match.

Jack Then call him and get him back here.

Anita I can't do that. It's a match.

Jack Unless you prefer me to go down there and bounce
him round the snug on his head . . .

Anita What's he done?

Jack Get him.

Anita picks up the phone and dials.

Anita I'll dial him on his mobile, he always has it with him.

Jack Well, he would do. He's a busy lad, isn't he?

Anita I don't know what he's supposed to have done . . . (*The phone connects.*) Hallo, Cliff? It's me . . . Listen, can you come back? No, now . . . No, I'm sorry but it's urgent . . . No, I can't explain on the phone, it –

Jack (*snatching the phone from her*) Cliff, this is Jack. Now get back here, sunshine. (*He hangs up.*)

Anita (*slightly intrigued*) I've never seen you like this before . . . You're quite masterful, Jack. (*She giggles.*)

Jack You haven't seen the half of it yet. Wait till little brother arrives, I'll –

Giorgio, on the landing, having managed to put on his socks and one shoe, now drops the second with a clatter. He stands appalled.

What was that?

Anita What?

Jack He's here, isn't he? He's upstairs. (*charging for the stairs*) He's not in the pub at all, he's upstairs . . .

Anita No, that's not him . . .

Jack thunders up the stairs. Giorgio, hearing this, dives for the near bedroom, looks round, panic-stricken, and decides, with certain unoriginality, to hide in the fitted wardrobe. He slides open the door and is all but engulfed in Anita's numerous frocks that spring from their confined, undersized quarters.

Giorgio Ah! (*He fights his way in with difficulty.*)

Jack (*reaching the landing*) Cliff! I know you're here!

Anita (*following him upstairs*) Jack, he's not up there, I swear he isn't. Jack!

Giorgio (*during this*) Oh, Madonna santissima, fa che non mi spari. Te ne prego, non lasciare che mi ammazzi.

> *Unable to close the door, Giorgio crouches behind the dresses, muttering a prayer. Jack enters the bedroom and stops short as he hears this.*

Jack Who's that in there? That's not Cliff.

Anita I told you it wasn't.

Jack Who is it, then?

Anita It's Giorgio.

Jack That Italian? The one I met the other night?

Anita No, that was Uberto. This is his youngest brother, Giorgio.

Jack How many of them are there?

Anita Five.

Jack Five?

Anita Uberto, Vincenzo, Orlando, Lotario and Giorgio.

Jack All called Rivetti?

Anita Yes.

Jack And you're working your way through them all, are you?

Anita Mind your own business . . .

Jack This is very much my business, Anita. I have one or

two urgent matters of my own to discuss with the Rivettis
. . . (*advancing on the cupboard*) Oy, you! Out!

A terrified scream from Giorgio.

Anita Don't frighten him, Jack, he's only a kid. He
hasn't done any harm. He's a good boy, he's very
religious . . .

Jack Yes, I can see he is. Says his prayers regularly in
married women's wardrobes. Anita, does Cliff know this is
going on?

Anita May I get dressed, please, Jack?

Jack Poor bastard. He doesn't, does he? He's down there
playing his darts match and he hasn't got a clue, has he?

Anita Please let me get dressed, Jack.

Jack What's this doing to Cliff? What's it done to him
already? Ask yourself, Anita. What is this doing to
yourself as a human being? Your husband's due back any
minute, you've got a 14-year-old Catholic Boy Scout in
your cupboard and you don't give a stuff, do you? You
defy belief.

Anita (*wearily*) Oh, God. Hold on a minute, Jack, I'll go
and put on some organ music.

Jack I'm not a prude. If people want to bore themselves
rigid with soft-porn movies or read newspapers full of tits,
I don't mind. I don't want to interfere with that. But surely
somewhere, Anita, there's got to be a minimum level of
decent human behaviour, hasn't there? Beneath which
none of us sink? Like not screwing around in your own
marriage bed with men who are busy swindling your own
family out of thousands of pounds? Something around
that level, eh?

Anita (*calmly*) Oh, I see. That's what all this is about.

Sorry, Jack, I was being a bit slow. My mind was still on other things.

Cliff comes in the front door and closes it.

Cliff (*calling*) Hallo?

Anita (*calling*) We're up here.

Cliff (*starting up the stairs*) This had better be important. It was a vital match tonight . . . Semi-finals. If we beat the Young Farmers this evening, we meet the CID in the final . . . Oh hallo, Jack.

Jack Evening.

Cliff What's the problem? (*to Anita, without undue surprise*) What are you doing?

Anita Jack's just been telling me that someone's swindling the family out of thousands of pounds, Cliff. Do you know anything about that?

Cliff No such luck. Hasn't come my way. What are we talking about then, Jack?

Jack We're talking about furniture, Clifford. We're talking about Ayres and Graces having their designs ripped off and reproduced elsewhere. We're talking about them being resold under a fancy foreign label. Most important of all, we're talking about my own brother organizing the whole bloody racket.

Cliff Who, me?

Jack Are you denying it?

Cliff Jack, you know I wouldn't do that. I'd never rip old Ken off like that. You know me . . .

Jack You are lying to me, Clifford. I've known you since you were one day old, boy. Never lie to me.

Jack advances. Cliff retreats.

Cliff Now, hold on . . .

Anita Jack, don't hit him . . .

Jack (*loudly*) I want the truth, son, the truth.

Jack thumps the cupboard to make his point. A cry of fear from Giorgio inside. They stop.

Cliff Who's that then? Is that that Giorgio.

Anita Yes.

Jack (*surprised*) You know about him?

Cliff What's he doing in there? Trying on dresses?

Anita He's hiding from you. He's frightened you'll kill him.

Cliff Me?

Anita It's all right. He's seen too many foreign films.

Cliff Stupid pillock. We'd better all go downstairs before he suffocates. Jack, I'm sure we can sort this out. Let's go down. I've got a nice single malt down there. (*to Anita*) You going to join us, or what?

Anita I'll be down in a second. Wait till I'm there.

Cliff leads Jack downstairs to the sitting room. Anita goes back along to the spare bedroom.

Cliff (*as they go*) When I explain it, Jack, you'll see. It's not as bad you think, I promise.

Jack (*his mind still on the other matter*) You mean to tell me you knew about Anita? And that boy?

Cliff Yes, I knew.

Jack And it doesn't worry you?

Cliff It's a free country, Jack. She does what she likes, I do what I like.

Jack You're happy the way things are, then?

Cliff You know me, Jack. I never expected much from life. Why should I expect to be happy, for God's sake?

Anita emerges from the far bedroom in a dressing gown. She comes downstairs, under the next.

Jack Don't you still love her at all?

Cliff Jack, before you leave, have a look out there in the front drive. You'll see a black Porsche 944S Coupé, brand new registration, personalized number plates. That I love. Just through there, I have over three thousand quids' worth of sound gear and a couple of hundred compact discs. That I adore. Just outside Chichester I have a small sailing boat that I would willingly lay down my life for. I am even in love with my new liquid-crystal display digital wrist computer. But Anita? Who needs all that, Jack? I don't. If I want pleasure, I can go for a drive, I can go for a sail, I can blow my head off listening to the Ninth Symphony, or I can even calculate the correct time in Vladivostock if I am that stuck for something to do. Women? Forget them. Quite frankly, I'd sooner play darts.

Jack Well, it's not for me to interfere, but I'd say you definitely have problems, Cliff.

He breaks off as Anita comes into the sitting room. Her manner now is brisker, less coquettish.

Anita What's all this about, then?

Cliff Look, get us all a malt, sweetheart, and I'll try to explain things to Jack.

Anita No. You get the drink. I'll explain.

Cliff hesitates.

Go on.

Cliff Fair enough. (*He goes into the far sitting room.*)

Anita What was it you wanted to know?

Jack You don't deny you're doing business with this Rivetti family?

Anita No. We don't deny that.

Jack By helping them to manufacture and sell exact copies of our furniture under their own label?

Anita No. Any furniture we sell, or rather any furniture we resell to the Rivettis and they then resell, that all comes straight from your factory and is delivered to us in your lorries, driven by your drivers.

Jack Just a minute. Are you saying you are reselling our actual furniture . . .

Anita Yes. We're buying it quite legitimately. And then we're reselling it. What's wrong with that?

Jack Selling it under another label?

Anita No.

Jack You know you bloody well are.

Anita When it leaves us, it hasn't got any label on at all.

Jack But it has when it arrives from our factory.

Anita No, it hasn't.

Jack How the hell are you buying goods from our factory without a name on?

Anita I don't know. You'd better ask your factory that, hadn't you? We're doing nothing illegal.

Cliff returns with a bottle of malt whisky on a tray with three glasses.

Jack Well, somebody's selling off our furniture via the back door. Presumably at give-away prices?

Anita I don't know.

Jack And who relabels it, then?

Anita I don't know.

Jack Presumably the Rivettis?

Anita I don't know.

Jack (*losing patience*) Now, look . . .

Cliff (*pleased at how Anita is handling this*) All we know is, Jack –

Anita (*cutting him off*) We don't know anything, Cliff. Nothing.

   Silence.

Cheers!

Jack (*not drinking*) Well, we'll get one thing straight. This is only the start. I shall follow this right the way through. I shall turn that factory of ours upside down till I find who's responsible for selling us short and, when I've sorted them out, I shall settle the brothers Rivetti, right? There will be no cupboard on this planet big enough to hide them. And if you two happen to be in the line of fire, then all I can say is, God help you.

Cliff (*nervously*) You wouldn't do that to us, Jack.

Anita He would.

Jack And it's not only me you've to deal with. Starting Monday, there will be this voracious little ferret in our midst, diving down rabbit holes, flushing out the black sheep left, right and centre. And I warn you, he's an unstoppable little bastard.

Anita That'll be Mr Hough?

Jack (*startled*) How did you know that?

Anita I go shopping with your wife, Jack. We're friends. I help her choose her clothes. Greater trust hath no woman . . .

Jack (*disconcerted*) Well. That's as may be.

Anita She also told me how you came by him, your Mr Hough. It sounds a bit underhand, Jack. Not like you at all. I mean, I'm sure people would be amazed if they heard . . .

Jack Oh. Oh, now. Don't you try that. Oh. Oh. Oh. Don't think you can try that. Not with me. You won't find me yielding to that sort of blackmail ever, I can tell you. (*Pause.*) Hardly ever. If at all. (*Pause.*) Very, very, very rarely indeed.

Anita Excuse me. I'm getting rather chilly. Switch off when you've finished, Cliff, won't you?

Cliff Right you are.

Anita goes upstairs.

(*smiling rather nervously, now he is alone with Jack*) Bit of a stalemate then, eh?

Jack Who is it selling you our stuff, Cliff?

Cliff I don't know.

Jack No, don't you try that. You're not as clever at it as she is. Now who? Who's behind it all? There's got to be one person, somewhere, hasn't there, fairly high up? Who?

Cliff I don't know.

Jack (*moving closer*) Cliff . . .

Cliff (*covering his head and retreating*) It's no use hitting me – I won't tell you.

Jack I'm not going to hit you.

Cliff You are.

Jack I've never hit you. When in the whole of our lives have I ever hit you? Even as kids . . .

Cliff You used to tickle me . . .

Jack Listen, Cliff. If I promise – if I give you my word as a brother that I'll keep you out of it, will you tell me?

Cliff I daren't.

Jack My solemn promise. Now you know my promise, Cliff. Since we were kids, have I ever broken it?

Cliff Your solemn promise?

Jack Yes.

Cliff All right. (*A nervous glance after Anita.*) Des.

Jack Des? You mean Desmond?

Cliff Yes.

Jack (*incredulously*) Are you talking about *Desmond*? Desmond?

Cliff Yes.

Jack My partner, Desmond Ayres? My so-called bloody partner? Desmond-bloody-Ayres? The man's own son? I don't believe it. I just don't believe it.

Jack storms out of the sitting room and towards the front door.

Cliff Jack? Where are you going?

Jack Heads are going to roll. I can promise you, heads will roll. Desmond Ayres!

Jack goes out of the front door, slamming it behind him. Cliff stands a little bemused in the hall, Anita comes out of the far bedroom. She now has her nightdress on.

Anita What's going on?

Cliff I'm afraid I had to tell him. About Des –

Anita Yes, I thought you might. Where's he gone?

Cliff You know how Jack can . . . I think he's on his way round to Des's . . .

Anita You'd better phone Des. Warn him Jack's coming.

Cliff Right.

Anita And then phone round everyone else. We'll have to have a meeting.

Cliff Tonight?

Anita As soon as we can. I'll get dressed.

Cliff goes to the sitting room phone and starts to dial. Anita enters the near bedroom and goes to the cupboard to select herself something to wear. Giorgio's startled face appears as she ruffles through her dresses.

Anita (*startled*) Oh, hallo, lover, I'd forgotten all about you. (*selecting a dress*) Later. I'll be back soon. *Presto. Presto.*

Giorgio (*kissing her hand, eagerly*) Presto! Presto!

Anita (*more interested in deciding what to wear with the dress*) Yes . . .

She absent-mindedly closes the cupboard door on him

*and moves off to the far bedroom. A telephone bell
rings as Cliff is connected and the lights come up on the
kitchen. Desmond comes in through the back door. He
has been to empty the rubbish-bin. He is in his shirt-
sleeves and is wearing his cook's apron. He answers the
kitchen phone.*

Desmond Hallo. Desmond Ayres speaking.

Cliff Des? It's Cliff. I'm just phoning to warn you. He's on
his way.

Desmond What? Who's on his way?

Cliff Who the hell do you think?

*Before he can speak further, a massive hammering is
heard on the front door, together with Jack's angry
voice. From the dining room, the yapping of a small
dog.*

Jack (*from outside the front door*) Desmond! Open this
door! Desmond!

Desmond What on earth's that?

Cliff (*fearing he is disconnected*) Hallo . . . hallo . . .

Harriet's head appears through the hatchway.

Harriet (*alarmed*) Demsond, there's someone at the front
door. (*to the dog behind her*) Quietly, Peggy, quietly.

Desmond (*petulantly*) Well, you'll have to let them in,
Harriet. Let them in. I'm on the telephone.

Harriet I don't know who it is. Oh. (*Disappears back
through the hatch.*) Peggy, stop that.

*Jack continues to hammer on the door, shouting
occasionally. The dog continues to yap. Desmond
returns to the phone.*

Desmond Hallo. Sorry, Cliff, someone was at the door. What were you saying?

Harriet comes out of the dining room, gently pushing the dog back with her foot and closing the door. She prepares to open the front door.

Cliff It's Jack. He knows everything. He knows about you.

Desmond Jack does?

Cliff It's probably him at your door . . .

Desmond Oh my God. (*dropping the phone*) Harriet! Don't open the –

Harriet has opened the hall door. Jack stands in the doorway like an avenging angel.

Jack (*with a terrible roar*) Desmond!

Harriet cringes, Desmond steels himself, Cliff listens alarmed and the dog yaps on as: Blackout.

Act Two

*The same. It is afternoon. Upstairs Poppy is round at
Anita's. The dresses we saw crammed in the wardrobe are
now strewn around the near bedroom. Poppy is trying one
on. Anita, who is dressed as if ready to go somewhere, is
perched on the bed watching. Downstairs, Harriet sits in
the near sitting room resting on the sofa. Nearby, an
enclosed dog basket with presumably an unseen animal
inside. In his kitchen, Desmond is busy preparing supper.
As he does so, he listens to a Teach Yourself Spanish
cassette on his portable player. Occasionally, he attempts
to join in rather unconvincingly. He checks the casserole in
the oven and, fetching a cookery book from a shelf, settles
at the table and studies it during the next, switching off the
tape.*

Poppy What do you think?

Anita Yes. It's all right. It's only pulling very, very slightly
round the hips.

Poppy Yes, they all do a bit. I keep meaning to lose some.

Anita It would let out. I know it would. I had it taken in
for me.

Poppy It's lovely.

Anita Take it if you want it.

Poppy Sure?

Anita I'm sick of it.

Poppy It's hardly been worn.

Anita Oh, I'm like that, I'm afraid. Three days and I can't stand the sight of most of my clothes.

Poppy I hate all mine, too, but I still keep wearing them.

Anita Depends what you choose to spend your money on, I suppose. With me, it's clothes. And shoes. (*reflecting*) And jewellery. You choose to spend it on something else. Presumably.

Poppy (*rather sadly*) I don't spend mine on anything.

Anita Mind you, I don't pay full price for anything. It's all back door.

Poppy (*surveying herself again*) Yes, I like this very much. I don't know if I've any shoes, though.

> *Anita opens a bedside drawer and produces a box of expensive jewellery – evidently her cast-offs. During the next, she tries various items on Poppy.*

Anita Pity we're not the same size. I could have given you those.

Poppy He must be doing very well.

Anita Who?

Poppy Cliff.

Anita He does all right.

Poppy I mean, for you to be able to afford all this.

Anita This? This is nothing to do with Cliff.

Poppy Isn't it?

Anita (*trying a necklace on Poppy*) No. I bought all this.

Poppy Oh, I see. I'm sorry, I –

Anita I'm a hard-working girl, me.

Poppy I see.

Anita Who do you think runs our business then? Cliff?

Anita holds a brooch to Poppy's breast.

Poppy I am sorry. You know, I never realized . . . Well, I knew you worked but I never realized . . . I thought you must have – Well, I don't know what I thought really – I thought you just had a job like mine. You know. Ordinary. Sorry.

Anita (*reproachfully, as she tries ear-rings on Poppy*) You'll have the heavy women after you, you know . . .

Poppy Yes, I know. Awful. I'm sorry. It's just, you know, you see Cliff driving around in his smart car and you naturally think . . .

Anita The reason he drives round in that, dear, is because I bought it for him for Christmas. Only don't let on I told you or he'll die of shame.

Poppy Well.

Anita Mind you, I mustn't lie. I do accept the occasional little gift – occasionally. (*displaying the gold bracelet she is wearing*) Now, I didn't buy this. Pretty, isn't it?

Poppy Lovely. Where did it come from?

Anita (*putting away the rest of the jewellery*) I don't know. Italy, I suppose.

Poppy (*slightly embarrassed*) Oh, yes. Of course.

Anita Well, if you ever feel like a bit of relaxation. A nice evening out – just let me know. I could probably fix you up.

Poppy What?

Anita With someone nice.

Poppy What, a stranger?

Anita He needn't be strange for long.

Poppy You mean for – money . . . ?

Anita No, no, no. Amateur status, love. Must keep that, mustn't we? Otherwise you are on the slippery slope. No, you can accept heartfelt tokens of appreciation, that's all. But they've got to be heartfelt. (*glancing at watch*) Where's Cliff got to? We must go soon. Anything else you want while you're here? (*selecting another frock*) What about this one. This'd suit you . . .

Poppy Well, if you're going out . . .

Anita You've got time to try this on. Look, come into my bedroom. I've got the full-length mirrors in there. You can see yourself properly.

Poppy Are you sure?

Anita (*gathering up the dresses*) I'll bring them all through, just in case . . .

Poppy This is very generous of you – I feel so guilty.

Anita (*moving to the landing*) Along here. You haven't seen my bedroom, have you?

Poppy (*following her and taking her own rather dull original dress with her*) No, I don't think I have.

Anita Now, this I'm rather proud of – What do you think?

Anita leads Poppy to one of the far bedrooms and goes in. Poppy reaches the doorway and stops momentarily.

Poppy (*in total amazement*) Oh, my goodness! Oh good Lord. What are they all for?

Anita laughs. Poppy cautiously enters the bedroom.

Harriet comes swiftly into the hall from the near sitting room and opens the front door. Desmond, unaware that this is happening, continues his reading. Jack is standing outside, on the point of knocking.

Harriet (*slightly frostily*) Hallo, come in, Jack.

Jack Oh, thank you, Harriet. Saved me from using the knocker.

She closes the front door. Jack waits to be directed somewhere.

Harriet If you could be as quiet as you can, Jack. Peggy's asleep in the front room . . .

Jack Peggy?

Harriet Ssssh!

Jack Oh, the dog. Yes, of course.

Harriet That's why I was looking out for you. To prevent you from using the knocker. Otherwise she'd have been disturbed again.

Jack (*solicitously*) Yes, I see.

Harriet She was up all last night, you know. Three thirty a.m. before she settled. Before either of us could settle, come to that.

Jack You and Des?

Harriet Me and Peggy. Desmond slept all right. Out like a light as usual. Take more than that to give him a sleepless night.

Jack Yes. (*awkwardly*) Harriet, I presume I was the cause of the trouble. I just want to apologize for yesterday. Bursting in here like that. I can only say – I'm sorry.

Harriet Well.

Jack Truly sorry. The point is that, overnight, I've thought about things in a more – calm – light and –

Harriet (*coolly*) I think you had better say all that to Desmond rather than to me, Jack.

Jack Certainly, yes. Where is he then? In the kitchen, I presume. (*He laughs.*)

Harriet (*unamused*) Would you step in here for a moment first, please? (*She indicates the near sitting room.*)

Jack (*rather startled*) Yes, by all means.

He and Harriet go into the near sitting room.

Harriet (*once they are safely inside*) I wanted to say this out of Desmond's earshot . . . Whatever it is that's going on – and you will appreciate that I realize something is going on with Des and his business – whatever it is, I am no part of it whatsoever.

Jack No, I didn't for a minute think –

Harriet I have no knowledge of it, I have had no benefit from it. Anything at all that Desmond has accrued as a result of his – dealings – I have seen not one penny of.

Jack That's entirely understood.

Harriet I am blameless. I am not to be implicated. Any criminal proceedings that may arise from all this cannot involve me . . .

Jack Harriet, listen. There is no question of criminal proceedings.

Harriet (*a trace of disappointment*) There aren't?

Jack Well, I hope not.

Harriet But surely –

Jack What I'm hoping is that we can sort this out as a family matter. Agree, between us, to put our own house in order. We shouldn't need to resort to the law.

Harriet But surely, what has been going on is criminal . . .

Jack I thought you said you had no knowledge of what was going on?

Harriet I don't. But I'm not a fool. I've had my suspicions. You can't live with the man without having those.

Jack (*a slight pause*) You didn't, by any chance, mention your suspicions to your sister?

Harriet Whatever do you mean?

Jack Did you mention this to Yvonne?

Harriet I can't remember offhand. I may have done.

Jack Even though you know she was bound to tell Ken?

Harriet Well, he had a right to know, anyway. He had to be told something was going on.

Jack Well, he was told. And sooner or later, he's bound to find out that Des is involved.

Harriet Perhaps he will.

Jack I don't know what it is Des has done to you, Harriet, but you've certainly got it in for him, haven't you?

Harriet (*defensively*) That's completely untrue. I'm not the one who shuts myself away – who refuses to talk, refuses to communicate at all unless it's about – onion soup.

Jack I'm sure that's not true, Harriet.

Harriet You live with him. You try living with him. You know something? Do you want to know how I feel about food and eating recently?

Jack No?

Harriet I saw a film about this once by that man who's dead. And I agree with him. Eating is an obscene act. That's what I think. Restaurants and cafés with people sitting in front of each other in public, shovelling food into their mouths. It's actually pornographic, isn't it? Don't you agree?

Jack Er – no, I don't think I do really . . .

Harriet I do. I think it's disgusting. Looking at all their fillings and – bridgework and tonsils . . . I'd sooner watch people do – you know – the other thing, than that.

Jack What other thing?

Harriet In the . . . you know . . . in the little girls' room.

Jack Would you really? Well. There's no accounting for taste, Harriet. I think, on the whole, I'd still prefer a meal . . .

Harriet It's the chewing, I think, all that masticating in front of each other . . .

Jack Yes, OK, Harriet. I really must get a word with Des now.

Harriet Look. Look. Ssh. Ssh. Before you go. (*She beckons him.*)

Jack (*warily*) What now?

Harriet indicates the dog basket.

Harriet Look. Look at her. Sound asleep. Have you ever seen anything so daft?

Jack Oh, yes. Incredible to be able to sleep like that, isn't it?

Harriet (*gazing with real love*) Yes.

Poppy and Anita come out of the bedroom. Poppy has changed back into her own clothes and carries a couple of dresses she has chosen. Anita has her coat on.

Poppy I've never seen such a collection of – things. I must be terribly innocent, I don't even know what half of them are for . . .

Anita Oh, darling, don't ask. Over the years I've accumulated so much gear. You need a degree in engineering just to lie down in that bedroom.

Poppy It's more like a stable. Does Cliff go for all that, then?

Anita I wouldn't know, love, I've never asked him. Don't forget your handbag.

Poppy Oh, heavens.

Poppy goes into the near bedroom. Anita steps into the bathroom and checks her appearance in the mirror.

(*alone to herself*) Well, I don't know, I'm sure.

Jack Yes. It's an unusual-looking dog, that. Quite old, is he?

Harriet She's thirteen.

Jack Unusual. Those pink areas, are those the natural markings?

Harriet No, her fur's rubbing off there. It's where she scratches herself. Can you hear her? Snoring?

Jack Oh, yes.

They stand listening. Anita and Poppy have now reached the hall. As they do so, Cliff opens the front door with his key.

Cliff Come on then. Come on.

Anita We're going to run Poppy home first, OK?

Poppy It's very kind of you . . .

Anita Then I said we'd pick up Orlando . . .

Cliff (*noticing Poppy's armful*) What have you got there?

Anita I've been introducing Poppy to the spoils of the good life . . .

Cliff Naughty, naughty.

Anita And not before time, poor woman.

They go out of the front door closing it behind them.

Jack Well, I'd really love to listen to her snoring all day, Harriet, but . . .

Harriet Yes, of course. He's in the kitchen. Can you find your way? I'm afraid I can't go anywhere near the place myself, I hope you'll understand. If I were to go in there, I'd –

Jack Yes, yes, yes, yes. Quite all right.

Jack hurries across to the kitchen and opens the door gently. Harriet, after a moment, gathers up the dog basket and retreats to the far sitting room.

Des?

Desmond (*looking up from his book*) Oh. Hallo, Jack.

Jack (*sniffing the air*) Smells interesting.

Desmond Yes. I think this might turn out quite interesting. Lancashire Hot Pot.

Jack Ah. Yes, lovely . . . Yum-yum.

Desmond I didn't hear you arrive.

Jack No. Harriet let me in. She was anxious I didn't

disturb her dog.

Desmond Oh yes? Well, she had a bad night.

Jack Yes.

Desmond So did I, actually.

Jack I think we all did.

Desmond Well . . .

Jack I wanted to say, I'm sorry about – last night – I –

Desmond No. That's all right. Quite. I mean, no.

Jack I mean, I said a lot of things . . .

Desmond No, no, no. I mean. No. It's me who's – Yes. (*Pause. Rather nervously*) What are you planning to do then?

Jack I'm planning to sort things out, Des. Get things back on the straight and narrow.

Desmond Yes. (*seeing Jack isn't going to reveal much more*) I've arranged for the others to be here. They shouldn't be long.

Jack Then I'll save it all till then.

Desmond Yes.

Pause.

Jack I feel you ought to know that it was Harriet who told Yvonne about all this. Who subsequently tipped off Ken. Who subsequently told me.

Desmond Yes. That's logical. I think she went through my things while I was at work. My papers. My own fault, I shouldn't have left them lying about. She obviously felt I was salting it all away somewhere.

Jack But weren't you?

Desmond Oh yes, I was. She was quite right. But I wouldn't have seen her short. I'd have left her well provided.

Jack Left her?

Desmond When I went.

Jack (*startled*) Went where?

Desmond goes to a kitchen drawer and after rummaging under a layer of tea towels, etc., produces a creased colour prospectus for a new holiday village.

Desmond I keep everything in here, she never comes in here . . . (*showing the leaflet to Jack*) Look. See.

Jack Where's this? Greece?

Desmond No. The Balearics. Minorca.

Jack Oh.

Desmond See that? That's partially finished. It's going to be part of this new complex. You see, it's got the golf course, shops, swimming pool, social club. These are the villas. And that there – (*pointing*) – that's my restaurant.

Jack What are you saying? You're going to work in a restaurant?

Desmond No, I've bought it. I've bought the lease. I own the franchise.

Jack You're going to run it?

Desmond Chef owner. It's been a dream, Jack. For years.

Jack You put all that money into this?

Desmond And the villa. That's mine, see? (*pointing to the map*) Number 78C.

Jack Looks a bit small.

Desmond Well, I don't need much. There's only me.

Jack You're going to live there on your own?

Desmond Yes.

Jack Serving Lancashire Hot Pot to a load of ex-patriate, golf-playing old age pensioners? You'll be up the bloody wall in ten minutes, Des.

Desmond I'm halfway there now, Jack. Look, if you try and stop me from doing this, it would kill me, it really would. The thought of this is the only thing that's holding me together these days.

Jack What about Harriet? I mean, she's – she doesn't seem so good, now. What's she going to be like if you suddenly take off with your chef's hat in your suitcase? I mean, when did she last eat, for God's sake? She's like a praying mantis . . .

Desmond (*suddenly quite savagely, for him*) Oh, she eats, don't worry about her. She just likes people to think she doesn't. But I've caught her. Kendal Mint Cake.

Jack Really?

Desmond Packets of it. She hides them in the dining room behind the dog food, but I've seen her through that hatch.

Jack She can't survive on just Kendal Mint Cake, can she? All her hair'll start falling out or something.

Desmond That wouldn't bother me. She'd match that dog of hers then, wouldn't she? (*agitatedly*) Look, she can eat in here any time she wants. It's up to her. I've said to her, any time you want. I've even offered her a choice of menu.

Jack You mean to tell me, you've been bleeding dry your own business, the business your father spent fifty years of his life putting together, a business dozens of people have given the best part of their lives to – just to open a bloody restaurant . . .

Desmond (*angrily*) It's my business.

Jack It's not your business, it's his business. No, it's not even that, it's ours. All of ours. It's our business.

Desmond (*shouting like a child*) Well, it ought to be mine. That's all. It ought to be mine, so there. (*Starts to cry.*) What does a man have to do . . .

Jack Oh, Des. Don't do that, please. It's hard enough without – (*The door knocker sounds.*)

Desmond (*sobbing*) I've given up a lot of my life as well. Bloody chairs and tables and sink units and bidets –

Harriet hurries from the sitting room to open the front door.

Jack That someone at the door, is it?

Desmond Yes, I'll . . .

He grabs a handful of kitchen towel and makes his way to the hall, blowing his nose as he goes. Harriet, meanwhile, has opened the door to Roy.

Roy (*cheerfully, to Harriet*) How do you do?

Harriet (*frostily*) Hallo. (*to Desmond*) I wonder if you could ask your friends to come to the back door, please. Peggy is trying to rest and so am I.

Desmond All right, dear, all right, I will . . .

Roy You want me to go round the back door?

Harriet Ssshhh!

Roy Sorry.

Harriet How many more times? Peggy is asleep.

Desmond (*whispering*) Go through, Roy.

Roy (*stepping inside*) Wilco. Thank you.

Desmond I'll wait out here and redirect the others when they arrive.

Desmond goes out of the front door.

Harriet (*to Roy*) Shut the door, then. Or Peggy'll be out on the main road.

Roy Sorry. (*Closes the door.*) Walks in her sleep, does she?

Harriet (*icily*) You know the way.

Harriet goes into the dining room. Roy enters the kitchen. Jack, who has been reading the leaflet, looks up in surprise.

Roy (*rather sheepishly*) Hallo, Jack.

Jack Oh, no. Not you as well?

Roy Yes.

Jack It's just about everyone, isn't it? All we need now is the Pope.

Roy Didn't you know? That I was involved?

Jack No. Des just said he was going to get everyone round here.

Roy Everyone?

Jack Well, all the – important ones.

Roy I was going to say. Not everyone. You'd need to book the football ground.

Jack (*sharply*) This is not a joke, son.

Roy (*hastily*) No, no. I know it isn't.

Jack It is no laughing matter at all. So wipe that bloody silly smile off your face . . .

Roy Right.

   Pause.

Jack Where's Desmond?

Roy He's re-directing the others.

Jack (*irritably*) What?

Roy To the back door.

Jack Oh.

   Pause.

Roy If you – if you didn't know I was involved – I needn't have come round, had I?

Jack Too late now, isn't it? You should have worked that out before you came.

Roy I didn't know before I came. I only knew when I came. Too late then. I'd have to have known before I came. Then I wouldn't have come if I'd known.

Jack (*studying him for a second*) You've got all the reasoning powers of a draught excluder, haven't you? How much does Tina know?

Roy Nothing.

Jack Is that the truth?

Roy Promise. She doesn't know a thing about it. I was frightened she wouldn't approve.

Jack (*rather bitterly*) Oh, I don't know.

Roy There's a horrible smell in here. What's he cooking?

Jack Lancashire Hot Pot, I think.

Roy So long as he's not expecting us to stay and eat it, that's all. He's a horrible cook.

Jack Is he?

Roy He's motorway material, I tell you. Haven't you been round here to eat since he got on this chef kick?

Jack No, I don't think we have. Poppy doesn't get on too well with Harriet . . .

Roy (*looking at the cookery book*) Lancashire Hot Pot. That could start the Wars of the Roses all over again, couldn't it?

A rapping on the back door and a rattling on the handle. It is Desmond accompanied by Anita, Cliff and **Orlando**, *30, the middle-most of the five Rivetti brothers. He is the family man, plumper and jollier than the two relatives we met previously, but with no better command of English.*

Hang on.

He unlocks the back door. All troop into the kitchen. Desmond follows them up and closes the door.

Anita Hallo, Jack.

Cliff Jack.

Jack Hallo.

Roy Afternoon, all.

Anita This is Orlando, Jack. Orlando Rivetti. *Questo è* Jack.

Orlando *Salve.*

Jack *Ciao.* How do you do?

An awkward silence.

Desmond Well, shall we all sit down?

They all do so. All are understandably wary of Jack.

Excuse us having to meet in here, everyone. Only Harriet's having to be with Peggy in the living room and besides, I need to keep an eye on the stove.

Roy A thieves' kitchen, eh?

He laughs. Nobody else does. Slight pause.

Desmond Perhaps you'd all like to stay for a bite to eat after our meeting?

Nobody responds to this offer.

You'd be very welcome. Obviously, we'll have to see how the meeting goes first. (*looking nervously towards his brother-in-law*) Jack? Do you want to kick things off?

Jack If this is everyone who's meant to be here . . . I gather it is – I don't want to say much. Most of you must have guessed how I feel about this. I think probably disgust is the word that springs to mind. Disgust that a group of people whom I regarded not only as friends but also as relatives – most of you – should conspire to swindle an old man, a sick old man out of his life's work.

Desmond We were always going to see him right, Jack.

Jack (*ignoring him*) That is all I have to say on that matter. All right? We are going to clean this up, all right? We are going to sponge the shit off the family name, all right? That's what we're here to do today. We are going to put the business back together as it was. As a decent, honest, small family business. So. How do we go about that?

Roy Difficult.

Jack I'll tell you. We start with that end. (*indicating Orlando*) We stop doing business with them to start with. *Arrivederci* Donizetti, all right?

Anita (*to Orlando*) *Dice che dobbiamo smettere di fare affari con voi* . . .

Orlando *Si Arrivederci* Donizetti.

He laughs.

Jack Oh, we've got the laughing one today, have we?

Anita He doesn't speak much English . . .

Jack Never mind, they seem to muddle through, don't they? (*to Cliff and Anita*) Secondly, there will be no more cut-price sales to your lot, all right?

Cliff If you say so, Jack.

Jack I do. Thirdly – (*turns to Desmond*) – we put our production line back to producing *bona-fide* company products, all right? Sold through the proper outlets at the correct prices. All right?

Desmond Yes. (*looking at Roy*) All right, Roy?

Roy Well, the lads aren't going to like it . . .

Jack (*outraged*) The lads aren't going to like what?

Roy Well, you know, losing the extra. I mean they'd sort of come to rely on it.

Jack Then they're going to have to rely on working for their money instead, aren't they?

Roy But they're bound to take a drop, Jack . . . I mean, their basic wage is only –

Jack If their basic isn't enough they'll have to clock overtime, won't they?

Roy They'd have to do another seventy hours a week to make up what they'd be losing . . .

Jack Too bloody bad!

Roy All I'm saying, Jack, is they're not going to like it . . . You could have trouble.

Jack (*excitedly*) I don't believe this. Are you threatening me with industrial action because the workforce object to being told they can no longer swindle the firm they're working for? It defies belief. It –

The hatch slams open and Harriet sticks her head through.

Harriet Would you mind keeping your voices down in here, please? There are other people in this house.

A startled silence.

Thank you.

Harriet closes the hatch sharply, comes out of the dining room and returns to the far sitting room.

Desmond Best to keep our voices down a bit. It's safer if Harriet doesn't hear what we're . . .

Anita She knows far too much already –

Desmond Ah, now, we don't know that necessarily –

Anita Of course we do. Who else told Yvonne?

Jack (*anxious to proceed*) So.

Desmond Sorry, Jack.

Jack So. That is what's going to happen. All right?

Anita Could I just – ?

Jack No. No discussion. No choice in the matter. That is it. Close of meeting.

Anita Please. (*faintly sarcastic*) Mr Chairperson, sir?

Jack (*suspiciously*) What?

Anita Just before we go, I just wanted to ask what you intend we do about our friend Mr Hough? In considerably less than a week, he seems to have found out quite a lot about us. He's either got supremely good powers of detection or he's had the good sense to talk to Yvonne . . .

Desmond Now we don't know that necessarily . . .

Jack (*over-riding this*) He doesn't know much. He knows about the Rivettis, that's all.

Anita He knows Des and I are supplying them. Because he phoned me this morning. He wants to meet me tomorrow sometime.

Jack And he starts with our firm tomorrow morning.

Desmond Oh my God . . . That's it then, isn't it? That's it (*He rises agitatedly.*)

Jack All right, all right, Des . . .

Desmond That's it! It's all over!

Anita (*sharply*) Desmond! Sit down and shut up!

Desmond sits again. They reflect.

Jack All right then, I'll cancel him. I'll phone him tonight and tell him we no longer require his services. That solves it.

Cliff You'll need to pay him off.

Jack I will. I'll tell him to submit his account for the work done to date.

Roy He'll need more than that.

Jack What are you talking about?

Anita (*as to a child*)What they're saying, Jack, is Mr Hough might not be totally satisfied with his standard payment. Considering the amount of information about us he has already gathered . . .

Jack Are you suggesting he'll try to blackmail us? (*Slight pause.*) Again?

Anita I'm suggesting he'll probably need paying . . .

Jack watches the next in stunned amazement. The ensuing business discussion happens with great rapidity.

Desmond How much are we talking about, then?

Anita Ten maximum.

Cliff How many of us are there . . . one, two . . . don't count Jack . . . three, four five . . . Five? Can we go to ten?

Desmond Ten? I can't go to ten . . .

Cliff No, two . . .

Desmond Still a lot.

Anita We could start with five. Hold back five.

Cliff In reserve.

Roy Two maximum.

Desmond Five up front.

Anita Five behind. Right?

Roy Done.

Cliff Carried.

Desmond OK.

Jack What's going on? What's going on?

Anita (*to Orlando*) *Duemila lire sterline. Ciascuno.*

Diecimila come assicurazione. D'accordo?

Orlando (*laughing at this*) *Con un premio simile mio fratello ti combinerebbe un'assicurazione molto più permanente.*

Jack What's he saying, now?

Anita Orlando says for that sort of premium his brother could arrange something more permanent . . .

Cliff laughs.

Jack Like what?

Orlando (*laughing*) *Un'assicurazione contro gli incidenti, eh?*

Anita (*laughing*) He says, accident insurance . . .

Cliff What? Like accidentally falling out of a fifth-floor window . . . ?

Roy Accidentally swallowing his magnifying glass?

Orlando makes a cheerful choking gesture with his hands, for Jack's benefit.

Jack If this is intended in any way as a serious suggestion – ?

Anita No, no, Jack. Orlando's joking, isn't he? (*kissing Orlando on the top of his head*) Oh, I love this one best of all. Do you know he's got six children? *Sei bambini, si?*

Orlando (*reaching for his wallet*) *Sei bambini, si . . .*

Jack Look, just a minute. Just a minute . . .

Under this, Orlando is passing round photos of his family to any who are interested.

Orlando (*during the next*) *Questa è la più piccola, Maria. Ha due anni. Quella è sua madre. E' una bella donna,* *vero? Questo è mio figlio maggiore, Rodolfo. Ha otte anni e già vuol fare l'architetto. Queste sono le gemelle, Lucia e Lucrezia, il giorno del loro quarto compleanno . . .*

Jack . . . What is going on here?

Roy We're just sorting out how much we need to give him, Jack.

Jack Give who?

Roy This Mr Hough.

Jack We're not giving him anything. Except what he's earned . . .

Desmond But, Jack –

Jack No. I've had enough of this. No more of it. You understand.

Orlando tries to interest Jack in a family snapshot.

No, I don't want to see. Put them away. *Avanti!* (*to the others*) Let me make this quite clear. I have no intention of indulging in any more blackmail, bribery, corruption or anything else. Is that understood? From now onwards, all our business is going to be conducted above board. My God, if we start giving five hundred quid here and five hundred quid there to every –

Roy Thousand.

Jack What?

Roy I think we're talking about thousands, Jack. Ten thousand.

Jack (*stunned*) Ten thousand quid. You're joking.

Desmond It might be only five.

Jack You are joking . . . I am boggled . . .

234

Cliff It's about the going rate, Jack . . .

Jack I am just – boggled . . . I mean . . .

Desmond (*hopefully*) You don't think Jack could get him for five hundred, do you?

Anita Never.

Cliff Jack ought to do it, though.

Jack What?

Anita Yes, you'll have to be the one to deal with it, Jack.

Jack You want me to do the bribing as well?

Anita Seriously. It'll have to be you.

Jack (*rising in fury*) That's it. No more. Not another word . . .

Cliff Wait a second, Jack. Wait a sec . . .

Anita It has to be you, Jack. You're employing the man.

Jack Good day. I am leaving now before I commit damage.

Desmond (*vainly*) Jack! Don't go that way, please . . .

Jack Goodbye.

Despite their protests, Jack stamps out through the hall and out of the front door, which he shuts with a thunderous slam. From the sitting room, the dog starts yapping. They look alarmed.

Harriet (*shouting angrily from the sitting room*) Who did that?

Desmond Quickly. Out the back.

Desmond goes swiftly to the back door, opens it and starts shooing his remaining guests out. As he does this, a furious Harriet comes out into the hall.

Harriet Someone did that deliberately . . . Deliberately . . .
(*She goes back into the far sitting room.*)

Desmond Quickly . . .

Roy Don't forget your Hot Pot . . .

Desmond (*turning, appalled*) Oh, my God, My Hot Pot!

*Harriet returns to the hall clasping the dog basket. She
opens the front door. There is no one there. Desmond
searches about for his oven gloves.*

Harriet Deliberately . . . You did that deliberately!

*Harriet goes out of the front door closing it behind her.
Desmond works to salvage his meal. He opens the oven
and withdraws a blackened, smoking, open casserole
dish of what was once Lancashire Hot Pot. Harriet,
meanwhile, has come round the house to the back door,
still clasping the dog basket.*

(*as she approaches*) Desmond! I will never forgive you for
this, Desmond . . .

She appears in the back doorway.

Desmond (*turning to her, the casserole still in his hands*)
Harriet, I'm sorry I . . .

*Harriet sees what he is holding and recoils in horror,
covering her mouth with her hand to stifle a scream.
Then, overcome with nausea, she rushes back into the
garden with a final, terrible moan. Desmond follows her
out, clasping his ruined casserole to him like a child.*

Harriet . . . ?

*It is now evening and we are back at Jack's and Poppy's.
Tina, dressed to go out for the evening, comes from the*

dining room. She carries a children's picture/story book.
She starts up the stairs. As she does so, Poppy comes out
of the spare bedroom (i.e. not Samantha's). She is wearing,
just a trifle self-consciously perhaps, one of the dresses
Anita has given her. A child's voice is heard from the spare
bedroom.

Poppy All right, Mummy's coming. Stay in bed.

> *Samantha comes into the kitchen through the open back*
> *door. She is wearing her school clothes and a*
> *motorcycle helmet. She carries a piece of electrical*
> *equipment – we can't tell what it is – wrapped up in an*
> *old sheet. A plug dangles from a mains lead, which is*
> *the only indication as to what it might be. Samantha*
> *places her load on the kitchen table, having checked the*
> *coast is clear. She now hurries out again, leaving the*
> *door open. Tina and Poppy meet on the landing.*

Oh, he's been calling for you . . .

Tina It's all right, I'll read him this. It's so boring it always
sends us both off to sleep. He hasn't woken Michelle, has
he?

Poppy No, she's well away. I'm sorry they've got to be in
the same room tonight but I couldn't face Sammy again . . .

Tina It's all right. It's not a problem (*regarding Poppy*)
That's really nice, you know, that suits you.

Poppy (*doubtfully*) You sure? I think it probably looked
better on Anita . . .

Tina Why? Why should it? You've got as good a figure as
she has.

Poppy Oh, I haven't really. (*studying herself*) I think I'm a
bit too old for it really.

Tina Rubbish. You look amazing. Really.

Poppy Really?

Tina Really.

Poppy (*still doubtful*) Well. (*then, giving up worrying*) You and Roy going to the cinema, did you say?

Samantha, helmetless, comes back into the kitchen under the next.

Tina Yes. We haven't been for years. Be nice. We're going to see – oh, what's it called – you know. With whatsisname. With the – with the thing. You know.

Poppy That'll be nice.

Tina Yes.

Samantha shuts the back door. The sound of a two-stroke motorcycle starting up and receding is heard.

Poppy Well, I (*Stops as she hears this. Calling*) Sammy? Is that you?

Samantha freezes in the kitchen. They listen.

I thought that was her.

Tina Late, isn't she?

Poppy You know what that school's like. All these societies and clubs and things. She often stays on late. She's got a friend who gives her a lift home.

Tina Eastwood. Clint Eastwood.

Poppy That's the one. I must go down. Jack'll be back soon. He's got this man coming.

She starts downstairs.

Tina (*stopping her*) Roy told me, you know, about all that at work.

Poppy Oh, did he? I didn't know if he'd –

Tina Yes. Last night. (*smiling*) I don't know, I'm sure . . .

Poppy (*half amused, despite herself*) Terrible, isn't it? I mean, all that going on. And your Uncle Desmond as well.

Tina And Uncle Cliff.

Poppy What a family, eh?

Tina And Auntie 'Nita.

Poppy Yes, well. Her. I don't think anything would surprise me any more as far as she's concerned.

A child calls from the spare bedroom.

Tina (*calling to the bedroom*) All right, I'm coming, love. (*to Poppy*) You know it's awful really but – ever since Roy told me about all this business and him being involved – I sort of respect him more for it. Not less. Isn't that awful?

Poppy Well . . . It is, really.

Tina I mean, I'd – I'd got really sick of him, I can't tell you. I mean, that's dreadful, isn't it? The man I loved – had my children with – promised to share my life with – and my heart used to sink when I heard him at the door. I mean, some evenings I used to sit and pray he'd been run over, just so's we wouldn't have to talk to each other . . . There. Isn't that awful? I feel so ashamed even saying it. But now all this business. Well, he can't be completely daft, can he? Otherwise he couldn't . . . Well, if you're going to be a criminal you've got to have some sort of brain, haven't you? I mean, any fool can be honest, can't they? You know what I mean?

Poppy (*doubtfully*) Yes, I think so. I don't know your Dad would agree, though.

Tina (*laughing*) Well, he wouldn't, would he? That makes him out a complete idiot, doesn't it?

Poppy (*laughing with her*) True.

A child calls again from the spare bedroom.

Tina All right, Kevin, here I come.

She moves off along the landing. Poppy starts downstairs and goes into the sitting room to turn on a couple of lights. Samantha listens till she is sure her mother is in there.

(*as she goes into the bedroom*) What do you want, darling?

Samantha picks up her bundle from the kitchen table and starts upstairs. Poppy comes out of the sitting room with the ice bucket on her way to the kitchen.

Poppy Sammy?

Samantha (*nonchalantly*) Oh hallo, Mum.

Poppy You're late, aren't you?

Samantha I had a meeting.

Poppy Oh, that's nice. Which one was it tonight?

Samantha The Musical Appreciation Society.

Poppy Lovely. What have you got there?

Samantha Gramophone records. My friend lent them to me.

Poppy Well, don't play them too loud, will you?

Samantha No.

Poppy Use the headphones Uncle Cliff gave you.

Samantha continues up the stairs. Poppy goes into the

*kitchen and fills the ice bucket. Tina, at the same
moment, comes out of the bedroom with an empty
water glass.*

Tina (*calling behind her*) Well, you're not having much
more of this or you'll wet the bed . . . Oh hallo, Sammy.

Samantha (*scowling*) Oh no. You haven't dumped your
foul, horrible, disgusting baby in my room again, have
you?

Tina No, I have not. And don't be so rude. She is very
beautiful. What have you got there?

Samantha Nothing.

Tina What? What have you stolen now?

Samantha Don't tell Mum.

She unwraps the bundle partially to reveal its contents.

Tina Whatever is it?

Samantha CD player. Compact disc.

Tina Sammy! Honestly, you're mad. Haven't you got
enough sound gear already? It's like Abbey Road Studios,
your room.

Samantha I'm not having this, I'm reselling it.

Tina Why?

Samantha Because I need the money, that's why.

Tina What for?

Samantha To buy things.

Tina What things?

Samantha Things. Mind your own business. (*Pause.*)
Things.

Tina Oh, Sammy, you're not into that, are you?

Samantha Into what?

Tina You know what I'm talking about. Those things – whatever you call them. Drugs. Are you into drugs?

Samantha Sssh! No.

Tina Truthfully.

Samantha No! Not seriously, anyway.

Tina Sammy, they're terribly dangerous. They keep telling you . . . They can kill you, you know.

Samantha So can picking your nose with a screwdriver . . .

Tina Oh, don't be so childish . . .

Samantha Look, you don't know anything about it. It's only if you do it regularly. I'm not going to do it regularly. I can't afford to, anyway.

Tina Sammy . . .

Samantha Bugger off, Tina. Go and pot your baby . . .

Samantha goes into her bedroom and shuts the door. Tina looks worried. She goes into the bathroom, fills the water glass and then returns to the other bedroom. As she does this, Jack enters through the back door. He is wearing his coat and carries an attaché case which he clutches rather tightly, while holding it slightly away from him as though it were red hot. Cliff follows a little way behind. He has on his driving gloves but no coat. He carries a heavy-looking adjustable spanner.

Poppy (*going to kiss him*) Hallo, love. Just in time for a drink.

Jack Oh, good. I – er – brought Cliff back.

Cliff appears round the door.

Cliff Hallo.

Poppy Oh hallo, Cliff.

Cliff Hallo.

An awkward pause.

Poppy How was your day, then?

Jack What?

Poppy Your day. How was it?

Jack Oh, my day? My day was fine, yes.

Pause.

Cliff Nice dress.

Poppy Thank you. (*Slight pause.*) It's your wife's.

Cliff Really? I don't think I've seen it before. I must have been glancing at my watch while she was wearing it. (*He laughs.*)

Poppy Are you going to take your coat off, Jack?

Jack Oh, yes.

Poppy (*helping him*) Here. Cliff? Can I – take your . . . (*Eyes his spanner.*) No . . . you want to keep all that, do you?

Cliff Yes, thanks.

Poppy Well, shall we move through to somewhere more comfortable, shall we?

Jack (*starting to move into the hall*) Right.

Cliff does not move.

Poppy Cliff?

Jack No, Cliff'll stay there.

Cliff I'll stay here.

Poppy What, in the kitchen?

Cliff Fine.

Poppy (*baffled*) Yes. Suit yourself. Would you like a drink?

Jack No.

Cliff No.

Poppy No. I can leave the light on, can I?

Jack No.

Cliff No.

Jack But leave the door.

Cliff Please.

Poppy Yes . . .

Poppy is mystified. Jack stands awkwardly in the hall, still clutching his attaché case for dear life. Cliff paces round the kitchen a couple of times and finally sits.

Jack, what's going on? Why's Cliff . . . ?

Jack Sssh. Come in here a second.

He indicates the sitting room.

Poppy Just a minute.

Poppy goes to hang up Jack's coat. Jack puts the briefcase down on the table and stares at it.

(*from the hall*) Did you say you wanted a drink?

Jack Yes, I did. Thanks.

Poppy I'll get you one.

Jack produces a key and swiftly unlocks the attaché case. A few bundles of ten pound notes spill on to the floor. He stuffs them back in the case and stares at the contents in horror. Then, shaking his head in disbelief, he closes the case again as he hears Poppy returning with the drinks. She stares at him.

You all right?

Jack Cheers.

Poppy Cheers.

They drink.

Jack I've got this – man – turning up in a minute.

Poppy Mr Hough? Yes, you told me.

Jack Did I?

Poppy On the phone.

Jack Oh, yes.

Poppy At lunchtime. (*Slight pause.*) What's that?

Jack What's what?

Poppy (*indicating*) That. What's that?

Jack That? That's a – that's a briefcase.

Poppy Is it yours?

Jack No.

Poppy Oh. What's in it, then?

Jack Nothing. Just paper. Bits of – bits of paper.

He stares at the attaché case unhappily.

Poppy Jack, you're lying, I know you are. Tell me. We never lie to each other. What have you got there? Tell me.

Jack It's – only money. Just money. That's all.

Poppy Money? How much money?

Jack (*hoarsely*) Masses. Masses and masses and masses of money. Quite frankly, I have never seen quite so much money in one small space. It makes your eyes water, I can tell you.

Poppy (*awed*) Jack, what have you done?

Jack Nothing.

Poppy You didn't steal it, did you?

Jack (*indignantly*) Of course I didn't steal it.

Poppy I'm sorry. Of course you didn't. I don't know what I'm saying . . .

Jack It's just to – it's just to pay Mr Hough, that's all. When he comes. I'm going to have to pay him.

Poppy Jack, what's happening? Suitcases full of money and people hiding in the kitchen with spanners . . . ?

Jack That's just protection, love. Cliff's my protection, that's all.

Poppy You never used to need protection –

Jack No, well, this is a special circumstance. I'm walking around with a lot of . . . It's a one-off, I promise. I pay him the money. Clear the family name. Then that's it. No more. Back to normal. I'm having no more of this, I can tell you. I'm really not, Poppy.

Poppy I wish I believed that.

Jack It's true. This is the last bloody favour I'm doing that lot, I can promise you.

Slight pause.

Poppy It's my fault. I got you into this.

Jack That's rubbish.

Poppy You should never have listened to me. They say this is what happens. Right through history. With all great men. Brought down by a woman. I'm just like whatsername in the Bible . . .

Jack What are you talking about?

Poppy (*tearfully*) Whatever she's called. You know, the one with the scissors . . . I'm as bad as her . . .

Jack Poppy, I don't have the faintest idea what you're talking about, I'm sorry. Scissors? Look, I'll deal with this bloke and then, if you like, why don't we both . . . ?

The doorbell rings.

Oh, hell . . .

Poppy All right. I'll let him in.

Cliff opens the kitchen door cautiously.

Cliff (*calling across the hall to Jack in the sitting room*) All right, Jack?

Jack (*urgently*) Stay in there! I'll shout if I need you . . .

Poppy goes to the front door. Jack paces about nervously and arranges the case on the coffee table. Poppy admits Benedict.

Benedict (*heartily*) Good evening, Mrs McCracken. My, don't we look attractive tonight?

Poppy Do we? Thank you very much, Mr Hough.

She relieves him of his coat.

Benedict I believe your husband is expecting me.

Poppy Yes, indeed he is. (*leading him towards the sitting room*) Can I get you a drink of any sort, Mr Hough?

Benedict Well, perhaps a small gin with just a dab of tonic would be very pleasant . . . Ah, good evening, Mr McCracken.

Jack Mr Hough.

Jack invites him to sit. Benedict does so. Poppy goes and pours Benedict his drink.

Benedict I trust you've had a good day?

Jack Yes. Thank you. And you?

Benedict Extremely successful, I'm pleased to say, Mr McCracken.

Jack (*disappointed*) Oh. Good.

Benedict I think you're going to react to some of my findings with some consternation, Mr McCracken. Probably even a little shock . . .

Jack Really?

Benedict (*slyly*) Unless, of course, you've already heard something?

Jack Depends what *you*'ve heard, Mr Hough.

Benedict Precisely. (*Laughs.*) We shall see.

Poppy has entered and now hands him his drink.

Thank you so much, Mrs McCracken.

Jack Thanks a lot, love. Don't hang around on our account. I know there's things you want to be seeing to . . .

Poppy (*who was about to sit down*) What? Oh. So there are. Yes.

Benedict Aren't you staying with us to . . . ?

Jack No.

Poppy No. I have – things to be getting on with. In the kitchen. Excuse me.

Benedict Of course.

Poppy leaves, seems a little lost as to where she should go. She contemplates the kitchen but, remembering Cliff is there, she finally opts for the dining room.

Good health.

Jack Cheers.

Benedict drinks. He then puts down his glass and opens his notebook.

Benedict Now, then. If I may proceed . . . ? The first thing I set out to discover, having successfully located the existence of the Rivetti connection –

Jack Er . . . Mr Hough –

Benedict – was whether . . . Sorry?

Jack I think, actually, there's little point in going on with your report.

Benedict No?

Jack You see, in fact, I've decided – against proceeding any further. Under the circumstances. I hope you'll understand my reasons.

Benedict Oh yes. Right. That's perfectly understood. (*Puts away his notebook.*) Saves a lot of time.

Jack I had no idea when I first asked you, of course.

Benedict No . . .

Jack Otherwise I would never . . .

Benedict Oh, no . . .

Jack So, what I'm saying is . . . we're trying to keep this in the family as it were . . . Not involve too many outsiders.

Benedict Such as myself?

Jack Precisely.

Benedict Or the police?

Jack Yes. No.

Benedict None the less, we are talking about a large-scale fraud, are we not?

Jack Oh, it is in hand. Let me assure you things are in hand.

Benedict So, I take it Mr Ayres has been informed about it –

Jack Er. No, no. Under the circumstances, what with . . . with certain persons being involved –

Benedict His whole family, for instance . . .

Jack Yes . . . if you will . . . we felt . . . it could be very upsetting for an elderly man in frail health, on the verge of celebrating his seventy-fifth birthday –

Benedict Yes. But I do feel Mr Ayres should know, though. Someone should tell him. He ought to know, oughtn't he?

Jack Well, that's a – that's a family decision, Mr Hough. We shall no doubt all be discussing it fully, in due course. All I need to say to you at this stage is, thank you for your help and impressive – assistance and . . . perhaps you'd send us your account. In your own good time.

A silence. Benedict stares at him.

(*slightly nervously*) Does that seem fair enough to you?

Benedict Frankly no, Mr McCracken. It doesn't seem fair to me at all.

Jack Ah.

Benedict Not fair to anyone, in fact. Not to the firm, not to Mr Ayres, not to me nor indeed, most important, to the course of justice.

Slight pause.

Jack Yes, well. Fair enough. I meant to add, of course, that – that we were all – when we talked – so impressed with your – work to date – Mr Hough – that it was generally felt overall that a – bonus would be in order. A cash bonus. (*Pause.*) A large cash bonus.

Benedict I see.

Jack The figure talked of was five thousand pounds. (*Slight pause.*) Five thousand five hundred pounds. Cash.

A chilly pause.

I don't know how that strikes you.

Benedict It strikes me as most offensive, Mr McCracken.

Jack Ah. (*Pause.*) I – er . . . now, where did I put it? – (*He slaps his pockets.*) . . . I may have got it slightly wrong, the sum . . . You know, I've had a head full of figures all day . . . It could have been nearer six thousand, now I come to think of it . . . where did I – ? I wrote it down somewhere . . .

Jack opens the attaché case so that Benedict gets a clear view of the contents, then closes it again.

No. It's not in there. No, I'm almost certain now I think about it, that it was six. Six, seven, something like that.

Benedict (*quietly*) Mr McCracken, what is the maximum sum you have been authorized to offer me?

Jack Ten.

Benedict Ten?

Jack Yes. Thousand. (*with sudden courage*) That's it. Take it or leave it.

Benedict I'm afraid you're left with it, Mr McCracken.

Jack Well, that's that. (*making to shake hands*) It's certainly refreshing in this world, Mr Hough, to meet an incorruptible man. I'm sorry I –

Benedict Oh no, Mr McCracken, I'm eminently corruptible, don't worry on that score. It's just that I do have a very good assessment of my own worth.

Jack Yes. I see. And that . . . ? Roughly? Would you care to put a value on that, Mr Hough? On your worth?

Jack Shall we say fifty thousand?

Jack (*blinking*) Yes. Well, I have to tell you, Mr Hough, you can take it from me, right now – that you are whistling up a gum tree, old chum.

Benedict Believe me, Mr McCracken, if this is not resolved to my satisfaction, I shall be whistling on every street corner until you cannot see across this room for blue uniforms. I have some idea of the sums involved over the years – maybe you don't. Just thank your lucky stars I'm not demanding a 10 per cent finder's fee or I could be into you to the tune of a quarter of a million pounds. You tell that to your – associates.

Jack (*rather shaken*) Yes. I will. Right. Now, you mean?

Right. I shall need to – telephone, you understand. Will you excuse me a moment?

Benedict Of course. (*glancing at his watch*) I don't have a lot of –

Jack Neither do I. Excuse me.

He goes to the door, remembers the briefcase, returns and walks out with it, maintaining as much dignity as he can muster.

Excuse me.

Benedict remains calmly seated and relaxed, sipping his drink. Jack goes into the hall, closing the door behind him. Cliff comes out of the kitchen. Poppy comes out of the dining room.

Cliff Well?

Poppy Well?

Jack (*indicating that Benedict is still there*) Shhh!

Cliff Did he take it?

Jack No, he did not.

Poppy He didn't?

Jack (*to Poppy*) Shhh! (*to Cliff*) He wants thousands.

Cliff How much?

Jack Fifty grand.

Cliff Fifty!

Jack I'll have to contact Des. See if he can raise any more.

Cliff What now?

Jack He's waiting for an answer.

Cliff Des won't be able to raise ten grand. He's got it all invested in saucepans . . .

Jack Sssh! Well, he's going to have to find it . . .

He picks up the hall phone and dials.

Cliff Who are you phoning?

Jack Des.

Cliff Well, don't say too much –

Jack Why not?

Cliff Certain dog lovers listen on the extension.

Jack (*replacing the phone*) What are we going to do, then? This bloke's waiting for an answer.

Cliff Go round and talk to Des.

Jack Now?

Cliff Sssh! Won't take a minute.

Poppy (*indicating Benedict*) What about him in there?

Cliff He can wait. We won't be long. Come on, we'll take my Porsche . . .

Jack I'm not riding in that thing.

Cliff Come on.

The doorbell rings. Benedict reacts briefly, then returns to his drink.

Poppy That's probably Roy.

Poppy goes to open the door.

Cliff Good, we'll need him . . . See how much he can raise.

Jack What about you and Anita?

Cliff What?

Jack Can you find ten grand apiece?

Cliff I greatly doubt it. I'll have to check with Anita. She handles the joint account.

Poppy lets Roy in the front door.

Roy Hallo, then. Is she ready to go?

Poppy Er . . . no. There's been a slight . . .

Jack (*moving to the sitting room, still clutching the attaché case*) I'll tell him to hang on here.

Cliff Roy, come on, lad, you're coming with us . . .

Roy No, we're going down the Odeon –

Cliff Business, Roy, business . . .

Roy Oh, right, wilco.

Tina comes out on to the landing from the children's bedroom. Cliff picks up the phone in the hall. Jack opens the sitting room door. Benedict turns.

Jack Excuse me, one moment, won't you, Mr Hough? I'll be just five minutes.

He closes the door.

Benedict Yes, I . . .

He frowns, then returns to his drink.

Tina (*calling downstairs*) I'm coming . . .

Roy Just a sec, love, there's a change of plan –

Tina (*indignant*) A what?

Jack Sssh! (*indicates the sitting room. To Cliff*) What are you doing?

Cliff Warning Des we're coming.

The phone rings in the kitchen.

Jack I thought we weren't to use the phone.

Cliff It's all right if you use the code . . .

Jack The code?

Tina What is happening, please? Exactly?

Jack Sorry, Tina. We'll bring him back in ten minutes.

Desmond comes breathlessly in through the back door. He is in his shirt-sleeves and apron. As he does so, the hatch opens and Harriet's angry face appears.

Harriet Desmond, are you going to answer that or not?

Desmond Yes, love, I was just recataloguing the deep freeze –

Tina We've missed the start now, anyway. It's hardly worth going. He'll have shot everyone by the time we get there.

Tina goes back to the bedroom rather crossly. Desmond answers the phone.

Desmond Hallo. Desmond Ayres speaking.

Roy (*after Tina*) Sorry.

Cliff Hallo. Des mate, it's Clifford. I won't talk for long. We may have another crossed line.

Desmond (*looking round apprehensively*) Yes, yes. Could be.

Cliff Just wanted to check the recipe you gave us a couple of days ago.

Desmond Oh, yes?

Cliff I'm afraid you might not have given me the correct quantity of sugar . . . We're coming round. All right?

He hangs up.

Desmond (*alarmed*) But you can't have any more sugar – (*realizing he is speaking to no one*) Oh, my God . . .

Cliff OK, we're on our way, come on.

Cliff moves to the front door. Roy follows him. Desmond locates a cashbox which he keeps concealed beneath his oven. He sits during the next and studies the contents – mostly bonds, bank statements and share certificates.

Jack (*meanwhile, aware he still has the attaché case*) Hang on. What about this thing? I'm not carting this all round the houses.

Cliff (*from the front doorway*) Leave it behind.

Jack Poppy, listen, love. Hide this. Put it somewhere safe.

Poppy Why?

Jack Look, there's ten thousand quid in here, right . . .

Poppy Oh, dear God. (*She looks faint.*)

Jack Easy, easy . . . (*changing his mind*) No. Look, it's all right. I'll take it with me, it's just as easy.

Poppy No, no. I was just being stupid. I'm a grown woman and I got you into this. Now, give it to me at once.

Cliff (*calling*) Come on.

Jack, slightly startled, hands her the briefcase.

Jack All right, love, fine. Good. (*indicating Benedict*) But whatever you do, don't let him near it, will you?

Poppy No, I won't.

Jack Don't even let him know you've got it. Hide it, then there won't be a problem, all right?

Poppy Yes.

Jack Guard it with your life, girl.

Poppy I will.

Jack kisses her.

Cliff Come on, Jack. We're only going round the corner.

Jack (*as he goes*) How are we all going to fit in that thing?

Cliff We'll fit, we'll fit. It's a two plus two.

The front door closes. Poppy is left holding the attaché case which she handles as though it were filled with dynamite.

Desmond (*studying his papers*) Oh, my God . . . I can't sell that. I can't possibly sell that. How can I make croissants?

Benedict comes to the living room door and opens it. Poppy instinctively flattens herself to the wall to avoid him seeing her.

Benedict (*calling, softly*) Hallo . . . Mr McCracken? (*Listens.*) Mr McCracken?

Puzzled, Benedict goes back into the room, closing the door. After a moment he sits down again. Poppy cautiously creeps upstairs. When she reaches the landing she looks around for somewhere to hide the attaché case. In the end, she decides to slide it under the bed in the near bedroom. As she walks on the floor above, Benedict looks up. Tina comes along the landing.

Tina Mum?

Poppy (*jumps*) Oh! Hallo, dear.

Tina I wondered who it was creeping about. Have they all gone out?

Poppy Yes, all except . . . Mr Hough. He's still here.

Tina What, down there on his own?

Poppy Jack won't be long.

Tina You sure you're all right?

Poppy Of course. Is Kev asleep yet?

Tina Very nearly.

Poppy I'll say goodnight, then . . .

Tina You've said it once.

Poppy goes off to the far bedroom. Tina follows, puzzled. As they go, there is a knocking on the back door. Desmond jumps, stuffs away his papers, hastily reconceals the cashbox and opens the door. Jack, Cliff and Roy enter. Roy appears to be suffering from the confinement of the journey.

Roy (*as they enter*) Bloody hell, Cliff, couldn't you find a smaller car, mate . . .

Cliff There's plenty of room . . . Hallo, Des.

Desmond Hallo, Cliff. Jack . . .

They close the back door. Desmond stares at them apprehensively. A pause.

Jack I don't know how I got into all this, I really don't.

Desmond Well?

Jack Our Mr Hough wants more, Desmond. You underestimated. How much can you raise?

Desmond How much does he want?

Cliff Fifty.

Desmond Fifty! Oh, no, Jack . . . that's impossible . . . there's no way I could . . . Fifty? No . . .

Cliff Then how much could you?

Desmond Well . . . Four.

Cliff Four? You miserable –

Desmond Seven if I sell the confectionary oven. But it's a German make, they're like gold to get hold of . . .

Jack Then you should get a good price for it. Right. That's seven from you. Plus two from Roy . . .

Roy By selling the rotary mower . . .

Jack Plus ten we've got already. Nineteen. We've got thirty-one grand to find, haven't we, genius?

Desmond (*pointing to Cliff*) What about him? What about those two? They're rolling in it.

Roy You could sell that car . . .

Cliff I'm not selling that.

Jack If needs be we will auction your internal organs round the back of the General Hospital, Clifford.

Cliff Well, we'd better talk to Anita. She knows better than me . . .

Cliff takes the kitchen wall phone and starts to dial.

Desmond You're not phoning her? Not on the phone?

Cliff Just to warn her we're coming . . .

Jack Come on. Get your pinny off . . .

Desmond Me?

Jack We need everyone.

The phone starts ringing in the near bedroom.

Roy There's no room for him in the back of that thing.

Jack You can manage, it's only half a mile.

Roy I'm running behind you.

Jack You're staying with us.

From the far bedroom, Anita comes along the passage. She has on her black basque corset and leather thigh boots, one of which she was apparently only halfway into when the phone rang. She is cursing as she limps and hops to the phone.

Anita All right, all right. Just a minute, just a minute. I knew these bloody things were a size too small . . . (*savagely, into the phone*) Hallo.

Cliff Hallo . . .

Anita Cliff? Look, what the hell do you mean by ringing up . . . ?

Cliff Hallo, cherub, I'm at Des's so I won't talk for long. It's a very bad line. We need your advice on the recipe –

Anita On the what?

Cliff The recipe. R–E–double C–

Anita All right, I know how to spell it, what about it?

Cliff I'm afraid it's going to need gingering up –

Anita All right. Come on round then.

She hangs up.

Cliff She's in a filthy mood . . .

Anita Oh, balls, balls, balls and bugger. (*calling*) Vinchy!

Vincenzo! We're going to have to stop for business, love, I'm sorry.

Vincenzo (*distant, muffled*) *Aiuto! Venite!* Anita! *Aiuto!*

Anita Oh, hang on, sorry. I'd better let you out of there, hadn't I? *Vengo . . .* Don't jump about, for God's sake, or you'll strangle yourself.

Anita goes back into the far bedroom. Desmond has taken off his apron and rolled down his sleeves.

Cliff Come on, Des.

Roy How are we going to fit him in?

Cliff It's not far.

Desmond Do I need a coat . . . ?

Jack If he puts an overcoat on, he's riding on the roof.

Cliff (*leading the way out*) Away we go, then . . .

Roy (*as they leave*) See you, Harriet!

They go out, closing the door. The hatch opens and Harriet glares out.

Harriet More sugar? Ginger? What's he making now?

She closes the hatch. Benedict, meanwhile, has risen and moves to the door again. He opens it and steps into the hall.

Benedict (*calling again softly*) Hallo! Anybody about?

*He seems worried. He moves to the kitchen door, opens it and goes in. During the next he looks round the kitchen and opens the back door and peers into the darkness outside. Meanwhile, Anita comes along the landing, fastening her dressing gown. She has both her boots on properly now. She is followed by **Vincenzo**. He*

is a thin, stooping, rather nervous figure of 28.
Bespectacled, academic and rather shy. He, too, is
pulling on a bathrobe but is barefoot, with just his
trousers on underneath.

Anita *(as they come downstairs)* Siamo nei guai col
detective . . .

Vincenzo Chi?

Anita L'investigatore privato che ha fatto l'inchiesta.
Vuole altri soldi . . .

Vincenzo Dovreste dire a mio fratello Lotario di farlo
fuori. Vi costa meno che pagare quello lì, a lungo
andare . . .

Anita I don't know what you're saying, love, but you're
probably right. Come on, we'll have a drink. *Qualcosa da
bere.*

Vincenzo Si, beviamo qualcosa.

Anita and Vincenzo go into the far sitting room.
Benedict comes out of the kitchen and moves towards
the dining room.

Benedict Hallo?

Benedict goes into the dining room. As he does so,
Poppy comes out of the far bedroom a little way. She
stands listening. Tina follows her on to the landing.

Tina What is it?

Poppy Nothing, I thought I . . . heard something. I –
Nothing.

Tina Shouldn't you see if he's all right down there? That
man?

Poppy He's all right. He's got a drink. *(Slight pause.)*

Actually, I don't really want to be with him on my own, really. He gives me the creeps a bit.

Tina What him? That little man? (*Laughs.*) Want me to come down with you, then?

Poppy Yes. All right. Once you've got him to sleep.

Tina I don't think he intends to tonight. Little horror. I wish he slept like Roy.

Tina and Poppy return to the far bedroom. As they do so, Cliff opens the front door with his key and lets in all the others, Jack, Roy and Desmond – all of whom are now suffering the after-effects of their constricted journey.

Cliff Come in. (*calling*) 'Nita?

Anita (*coming out of the far sitting room*) We're in here.

Roy (*gaping at her*) 'Strewth!

Anita What are you gawping at?

Cliff For God's sake, love, couldn't you even find time to put your clothes on? What do you think you're doing?

Anita A little light housework, my angel.

They troop into the far sitting room. As they do so, Benedict comes out of the dining room and looks about the empty hall.

Benedict (*to himself*) Curiouser and curiouser . . . Mrs McCracken?

He starts climbing the stairs. The group in the sitting room, Jack, Anita, Roy, Cliff, Desmond and Vincenzo come through to the near sitting room. They seat themselves during the next. Only Anita and Vincenzo have drinks.

Anita Well, what's all this in aid of? He wants more money, I take it.

Jack He wants fifty. You're thirty-one light. Can you make it up?

Anita What? Ready cash?

Jack Yes.

Anita Absolutely not.

Desmond Not if you sold something?

Anita If we sold something we might, yes . . .

Roy That car of his for starters –

Anita (*thoughtfully*) No, we can't sell that. I didn't buy it through normal channels . . .

Desmond (*agitated*) Well, you've got to find it, somehow –

Cliff (*angrily*) Look, why is it us selling things –

Jack All right!

They pause for a moment. Benedict reaches the top of the stairs. He looks into the darkened bathroom.

Benedict Mrs McCracken?

He switches on the light and looks round the bathroom. After a second, he switches it off again.

Desmond All my money is already tied up. It's heavily tied up.

Cliff Well, untie it then . . .

Jack Listen. Listen, you lot. I'm going to say this once. You either come up with the money or that's that, all right? I'm leaving you to fend for yourselves.

Roy Oh, don't be like that . . .

Jack Sort it out between you. Because I don't intend to spend the rest of my life acting as your bagman and wandering round with trunk loads of small change.

Benedict goes into the near bedroom and turns on the light. He is now very wary.

Benedict Hallo . . . ?

He studies the room for a moment before turning out the light.

Jack You've got five minutes. Because I've left him sitting at home waiting for an answer.

Roy Well, I haven't got ten.

Jack What about him? Italy?

Anita This is Vincenzo. You met his brothers.

Roy If you get the set, you can trade them in for a gallon of petrol.

He laughs.

Cliff I don't think we can ask the Rivettis again. Apparently their mother got very upset about the last two grand.

Jack Well, I do look forward to meeting her as well, sometime. Coming back to my original question, where are you going to find it from?

Benedict (*starting along the landing towards the far bedrooms*) Mrs McCracken?

Anita Would – you . . . ? I wonder if you'd excuse us a second, Jack, while we sort this out between us?

Jack That's all you've got. A second.

Anita We'll be as quick as we can . . .

Jack (*making to rise*) Right, I'll . . .

Anita No, sit there. We'll go next door. All right? Come on everyone. Next door.

Anita leads them all except Jack back into the far sitting room. Jack sits waiting impatiently, now and again glancing at his watch. Benedict is almost at the far bedroom door.

Benedict Mrs McCracken . . .

Poppy comes out of the bedroom and nearly collides with Benedict. She yelps.

Poppy Oh!

Benedict Mrs McCracken . . .

Poppy Oh, I'm sorry. I do beg your pardon, Mr Hough, I –

Tina comes hurrying out of the bedroom.

Tina Mum? Are you all right?

Benedict No, I beg your pardon, Mrs McCracken. I had no intention of startling you . . .

Poppy No, I'm sure . . .

Benedict I was merely trying to ascertain if there was anyone left in the house besides myself . . .

Poppy I'm sorry we – abandoned you rather. I was just seeing to my grandchildren . . .

Benedict (*sentimentally*) Ah!

Poppy Have you met my daughter, by the way? This is Tina.

Tina How do you do?

Poppy This is Mr Hough . . .

Benedict Yes, she's as lovely as her mother. Hallo, Tina, I think we met briefly the other night.

Tina (*glaring at him*) Yes.

Poppy It's all right, Tina, I'm fine . . .

Tina Sure?

Poppy Yes.

Tina goes back into the bedroom.

I'm sorry. Shall we go downstairs? I'll pour you another drink. My husband shouldn't be much more than five minutes.

Benedict Well, quite frankly, Mrs McCracken, I don't think I can stay much longer myself . . .

Poppy Oh, dear . . .

Benedict I've one or two other evening commitments. I think I must be on my way.

Poppy Yes, of course. In that case, let me . . .

She indicates the stairs.

Benedict I wonder, just before I go . . . Your husband said it would be in order – if I could have the briefcase. To take with me.

Poppy Oh, no. I'm sorry. I was given to understand that –

Benedict I assure you, it is quite in order.

Poppy Yes. Well, the point is, he's taken it with him. Wherever he went. I'm sorry.

Benedict Oh dear, how inconvenient.

Poppy I am sorry. You'll have to wait till he comes back. With it.

Benedict I somehow feel that mightn't be in the best interests of my health.

Poppy I can put the fire on for you.

She tries to usher him downstairs again. Benedict seems reluctant to go.

Benedict This is all very unfortunate. So it's not here?

Poppy Sorry.

Benedict You know something, Mrs McCracken. When I was a little boy, whenever I went to parties, we used to play a game called hunt the slipper. Have you ever played it yourself? I'm sure you have. Perhaps even with your own children? Well, of all the games there were, that was my favourite. Because I was really very, very good at it indeed.

Benedict begins to drive Poppy slowly backwards along the landing towards the near bedroom. She seems nearly hypnotized by Benedict.

And do you know my secret? I'll tell you. I'd walk straight into the room where whatever it was had been hidden and I'd look straight at whoever I knew had hidden it and – try as they might, Mrs McCracken – they'd give themselves away. They just couldn't resist sliding their eyes round that little bit, to make sure it was still safely hidden. Rather the same as you yourself did just a moment ago, Mrs McCracken.

Poppy Listen, I don't know what you think you're doing –

They are now in the near bedroom.

Benedict Now my guess is, it's somewhere in here. (*Switches on the bedroom light.*) Am I right?

Poppy Look, I'm afraid I must ask you to leave now, Mr Hough.

Benedict Just as soon as I find my property, Mrs McCracken, I shall be happily on my way.

Poppy (*louder*) I'm sorry, I refuse to be intimidated . . .

Benedict Ssh! Mrs McCracken. We shall have to learn to play this game very quietly, shan't we? Otherwise we might frighten our grandchildren. And that would never do, would it?

Poppy (*starting to get indignant*) Now, you listen to me –

Benedict Sssh! (*Looks towards the cupboard.*) What about in here?

He passes Poppy who instinctively draws away slightly. Benedict looks in the cupboard.

Poppy My other daughter is here as well, you know. Just along there.

Benedict Who? Young Gladys? Well, we mustn't disturb her either, must we? (*examining the cupboard*) No, nothing in here.

Poppy I think that was my husband's car.

Benedict If you were a sport, you'd shout out 'warmer'. Or 'colder, colder' . . . Ah, now where did I catch those lovely eyes looking then . . . Eh? Under here perhaps?

He bends to look under the bed. From the other side Poppy grabs up the attaché case and runs for the door.

No, no. That's cheating. Unfair . . .

Poppy You can't have it . . . Get away!

Poppy rushes into the bathroom and tries to close the door. Benedict, hot on her heels, prevents her doing so.

Despite her efforts, he slowly manages to get the door open. He is evidently stronger than he looks.

Benedict (*quietly*) Now, now. Naughty, naughty, naughty, Mrs McCracken.

Poppy (*struggling*) You keep out of here . . .

Benedict (*as he slowly forces open the door*) When I used to go to parties little girls who cheated used to get smacked . . . Are you a believer at all in corporal punishment, Mrs McCracken? I must admit I've invariably found it most effective. Especially for little girls who – cheat!

With a last shove he forces the door open. Poppy recoils and all but falls into the bath. Benedict switches on the light. Poppy stands, panting, clasping the attaché case to her.

(*advancing on her*) Come on, now . . . Come on . . .

Poppy (*screaming*) Tina!

Benedict Oh, now that's really naughty. Smack! Smack! Smack!

Jack (*calling*) Come on, you lot. I want to get home and have my dinner.

Benedict grabs the attaché case and they wrestle semi-silently.

Benedict (*struggling*) You didn't really think I was just going to sit there waiting, while he rounded up your whole family . . . Come on. Let go . . .

Poppy (*simultaneously, with him*) I'm not going to . . . I won't . . . you won't . . .

Tina, who has heard Poppy's cry, comes rushing along the landing.

Tina Mum? Mum, what's happening?

Poppy Don't let him get it, Tina. Help me stop him . . .

Tina (*pitching in to help*) You leave her alone. You let go of my mother . . .

Benedict (*enjoying himself*) Now, now, now. Two against one. This won't do, girls . . .

Poppy Give it to me . . .

Tina Give to her . . . Let go!

Benedict I warn you, ladies, I'm much stronger than I look. I don't want to hurt you. But I may be forced to if you don't – Aaah!

The three topple over on to the floor with a cry.

Now, this is becoming very undignified . . . (*to Tina*) Ow, now. Mustn't bite, must we?

They struggle on the floor for a moment. Their combined strengths are more or less equally matched. A deadlock. During this, Anita comes from the far sitting room.

Anita Sorry, Jack.

Jack Well? You come up with a solution?

Anita Yes, we have. But I'm afraid it's not one you'll like.

Jack (*sarcastically*) You mean, I've got to find the money myself?

Anita The only solution, as we see it, and we've talked it round and round, is that we hand the original money over to Vincenzo in there and he'll get his brother to do the rest. Arrange for Mr Hough to have a little accident. Nothing dramatic.

Jack stares at her.

Tina (*yelling*) Sammy! Sammy! For God's sake, come and help us!

Jack I don't think I can have heard you correctly . . .

Poppy Sammy! She's got those bloody headphones on, I bet.

Jack Arrange an accident? You're actually talking about murdering him, aren't you? That's what you're talking about?

Poppy and Tina (*yelling in unison*) Sammy!

Anita Jack, it's the only solution . . .

Jack If that is the only solution, God help us . . .

Anita If you don't want to see us all in prison . . .

Jack (*storming out through the hall*) That's it. That's it. We have reached the pit. We have touched the sewage. We are back on all fours. Not another word on the subject. Good night.

Jack slams the front door. Anita stands looking after him. Cliff comes out into the hall from the far sitting room.

Cliff I gather he didn't take it too well?

Anita Oh, he'll come round to it. You know Jack . . . Let's all have another drink, shall we?

She goes back into the far sitting room with Cliff. Meanwhile, in the bathroom the fight continues.

Benedict Come on now, girls, you've had your fun. That's enough. Or someone will get hurt . . .

With a huge effort he heaves the three of them off the

*floor for a second. They now teeter on the edge of the
bath. The attaché case comes open at this point and the
bathroom is filled with notes.*

Poppy (*alarmed*) Hold on, Tina.

Tina (*struggling*) I am, I am, I am . . .

*Samantha comes out from her bedroom, rather blearily,
her headphones still round her neck.*

Samantha Somebody call . . . ? (*calling as she comes
along the landing*) Mum? Mum?

Poppy Sammy, come and help us.

Tina (*with her*) Sammy!

Benedict (*still enjoying himself enormously*) Oh, not
Gladys as well. This is getting very unfair . . .

*Samantha enters the bathroom and surveys the scene in
amazement.*

Samantha What are you doing?

Poppy Sammy, will you please help us . . .

Tina Sammy, for Christ's sake . . . He's trying to kill us.

Samantha Oh, it's you, is it? Sodding pukeface . . . (*Leaps
in vigorously.*) Right . . .

Benedict Hey! Hey! Gladys . . .

*Under the weight of this latest assault, Benedict topples
backwards into the bath and out of sight. There is a
sharp cry and a terrible thud. Tina and Poppy cease the
struggle. Poppy recoils holding the nearly empty
briefcase. Tina slides back on to the floor, exhausted.
Samantha continues her onslaught.*

Poppy Sammy! Sammy! That'll do! That'll do!

Tina (*with a yell*) Sammy!

Samantha stops. Out of breath. She sits with the others on the floor. One gathers she was in a fairly dazed state when she started. A silence.

(*panting*) My God. Will you look at all this money?

Samantha Where's it come from?

Poppy It's your Dad's . . .

Samantha Did he nick it?

Poppy No. Not your Dad. You should know better than that, Sammy.

Tina How is he? That man . . .

Poppy I don't know, I'll . . . (*Examines Benedict.*) He doesn't seem to be breathing. (*Listens.*) He's not breathing. (*stunned*) He's dead.

Tina (*in an appalled whisper*) Oh, God.

Samantha Good.

Poppy Sammy! He's got this great cut in his head from somewhere, he's . . . Look at all this blood. (*appalled*) Oh, dear heaven, what's Jack going to say?

They all stay there in various attitudes of collapse, unable to move due to exhaustion and varying degrees of shock. Jack comes in the front door and closes it. The women react. Jack goes straight to the sitting room.

Tina (*softly*) It's Dad.

Jack (*seeing the sitting room is empty*) Poppy!

Poppy What's he going to say . . .

Jack (*glancing into the empty kitchen*) Poppy!

He grows slightly more alarmed.

Tina (*indicating Benedict*) Perhaps we can hide him somewhere . . .

Poppy No, he'll have to know. Your Dad will have to be told.

Jack (*at the foot of the stairs, calling*) Poppy! Tina!

Poppy (*calling back feebly*) We're up here, Jack . . .

Jack (*starting up the stairs*) What?

Tina In here, Dad . . .

Jack reaches the landing, uncertain as to where to locate them. He looks in the near bedroom, then the bathroom. He stops short, startled, as he sees the state of the three women.

Poppy Hallo, Jack . . .

Tina Hallo, Dad.

Samantha Hi . . .

Jack What are you doing? What are you all doing in here?

Poppy We were . . .

Jack What are you doing with all that money? What the hell's been going on?

Poppy We were trying to save it for you, Jack . . .

Jack And where's Mr Hough, then?

Poppy He's –

Samantha He's in the bath.

Jack What?

Poppy (*pointing; almost inaudibly*) In the bath.

Jack steps over them to see for himself.

Jack Oh, shit. (*Stares at Benedict.*) Oh, shit. Poppy, what have you done? (*Pause.*) Oh, shit.

Poppy (*very penitent*) I'm very sorry, Jack.

Jack Oh. (*Sways.*) I'm a bit dizzy . . .

Poppy Don't faint, love, don't faint in here . . .

Tina Steady, Dad . . .

Poppy He faints at blood . . .

Jack No, it's all right. I'm all right. (*recovering*) What are we going to do . . . ?

Poppy (*smiling feebly*) At least he's in the bath. Not so much of a mess . . .

Jack (*dully*) Good thinking, Poppy, yes.

This strikes Poppy as funny. She laughs. First Tina, then Samantha follow suit. They scream with laughter. Jack stares at them incredulously.

All right, That'll do. That'll do. THAT'LL DO!

They stop. A silence.

Blimey O'Reilly. It's like the bloody Borgias' bathroom in here. What's the matter with you all?

Poppy (*the tears coming now*) What are we going to do, Jack . . . ?

Tina (*starting to cry, too*) What are we going to do, Dad?

Jack (*stronger at once*) It's all right. It's all right. We'll sort it out . . .

Poppy (*weeping*) I'm terribly sorry –

Tina (*weeping*) It wasn't your fault, Mum.

Samantha seems to have gone into mild shock.

Jack Now, it's all right. It's all right. Now, come on. Let's get organized. Tina, you see to Kevin, it sounds as if he's calling for you. Sammy, I want you to pick all this lot up. Every penny, do you hear . . .

Samantha Oh, Dad. Why's it always me?

Poppy (*between tears*) What about . . . What about him?

Jack Leave him just as he is, I'll deal with that. Sammy, draw the curtains round him, there's a girl.

> *Samantha draws the shower curtain and then begins to pick up the notes, under the next. Tina returns to the far bedroom. Jack leads Poppy from the bathroom and downstairs.*

And you're coming downstairs with me, all right?

Poppy (*snuffling*) Yes . . .

Jack (*gently*) You know what we're going to do?

Poppy (*faintly*) No . . .

Jack (*as to a child*) We're going to get things cleared up and then we're going to put all this lot behind us, you see? Anita's got some friends who'll get rid of him. Him in the bath . . . They'll know how to do that, they're used to that . . .

Poppy Are they?

Jack Oh yes, they do that sort of thing in their sleep. And do you know what the day after tomorrow is?

Poppy No . . .

Jack It's your Dad's birthday, isn't it?

Poppy Oh, yes, I'd forgotten . . .

Jack Well, we mustn't forget that, must we? We've got to give old Ken a real treat, haven't we? For his seventy-fifth? Us and all the family? Eh?

Poppy (*smiling bravely*) We will . . .

Jack We'll have a real party. Des and Harriet and Anita and Cliff and Roy and Tina . . .

He is swamped by the next. As Jack speaks, the events start to occur. Slowly the scene transforms as people gather for the party. Music also starts from the hi-fi, as before. Cliff, Roy and Desmond come out of the dining room, both with plates from the cold buffet. From the far sitting room into the near sitting room come Anita, Harriet and **Lotario,** *32, a smartly dressed, sharp-featured man, looking very much like a representative of an organized crime syndicate. They are all talking together.*

Anita This is Lotario Rivetti . . . this is my – I don't know what to call her, really . . . she's my brother-in-law's wife's brother's wife . . . Does that make any sense?

Lotario (*who speaks perfect English, laughing*) I think so. I think so. We have similar family complications in my country, as you can well imagine . . .

Harriet (*who seems to be making a slight effort*) Yes, I can see you might . . .

Anita We're going to get something to eat. Are you going to join us, Harriet?

Harriet No, I won't. Not just at the moment . . .

The last is played under the following.

Cliff (*as he comes out of the dining room*) Poppy, my darling – (*kissing her*) – you have excelled yourself yet again. That spread is sumptuous. Is that the right word – sumptuous?

Poppy Thank you . . .

Cliff Is that not so, Des?

Desmond Oh, yes indeed.

Cliff There you are. There speaks the expert.

Jack No higher praise . . .

Poppy Well, thank you. Excuse me, just one second . . .

Poppy goes into the dining room.

Cliff You got a drink, Jack? Can I get you one?

Jack Ta, yes. Large scotch and water.

Cliff Right.

*Cliff goes into the far sitting room. Anita and Lotario
have left Harriet in the near sitting room and are
heading towards the dining room. They meet up with
Jack on their way through the hall.*

Desmond Jack, is it possible to have a quick word . . . ?

Jack Could it wait a second, Des? I need to freshen up.

Desmond It'll only –

Anita Jack. You haven't met Lotario, have you? Lotario,
this is my brother-in-law, Jack McCracken.

Jack (*speaking slowly and loudly*) Hello. Welcome to our
party. *Ciao.*

Lotario Hallo. It's a splendid do. Absolutely wonderful. I
was just telling Anita, it reminds me very much of our own
family parties back in Milan.

Jack (*startled*) Ah.

Anita This is the one that speaks English.

Jack Yes. I noticed.

Lotario Yes. I was very fortunate. I was educated privately in Dorset . . .

Jack Great.

Anita (*dragging Lotario away*) Come on. We're going to get something to eat . . .

Lotario Talk to you later on, old boy.

Jack Yes, rather. You betcha.

Anita and Lotario go into the dining room. Jack goes upstairs before Desmond can grab him. Cliff comes out of the far sitting room with Jack's drink.

Desmond (*vainly, after Jack*) Jack . . . (*seeing Cliff*) Cliff, could I have a quick word?

Cliff Yes, right you are, Des. I've just got to give Jack his drink . . .

Desmond ignores this and draws Cliff to one side. Upstairs, Jack has gone into the near bedroom and starts to change his shirt, as before.

Desmond It's just – I need Jack's OK to – you know – move off. You know. Leave the country. Set my overseas interests in motion. Only I don't want to do anything to jeopardize things, Cliff. Or the business, obviously.

Cliff You're going to have to wait a bit, Des.

Desmond Yes but, Cliff, you must appreciate the situation between me and Harriet is increasingly . . . You know how things are . . .

Cliff You're just going to have to be patient, old son. Grin and bear her for a bit longer. We can't have you doing a bunk now. It'd look all wrong, Des. First Mr Hough, then you. We can't have everyone disappearing. Hasn't she been a bit more reasonable lately? I thought Anita'd had a word with her . . .

Desmond Oh yes, she's been much better. That certainly helped. I was grateful to Anita for that, Cliff. I don't know what she said but . . .

Cliff has now started up the stairs with Jack's drink. Tina comes out of the dining room. Desmond goes, rather unhappily, into the near sitting room.

Tina I'll get some more. Where are they? In the drawer?

Tina goes into the kitchen.

Desmond (*to Harriet*) You going to have something to eat, dear?

Harriet (*wincing*) Certainly not.

Desmond Are you sure? It's really delicious. There are things there you'd like. There's a nice trifle. You like trifle, don't you?

Harriet Desmond, please leave me alone. Go away.

Desmond I was only trying to . . .

Rather dejectedly, Desmond goes into the far sitting room, leaving Harriet alone. Tina finds the forks and passes them through the hatch.

Tina Here we are, Mum . . .

Poppy (*from the dining room*) Oh, thank you, dear.

Tina returns to the dining room. Under the next, Anita and Lotario cross from the dining room to the near sitting room with plates of food. Cliff arrives in Jack's bedroom.

Cliff (*presenting the drink*) There you go.

Jack Shut the door.

Cliff (*doing so*) The Italians are proving a bit difficult . . .

Jack Never mind them. What about Harriet? Is she safe now?

Cliff Yes, she's all right. For the time being . . .

Jack I mean, if she gets wind of all this from Des and goes blabbing off to Yvonne again, we're back to square one, aren't we? In spades.

Cliff Harriet's all right. Anita's talked to her.

Jack I hope she talked her round.

Jack goes out of the near bedroom and into the bathroom to rinse his face. Cliff follows him. Anita and Lotario enter the sitting room from the hall.

Anita Where did we put our drinks then?

Lotario I think they're through here . . .

He leads the way through to the far sitting room.

Anita Oh, yes. So they are. Hallo, Harriet. All alone?

Harriet I'm all right.

Anita (*smiling*) Good.

Anita goes through to the far sitting room. Jack and Cliff are now both in the bathroom.

Jack Shut the door.

Cliff does so.

What's the matter with the Italians, then?

Cliff They're proving a bit expensive, Jack, that's all. I mean, their bill for the removal and disposal of our friend is costing an arm and a leg, if you'll pardon the expression.

Jack How much?

Cliff Fifty.

Jack That's blackmail, that is.

Cliff I know. But we weren't in much of a position to argue, Jack. And, I mean, with the Rivettis you got all the equipment, the van, the boat. They probably even had the proper lead weights.

Jack Right. So where's that leave us? Overdrawn, doesn't it?

Cliff Well, I took the liberty, Jack. I took the liberty of doing a deal in kind.

Jack What deal?

Cliff It appears that they could find a use for our own domestic furniture distribution network for the circulation of urgent medical supplies.

Jack Urgent medical supplies? What are we talking about here? Are we talking about drugs?

Cliff No, medical supplies.

Jack Don't try telling me the Rivettis have joined the International Red Cross. They mean drugs. No way.

Cliff Now, Jack –

Jack Forget it.

Cliff Jack. I know it's a dirty, filthy, stinking business –

Jack Right.

Cliff And normally, I would say no, with you. Categorically no. But these are what they term urgent medical supplies. Meaning they are only intended – and I have their solemn vow on this – they are only intended for established users who, if denied their regular supply – well, it would entail a great deal of unnecessary suffering . . .

Jack No, I'm sorry, I . . .

Cliff Yes, I know it's a dirty, filthy, stinking, lousy, disgusting business, Jack – but we do have a solemn undertaking that there will be no first-time users involved here, Jack. Otherwise, I would say no with you. No, no and again categorically no.

Jack We have that undertaking?

Cliff We do.

Jack Well. This is just a one-off, you understand. You tell them I'm not doing this on a regular basis. It's only till we've paid them off.

Cliff Absolutely. Yes . . .

Jack starts to leave the bathroom.

There should be quite a bit in it for us as well, incidentally. But that's only incidental.

They both return to the bedroom where Jack puts on his clean shirt. Anita comes in briefly to the near sitting room.

Anita Come on, Harriet, come and keep Desmond company. He's all on his own, poor man . . .

Harriet (*drily*) Oh, dear . . .

Anita (*pleasantly enough*) Now, Harriet. Remember our talk? You must look after Desmond, otherwise he'll start finding new friends, won't he? And before you know it, these new friends of his, they'll be round at your house at all hours of the day and night, leaving doors open, so that Peggy could so easily run straight out into that busy main road. Straight under the wheels of some great big lorry . . .

Harriet has risen during the last of this and hurries into the far sitting room.

(*cheerfully*) Here she is . . .

Anita goes back after her.

Jack Anything else?

Cliff No, that's it for now . . .

Jack Right. Well done.

Cliff makes to leave the bedroom.

Incidentally, Cliff – close the door, will you – I think, in due course, I'd like you and Anita to consider coming on to the board –

Cliff Oh. What, you mean – ?

Jack As full directors. To join me and Desmond. With a view to taking over from him later when he leaves.

Cliff I hope he won't be leaving us for a good bit yet, Jack.

Jack Well, frankly, he's worse than useless, Cliff. The sooner he starts polluting the Mediterranean with burnt cooking fat, the better.

Cliff No. Still, we'd all prefer to have him around just the same, wouldn't we? Where we can see him? I mean, you're the guv'nor, Jack, but it seems to me we're the sort of family that needs to stick together . . .

Jack (*rather moved*) You're dead right, Cliff. (*embracing him*) We're a family, for God's sake.

Cliff (*rather bemused by the force of this reaction*) True. See you down there then, Jack.

Cliff goes out and along the landing. As he does so,

Samantha, in her party outfit, comes along the landing from her bedroom.

Hello, Sammy. How are you doing?

Samantha Hallo, Uncle Cliff.

Cliff Coming to join the knees up?

Samantha (*staring at him blankly*) What?

Cliff (*studying her for a second*) Right, I'll see you down there . . .

Cliff goes downstairs. Poppy hurries from the dining room. She is dressed in her boldest party dress yet. This one obviously was bought for her, not for Anita.

Poppy (*calling upstairs*) Jack? (*to Cliff*) Is Jack coming down?

Cliff On his way.

Poppy I think they're here . . .

Poppy hovers in the hall. Cliff goes to the far sitting room. Jack finishes dressing in the bedroom and meets Samantha as he sets off downstairs.

Jack Hallo, Sammy. All right, then?

Samantha I'm all right.

Jack Right. (*Pause.*) Good. See you downstairs.

Jack hurries downstairs.

Samantha See you downstairs.

During the next, she stands for a time at the top of the stairs, and then, as if unable to face the throng below, goes into the darkened bathroom where she sits for the remainder of the play, staring ahead of her blankly.

Jack (*reaching the hall*) Now then. Where is everyone?

Poppy Oh, there you are. Quickly. He's arrived . . . He's just driven up with Yvonne in the taxi.

Jack Oh, good. Just in time.

Jack goes into the far sitting room and shoos people through to the near one.

Jack Come on, everyone, Ken's arrived.

Poppy (*waving Tina out of the dining room*) Come on, Tina. Quickly.

Tina scurries across the hall and into the near sitting room where she joins Cliff, Anita, Lotario, Harriet, Desmond, Roy and Jack. Poppy hovers in the hall, waiting.

Anita (*as someone touches her*) Oooh!

All Sssh!

Anita Here we go again . . .

The doorbell rings. Poppy opens the door immediately. Ken and Yvonne enter. Ken is much the same, perhaps a little vaguer. Yvonne is like a Christmas tree. She sparkes with expensive jewellery, everywhere.

Poppy Hallo, there. Come in, come in.

Ken Hallo, my flower. Hallo, my dearest.

Poppy Let me take your coats.

Yvonne (*winking*) Are we the first?

Poppy I think you are, yes.

Ken Happy birthday, my dear. And very many more.

Yvonne No, it's your birthday, Ken. It's yours. (*to Poppy*)

He keeps forgetting. He kept wishing the taxi driver many happy returns.

Ken Mine? Is it my birthday, then?

Poppy Yes, it's yours. Not mine.

Ken I know that, girl. Seventy-five. Seventy-five today. Right?

Poppy That's right. Now you come on through.

Ken This is very nice. Who lives here, then?

Poppy leads them across the hall. As Ken enters the near sitting room, the lights are switched on. A great cry from everyone.

All (*singing*)
Happy birthday to you,
Happy birthday to you, *etc.*

At the end, applause. People cluster round Ken with good wishes. He seems quite overwhelmed. Poppy draws Jack to one side.

Poppy Jack! Have you seen what that woman's wearing? Have you seen what Yvonne's wearing?

Jack What's that?

Poppy That's all Grace's jewellery. Those are my mother's diamonds she's got on.

Jack Perhaps Ken lent them to her.

Poppy (*with some venom*) Nonsense. Jack, she's stolen them. If they belong to anyone, they're mine. That woman has stolen them and she thinks we daren't do anything about it. Little thieving bitch . . .

Jack It's all right, love. If she has stolen them, then she'll answer for it. I'm having no more of that, ever again.

From now on this family's going to be subject to a few hard and fast rules. And anyone who breaks them is going to have the family to answer to. I'll get Anita to have a word with her later. Now come on, stop worrying and enjoy the party . . .

Poppy (*lovingly*) You're a good man, Jack. You're such a good man.

She kisses him lightly. They both return to the throng.

Ken (*above the chatter*) Ladies and . . . Ladies . . .

Cliff Speech! Speech!

Anita Ssshh! Quiet!

A silence. Ken and Yvonne have both been given drinks.

Ken Ladies and Gentlemen . . . I just want to say . . . now, I'm not saying very much. Because it's not my place to. It's not my day. All I want to say is . . . Jack.

He looks towards Desmond.

Desmond (*pointing, gently*) That's Jack, Dad . . .

Ken Yes, it's Jack I'm talking to, not you, you fool. (*turning to Jack*) Jack. Thank you, for everything. And you know what I mean by everything. And, happy birthday, son.

He raises his glass. Everyone, rather startled, toasts Jack.

Jack Well. This is an unexpected anniversary pleasure. (*Reflects.*) I've made my speech for this year. It still stands. I'd simply like to propose this toast. Here's to you, Ken. Here's to us. Here's to the family. And finally, here's to the business. We've had our share of troubles and we've seen them off. And together, I can promise you this, we will continue to see them all off – whoever they are and wherever they come from. Ladies and Gentlemen, I give you – the family business!

All The family business!

*As they drink, the lights fade on the party guests –
leaving, for a few seconds or so, the image of Samantha,
huddled and alone. Then, as we lose her too:*

Blackout, Curtain.

HENCEFORWARD . . .

Characters

Jerome, *a composer*
Corinna, *his wife*
Geain, *their daughter*
Zoë, *an actress*
Mervyn, *a welfare officer*
NAN 300F
Lupus ⎱
Young Geain ⎰ *(Video only)*

Note
NAN 300F is played by the same actress as Corinna in Act One and by the same actress as Zoë in Act Two.

Setting: Jerome's studio.

Act One: Friday night/Saturday morning. Sometime quite soon.
Act Two: A few days later

Henceforward . . . was first performed in Scarborough at the Stephen Joseph Theatre in the Round on 30 July 1987. The cast was as follows:

Jerome Barry McCarthy
Lupus Robin Herford
Zoë Serena Evans
Geain, aged nine Victoria Horsfield
Geain, aged thirteen Emma Chambers
Corinna Penny Bunton
Mervyn Michael Roberts

It was subsequently performed at the Vaudeville Theatre, London, on 16 November 1988. The cast was as follows:

Jerome Ian McKellen
Lupus Robin Herford
Zoë Serena Evans
Geain, aged nine Victoria Horsfield
Geain, aged thirteen Emma Chambers
Corinna Jane Asher
Mervyn Michael Simkins

Notes on the Music

Paul Todd's music which was used in both the
Scarborough and West End productions of **Henceforward**
. . . is available for hire from Casarotto Ramsay Limited
on cassette tape. Should the production require the actual
voices of an individual company this, too, can be arranged
through Casarotto Ramsay Limited. Care should be
exercised in attempting special composition: the original
score was constructed on a Synclavier, and the text
requires an instrument of similar sophistication.

Act One

SCENE ONE

A darkened living room of a flat. The only light is from a video/sound console system, at present inactive. We can make out very little or guess the time of day. All at once, a large wall-mounted video screen lights up. Or perhaps a series of screens. We see the picture as from a front-door video entryphone system. **Jerome**, *a man of about forty, can be seen at the door. He is carrying three carrier bags, together with a somewhat incongruous walking stick. We see Jerome inserting his key and struggling and muttering as he opens his front door. He enters the flat. As he closes the front door the screen blanks again. After a second, the hall lights come on and Jerome approaches down the hall. Then the lights come on in the living room.*

It's a curious room. No windows, or, at least, what there were are curtained off and no light comes through the heavy steel shutters outside. There is a sofa, two swivel chairs and a low coffee-type table – all modern. That's really the extent of the recognizable furniture. The remainder of the room is filled with some very sophisticated electronic equipment. Not an amateur electronic rat's nest of wire and cable but custom-built units containing computers, tape and disc recorders – racks of amplifiers, filters, reverb units and gismos of all descriptions. At one end, several keyboards. Some of these are covered and remain so until much later in the play when we realize for the first time what a vast array of equipment Jerome actually owns. The room, in fact, betrays the contradictions in his own character. For while the immaculate technical equipment is kept lovingly protected from the slightest speck of dust, the rest of the room – the living area – is in fair chaos. Remnants of instant meals, old tea and coffee cups, the odd item of clothing. The signs of someone who lives alone and has stopped caring much. And, strangely, the overall impression given off, despite all the modern paraphernalia, is of something faintly Gothic. Three ways off, one to the hall and front door, one to the kitchen and one to the rest of the flat – the bedrooms, bathroom, etc.

Jerome is standing in the hall doorway having just switched on the lights. He dumps his packages on the sofa and replaces his stick near the hall doorway. Also on the sofa, slumped, face down in a somewhat undignified posture is **Nan**, *who remains motionless for some time. Jerome, ignoring her, crosses to the console, where he switches on his answering machine. As he moves back to the sofa, on the screen and through the speakers, the machine fast-rewinds. He doesn't take much notice of it, though. He gathers up two of the carriers which appear to be filled with tinfoil-sealed instant meals and goes off into the kitchen. As he does so, the answering machine starts to play back both sound and vision. An introductory beep. A logo appears:* The Department of Social Services. ECONOMY. Except in special circumstances all calls made are NVR. 01–993–9000.

Mervin's voice Mr Watkins, this is Mervyn Bickerdyke from the Department of Child Wellbeing . . .

Jerome groans.

I've been trying to get hold of you for some days now, regarding a meeting. The time is nine forty-six. I wonder if you would call me. My number is on screen. Thank you.

He hangs up. The screen blanks, the audio beeps. In a second, the next message appears.

Jerome (*On his way to the kitchen, in reply to* **Mervyn**) No, I won't and I'm not.

A fanfare-like tune from the answering machine and a logo appears: BLAISE GILLESPIE – Escorts for the Discerning.

Choir (*singing, from the video*) Blaise Gillespie! A call from Blaise Gillespie!

Voice (*cheerfully*) Hallo, Mr Watkins, this is Mary Hope-Fitch, calling once again from the Blaise Gillespie Agency. It's ten forty on Thursday. Just to remind you of your appointment today with Zoë Mill who plans to be with you by fourteen hundred this afternoon. I hope that's still convenient. She's looking forward so much to meeting you. We feel certain she'll answer all your rather specialized requirements. If there's any problems at all, please don't hesitate to call. Thank you.

Jerome returns from the kitchen for his third carrier bag.

Choir (*singing, from the video*) Blaise Gillespie! A call from Blaise Gillespie . . .

Jerome (*mimicking them*) From tone-deaf Blaise Gillespie . . .

Another couple of beeps as the message ends and moves on to the next. It is the same logo as the first call.

Mervin's voice Mr Watkins, this is Mervyn Bickerdyke from the Department of Child Wellbeing . . .

Jerome groans. And he goes into the kitchen with the carrier.

It is urgent that I speak to you. I realize you may be – busy with your compositions – but it is a matter of some importance. It's eleven seventeen and my number is on screen. Thank you.

*Jerome returns with one of the tinfoil food packages in
one hand, a palm-sized section of printed circuitry in the
other. A beep as the message ends on the answering
machine.*

Jerome Look what I've brought for you. (*He balances the
circuitry casually on Nan's back as he passes her.*) Who's a
spoilt girl, then?

*Jerome sits on the sofa and studies his purchase.
Another beep. The screen crackles and flickers with a
fuzzy image that could be anyone's.*

Zoë's voice (*faintly*) Hello, this is Zoë Mill. I'm from the
Blaise Gillespie Agency. And it's eleven fifteen . . . Hallo?
Hallo, this is Zoë . . . Hallo? Can you hear me? Oh,
dammit . . .

*Another beep. The screen clears. Jerome, unperturbed,
continues to read. Another beep. Interference as before,
if not worse.*

Hallo, this is . . . Oh, Jesus! Don't any of these bloody
things work at . . . ?

*Another beep as Zoë is cut off. Jerome reads on. As he
does so, there is a swift beep – a yell from Zoë and
another beep – qualifying as the shortest message ever.*

(*in fury*) Aaarrrgggh!

*From the machine, another beep and **Lupus** appears on
the screen. He is a forlorn sight, a harassed, careworn
man in his forties. He wears a T-shirt reading MUSIC IS
A LIVING THING. It appears he is at home, from the
background we can see behind him. The sound of a
child playing out of sight.*

Lupus Hallo, Jerry. It's me. Lupus. I thought I'd just call
you, mate . . .

Jerome, reacting to Lupus's voice, gives a terrible groan.

. . . keep you up to date with how things are –

A ball, presumably thrown by a child, bounces of Lupus's head. The child laughs.

(*ineffectually*) Ah, now don't do that, Orson . . . That hurt Daddy. The point is, Jerry, it's come to the big N.C.H. Ultimatums from Deborah. Threats from the Bank Manager. I mean real threats, Jerry. Two heavy lads in camel-hair coats kicking at my front door. So it looks like I'm going to have to take that job with those geriatrics. I never thought it would get this desperate, Jerry. Look at me, I'm a top session-player –

He is struck again by a projectile.

Orson – don't do that, darling, Daddy's talking – Jesus – what am I reduced to – ? – relief drummer in a three-piece band for an old folks' dance in Finchley. Who needs it, Jerry? Answer. I need it. Desperately I need it.

Jerome, apparently following the instructions he has been studying, removes the tinfoil package from its sleeve and searches for an insulated surface. In the end he decides to place the container on one of his discarded items of clothing, a shirt, which he spreads on the coffee table.

My God, I do. Because there's nothing else. But I don't have to tell you.

Jerome, having positioned his container, holds it in one hand, and tugs at a red ring in the lid. This pulls out a length of metal strip which he is left holding in his other hand. He stares at both items suspiciously. Jerome, during the next, goes to the answering machine, tossing aside the packet.

And if Deborah leaves me, Jerry, which it looks as if she's going to – it's sorting out the suitcases time, you know – but if Deborah goes – on top of everything else . . . I mean, I've been a loving husband. I've been a forgiving husband. God, have I been forgiving? I let her play around with – every bastard who could make it up our stairs. Present company excepted. I just don't know what I'm going to do, old mate . . .

> *Jerome pushes a button on the console and Lupus goes into fast-forward mode. He spools jerkily on for some time. The odd child-aimed missile hits him on the head as his high-speed voice twitters on. Jerome finishes his instructions. He shrugs and moves over to Nan, picks up the printed circuit card and examines it. He goes to a cupboard beneath the console and gets out a large loose-leaf manual. He studies this. As he does so, Lupus's message on the tape ends, the machine beeps and resumes normal speed. Another beep. The screen reads:*
> FAULT: VISION TEMPORARILY INOPERATIVE.

Zoë's voice (*rather distraught*) Hallo. This is Zoë Mill from the Blaise Gillespie Agency at – God, what's the time? – it's twelve thirty-one – All right? I've been trying to phone you for ages – Only none of the – And I keep getting your machine. My train is – my *bloody* train – pardon the language – is delayed – and I'm now at – God knows where I am – Oh, where the hell am I? Just hold on a second.

> *Station sounds as, apparently, she opens the call-box door.*

(*calling to someone*) Excuse me! I say, excuse me. Could you tell me where I am, please? . . . Where? . . . Hendon Central? Thanks so much.

> *Door closes.*

Hallo, I'm at a place called Hendon Central, apparently. So I don't know when I'll reach you. More important, I hope you're there because I'd hate to think I –

She is interrupted by a series of beeps.

Oh, I've no more on my card, that's it. See you shortly. I hope. Otherwise I –

The screen goes dead and then reads: MESSAGES END.

Jerome remains impervious to this. He is still intently studying the manual. After a second, the screen blanks.

Jerome (*at length*) All right. Let's see what we can do.

He rather unceremoniously puts his hand up the back of Nan's skirt and fumbles for a moment.

Pardon me.

There is a click and his hand re-emerges with an identical piece of printed circuitry.

Ah-ha!

He studies it critically for a moment and then throws it aside. His hand goes back under her dress as he replaces the circuit with the new piece. There is a series of clicks.

(*as he does so*) Now . . . I'm not supposed to be doing this, you know . . . if they caught me doing this . . . they'd . . . aaah! . . . get in . . . they'd probably lock me up and melt you down for scrap . . . I had to steal this from a check-out machine at the supermarket when their backs were . . . aah.

A final click.

Nan (*a little sigh*) Aaah!

Jerome Ah! There you go. Good girl. Now.

He heaves Nan round and sits her up on the sofa.

God, you're a heavy old bag of bits. Come on.

He grabs her neck on either side brings it sharply forward and then back. Nan clicks. A male voice, dedidedly not hers, probably a long forgotten technician's, emanates from somewhere in Nan.

Voice NAN 300F, series four, model 99148622G for Gertie. System check commencing – Go.

Nan goes through her pre-check routine. This is rapid and comprehensive. A great deal of internal computer chatter as systems load. Her eyes blink rapidly, her mouth flaps, every joint of her body tenses then relaxes. She rises, sits, her limbs jerk.

Nan (*In her own voice, very rapidly*) Modified Sampling Commences. Oh–for–God's–sake–Jerome–can't–you– think–of–anyone–else–but–yourself–for–a–change–just– for–once–I–mean–what–sort–of–a–person–are–you? Modified Sampling Ends.

A few more whirrs and clicks.

System check complete. Operational eighty-three point one seven. We are sixteen point eight three per cent unstable and are within eight point one seven per cent of permanent shutdown. (*cheerfully*) Clock set o-eight-hundred hours. Good morning. Rise and shine.

Jerome Nan, walk about.

Nan Walk about, Nan.

She does so. She walks with a rather bouncy stride but has a slight limp. She clanks a little as she goes down on her bad leg. Jerome watches her critically as she circles a couple of times.

Jerome That's better. You're not bumping into things like you were. I've still got to fix your leg, though. It's the pivot. You need a new pivot, old girl. Only they've stopped making them, you see.

Nan (*banging into a piece of furniture*) Oh, for goodness' sake, you extremely stupid old bat. Who put that there, then?

This last reveals the slightly tetchier side of Nan. In fact, as time goes on, we see that she is rather a Jekyll-and-Hyde creature. Her sunnier nature is the result of her initial 'nanny' factory programming; her darker side the result of subsequent modifications by Jerome himself – the source of which will become clearer later.

Jerome Nan, come here.

Nan Coming, Nan.

Nan comes to him and stops in front of him.

Jerome That's it.

Jerome crouches down and lifts her skirt to examine her knee. We see that at the knee joint her legs cease to be humanoid and are exposed metalwork. Nan licks her fingers and starts to smooth Jerome's hair.

Nan That's better . . .

Jerome Don't do that . . .

Nan That's better.

Jerome Nan, stop.

Nan Stop, Nan.

Nan stops. He rises.

Jerome Nan, watch my finger.

Nan Watching your finger, Nan.

He moves his finger to and fro in front of her eyes. She follows it with her eyes very slowly.

Jerome Yes, I think we can sharpen your reflexes a bit.

He places his hand inside Nan's blouse while continuing to move his other hand in front of her eyes. Nan's response quickens noticeably.

That's it . . . that's better . . .

Nan suddenly twitches violently.

Whoop! Too much. Sorry. That's it. Nan, thank you.

Nan Thank you. Lovely glass of orange? Lovely orange?

Jerome Nan, lovely.

Nan Lovely. Lovely morning. Rise and shine.

She bounces off to the kitchen.

Jerome (*glancing at his watch*) Oh, I never set your clock, did I? Never mind. You're better than you were.

He goes to the console and plays with a few switches. From the kitchen a crash.

Nan (*off*) Oh, for goodness' sake, you extremely stupid old bat. Who put that there, then?

Jerome frowns but ignores the sound. He puts on some Bach. It relaxes him. The phone rings. He makes no effort to answer it. It continues to ring.

Jerome Go away, Lupus, I'm not here.

He notices suddenly that his meal is still sitting there in its tinfoil.

Oh, no!

He grabs hold of the tinfoil package. It is very hot.

(*dropping it*) Ah!

He picks it up with the shirt it was standing on and cautiously, still protecting his hands, he opens the lid. The contents are black and charred and smoking.

(*disgustedly*) Oh, miraculous.

He drops the tinfoil back on the table. Nan comes in with a mug in her hand. It is unfortunately empty since she is holding it upside down.

Nan (*placing the inverted mug on the table by Jerome*) Lovely glass of orange. (*heading towards the bedroom*) Lovely morning, wakey-wakey.

Jerome (*staring at the mug in disgust*) You load of old scrap.

He is about to drop the shirt, too, when he observes that it now has a burn mark on it, left from the heated tinfoil.

(*equally*) Oh, mind-numbing.

He lies on the sofa for a moment absorbing the music. Nan re-enters with a face flannel in her hand. She makes a beeline for Jerome.

Nan (*playfully*) Booo! Nan's coming to getcher!

Nan attacks his face vigorously with a flannel. Jerome struggles. She is apparently quite strong.

Jerome Waah! Noff.

Nan Come along, wash your face and hands before your breakfast!

Jerome Wah! Noff! (*getting his mouth clear*) Nan off! Nan off!

Nan stops at once.

Nan That's better.

Jerome I am reprogramming you. You've taken a layer of skin off my face. You do that again and I'm stripping you down for spares and then dropping you off a twenty-storey building –

Nan Story-time, now . . .

Jerome Oh, God . . .

Nan Once upon a time there were three bears called Jack and Jill who wanted to go to the ball only the other ducklings wouldn't let her play with them . . .

Jerome Nan, stop.

Nan Stopped, Nan.

Jerome Nan, register.

Nan Register, Nan.

Jerome (*standing in front of her so she can scan his face*) Not child. Not child.

Nan Not child. Registered, Nan.

Jerome Nan, take a nap.

Nan Take a nap, Nan.

Jerome (*muttering*) I don't know why I bothered to switch you on again, really.

She heads back to the bedrooms.

Nan (*turning suddenly tearful, in her other tone*) I don't know why I bother, Jerome, I really don't. When you treat me like this. I've done everything I possibly can. I can't cope any more. If you want to go and live with her, I don't care. Go on! Go on! Go and live with the bloody woman.

See if I care.

> *She goes out to the bedrooms. Jerome frowns. He sits.*
> *The Bach continues to play. After a moment, there is a*
> *crash from the bedroom.*

(*off*) Oh, for goodness' sake, you extremely stupid old bat.
Who put that there, then?

> *Jerome sits once again and closes his eyes, assured of*
> *peace at last. After a second, the doorbell rings. The*
> *screen lights up once more. It is the video entry-phone*
> *system again. Zoë is at the front door. She is breathless*
> *and dishevelled.*

Zoë (*from screen*) Mr Watkins . . .

Jerome (*disturbed again*) I don't believe this . . .

Zoë Mr Watkins! This is Zoë Mill from the Blaise
Gillespie Agency. Would you let me in, please?

> *She looks anxiously over her shoulder and rings the*
> *doorbell again. Jerome crosses to the console. He*
> *switches off the music.*

(*urgently*) Mr Watkins! Please!

Jerome (*pressing the door button at the console*) All right!
Push the door.

Zoë Mr Watkins, open the door . . .

Jerome Push it. It's open . . .

Zoë Oh, please say you're in. Please God you're at
home . . .

> *She rings the bell again.*

Jerome (*yelling*) It's open. Push the door!

Zoë I'm going to break it down, Mr Watkins.

*We see her, on screen, step back and run at the door.
Jerome presses the door button long and hard. Zoë hits
the door which opens easily. She disappears. A second
later, she appears in the room, a tattered, breathless
wreck. She pulls up short, breathing heavily. Jerome
stares at her incredulously.*

(*attempting a semblance of dignity*) Mr Watkins? How do
you do? I am sorry to burst in like this. My name is Zoë
Mill. From the Blaise Gillespie Agency.

Jerome stares at her stupefied.

(*after a pause*) I hope they advised you I was coming, I . . .

Jerome (*suddenly aware of this*) You've left my front door
open . . .

*He rushes out of the room into the hall, seizing his
walking stick as he goes. Zoë, alarmed, flinches slightly
as he dashes past her. Jerome appears briefly on the video
screen. We see that his stick is in fact a swordstick which
he has now drawn. He checks to left and right, then
closes the door. The screen goes blank. Jerome returns,
sword still drawn. Zoë watches him, transfixed. Jerome
sheathes his sword and replaces the stick near the door.*

Never leave my front door open.

Zoë (*muted*) No. I'm sorry. (*Pause.*) You see, there were
these people –

Jerome I know there are these people. Why the hell do
you think I keep it shut?

Zoë Yes.

*Another pause. Jerome stares at her. Zoë tries to pull
herself together. It is difficult for her. Her clothes are in
ribbons, her face is bleeding from a cut and her hands
are torn and filthy. She has lost one shoe and is holding*

the other. Her stockings are in shreds. She obviously started out looking quite elegant in her smart suit and crisp blouse.

Jerome (*aware he has been rather rude*) Sorry.

Zoë No, no. I'm sorry. (*brightly*) Well, here I am. At last. (*She laughs nervously.*) What a super room.

Jerome is staring at her. A pause.

(*nervously indicating a seat*) Is this – for sitting on?

Jerome (*guardedly*) Yes.

Zoë Well. Would you mind if I – ?

Jerome No.

Zoë Thanks very much.

She sits. Jerome continues to stand, staring at her. She gives a sudden, quite unexpected, reflex sob as the shock begins to take hold but elects to continue as if it hadn't happened.

I'm sorry if I'm looking a bit of a – I must do a bit. I'm sorry. Anyway, I understood this was just an initial interview. Mrs Hope-Fitch told me you just wanted to look at me. See if I was suitable. But I believe the actual job's not for a week or so? Have I got that right? (*She sobs.*) Excuse me. Yes?

Jerome (*thoughtfully*) Yes.

Zoë (*indicating herself*) Look, you'll just have to disregard all this. I mean, *this* is ghastly. But I can – you may not believe this – I can look pretty good. Although I say it myself. Yes? But as I say, not – Don't, for God's sake, go by this. (*She sobs.*) Sorry.

Silence.

Would you like me to – walk up and down? Give you an overall picture? People sometimes find it helps them to – get a more general . . . Of course, I don't know quite what you're looking for so it's a bit . . . I understand it was slightly unusual? Is that so? (*She sobs.*)

Jerome (*thoughtfully*) Yes.

Zoë I'll stand up. (*She does so.*) There.

Jerome studies her.

Five foot four and a bit. I can lose a bit more weight if you like. I'm a bit over my usual . . . (*She sobs.*) I'll walk about for you. In case you need me to walk. (*She walks about, limping slightly.*) By the way, I don't usually limp, of course. Please, disregard that. I just seemed to have bashed my knee – Anyway. And, naturally, with heels on I'm that bit taller. They help no end, of course, with all sorts of things. God, look at my legs. Don't look at those, either. I'm sorry, I'm afraid you're just going to have to take my word for an awful lot of things. (*She sobs.*) Look, I'm awfully sorry, I think I'm just going to have to go away somewhere and have a quick cry. I'm sorry, I'm just in a bit of a state. I am sorry. Is there a – ? Have you got a – ?

Jerome Oh yes, yes, sure. There's one just out there. First on the left.

He indicates towards the bedrooms.

Zoë I'll be as quick as I can. I'm so sorry.

Zoë plunges out of the room. As she reaches the offstage bathroom, we hear the sudden start of her tears, then the slamming of a door. Jerome stares after her, thoughtfully. He goes to his console and winds back a tape. He replays a section.

Zoë's recorded voice . . . all sorts of things. God, look at my legs. Don't look at those, either. I'm sorry, I'm afrai–

Her voice cuts off as Jerome stops the tape. He shrugs. He switches the machine back to record. He waits. He fades up a fader on the panel. Zoë's sobs are heard over the speaker and the sound of her blowing her nose.

Zoë (*over the speakers*) Oh, dear God . . .

Jerome fades her down and moves away from the console. After a moment, Zoë returns with a handful of tissues, wiping her nose.

Sorry about that. Here I am. Back again. Anyway, where was I? Yes. Let me tell you about me. I'm originally an actress. Still am, actually. Only I also model to keep the wolf occasionally from the door. And I've been doing this escort thing lately which has been very interesting. Only I understood you didn't just want an escort, you wanted something slightly more. So that's probably why they thought of me. I did have some pictures and my CV to show you as well, only they took my briefcase. (*getting tearful again*) It wasn't even as if there was anything in there . . . Sorry. There were these terrifying girls, you see . . .

Jerome Girls?

Zoë Who attacked me. Just now. On my way here.

Jerome Attacked you?

Zoë Girls. Women. I don't know.

Jerome What did you do to them?

Zoë (*rather indignantly*) I didn't do anything. I was just quietly walking here from the station. It was a lovely day and I –

Jerome *Walked?*

Zoë Yes.

Jerome You walked from the railway station to here?

Zoë Yes. I've just said. And then these monsters – came from nowhere. What sort of area is this? Don't you have any police at all? Any security patrols?

Jerome Not any more.

Zoë Neighbourhood vigilantes?

Jerome Not lately.

Zoë You mean, this area is not protected? At all? What about this building?

Jerome The security staff kept being found dead. It got very expensive . . .

Zoë My God. Mrs Hope-Fitch might have warned me.

Jerome What did these people look like?

Zoë Oh. (*She shudders.*) Awful. No hair at all. Not on their heads, anyway. Masses of it everywhere else. And sort of purple paint across here. (*She indicates a band across the middle of her face.*)

Jerome No, that's a tattoo.

Zoë Really?

Jerome They're the Daughters of Darkness.

Zoë Oh. They were female then.

Jerome Most of them.

Zoë Well, whatever they were. I didn't stop to introduce myself. I hit the biggest of them and ran as fast as I could.

Jerome (*stunned*) You hit a Daughter of Darkness.

Zoë Yes. On the head. With my shoe.

Jerome Ah.

Zoë Am I supposed to have done something wrong?

Jerome Well, I don't think you should have done that.

Zoë Why not?

Jerome Well, you may have got them angry.

Zoë Angry? What about my briefcase . . .

Jerome Was there anything important in your briefcase?

Zoë No, I've just said, just my –

Jerome Then it would have been simpler to have given it to them.

Zoë But I don't see why I should have just handed it over. It was a present from my ex-boyfriend.

Jerome You may have made things difficult.

Zoë (*sarcastically*) Well, oh dear, oh dear. That's all I can say.

Jerome For you.

Zoë How do you mean?

Jerome Well. When you want to get back, they may not let you back . . .

Zoë You mean . . . ? But . . . ? How do I . . . ? I can't stay here indefinitely, can I?

Jerome No, no . . .

Zoë If they won't let me out, then we'd better call the police, hadn't we? Or whatever it is that passes for the law round here . . .

Jerome I'm afraid that's them. They pass for the law round here. They are the law.

Zoë The Daughters of –

Jerome Darkness. Yes. Currently.

Zoë Well, in that case, I'm sorry. I had no idea I was hitting a policeman, I can assure you. Where I come from they don't have purple stripes tattooed across their faces. You mean this is a genuine no-go area? My God, I've only read about them till now. Mind you, I've never been this far up the Northern Line before. Where are we? Somewhere extraordinary. Edgware. I went to Balham once but that's the other way, isn't it? How absolutely terrifying. So what happens now?

Jerome It's all right. I'll talk to them. I have a relationship with them. Of sorts. I do things for them, now and then.

Zoë Do what?

Jerome I help rig their sound gear when they have their big concerts. Things like that.

Zoë Oh, how interesting. Are you a roadie?

Jerome Not really. It's just a hobby.

Zoë What is it you do?

Jerome I'm a composer.

Zoë How amazing. Well. Hence – (*She indicates the sound console.*) – hence all that.

A sudden violent clang from one of the windows. Zoë is startled.

What on earth is that?

Jerome That's the Daughters.

Zoë What are they doing?

Jerome Throwing bricks at the window shutters. They're showing their displeasure.

Another clang. Zoë winces.

It's all right, they're half-inch steel. They'll probably keep this up for an hour or two. Till they think of something else to do.

Another clang.

Zoë Lucky you had your shutters closed.

Jerome Hardly lucky. They're welded to the window frames. They haven't been opened in four years.

Another clang. She winces.

Zoë They can't get in, can they?

Jerome Not unless they can jump thirty feet. It's all right.

Another clang. A silence.

I think they've gone.

They listen again.

Yes.

She relaxes slightly. A pause.

It's quieter where you live, then?

Zoë Yes, we're – pretty lucky in Kilburn. Regular armed patrols, masses of security cameras and so on. Very well lit, most of it. I mean, actually, the High Street's brighter at night than it is in the daytime. Providing you're in by dusk you're fine. I've had no trouble. Not really. Couple of burglaries, that's all. Oh, and my dog was shot, that was sad, but we think that was an accident. We think someone must have mistaken him for a police dog.

Jerome Shame. We?

Zoë My ex-boyfriend.

Jerome Ah.

Zoë He's still living with me but he's definitely my ex-boyfriend. Still. Enough about me. To business.

Jerome Yes.

Zoë You must tell me about this job you'd like me to do. Assuming you'd like me to do it, of course?

Jerome Yes.

Zoë You're still deciding?

Jerome Yes.

Zoë Oh, right. Sorry. Do you want me to walk up and down again?

Jerome No.

Zoë (*laughing*) I could do you a bit of Shakespeare. Any good? No.

Jerome I wonder if you'd mind – trying on some clothes.

Zoë (*suspiciously*) What sort of clothes?

Jerome Just normal clothes. Women's clothing.

Zoë I'm the one trying them on?

Jerome Yes.

Zoë Where? I mean, where do you want me to try them on?

Jerome Here.

Zoë You mean in front of you?

Jerome Yes.

Zoë You want me to change my clothes in front of you, is that it?

Jerome No. I want you to change into different clothes elsewhere. And then come in here so I can look at you wearing those different clothes in front of me. That I'll give you. To wear. You.

Zoë (*considering this proposition*) Yes, that sounds OK. I'm sorry. It's just occasionally, you know, we get – sort of weird requests, you know. The old favourites, you know. Nuns and gymslips.

Jerome Oh, no.

Zoë Fine.

Jerome Nothing like that.

Zoë No, sorry. Just thought I'd . . .

Jerome These are my wife's clothes.

A silence.

Zoë Your wife's?

Jerome Yes. They're quite ordinary clothes. They may be a bit out of fashion but –

Zoë Your wife, is she – ?

Jerome What?

Zoë Is she dead at all?

Jerome Dead?

Zoë Yes.

Jerome No, she's –

Zoë She's still alive?

Jerome Yes.

Zoë Living with you?

Jerome No. We're separated.

Zoë Oh. (*She breathes more easily.*) I'm sorry.

Jerome If you don't mind my saying so, you seem rather wary.

Zoë Well. Yes. I'm sorry. Look, this is my first time. As an escort. And I was assured that there was nothing further entailed, other than escorting. But then I get here and find you on your own, asking me to try on clothes. I got panicked. Sorry. I'm a little bit shaky still, I – Give me the clothes. I'll put them on for you. No more questions. (*slapping her own face*) Zoë, grow up and be your age.

Jerome Wait there.

He goes out to the bedrooms. Zoë looks about her.

Zoë (*to herself*) Nevertheless. This is a very, very creepy set-up. It has to be said.

She wanders about looking at the room for the first time, intrigued by the console. She is examining this when the doorbell rings and the nightmarish face of one of the Daughters of Darkness appears on the screen, leering into the video camera.

Oh, dear God, it's them . . . (*She hurries towards the bedroom doorway.*) Mr Watkins . . . Mr Watkins . . . I think it's them. They're at the door –

Jerome hurriedly returns with a long dress, similar to the one that Nan was wearing, a blouse and a pair of shoes. The face remains on the screen murmuring inaudible obscenities.

(*indicating the screen*) There! That's one of them.

Jerome Oh, she's OK. That's Rita. She's our local representative. She's fairly friendly. I'll have a word with her. (*handing her the clothes*) Try these. The dress should be all right. I don't know about the shoes. We can always buy some others.

Zoë Don't let her in here.

Jerome Certainly not. She's not that friendly.

She takes the bundle. He picks up his swordstick and goes out. After a second he appears on the screen and we see him and the Daughter of Darkness engaged in an inaudible, urgent-looking conversation. Zoë, rather nervous now she's alone, glances at the screen, notes Jerome is busy and decides to change where she is. She undresses to her slip. There is a small sound from the direction of the bedrooms. Zoë starts, glances at the screen and, hearing nothing more and seeing Jerome, relaxes again. She sits and taking up the clean blouse is fiddling with one of the fastenings on it, prior to putting it on, when Nan appears in the bedroom doorway. Zoë does not see her. Nan watches her for a moment, then produces her face flannel.

Nan (*playfully*) Booo! Nan's coming to getcher!

Zoë turns, sees her, but is too late to dodge. She screams. Nan sets about Zoë's face with her flannel. Zoë screams and struggles but her cries are mostly muffled. Unnoticed, Jerome finishes his on-screen conversation. In due course, he closes the front door on Rita and the screen blanks again.

Zoë (*spluttering*) Hot hoo hooing hoo hee? Het ho! Hoff! Het Hoff!

Nan That's better. That's better. There's a nice clean face.

As she says this, Nan goes off at speed to the kitchen.

Zoë (*calling after her, indignantly*) What were you doing?

What did you think you were doing? Oh, dear God.

She grabs up the clothes and prepares to flee towards the front door. She all but runs into Jerome.

There's a – There was a –

Jerome Anything wrong?

Zoë A woman just came in and washed my face –

Jerome Oh, yes.

Zoë What do you mean, 'oh, yes'? Who is she? What was she doing?

Jerome It's all right, she registered you as a child, you see. That's all.

A crash from the kitchen.

Unless she's told otherwise she registers everyone as children.

Zoë Who is she? Is she your wife?

Jerome No, no. She's a NAN 300F. She's a machine. She's just a machine.

Zoë *That* – was a machine? I don't believe it.

Jerome Oh, yes.

Zoë Well, what is it? Where did it come from?

Jerome It – er – it came from the man just down the hall, actually.

Zoë The man down the hall?

Jerome Yes.

Zoë I'm going. All right? I'll borrow these clothes. I promise to post them back. I'm sorry, I don't think this job is for me after all. I think I'll just stick around a little longer and hope for a fringe revival of *Hedda Gabler*. (*She makes to go into the hall.*)

Jerome Are you thinking of leaving?

Zoë I most certainly am. I'm not stopping here with that – deranged machine, thank you very much.

Jerome I – wouldn't go just yet –

Zoë Why?

Jerome Well, I don't think the Daughters would be too happy if you tried to leave. Not until your case comes up before Council.

Zoë Council?

Jerome They're considering it at the next Council.

Zoë When's that?

Jerome Midnight.

Zoë Midnight? I'm not sitting here till midnight . . . I mean, they can't . . . I've got masses of . . . They can just – they can simply go and –

   A single loud clang on the shutters.

(*facing the inevitable*) What happens at midnight, then?

Jerome They'll consider your case.

Zoë Do I have to be there?

Jerome Not unless you want to be.

Zoë No, thanks very much. What'll happen?

Jerome Rita thinks you'll get away with a fine. It would have been worse but – I put in a word.

Zoë (*sarcastically*) Lucky I met you, really.

325

Jerome Do you have money with you?

Zoë I'm not a complete idiot . . . I have credit cards on me.

Jerome (*curious*) Where?

Zoë Never you mind. Will they do?

Jerome Possibly. I know they take cheques. Listen, do you want to –

He indicates her state of undress.

Zoë Oh, yes. Since I appear to be here for the night, I'd better get dressed, I suppose.

Jerome There's a bedroom along there if you –

Zoë Where is the thing?

Jerome In the kitchen. It's all right, I'll keep her away.

Zoë Please do. (*She moves to the doorway.*) There aren't any more of them, are there?

Jerome No. Second door on the right.

Zoë Won't be long.

She goes off to the bedrooms. Jerome frowns, as he is still undecided about her. He crosses to the console and fades up a fader.

(*through the speakers, muttering*) . . . trapped in this place till midnight with a raving lunatic and a homicidal tin woman is hardly my idea of a good time . . .

Jerome fades her down. He stops a tape machine and rewinds it a little. He replays a section. The voices come over the speakers.

Zoë's recorded voice (*spluttering*) Hot hoo hooing hoo hee? Het ho! Hoff! Het Hoff!

326

Nan's recorded voice That's better. That's better. There's a nice clean face.

Zoë's recorded voice (*indignantly*) What were you doing? What did you think you were doing? Oh, dear God.

> *Jerome stops the tape and rewinds a fraction. He replays again.*

What were you doing? What did you think – (*He rewinds.*) What were you doing? (*He stops the tape.*)

Jerome No. (*He shakes his head.*) No, no, no.

> *He hears Zoë returning. He hastily switches on the recorder again and moves away from the console. Zoë enters. She has on the dress, blouse and shoes.*

Zoë The clothes are fine. The shoes are a fraction large but – What do you think?

> *She poses to allow him to inspect her. Jerome studies her from several angles.*

Jerome Does your hair – Does it come down at all?

Zoë Oh, yes. Do you want me to – ?

Jerome Would you mind?

Zoë No. (*She takes the clips from her hair.*) I don't usually wear it down because it makes me look about ten. But – if that's what you're looking for . . . There! Is that more the thing?

Jerome (*impressed*) It's – it's excellent.

Zoë Oh. Good. Well. Good.

Jerome Excellent.

Zoë You still haven't really said –

Jerome Would you mind laughing for me?

Zoë Laughing?

Jerome Is that possible?

Zoë Yes. Hang on. That's one of the things I'm never very good at. I can cry very well. Floods of tears at the drop of a hat. No? OK. (*She tries.*) Ha! Ha!

Jerome looks dubious.

Sorry, that was awful. I can do miles better than that. Ha! Ha! No. Think of something funny, Zoë. Ha! Ha! You don't happen to know any jokes, do you? No, I didn't think you did. Ho! Ho! Ho! God, this is awful. Thank heavens my drama teacher isn't here. Haw! Haw! Haw! (*as her laughs get progressively worse*) Look, could we leave it for a second and come back to it. I could do you my piece of Shakespeare . . .

Jerome No, that's quite all right. Don't worry at all. I realize it must be very –

Zoë Well, it is very difficult if you haven't any real – motivation, you see.

Jerome Oh, yes.

Zoë I mean, frankly, not an awful lot's happened to me recently that makes me want to scream with laughter.

Jerome Please don't worry at all.

Zoë So, you want me to walk about with my hair down, laughing in a long dress . . . Any other requirements? I mean, what's it all for? Are we selling something?

Jerome Please. Sit down.

Zoë Thank you.

She sits.

Jerome Just a moment.

He moves to the console again, this time looking for a
video recording from the cupboards. Zoë waits
patiently. Nan enters from the kitchen. She carries a
drinking glass and a plate, both of which are upside
down. Zoë, frozen, watches Nan.

Zoë (*in a whisper*) Mr Watkins . . . Mr Watkins . . .

Jerome (*from the cupboard*) Hallo?

Zoë It's – it's back again.

Nan (*putting the things down and turning to Zoë*) There
we are, doesn't that look lovely? Doesn't that look good?

Zoë (*nervously*) Oh, yes. Lovely, lovely . . .

Nan moves swiftly to her, producing a coloured bow
from her pocket which she fastens in the protesting
Zoë's hair.

(*As Nan does this*) Ah, now – don't you – don't you start
that – Mr Watkins . . .

Nan There! There! There!

Jerome (*seeing what's happening*) Oh, yes. Sorry – it's all
right, you're perfectly safe . . . Nan, stop.

Nan Stopped, Nan.

Nan freezes by Zoë, who escapes, looking slightly
ludicrous with her hair now in a top-knot.

Jerome She's still registering you as a child, that's all. We'll
re-register you, then she won't bother you.

Zoë Anything. I mean, I know my hair like this makes me
look younger but this is ridiculous . . .

Jerome Could you just stand facing her, so she can scan
you.

Zoë stands some distance away.

Zoë Like this?

Jerome A bit closer. Would you mind?

Zoë (*moving closer*) I don't like the way it's looking at me.

Jerome That's just your imagination. She's not thinking of anything. She's actually on standby.

Zoë Yes, I think I've acted with one or two people like this.

Jerome Nan, register.

Nan Register, Nan.

Jerome Not child. Not child.

Nan Not child. Registered, Nan.

Jerome There we are.

Zoë (*stepping away*) Is that it?

Jerome Yes. She's now recorded you as an adult – well, rather as a non-child – so she shouldn't bother you at all now.

Zoë (*removing the hair bow gingerly*) Was it designed to look after children?

Jerome Yes. Well, technically, narrower than that. To look after a child. It was felt that the programming got too complex to deal with several children. So it was designed to deal with just one individual. Then that was it. It shut down automatically and you had to give it a whole new factory programme. It was a safety measure to prevent one being reused, you see. On a mismatched child. Well, so this man was telling me –

Zoë This would be the man down the hall –

Jerome That's right.

Zoë Why did he give it to you?

Jerome Ah, well. He was a designer for the firm that made them. But they went bankrupt and he moved away. He really only left me this for spares. I got her working again myself. Just for my own amusement, really.

Zoë But how can it still work? I mean, I thought you said they shut down once they . . . ?

Jerome Yes, they do. I don't think this one's ever been matched to a child, though. She's a prototype.

Zoë You mean that's why she thought I was . . .

Jerome Yes. She lives in hope. Don't you, Nan?

Nan reactivates at the sound of her name.

Nan I'll do the beds now. Time to do the beds.

Nan goes off towards the bedrooms.

Jerome Random programming. If you don't tell her what to do, after a time she just selects something from her memory.

Zoë Seems quite sad, in a way. Wandering about, looking for a child to look after. Unfulfilled, almost. In so far as a machine can be unfulfilled, of course. I suppose no more so than, say, a coffee grinder that can't find any beans to grind could be described as unfulfilled.

Jerome Well, there's more to her than a coffee grinder.

Zoë Oh, yes. But one mustn't empathize with machines, must one? They say that's fatal. Mind you, I do that all the time. I shout and scream at my washing machine. (*She laughs.*) There! That was quite a good laugh, wasn't it? Why did they go bankrupt? The firm that made them? I'd have thought they'd have sold like hot cakes. What happened?

Jerome Er . . . They were very expensive. And – (*he seems evasive*) – there were teething problems.

Zoë (*suspiciously*) Were there?

Jerome (*reflectively*) I think the biggest mistake they made was to make a machine so sophisticated and then give it too small a function. I mean, I think a machine that complex needed more than just a child to look after. Otherwise there's bound to be stress.

Zoë Possibly. Yes. What an interesting theory. You mean, a machine with a certain sized brain can actually have too little to do?

Jerome Too little to think about.

Zoë Yes. Quite a theory.

Jerome That's why I tried for a time to –

Zoë To what?

Jerome Give her some other thoughts. Feed in other memories. Particularly with her having no chlid, I thought it might . . .

Zoë Did it help?

Jerome I don't know that it did, really. Still. It was worth a try.

A silence. He seems steeped in thought again. Zoë studies him.

Zoë Did you say you were a composer?

Jerome Right.

Zoë What sort of music do you compose?

Jerome All sorts.

Zoë I mean, is it – you know – popular sort of music?

Jerome Not very, no.

Zoë No, you know what I mean – as opposed to classical music?

Jerome I don't write classical music, either. I'd need to have been dead several hundred years . . .

Zoë Well, what do you write?

Jerome I write – modern music.

Zoë Would I know it? I mean, would I have heard any? Only it would be nice to tell people when I get home – that's if I get home – I met *the* Mr Watkins.

Jerome Jerome.

Zoë Jerome, right. *The* Jerome. Do call me Zoë.

Jerome Tell your friends that if they remember those baby-powder commercials they showed two or three years ago, ten times a night, every night for about eight months – then you met the man who wrote that music and wished to God he hadn't.

Zoë What you mean – the one with the singing babies?

Jerome nods wearily.

(*excitedly*) All those sweet little singing babies? But that was absolutely brilliant. Did you do the music for that? But that was absolutely fantastic. That was wonderful. That was so clever. That was completely and utterly *brilliant*. You're an absolute genius.

Jerome Thank you.

Zoë Oh, I wish they'd bring that back. It was so good.

Brilliant. Gosh. I'm very impressed. What else have you written?

Jerome About three hundred other pieces.

Zoë Any more with singing babies?

Jerome No, no. No more singing babies.

Zoë What else?

Jerome (*wearily*) Three string quartets. An unaccompanied cello sonata. Several pieces for synthesizer.

Zoë No, I don't know any of those. Tell me, I bet everybody asks you this – how did you get all those babies singing in tune?

Jerome looks at her incredulously.

Or is that a closely guarded secret?

Jerome Yes. I'm afraid it's very – closely guarded.

Zoë (*disappointed*) Oh. Brilliant, anyway.

Jerome (*without malice*) Would you describe yourself as an intelligent person?

Zoë Me?

Jerome Yes.

Zoë Heavens! I don't know. As an actress friend of mine used to say – it depends on the script, dear. (*She laughs.*)

Jerome (*nodding*) Yes. That's a good point. That's a very good point.

Zoë It's an intellectual role this then, is it?

Jerome No. Just reasonably intelligent. I was just wondering –

Zoë Oh, I can come over as pretty clever, you know. I did

Arkadina in *The Seagull* – do you know it?

Jerome No.

Zoë Chekhov. I mean she's often played as quite stupid but I don't think she is. Of course, I was much too young for her . . . (*Pause.*) Shall I walk around again for you?

Jerome No.

Zoë restlessly walks about.

Zoë And I played the wife in *See How They Run*. She's no fool, either. (*Pause. At the console, pretending to play a keyboard*) Diddly-diddly diddly dom. Is this where you compose?

Jerome Uh-huh.

Zoë Brilliant. What is it?

Jerome It's a digital audio system.

Zoë Ah-ha!

Jerome Which I use primarily for sampling and synthesizing aural sounds.

Zoë Brilliant. Whey-hey. Diddly-diddly –

Jerome Please don't touch anything. Please.

Zoë No, no. Sorry. I promise.

Nan comes through busily with a bundle of dirty sheets en route to the kitchen, humming to herself.

What on earth is it doing?

Jerome Oh, she'll do that for hours. It keeps her happy.

Zoë Oh. (*Slight pause.*) Are you still deciding?

Jerome Yes.

335

Zoë OK. Don't mind me. I can't go anywhere, anyway. (*She studies the console; reading*) What do 'bedroom one', 'bedroom two' and 'bathroom' mean.

Jerome Just an experiment.

Zoë Something you were composing?

Jerome That's right.

Zoë A bathroom suite. (*She laughs.*)

Jerome (*meaning her laugh*) Very good, very good.

Zoë Pretty good for me. (*She laughs again.*) I very rarely make jokes.

Jerome Jokes?

Zoë Just then. I made a joke. Didn't you – ? Oh, you meant the laugh? You liked the laugh?

Jerome Very good. Excellent. (*He has risen.*)

Zoë Thank you. I'll put that on my CV. (*scowling*) When I get some more done. Special skills include laughing.

Jerome Let me show you something . . .

> *Jerome goes to the console and starts the video recording he has located earlier. In a moment, the screen lights up. A young girl of about nine appears on the screen. Conventionally pretty, fair-haired and slightly self-conscious.*

Young Geain Hallo, Daddy. This is Geain. I'm just calling to say thank you very much for all my presents. They were all really live. Especially the disc voucher which I'm going to spend on the new Jamie Butterscotch and one by The Grind. Mummy gave me a long dress which is really live. It's yellow and grey and Granny and Grandpa gave me some live jewellery to go with it and I'm going to wear that tonight because we're going out to dinner to Del – to Del something – I can't remember. I wish you were coming, Daddy. And I miss you very much. And I hope to see you soon. Bye. Love from Geain. (*She makes a big cross in the air with her finger.*) That's a kiss.

Jerome stops the tape and looks at Zoë who realizes she is supposed to comment.

Zoë That's your daughter?

Jerome Yes.

Zoë Lovely.

Jerome Thank you.

Slight pause.

Zoë I couldn't play her.

Jerome Oh, no . . .

Zoë You don't want that?

Jerome No.

Zoë Oh, good. (*Pause.*) How old is she?

Jerome Geain? She'll be thirteen.

Zoë Thirteen? She looks quite young for her age.

Jerome Oh, that was recorded – some time ago.

Zoë I see.

Jerome That was probably the last occasion I was permitted to see her.

Zoë Really?

Jerome Her mother – my wife wouldn't let her phone me after that. She wouldn't let me visit her. She wouldn't let Geain visit me.

337

Zoë Why not?

Jerome Why not? Because my wife is a selfish, vindictive, unforgiving bitch.

Zoë Oh, I see. Yes. (*A pause.*) Do you want me to play her, then?

Jerome (*angrily*) No, I don't want you to play her.

Zoë No, right. Sorry, sorry.

Nan comes through again with the same bundle of sheets, bound for the bedroom once more.

I think I'd better go and give her a hand in a minute.

She laughs feebly. Jerome is silent again.

It's a nice name, Jane. *Jane Eyre.* We did that one. I played the mad Mrs Rochester. Behind the panelling. Not much of a part. I should have played Jane, really. I'd have been really good.

Jerome G–E–A–I–N.

Zoë Sorry?

Jerome Ours is spelt G–E–A–I–N. At her mother's insistence.

Zoë How unusual. What is it? Gaelic?

Jerome No, just pretentious.

Zoë I'd love to have children of my own. Well, for about twenty minutes, anyway. Sometimes I think, wouldn't it be lovely to hear them rushing about the flat, laughing and yelling? And then – at about six in the morning I think, no, it wouldn't at all, I can't think of anything worse. But I suppose with the right man – someone who'd share them – do all the cleaning up – possibly they'd be everything I ever wanted. But I doubt it. I suppose you're either maternal or you aren't. I know which I am.

Jerome (*who has been staring at her, coming to a sudden decision*) All right. We'll give it a try. The proposition is this. I want you to live here with me for twenty-four hours as my loving, caring companion –

Zoë Ah, now, listen, I thought we'd been through all that –

Jerome In just about a week's time – my wife and my daughter, together with some – petty official from the Social Services – are coming here, to this flat, for the first time in four years. And between them, my wife and this official will decide whether or not they consider this a fit place and, more important, whether they consider me a fit person for her to spend time with in the future. On their one visit everything rests. If I fail to meet their high standards of homeliness and hygiene, then it's unlikely I shall be allowed to see my daughter again.

Zoë Unless you visit her.

Jerome Visit her? Where?

Zoë Where she lives.

Jerome She lives with my wife. How can I visit there? The woman loathes the sight of me.

Zoë She's coming here, though.

Jerome She's coming here to make damn sure she prevents any future visit by Geain. I've told you, Corinna is a very vindictive, unforgiving woman.

Zoë Unforgiving of what?

Jerome (*evasively*) Unforgiving of – anything you care to mention.

Zoë So you need to present them with a solid domestic front.

Jerome I want to present them with a relationship that's so perfect that not only can she not find fault with it, but it doubles her up with jealousy. It leaves her eating her heart out with envy and frustration.

Zoë Yes. (*tentatively*) If you don't mind my saying so – it's beginning to sound a wee bit vindictive on both sides –

Jerome How do you mean?

Zoë Well –

Jerome I have cause. I have cause to be vindictive –

Zoë Oh, yes. Only –

Jerome (*excitedly*) She's not the one who's been forbidden to see her own daughter. Denied all those precious moments watching her child grow up. She's not the one who's been left to live alone in an empty flat. Unable to work – unable to write a single note of music for four years. Four years!

Zoë (*alarmed*) Yes.

Jerome Nothing.

Zoë No.

Jerome And you talk about me being vindictive. (*turning on her, angrily*) Who's side are you on? You're taking her side and you haven't even met her . . .

Zoë No, I'm not. Honestly, I'm not –

Jerome Do you want this job or don't you?

Zoë Yes, yes . . .

Jerome Because if you don't, I can quite easily . . .

Zoë No, I do. I want it very much. I do honestly. Please, please, please!

A silence. Jerome simmers down.

Jerome (*muttering*) God, you bloody women. You don't half stick together, don't you?

Zoë Not really.

Jerome My sister, right or wrong. Yes?

Zoë Not at all. Don't be –

Jerome What? Don't be what?

Zoë (*changing tack*) I think I could be the perfect female companion. For twenty-four hours, anyway. I think I could do that. Not much longer though. Mind you, my ex-boyfriend would claim I couldn't even manage it for twenty-four hours. (*expansively*) Hallo! Welcome! Welcome! Welcome!

Jerome (*anxiously*) Yes, I don't want anything too . . .

Zoë No, well, I'll work on it. Do you think I should wear glasses? Do you think it's a glasses part?

Jerome No, I don't.

Zoë No. Still, I need something. I always need some little thing to start off with. Some actors always start with the shoes. (*gazing at her feet*) I don't think I'll start with these, somehow. I can do quite a deep voice. Shall I give her a deep voice? Like this?

Jerome (*alarmed by her enthusiasm*) No, no, please. Just your normal voice. Just be your normal self. Please.

Zoë (*calming down*) OK. I could do the limp like that thing out there . . . (*She mimics Nan's walk*) No, only joking. Well, OK. I accept.

Jerome Good.

Zoë Actually, it's quite handy me being stuck here. I

mean, it gives me a chance to research, you know. Talk to you. Find out what constitutes your perfect mate.

Jerome So long as we convince them.

Zoë Oh, yes. Only it helps if I don't pour you a large Scotch when you're a teetotaller. Those sort of things tend to give the game away. (*Pause.*) Or cooking you chicken when you're a vegetarian. (*finding the burnt tinfoil dish*) Or baking home-made cakes when you're on a diet . . . Is this one of those new self-cooking dishes?

Jerome That's right.

Zoë How was it?

Jerome Delicious.

Zoë (*doubtfully examining the burnt dish*) Yes. (*Pause.*) Talking of food and drink. Would it sound awful – ? Only I did start out very early this morning. And my ex-boyfriend had polished off the muesli.

Jerome Oh yes, certainly, I'll see what we have. I've just stocked up, there's quite a bit of frozen stuff.

Zoë No, I'll do it. Don't bother.

Jerome That's OK, I'll . . .

Zoë No, no, please. Let me. Start getting into the role. Little woman in kitchen. (*She starts for the kitchen, then stops.*) Where's the thing?

Jerome In the bedroom.

Zoë OK. Watch this then. A startling character transformation.

> Zoë *marches out to the kitchen while Jerome watches rather apprehensively. She comes straight back again.*

I'm sorry, I'm not going in there. My God, what have you

been doing?

Jerome What?

Zoë It's *disgusting* out there. It's *revolting*. It's swimming in – yuurrrk. Uggh! Ugghh! It's your ghastly machine. It must be.

Jerome She does – spill things.

Zoë Spill things? She's tipped whole piles of festering food all over everything. You should be dead, you know. It's a miracle you're alive . . . I tell you, that machine is a –

Jerome All right, I'll do it.

Zoë I'm not eating *anything* from there –

Jerome It's instant stuff. It's sealed. I'll just put it in the oven.

Zoë Well, make sure we open it in here . . .

Jerome Whatever you say.

He goes out to the kitchen. Zoë, left alone, decides to practise her role. She takes up the stance of a beaming hostess.

Zoë (*brightly*) Hallo! Hallo! Hallo! Welcome! Welcome! Welcome! Sorry. I completely lost track of the time. Typical. (*turning as if hearing someone calling*) What's that? Just a tick, darling. I'm coming, darling.

As she is doing this, Nan comes from the bedrooms. She has finally got rid of the sheets. She is heading towards the hall. But she sees Zoë and stops, staring at her impassively.

(*seeing Nan*) Oh, hallo, I was just . . .

Nan moves off to the hall and goes out.

Mind your own business, anyway.

She is about to start again when the phone rings.

Jerome (*off*) Leave that. It'll go on to answer.

Zoë waits. Lupus appears on the screen after the phone has rung a couple of times. He is seated at a drum kit which he has set up around his video machine. We can see part of this. He's slightly more wild-eyed than before and possibly suffering from the effects of some stimulant. Zoë stares at him incredulously.

Lupus (*from the video*) Hiya, Jerry. I seem to have got the old answering machine again – but on the offchance you're there and would like to register as the only person left in the world who is still prepared to talk to me, here I am. Calling on my final life raft, my only friend, my single ray of hope in the dark endless tunnel some of us laughingly refer to as life. I'm afraid it's down to you, Jerry. You stand between one man and the end of his tether. His final straw. His last burning bridge.

Under this, Jerome returns from the kitchen with two packets.

Jerome Do you want Breast of Grouse en Croûte or Gourmet Chicken with Almonds and Wild Strawberry Sauce?

Zoë (*not inspired by either*) Grouse.

Jerome There is Sliced Beef in Clam Sauce.

Zoë Grouse.

Jerome OK. I think I'll try this chicken.

Zoë There's an extraordinary man on your phone in a desperate state.

Jerome Yes, I know. It takes twenty seconds. Can you wait?

Jerome goes off to the kitchen. Lupus has been going under this.

Lupus You may have gathered that my wife has gone. My son has gone. Our furniture has gone. Everything. But for the last time, Jerry. Whoever she's with this time, she can stay with him. I'm not letting her back in. Not this time. She chose to leave, by the way, whilst I went for a job which incidentally I never got. The dynamic geriatric Finchley tea-dance trio decided they could manage without me. Their Arts Council grant came through and they celebrated by buying a drum machine. (*He laughs heartily and mirthlessly.*) So, here we are, sitting amongst this load of obsolete gear (*smashes a cymbal*) – that nobody wants – (*hits a drum*) – why hear the real thing when you can hear a synthesized mock-up – (*another whack of a cymbal*) – I thought you might like to hear it, Jerry, before I burn it all – the last live drum solo, as played by man. The very last.

Jerome returns. He holds a cloth round the two now very hot tinfoil dishes. Zoë, who has been watching the screen transfixed, springs up. Lupus is preparing himself to start a drum solo.

Jerome Look out, they're hot.

Zoë Sorry, I'll – clear some space . . . There's this extraordinary man. Is he all right?

Jerome (*dismissively*) Yes, he's fine. He's always like that.

Lupus starts to play the drums.

Oh, for God's sake, Lupus!

Jerome dives for the console and turns down the volume. Lupus thrashes away silently for some minutes under the next.

Hang on. I'll get some cutlery.

Zoë gives him a look.

I'll wash it first, don't worry.

Jerome goes out. Nan has entered, holding the nozzle of a vacuum cleaner but unattached to any machine. She stops behind Zoë.

Zoë (*calling to Jerome*) I think I'd feel happier if you could boil everything before I touch it, please.

Nan (*quietly and venomously*) Making ourselves comfortable, are we, Deborah?

Zoë (*jumping round in alarm*) What?

Nan I know what you're after, dear, and you're not going to have him. If you want Jerome, the only way you're going to get him is over my dead body, you calculating little trollop.

Zoë (*very indignant*) I beg your pardon.

Nan You'd better watch your step, Deborah darling, or one of these nights you're going to wake up with your throat cut.

Nan moves away and goes off to the bedrooms. Zoë stares at her in horror. She clutches her throat. Jerome returns with some knives and forks and two tins of beer.

Jerome Here.

Zoë (*recoiling*) Ah!

Jerome You OK?

Zoë Yes – it was – hot.

Jerome Good. I brought some beer. I thought you'd prefer the can rather than our glasses. (*He opens both the meals.*) That's yours, I think.

Zoë Thank you.

Jerome (*examining his own dish*) Yes, I think these must be the wild strawberries. Do you want beer?

Zoë Please.

Jerome opens the beers.

Jerome Go ahead, do start. Before it gets rusty.

She tries it.

Zoë Mmm! Not bad.

Jerome Hot enough?

Zoë Perfect.

They eat.

How long were you married? To Corinna?

Jerome Eleven years.

Zoë God. A lifetime. Must have felt very strange. Splitting up.

Jerome Yes.

Zoë I mean, even if you loathed the sight of each other.

Jerome Yes.

Zoë Was she a musician?

Jerome Corinna? (*He laughs.*) No. She was my bank manager. Until I moved my account.

Zoë Do you miss her?

Jerome No.

Zoë Would you ever consider going back to her?

Jerome Look, what the hell is this? A census?

Zoë I just want to know. I need to know.

Jerome Why? Why do you want to know all that?

Zoë Because I'll need to. If I'm to behave like someone who's been living with you for some time, I'll need to know.

Jerome Well, you don't need to know all that. I'll tell you what you need to know, don't worry.

Zoë OK. Fine. Fire ahead.

A pause.

Jerome (*grumpily*) What do you want to know?

Zoë No, no. I'm not asking any more questions. You tell me.

Jerome It's all right . . .

Zoë No, if I ask questions you just bite my head off. You can tell me, go on.

Jerome I'm sorry. I – haven't really talked to anyone – well, not face to face – for some time, you see. Since they fully automated the hypermarket, I don't think I've spoken to anyone for months. So, you'll have to make allowances.

Zoë I understand.

Jerome So. If you want to ask questions. Please.

Zoë Right.

They eat.

Jerome Go ahead.

Zoë I will. I'm just trying to think of some. Why did your wife leave you?

Jerome I don't think that's any of your damn business.

Zoë Oh, terrific . . . Forget it. I'll just make it up. I'll make it all up. Just don't blame me if it all goes totally wrong. When it turns out that I don't know vital facts about you that I should know –

Jerome I just don't see that you need to –

Zoë Look. If it transpires that your wife left you because for eleven years – or whatever it was – you drove her absolutely mad whistling in the nude at breakfast time – then that's something I ought to know. Because it just might crop up in conversation between the two of us. 'Darling, doesn't he drive you mad the way he whistles in the nude at breakfast?' 'No, not at all, dear, I love it, I find it totally refreshing . . . '

Jerome All right, all right. My wife left me because . . . She claimed I drove her mad –

Zoë Whistling in the nude at breakfast – ? Sorry.

Jerome She wasn't, in the end, prepared to live with a creative person. That's what it boiled down to. She wasn't prepared to fit in with the lifestyle of a creative entity. Such as myself. That's all. I'm not saying she was a selfish woman. Nor am I saying she was a woman who refused to adapt or even begin to understand the pressures that – a creative person can undergo. I'm not saying that about her. After all, why should she? She's just a bloody bank manager.

Zoë (*sympathetically*) No. And you probably didn't understand a lot about banking, did you?

Jerome (*sharply*) What's that got to do with it?

Zoë (*quickly*) Nothing.

Jerome Still, I'm sure she'll make some – chief clerk – a very good wife.

Zoë (*deciding this isn't a line worth pursuing further*) I'd love to hear some of your music. Could I, possibly?

Jerome Yes. Perhaps. Sometime. As I say, I haven't written anything for – ages.

Zoë Since they left?

Jerome Nearly.

Zoë Four years. Heavens. You really did need them, then, in some ways? Well, your muse did.

Jerome Geain. I needed Geain. I need her back more than anything in the world.

Zoë, for the first time, notices the signs of his inner distress.

Zoë (*moved*) Well, I'll – do my best for you. (*Pause.*) Did she inspire your Singing Babies? I bet she did.

Jerome *First Sounds*. Yes. (*Pause.*) I recorded her over several days . . .

Zoë You mean it was actually her? Actually Geain you used?

Jerome Yes. That was the first occasion I started using purely natural sounds – sampling and treating them. It took months.

Zoë Fancy. And all that for what? Thirty seconds?

Jerome Thirty seconds? It was a forty-five-minute piece originally.

Zoë Oh, I see. There's more?

Jerome Much, much, much more.

Zoë You can't write at all, then? No ideas?

Jerome I know what I want to write. But I don't know how to do it.

Zoë What?

Jerome (*more to himself*) I know what it's going to be. I know what I want to say. It's how to say it. I haven't got the sound. I haven't heard it. Three years and I'm still waiting to hear the sound.

Zoë What do you want to say?

Jerome I want to say – what I want to say is – well, I want to say – love. Really.

Zoë (*mystified*) Love?

Jerome Yes.

Zoë I see. What sort of love?

Jerome Just – generally. Love. You know . . .

Zoë (*puzzled*) No, I'm not sure I –

Jerome (*tetchily*) Love. You've heard of love, I presume?

Zoë Yes, yes. Sorry, only you're not putting it awfully well.

Jerome (*irritably*) Of course I'm not putting it awfully well. If I could put it awfully well, there wouldn't be a problem. I want to express the feeling of love in an abstract musical form. In such a way that anyone who hears it – *anyone* – no matter what language they speak – no matter what creed or colour – they will rcognize it – and respond to it – and relate it to their own feelings of love that they have or they've experienced at some time – so they say – yes, my God, that's it! That's what it is! And maybe who knows, consequently, there might be a bit more of it.

Zoë is spellbound by this.

Zoë How wonderful. (*She reflects for a second.*) It must have been a bit like this, sitting with Beethoven.

Jerome I doubt it.

Zoë That's how I imagine it, anyway.

Jerome I don't think Beethoven sat down all that much. He used to stamp about the place, shouting.

Zoë There you are, then. You're both terribly similar.

Pause. They have both finished their meal.

Oh, it must be just so awful for you. Having all those ideas and not being able to express them. Poor you.

Jerome looks at her.

I mean, I know sort of how you feel. I get that way if I'm just writing a letter. I want to say something really – I don't know – heartfelt to someone. And it all comes out like the inside of some awful Christmas card. Happy tidings, boyfriend dear. At this joyous time of year. When what you mean to say is – I love you incredibly much and I'd do just about everything I could in the world to make you happy and I just want to be with you and stay close to you for ever and ever and ever – And you try and write that down so it makes sense and what do you get? Happy tidings, boyfriend dear . . . (*aware of his gaze*) What's the matter?

Jerome Nothing.

Zoë Are you having second thoughts?

Jerome No. Third thoughts.

Zoë (*slightly apprehensive*) Oh? What are those?

Jerome I was just thinking – you're a very nice person, really. Only, saying it like that, I think I sound rather like one of your Christmas cards.

A pause. Zoë is a little ill at ease.

Zoë I think I'll sing my song for you now, if you don't mind.

Jerome (*rather dismayed*) Really?

Zoë Well, it's either that or my Shakespeare. And I don't think Queen Margaret would go down frightfully well after chicken and strawberries. (*arranging herself*) It's all right, it's quite short . . . (*making a false start*) You're not my – Hang on. (*She sorts out her first note.*) Right. Here we go. (*Sings:*)
You're not my first love . . .
It would only be a lie if I pretended –
In the past there have been others
Who have slept between these covers
But I promise
Though you're far too late in life to be my first love,
You'll be my last love.
I swear to you, you're gonna be my last love . . .

She finishes her song. Silence.

Well. It has this great accompaniment. Diddly-diddly diddly dom.

She smiles at him awkwardly. Jerome rises and moves to her. He stands by her, then kisses her. They break and stare at each other.

You taste of wild strawberries.

Jerome You taste of grouse.

Zoë laughs. Jerome smiles one of his rare smiles.

Do you want any more?

Zoë More?

Jerome Food?

Zoë No.

Jerome Any more anything of anything?

Zoë (*without hesitation*) Yes, please.

Jerome Well, shall we . . . ? What would you prefer to do? I mean, would you like to – here? Or – ?

Zoë I don't mind. Here's fine if – you –

Jerome Or there's the bedroom, that might be –

Zoë Sure. That's fine. Will she have made the bed by now, do you think?

   She laughs.

Jerome Oh, no, that's no problem. Those sheets were just for her to –

Zoë Well, fine. Shall we go in there?

Jerome (*unmoving*) Yes, yes, yes.

Zoë You want to?

Jerome Oh, yes. You bet.

Zoë I mean, we don't have to if you – ?

Jerome No, no, no . . . (*laughing*) Useful research, whatever else . . .

Zoë (*drawing back, concerned*) Oh, I wasn't . . . just for that.

Jerome No, no. I was joking.

Zoë I mean, I really want to. I don't – if I don't want to . . . I don't do that sort of thing.

Jerome I know, I'm sure. Nor do I.

Zoë Good. (*Pause.*) Well – shall we . . . ?

Jerome Why not?

*They both move towards the bedrooms. As they do,
Nan enters clasping the section of vacuum cleaner. Zoë
jumps. Nan passes them, crosses to the hall and goes
out.*

She's OK.

Zoë I wonder. Would you think it awful of me – if I asked
you to switch it off?

Jerome Switch her off?

Zoë Just while we were – just while we were in –

Jerome It's not very good for her, to keep switching her on
and off, you see . . .

Zoë No, no, I'm sure. It's just if it did happen to come in
while we were – I think I'd probably scream or something –

Jerome Well, I could disengage her. That would put her on
standby. I'd disconnect her movement functions but leave
her brain working . . .

Zoë (*not wanting the details*) Yes, fine. That sounds fine. I
wouldn't want to damage her.

Jerome (*calling*) Nan, here.

Nan (*off*) Coming, Nan.

Nan enters from the hall.

Zoë Did that face come with it? I mean, is that how it
came out of the factory?

Jerome No, I – tinkered around with it. You can easily
alter it, you just heat it first with a hair drier.

Zoë Well, I think you could have chosen a better face. It
looks like Mrs Danvers.

Jerome Nan, sit.

Nan Sitting, Nan.

Nan sits.

Jerome Nan, Function Command Jerome Disengage.

Nan gives a slight beep.

Nan Disengaged.

Jerome Nan, walk.

She gives a little beep and a twitch but stays in the chair.

(*trying again*) Nan, walk.

Nan beeps and twitches again but stays still.

There you are, you see. Can't move at all.

Zoë No. (*She seems a little guilty at what she's requested Jerome to do.*)

Jerome I'll just check – things are off.

He goes to the console. He checks, unseen by Zoë, his recording machines. Zoë stands in the doorway, waiting for him. Nan's head turns slowly and looks at her.

Zoë Ah!

Jerome What is it?

Zoë She's just moved her head.

Jerome Well, yes, she can still move her head. That's all right, isn't it?

Zoë Oh yes, that's quite all right. I just wasn't expecting it.

She starts fumbling under her dress.

Jerome (*watching her*) Are you all right?

Zoë (*having difficulty*) Yes, I was – I was just going to show you my – Show you my – (*She produces a string of plastic credit-type cards from her thigh wallet.*) There. Better get it over with. (*pointing to one green card in particular among the string of others*) My Green Card. OK?

Jerome Oh, yes . . .

Zoë I had a full check. Last month. I'm all clear. CBH 1.

Jerome Fine. Good. Congratulations.

Zoë Well. You can't be too careful. Can you?

Jerome No.

    Slight pause.

Zoë Are you – ? Have you got – ?

Jerome Oh, yes – somewhere. It's in the – I put it in the – It's around . . .

Zoë (*slightly doubtful*) Good. (*making to move*) Well . . .

Jerome After you.

Zoë Thank you. (*as she goes*) You still want to do this, don't you?

Jerome (*switching off the lights and following her*) Oh, yes . . . You bet. Rather.

Zoë (*off*) Because if you don't, I shan't be hurt –

Jerome (*off*) Oh, I do. I do. Do you?

Zoë (*off*) Oh, yes . . . You bet.

    The bedroom door closes and their voices are cut off. Nan sits alone. She is lit, primarily from the console lights which start blinking and flashing in response to the unheard sounds in the bedroom. The light patterns become increasingly vigorous.

Nan (*slowly and with difficulty*) Deb–or–rah . . . Deb–or–rah . . .

As the lights continue to flicker on her face – blackout.

SCENE TWO

A few hours later. It is probably morning, though it's impossible to tell. Nan has gone. Jerome sits on the stool which is swivelled to one side of the console. He is working at a stretch of keyboard. He is wearing headphones, so there is no sound. He grunts occasionally to himself as he works. Nan swings in from the kitchen with another of her upside-down mugs of coffee. She puts it down near Jerome.

Nan Nice cup of cocoa. Don't let it get cold, now.

Jerome, even if he hears her, ignores her he is so absorbed. Nan returns to the kitchen. After a moment, Zoë, rather crumpled from sleep, comes from the bedroom wrapped in a blanket. She watches Jerome for a moment. She moves behind him and kisses the top of his head gently.

Jerome (*rather loudly because of his headphones*) Nan, stop! Stop that at once.

Zoë pulls back, hurt. Jerome realizes belatedly that it was unlikely to have been Nan. He turns and takes off the headphones.

Zoë Good morning.

Jerome Good morning.

Zoë How long have you been up?

Jerome (*shrugging*) Oh . . .

Zoë I've slept for hours.

Jerome Yes . . .

Zoë Well . . .

Jerome Yes . . .

Zoë (*kissing him*) Good morning.

Jerome Morning.

> *Zoë stands smiling at him. He seems rather embarrassed.*
> *There is a characteristic crash from the kitchen.*

Zoë (*drily*) Mrs Danvers is up bright and early, I hear.

Jerome Well, she's got a busy day ahead.

Zoë I'm glad she didn't bring me early-morning tea.

Jerome She's been known to. It's not an experience worth repeating. By the way, we had a visit from Rita. It's all fixed.

Zoë Thank goodness.

Jerome The Daughters have agreed your fine. Five hundred pounds.

Zoë (*aghast*) Five hundred pounds!

Jerome It was either that or fifty lashes. I said you'd prefer the fine.

Zoë Well, the Blaise Gillespie Agency is footing the bill for that, I can tell you. They should have warned me.

Jerome You'll need this. (*He picks up a grubby coloured card and hands it to her.*) It's your pass card. To get you back to the railway station.

Zoë (*reading*) 'This is to – certify – I the undersigned have paid my debt to society.' Oh, really.

Jerome Yes, you have to sign it, too. Don't lose it.

Zoë I'd be a lot more impressed if they could spell 'certify'.

She puts the card down.

Jerome I'll come with you. See you off. If you'd like me to. Do you want anything? Tea or anything?

Zoë No. I must get dressed. I need to be back by midday. I've got an audition. It's a new musical. Set in a women's prison. *Hooray for Holloway* – Well, that's what everyone's calling it, anyway. I think I'll do my song for them. What do you think?

Jerome Sure. Why not?

Zoë seems reluctant to move. They stare at each other.

I – don't know what to say, really.

Zoë I – was wondering. Whether I should be coming back? Whether you'd like me to come back again? I mean, sooner than – like this evening? Or tomorrow? We've still got a lot to discuss, haven't we? If we're going to get everything right for this meeting with your wife? And your daughter? What do you think? I mean, I'm not trying to push. Just as you like. What do you say?

A silence.

I don't mind. Only do say something. Please.

Jerome kisses her gently.

Is that a yes?

Jerome Is that what you'd like?

Zoë Yes.

Jerome Then, that's what I'd like.

Zoë Good. (*Pause.*) Just one thing.

Jerome What?

Zoë Who the hell is Deborah?

Jerome (*startled*) Who?

Zoë Deborah. Who is she?

Jerome No idea at all. Never heard of her.

Zoë Well. Somebody has, that's all I can say. Mrs Danvers keeps muttering her name at me every time she passes.

Jerome I can't think why she'd do that.

Zoë No, right. I must just remind her of something she used to know. Her old pal, Debbie, the deep freezer perhaps. (*She watches him for a second.*) Last night, was that the first time you – you hadn't made love to anyone for some time, had you?

Jerome Three years.

Zoë (*not unkindly*) Well, you'll soon get the hang of it again, I'm sure. (*realizing she may have put this rather badly*) So. I'll get dressed. OK?

Jerome Yes.

He plays with some of the knobs on the console.

Zoë You all right?

Jerome Yes.

Zoë What were you doing? You weren't composing something were you?

Jerome Not really. I – er – (*He waves his hand at the console and presses a start button. From the speakers a fragment of a composition that Jerome has been working* *on. It is, recognizably, Zoë's laugh, recorded, sampled and re-treated in a simple, gentle, melodic line.*)

Zoë (*recognizing herself*) Is that me?

Jerome Yes.

> *They listen. It is quite short. It finishes. Jerome stops the machine.*

Zoë That was me.

Jerome That's right.

Zoë When did you do that?

Jerome While you were asleep.

Zoë But when did you record me? Yesterday?

Jerome That's right.

Zoë You secretly recorded my laugh? My awful laugh?

Jerome It's a very nice laugh.

Zoë Watch it. I shall demand repeat fees. (*She smiles.*) It's very good.

Jerome (*smiling*) Thank you. It's a sketch at the moment.

Zoë Terribly clever. It's all done with that machine?

Jerome Yes.

Zoë Brilliant. Brilliant machine. I'll tell you something, do you think when it goes – (*hums a few notes*) – it wouldn't be better if it went – (*demonstrates something different*) – don't you think?

Jerome (*guardedly*) How do you mean?

Zoë Like – (*hums her improvement again*).

Jerome It doesn't go – (*hums her improvement*).

Zoë I know it doesn't. It goes – (*hums her version of the original*).

Jerome No, it doesn't go – (*hums her version of the original*). It goes – (*hums the original*).

Zoë Well – (*hums the original*) – then. I still think it would be better if it went – (*hums her improvement*).

Jerome No, it wouldn't.

Zoë It would.

Jerome It wouldn't.

Zoë Why not?

Jerome Because it doesn't go like that. That's not the way it goes.

Zoë I know it doesn't. I'm saying, perhaps it should.

Jerome (*angry now*) No, it shouldn't. It goes the way it goes because it goes that way –

Zoë Why? Why does it, necessarily?

Jerome (*yelling*) Because that's the way it goes, that's why. Because I wrote it that way and I'm the one that matters.

Zoë (*defensively*) All right! Yes! (*A pause.*) There's no need to shout at me. I'm not your machine, you know.

Jerome (*muttering*) At least she doesn't try and rewrite my music for me.

Zoë I'm sorry. I thought you might like a suggestion. Obviously you don't. Fine. (*Pause.*) Obviously, you think that's perfect. Fine. You're the expert.

Jerome (*testily*) Right.

> *Nan comes from the kitchen to the hall carrying a floor-mop handle without the mop attached. She goes out*

busily. Zoë stares.

It's her day to mop the hall.

Zoë Oh, good. I'm sure that floor could really do with a good scrape. Is that all you've done, then?

Jerome What?

Zoë Just that bit? Is that all you've written?

Jerome No.

Zoë Oh.

Jerome I started a second sketch.

Zoë Good. (*Pause.*) Well, let's hear it then. I won't say a word, I won't say a word, I promise.

Jerome (*reluctantly*) It's not finished.

He plays her the second sketch. It is, like the first, based on Zoë but is very different in mood – obviously this time based on a recording of Zoë's love sounds. She listens thunderstruck. It finishes. Jerome switches off the machine again.

Zoë Is that what I think it is?

Jerome Yes.

Zoë You recorded that while we were – ?

Jerome Yes.

Zoë I don't believe it. You mean, while we were making love you just calmly leant out of bed and switched on a tape recorder?

Jerome No –

Zoë No wonder you didn't seem to have your mind on the job –

364

Jerome Of course I didn't.

Zoë Then how else did you – ?

Jerome I didn't switch it on specially. They're on all the time.

Zoë All the time?

Jerome Yes.

Zoë What, you mean like now?

Jerome Yes. All the time.

Zoë What, everywhere? In the – everywhere?

Jerome I keep saying. Yes.

Zoë (*aghast*) You're sick. You're diseased. You're perverted –

Jerome That's the way I work – That's how I work.

Zoë Well, I'm sorry, that's not the way I work. You switch that thing off right now or I'm leaving.

Jerome I can't switch it off. Look, it has to be on, don't you see? What's recorded here is – is what I use later. Some of it. Not all of it, obviously.

Zoë Then you can just record parts –

Jerome How do I know which parts to record? Jesus –

Zoë Well, I can tell you the parts you're not going to record. You are not recording me making love, me having a bath or me in the loo – that's three for a start . . . My God, did you do this sort of thing to your wife? To your daughter?

Jerome Yes.

Zoë Didn't they mind? Yes, of course they minded, they

walked out on you. What about Deborah, what did she have to say?

Jerome (*shouting*) For the tenth time, I don't know any Deborah!

A loud crash from the hall.

Zoë Well, somebody evidently does. Why don't you ask old Mrs Danvers about her?

She stamps off to the bedroom. Nan comes from the hall, almost immediately.

Nan I know what you're after, dear, and you're not going to have him. If you want Jerome, the only way you're going to get him –

Jerome Nan, stop!

Nan Stop, Nan.

Jerome stares after Zoë. Nan goes out to the kitchen with her mop handle. Jerome slides up a fader on the desk. Zoë's voice in the bedroom can be heard coming over the speakers.

Zoë . . . never known anything so sick in my life . . . it's disgusting . . . I mean, there is such a thing as basic privacy . . . just to record someone without even . . . I mean, recording us when we were . . . If you're recording this now, Jerome, which I presume you must be – when you play this back I want you to know that you are a sick, twisted voyeur . . . or whatever the listening equivalent is . . . an auditeur . . . a Listening Tom . . .

The sounds of her moving out of the bedroom. Jerome hastily fades down the bedroom mike. Zoë is heard approaching. She is finishing fastening the clothes she borrowed.

I was just saying, you are a Listening Tom.

Jerome I don't know why you're suddenly behaving like this.

Zoë If you honestly don't know, then that's probably the reason you are living on your own, Jerome.

Jerome What are you talking about?

Zoë I'm sorry to disappoint you but you're going to be very hard pressed, even today, to find any woman prepared to have an affair when she runs the risk of having the thing released later in stereo.

She makes to go.

Jerome Don't forget your pass, will you?

Zoë returns for the card, her anger giving way to genuine hurt. As she does this, Nan comes from the kitchen again and stops in the doorway.

Zoë God, I'm so upset, you've no idea. I really cared, you know. Did you know that? Oh, it was only supposed to be a job but I actually genuinely cared about you and your wife and your daughter and your music . . . And now, it's all been betrayed . . .

Jerome I don't see what difference it makes.

Zoë You can't see that there are things that people say and do with each other that they don't want other people to hear? And if they think that other people are going to be listening, then they just don't say them any more?

Jerome But as an artist my work entirely depends on the fact that I do repeat those things –

Zoë Well, then, pardon the language, but bugger your work. There are some things more important.

Jerome Like what?

Zoë Like me, for one. I am considerably more important than your bloody music, pardon the language. I'm sorry.

Jerome Why? What makes you so bloody important?

Zoë Because I'm a bloody human being, that's why. And if you can't see that, I'm sorry for you. I really am. Jerome – I know you don't like people giving you advice – but if you're still thinking of writing your piece about love, really, I should forget it.

Jerome Thank you so much, I'll bear that in mind.

Zoë I mean it, Jerome. Love? How could you ever possibly, ever, in a million years, conceivably describe something you can't even recognize. (*indicating the motionless Nan*) If you don't believe me, ask her. Even she knows more about it than you do.

> *Zoë stamps out. Jerome stares after her. The video screen springs to life as she goes out the front door. She glares at the camera for a second, pulls a face at it, then slams the front door. The screen blanks.*

Nan (*starting to move to the hall*) I'm going to clean in here today. Don't get under my feet.

> *A thought occurs to Jerome. He plays with the controls on the console. Sounds of fast replay.*

Zoë's recorded voice . . . for one. I am considerably more important than your bloody music, pardon the language . . .

> *Jerome spools slightly forward.*

. . . but if you're still thinking of writing your piece about love, really, I should forget it.

Jerome's recorded voice Thank you so much, I'll bear that in mind.

Zoë's recorded voice I mean it, Jerome. Love? How could you ever poss–

Jerome stops the tape and spools slightly back again.

. . . it, Jerome. Love? How cou–

He plays the tape again, then winds it back by hand. Then forwards again, then back several times, playing and replaying the single word at various speeds, back and forth.

. . . love . . . ev–ol . . . l . . o . . v . . e . . .

Jerome has a couple more goes, then gives up.

Jerome No. Never in a million years. No truth. No sincerity. Nothing.

The phone rings. The screen lights up with the Department of Social Services logo. Jerome stares at the screen dully.

Mervyn's voice Mr Watkins, this is Mervyn Bickerdyke from the Department of Child Wellbeing. Calling yet again regarding a proposed meeting. This can't go on, Mr Watkins, it really can't. The time is nine o-three. Please, please, call me . . .

Jerome Mr Bickerdyke, I would call you with pleasure, only what would be the point?

Mervyn's voice . . . my number is, as ever, on screen. Thank you.

Nan has entered and started to vacuum aimlessly around Jerome's feet, using just the disconnected telescopic tube to do so.

Jerome (*irritably*) Nan, give it a rest, please . . .

She stops.

Nan Think I'll have a little rest.

Nan sits down near Jerome. He regards her.

Jerome What do you know about love then? You pile of old junk?

Nan is silent.

(*really for want of anything better to do*) Nan, copy.

Nan Copying.

Jerome Love . . .

Nan Love . . .

Jerome (*more passionately*) Love!

Nan Love!

Jerome No, love!

Nan No, love!

Jerome (*giving up*) . . . useless.

Nan . . . useless.

Jerome spools the tape machine idly. He stops and plays it.

Zoë's recorded voice . . . nice name, Jane. *Jane Eyre*. We did that one. I played the mad Mrs Rochester. Behind the panelling. Not much of a part. I should have played Jane, really. I'd have been really good –

Jerome stops the tape.

Nan . . . nice name, Jane. *Jane Eyre*. We did that one. I played the mad Mrs Rochester. Behind the panelling. Not much of a part. I should have played Jane, really. I'd have been really good –

During this, Jerome looks startled for a moment. Then inspiration strikes him.

Jerome Ah!

He goes to a cupboard under the panel. As he passes, he removes Nan's wig, revealing her silver skull beneath.

Nan (*echoing him*) Ah!

He takes from the cupboard a rolled bundle which he undoes and lays out carefully on the worktop. A neat row of electrical screwdrivers and spanners, etc., together with an open tobacco tin. Each gleaming like a surgeon's implement. He switches off a few general lights so that the illumination is concentrated around the console. He rolls up his sleeves.

Jerome (*softly, to Nan*) Well. What the hell. It's worth a try, that's what I say.

He selects a slender screwdriver and stands over her.

Nan (*cheerfully*) Well. What the hell. It's worth a try, that's what I say.

Jerome starts to remove a small grub screw from her temple. A sound as he drops the screw into the tin. The shutters clang several times as missiles strike them from outside, giving the impression of thunder. Jerome labours on, impervious, as – curtain.

Act Two

In the blackout, the first thing we see is Lupus's face on the screen. He looks terrible. He appears to be calling from a club, judging from the din in the background. The colour variation in the picture is also quite extreme, veering erratically from one vivid hue to the next.

Lupus (*from the screen*) Hallo, Jerry, old mate. Thought I'd roll into view, stick my nose over your horizon there. See how things were. I take it you're out or – busy – or something. I'm calling from the Blue Cockatoo. Thought I might look up one or two of the old gang, for old time's sake. Only there doesn't seem to be anyone here, tonight. A bit of a heavy mob round the bar – I hope this phone's working OK, I'm not –

He thumps the unit in front of him, out of our vision. The colour alters abruptly. As he continues, the lights come up on the room. It is a week later and it is much tidier than when we last saw it. A great effort has been made to turn the place into a suitable home for **Geain**. *Most of the equipment – except the main console – has been covered up. The coffee table is partly laid out for an informal tea party. Jerome comes in from the kitchen. He, too, has made a great effort with his appearance.*

That any better? Anyway, I'm down here at the old Cockatoo if you feel like a jar. Since I finally lost Deborah, I've been . . . (*yelling to someone out of view*) Hey, keep it down, fellows. Please?

He thumps the unit again. His colour changes once more.

Since I finally lost Deborah, I've been pretty near to – (*in response to someone off screen*) What? What's that? And you yours. Yes . . . (*back in the phone*) Jesus, who are all these guys? Anyway, as I was saying, since Deborah finally decided to go, I've been on the verge of playing the last waltz, I can tell you . . .

Jerome, as if by reflex, his mind on other things, fades Lupus down on the console. Lupus's image continues to chatter silently, changing colour once or twice more. Finally, he bangs the videophone once too often and the thing blanks out.

Jerome (*calling*) Darling!

Zoë's voice (*from the kitchen*) Hallo, darling?

Jerome Darling, what are you doing?

Zoë's voice (*off*) I'm just finishing off in here, darling.

Jerome Darling, come on in, they've arrived.

Zoë's voice (*off*) Right you are, darling. Just a tick.

A moment later and Zoë comes on. Or rather it is Nan made over into a version of Zoë. She looks a good deal like Zoë but still has Nan's distinctive walk – and several of Nan's old mannerisms which emerge from time to time. One improvement Jerome seems to have wrought is that she is carrying a plate of sandwiches the right way up. She, too, is very smartly dressed in the usual long frock and with a great deal of ribbons and bows in her new wig. Jerome has also rather emphasized her figure. She's a degree more voluptuous than Zoë and more shapely than Nan. She looks rather like a parody of an old-style Southern belle.

Nan (*brightly, as she enters*) Hallo! Hallo! Hallo! Welcome! Welcome! Sorry. I completely lost track of the time. Typical.

She puts the sandwiches down on the coffee table.
Jerome watches anxiously.

Jerome Good. Good girl. That's it. Darling, will you fetch the tea, or shall I?

Nan I'll fetch the tea, darling. Excuse me.

She goes off. Jerome watches her critically.

Jerome (*muttering*) There's nothing I can do with that leg.

Nan (*from the kitchen*) Just coming, everyone.

A crash from the kitchen.

(*Off*) Oh, for goodness' sake, you extremely stupid old bat. Who put that there, then?

Jerome Oh, for God's sake – (*calling angrily*) Darling!

Nan (*off, sweetly*) Yes, darling.

Jerome Darling, come here, you scrapheap.

Nan (*off*) Coming, darling.

Nan returns, empty-handed. Jerome gets out a small
screwdriver from his tool kit.

Jerome (*brusquely*) Darling, sit down.

Nan (*sitting*) Sitting down, darling.

Jerome selects a screwdriver and approaches Nan.

Jerome (*muttering*) They're going to be here in a minute, you useless heap. Darling, disengage.

Nan beeps and sits immobile in the chair as Jerome lies
on his back on the floor and disappears under her skirt.

(*slightly muffled, to himself really*) Sorry to switch you off but I'm not getting a hundred volts through me again. Yes . . . I keep adjusting this balance control but – it's such –

fine . . . tuning . . . I think it's this leg of yours . . . you keep shaking your works about . . . Darling, engage.

Nan beeps again.

Nan Reconnected. Operational seventy-eight point seven four. We are twenty-one point two six per cent unstable and are within three point seven four per cent of permanent shutdown.

She beeps. Jerome emerges again.

Jerome Don't you dare shut down on me. Not now. Darling, walk about.

Nan Yes, darling.

She does so.

Jerome That's better, that's better. Precious!

Nan comes immediately and kisses his cheek. She waltzes away again.

(*an experimental laugh*) Ha! Ha!

Nan responds with one of Zoë's laughs.

Good. (*calling again*) Precious!

Nan comes and kisses him on the cheek again, then moves away.

Good! Ha! Ha!

Nan laughs again. Jerome moves away to one side of her.

(*in a normal tone*) Zoë . . .

Nan's head turns to look at him, as if listening. She is programmed to do this whenever her name is mentioned. Jerome moves to the other side of her.

(*as before*) Zoë . . .

> *Nan looks at him again.*

(*rather amazed*) It works. Darling, it works!

Nan It works, darling!

Jerome Nan, still –

> *Nan ignores him.*

I mean, darling, still.

> *Nan stops still.*

Nan Still, darling.

Jerome Let me straighten your wig. Here . . . (*studying her*) I don't think I've got your mouth right even now.

> *He adjusts her appearance, trying to remould her face with his thumbs. The doorbell rings. Jerome jumps. The screen lights up to show* **Corinna** *and Mervyn waiting at the front door.*

Here we go, then. Darling, kitchen.

Nan Yes, darling.

> *She starts to go.*

Jerome No, no. Wait (*He moves to the console.*) Darling, here.

Nan Coming, darling.

Jerome (*standing her in front of the screen where she can study Corinna and Mervyn*) Darling, register.

Nan Register, darling.

Jerome Not child. Not child.

Nan Not child. Registered, Nan.

Jerome Good. Darling, kitchen.

Nan Kitchen, darling.

Jerome Darling, take the plate.

Nan I'll take the plate, darling.

Nan takes up the plate and goes off to the kitchen. Jerome straightens his appearance. The doorbell rings again.

Corinna's voice (*impatiently, through the speakers*) Jerome, come on, open the door. Please.

Jerome Here we go. Those warm vibrant tones . . .

Jerome presses the door button. They remain out there.

Corinna's voice Jerome! For heaven's sake!

Jerome Push the door! Push it!

The doorbell rings again.

Mervyn's voice (*from the speakers*) Mr Watkins!

Corinna's voice Jerome!

Jerome Push the bloody thing – ! Oh, for goodness' sake . . .

He runs out down the hall. We see, on the video screen, him opening the door to them.

Corinna's voice (*from the speakers, sarcastically*) Well, thank you so much.

Jerome's voice (*from the speakers*) Come in, then, come in.

Mervyn's voice (*from the speakers*) How do you do, Mr Watkins. Mervyn Bickerdyke of Child Wellbeing.

Corinna's voice (*from the speakers*) Yes, come on, let's get out of this hideous hall first . . .

The screen blanks as they all come inside and the door closes. Corinna enters first, followed closely by Jerome. Mervyn follows behind them. Corinna is, of course, very similar in looks to the original Nan but with little of Nan's submissive nature and a good deal more personal aura, not to mention neuroses. In her mid-thirties, she is formally dressed as though for a business meeting rather than a social event. Mervyn is about the same age. One of those big, gentle, good-natured, pleasant men, he obviously gets by in his job through kindness and tact and by offending no one – rather than through dynamic personality. At present, he is filled with a nervousness which he can't altogether conceal.

Jerome (*as they enter*) . . . I can't help it, there's a fault with the door . . .

Corinna There was a fault with the door when I left . . .

Jerome Probably because you slammed it so hard when you went, dear.

Mervyn Hallo, Mr Watkins, my name is –

Corinna If I slammed it, I had very just cause.

Jerome (*aware someone is missing*) Where's Geain?

Corinna If anyone had reason to slam a door . . .

Mervyn Mr Watkins, I think I ought to introduce myself – I'm . . .

Jerome Where the hell's Geain? What have you done with Geain?

Corinna Geain is coming.

Jerome What have you done with her?

Corinna She is coming. Geain is coming.

Jerome When? Because I'm not meeting without her. There's to be no meeting without Geain.

Mervyn Mr Watkins, if I could just nudge my way in a moment to introduce myself –

Corinna Geain went on in the car to buy something. She'll be here in a minute. Anyway, we need to talk without her first –

Jerome You left that child out there in a car on her own – ?

Corinna Jerome, don't be ridiculous. She is not on her own. It is an armour-plated limousine which cost a fortune to hire – but since that's the only way we could guarantee to get to this place these days . . . She has the driver with her and a man riding – whatever it's called – riding sidegun –

Mervyn Shotgun.

Corinna Shotgun. Thank you, Mr Bickerdyke. Besides which, she is thirteen years old and quite capable of looking after herself.

Mervyn I would endorse that, Mr Watkins.

Jerome (*slightly pacified*) I'm not agreeing anything without Geain having the chance to say what she feels.

Corinna I've no doubt she will. Don't worry.

A slight pause as Corinna inspects the place. Mervyn seizes his chance.

Mervyn Look, I'm going to nip right in there for a second, just to say hallo, my name is Merv–

Corinna I must say this place is looking remarkably tidy. You must have been scrubbing at it for weeks.

Jerome Well, we wouldn't want you picking up any nasty germs whilst you were visiting us, would we?

Corinna Us?

Jerome What? (*A great show of having forgotten.*) Oh, dear. Oh, heavens. Ah. How could I have forgotten? You haven't met Zoë, have you?

Corinna Zoë?

Jerome Zoë.

Corinna Who or what is Zoë?

Jerome Zoë is my – fiancée.

Corinna Fiancée?

Jerome Yes.

Mervyn Oh. Many congratulations.

Jerome (*to Mervyn*) Thank you very much.

Corinna Did you say fiancée?

Jerome Yes.

Corinna I don't believe it. This is a joke – This is an obscene, grotesque joke. A fiancée . . . ?

Jerome Before you meet her, dearest, could I ask you, please – she is very sweet, rather shy – and a little unused to strangers . . . So, please, don't try and be clever with her or embarrass her with awkward questions . . . because she couldn't cope with that. All right? Would that be remotely possible, do you think?

Corinna I don't believe any of this. Not one word.

Jerome (*calling*) Darling!

Nan's voice (*from the kitchen*) Hallo, darling?

Corinna My God!

Jerome Darling, what are you doing?

Nan (*off*) I'm just finishing off in here, darling.

Jerome Darling, come on in, they've arrived.

Nan (*off*) Right you are, darling. Just a tick.

Corinna (*rather shaken*) Well, this – certainly does alter things. Doesn't it?

Jerome (*smiling*) Doesn't it?

Nan comes in as before.

Nan (*brightly, as she enters*) Hallo! Hallo! Hallo! Welcome! Welcome! Welcome! Sorry. I completely lost track of the time. Typical.

Corinna and Mervyn gape.

Jerome Darling, this is Corinna.

Nan Hallo. Corinna. I've heard so much about you.

Corinna (*faintly*) Have you?

Mervyn has never seen anyone quite like her. Jerome is a little easier, now that he is past the first hurdle.

Jerome Well, now. I'm sure we'd all like some tea, wouldn't we? Darling, will you fetch the tea, or shall I?

Nan I'll fetch the tea, darling. Excuse me.

Mervyn (*stepping forward to Nan, hand extended*) Hallo, may I just say hallo. My name is . . .

Nan sweeps past him, unaware. He jumps back.

Corinna Are you telling me that she's living here voluntarily?

Jerome Of course she is. We're engaged.

Corinna Living with *you*?

Jerome Why not?

Corinna But she's – she's –

Mervyn Very much so. Congratulations again.

Corinna Where did you meet her?

Jerome She's an actress.

Mervyn (*impressed*) Really?

Jerome A classical actress.

Corinna Classical?

Nan comes back in unexpectedly. She is empty-handed.

Nan (*brightly, as she enters*) Hallo! Hallo! Hallo! Welcome! Welcome! Welcome! Sorry. I –

Jerome (*interrupting swiftly*) Darling, the tea!

Nan (*unflustered*) I'll fetch the tea, darling. Excuse me.

She goes out. A pause.

Jerome Excuse me.

He hurries out after Nan to the kitchen.

Corinna I think she's wearing one of my old dresses.

Mervyn Oh, yes?

Corinna She's certainly made herself at home here.

Jerome (*from the kitchen, shouting fiercely*) Darling, tea! Darling, tea!

Nan (*from the kitchen, equally fiercely*) Darling, tea! Darling, tea!

Several loud clangs. The others stare. Jerome hurries back.

Jerome Sorry. Just – lending her a hand. Please, sit down.

They sit. Silence. Jerome listens anxiously. He rises. Then sits again.

Corinna Does she need any help?

Jerome No, no.

Nan returns. She carries the tea pot and a plate of small cakes.

Nan (*to the seated assembly*) Do sit down, everyone.

Mervyn (*rising apologetically*) Sorry, I . . .

Nan Nice pot of tea.

Jerome Oh, super. Clever little cuddles.

Nan And some home-made cakes.

Jerome (*rather over-enthusiastically*) Home-made cakes! Wonderful! Wonderful! Yummy, yummy, yum-yum.

Mervyn You made these yourself?

Jerome Yes, she did. Didn't you, darling, you made these yourself?

Nan I made them myself, darling. (*She grabs the tea pot rather jerkily.*) Tea, everyone?

Jerome (*hastily taking the tea pot from her*) I'll pour the tea. (*as he pours*) You relax. You've been at it all day. Precious.

Nan rises at once and kisses him on the cheek.

(*rather coyly*) Oh, come on. Not in front of everyone . . .

He laughs. Nan laughs in response. Corinna stares in disbelief.

Corinna I think I'm going to be sick.

Jerome (*to the others*) She's been at it all day. Slaving away in that kitchen. Then she was up at dawn, scouring the place from top to bottom. She never stops. All day. Now, do we want milk or lemon? (*to Nan*) Darling, you won't have anything, I take it.

Nan I won't have anything, I take it, darling.

Jerome (*to the others*) Eats nothing at all. Fierce diet.

Corinna (*rather sourly*) Doesn't look as if she needs to bother.

Jerome She doesn't. Wonderful metabolism. Milk?

Corinna Lemon.

Mervyn I'll have milk, thank you.

Jerome finishes serving the tea, helping himself as he does so.

Could I stick a foot in the door here just to take this opportunity to say hallo, formally? I'm Mervyn Bickerdyke, Child Wellbeing, of course. I spoke to you on the phone, Mr Watkins. Eventually.

Jerome Yes, so you did. Sandwich?

Mervyn Thank you. (*smiling at Nan*) Seeing as they were made with your own fair hands.

Nan ignores him. Corinna grabs a sandwich, irritably.

I'm sorry. After you, after you.

All, except Nan, help themselves to sandwiches.

We were just hearing, Zoë, that you were an actress.

384

Corinna Classical, is that right.

Jerome That's right, isn't it, darling? You're a classical actress, aren't you, little blossom?

Nan Oh yes. Arkadina in Chekhov and Queen Margaret in *See How They Run*.

Corinna (*puzzled*) Really?

Jerome That was the – Royal Shakespeare production, of course –

Mervyn Of course. Now, to the reason we've all met –

Something starts to bleep somewhere about his person. Jerome checks Nan nervously.

– we've . . . Oh. Would you excuse me. My bleeper.

He rises.

Jerome (*waving towards the console*) Do you want to make a – ?

Mervyn No, no. I have my portable here. Thank you very much.

Mervyn moves away from them to a far corner of the room. He produces a wafer-thin pocket phone from his jacket and answers his call. He stops bleeping. He murmurs indistinctly while the others continue their tea.

Corinna Well, I have to confess, Jerome, that I am simply amazed. I didn't think anyone could do it, Zoë. Make a civilized animal out of this man.

She laughs. Nan laughs in response.

Jerome I'm putty in her hands, darling, aren't I, precious?

Nan Aren't you, precious?

She gets up and kisses him on the cheek and sits again.

Corinna glares at them, disgusted by this blissful scene.

Corinna Don't think I don't know why you're doing this, both of you. Trying to impress that – (*indicating Mervyn*) – limp lettuce over there . . . God, he's wet. Three hours we were in that car with him bleating away. That's when his bleeper wasn't going. He was either bleeping or bleating, like a radio-controlled sheep. God, I despair of men these days, I despair. They're all so lank. And dank.

Jerome (*to Nan*) My ex-wife airing her views in general.

Corinna Well, ask Zoë. I bet she feels the same. Zoë, outside this very special little love-nest, this haven of domestic fervour, don't you find most men these days utterly spineless and flaccid? I mean, that's just talking to them – I'm not even talking about bed. Don't you agree, Zoë?

Nan looks blank.

Yes, she does. She's just being loyal, poor thing.

Jerome She knows when to keep quiet, don't you, Zoë?

Corinna She'd need to. Living with you.

She laughs. Nan, responding to this laughs too. Corinna looks at her rather sharply, sizing up her rival afresh.

Yes, you're a deep one, aren't you, Zoë? Quite a lot going on in there, I imagine.

Jerome You bet.

Mervyn finishes the call and rejoins them.

Mervyn Sorry. Never far away from the office when you've got one of those.

He waves his phone.

Corinna I thought you said you had two of them?

Mervyn Ah, yes. I have my private home phone as well. In case my wife wants to get hold of me.

Corinna (*sweetly*) But that one doesn't ring very often, I imagine?

Mervyn (*missing that*) Right. Where were we? Yes. Young Geain –

Jerome Look, if we're going to start talking, I think Zoë would rather – get on with other things.

Corinna Oh, surely not?

Jerome Well, she was saying earlier she felt she'd feel a bit in the way. And she does have some work to get on with. Darling, if you want to go and study now . . .

Nan (*rising at once*) I want to go and study now, darling. (*She goes out to the bedrooms.*)

Corinna No, no, this is ridiculous, she must stay. Zoë! (*To Jerome*) Jerome, tell her to come back at once, for heaven's sake, she needs to hear all this.

Jerome No, she really does need to do some work. She has a big audition tomorrow.

Mervyn Really? What's that for?

Jerome For a musical.

Mervyn (*more impressed still*) Does she sing as well?

Jerome Like an angel.

Corinna How else? None the less, if she really is intending to live here with you, possibly even marry you – God help her – she ought to be in on the discussions –

Mervyn It would be advisable.

Jerome (*reluctantly*) Well. For a few minutes. (*calling*) Darling!

Nan (*off*) Hallo, darling!

Jerome (*calling*) Darling, come back.

Nan (*off*) Right you are, darling, just a tick.

Jerome She's coming.

Mervyn (*indicating the sandwiches*) May I – ?

Jerome waves for him to go ahead. Mervyn evidently enjoys his food.

Corinna Has she hurt her leg?

Jerome What?

Corinna She appears to be limping.

Jerome Oh, she damaged it – while she was rushing around dancing.

Mervyn She dances as well?

Jerome No one to touch her . . .

Corinna I'm longing to see her fly.

Nan re-enters.

Nan (*brightly, as she enters*) Hallo! Hallo! Hallo! Welc–

Jerome (*cutting her off*) Darling, we want you to sit here with us.

Nan (*sitting*) Yes, darling.

Mervyn Maybe we can persuade you to sing for us before we leave, Zoë.

Jerome I'm afraid not.

Mervyn No?

Jerome No. She's saving the voice.

Mervyn Oh, I see.

Jerome Professionals. They have to be very careful how often they sing.

Corinna Or even speak, apparently.

She smiles at Nan.

Mervyn Well. I think we ought to – make a start, then. The question we have to decide first, regarding Geain, is whether – (*He starts to beep again.*) I'm sorry. Please excuse me –

Corinna (*exasperated*) Oh, dear God.

Mervyn Don't worry, I'll put them on to answer. It's the office again, I'll put them on to answer.

He fumbles in another pocket as he continues to beep.

Jerome (*intrigued*) You have an answering machine on you as well?

Corinna If you turn him upside down, he also makes ice-cream.

Mervyn (*rather proudly*) I've got a few wires about my person, yes, I have to admit it. (*He finds his answering machine and switches it on. The beeping stops. Producing items from various pockets and holding them up to show them*) Answering machine. Neat, eh? Home phone. Office phone. Oh, this is an interesting one. Location finder. If you're ever hopelessly lost. Switch it on and it can pinpoint your on-ground position to within twelve square metres. French. Of course. Then you've got this – excuse me. (*He takes off his jacket to reveal that the whole of his neck and arms are encased in a criss-cross of wires.*) This is a personal alarm system. Latest type. West German.

Naturally. Made by Heisser-Hausen Zeiplussen. They're a subsidiary of Glotz.

Jerome (*vaguely*) Oh, yes.

Mervyn Any physical attack on my person and this thing screams the place down.

Corinna Do you need a machine to do it for you?

Mervyn (*putting on his jacket again*) Ah, but what if I was rendered unconscious? I couldn't scream at all, could I? Whereas this thing. Two kilometre radius – up to an hour, guaranteed. And it automatically phones the police.

Corinna And you certainly couldn't do that if you were unconscious, could you? Must take you ages getting dressed in the morning.

Mervyn Maybe. But I can get undressed quick enough, if called upon to do so, don't you worry about that.

> *He laughs at his own roguish wit. Corinna looks at him coldly. Nan responds, laughing.*

(*winking at Nan as he sits again*) Sorry. Mustn't get me on to these things. Fatal. My hobby, rather.

Jerome Have some more to eat.

Mervyn Thank you.

> *He helps himself.*

Corinna Lovely home-made cakes, Zoë. Clever you. Very, very like those new deep-frozen ones you bake in the packet. But yours are twice as good.

> *She smiles at Nan again.*

Mervyn Getting back to Geain, then. We mustn't get sidetracked, must we? We –

The phone rings in the room.

Ignore it. Ignore that. I'm on answer, ignore it.

Jerome That's my phone.

Mervyn Oh, is it? Yes, of course, that's your phone . . .

He laughs. Nan laughs as well.

Corinna That woman laughs at anything.

Jerome She's got a sense of humour. That's why I love her. Don't I, precious?

Nan kisses him.

Corinna Oh, do stop it, both of you.

The answering machine picks up the incoming call. On screen, Lupus appears. He is still in the club phone box but there seems to be some sort of riot going on round him. There also appears to be something on fire, judging from the smoke and the flames reflected on his face. He looks somewhat the worse for wear.

My God, it's not him . . .

Lupus Hi, Jerry, mate. I'll have to make this a quick one. Lupus, still at the old Cockatoo. I hope the answering machine doesn't mean you're on your way here. Anyway, this is to say, if you do get this message, don't bother coming down. It's got a bit rough here . . .

Jerome gets up and crosses to the console.

Jerome Excuse me.

Lupus Apparently, this afternoon the club was booked by two hundred members of the Motorhead Nostalgic Appreciation Society. I ask you, Jerry – Motorhead! Where have they been? I said to one of them, listen, if it's nostalgia you're into then do yourself a favour, treat yourself to the

Moody Blues and listen to real music. I mean, really –

His voice is cut off as Jerome fades him down.

Corinna Good old Lupus.

Mervyn Do you need to make any calls on his behalf? His lawyer or something? It looked quite serious . . .

Jerome No, no. He's all right. That's always happening to Lupus. Nothing out of the ordinary.

On screen, the phone booth topples on to its side. Lupus goes with it, still gesticulating and talking. None of them notices this. The screen goes blank.

There you are, you see, he's hung up.

Corinna The man is a walking state of emergency. Is he still with that woman? With Deborah?

Nan makes a little strangled sound.

Or is she off with somebody else's husband again?

Jerome I really wouldn't know. Look, let's –

Corinna Dear little Deborah, I wonder how she is these days?

Nan reacts again and does so every time Deborah's name is mentioned.

Heard anything from Deborah lately, have you, Zoë?

Jerome I don't think Zoë wants to talk about Deborah and nor do I.

Corinna I'm sure you don't. But how do you know Zoë doesn't?

Jerome Because she doesn't.

Corinna Have you asked her? Ask her.

Mervyn (*jocularly*) I think I'd quite like to hear about Deborah from the sound of things . . .

He laughs. Nan laughs. Jerome glares at him.

Corinna Go on. Ask her.

Jerome There isn't the faintest chance is there, darling, you want to hear about Deborah?

Nan I want to hear about Deborah, darling.

Corinna (*scenting blood*) There you are. I told you she did. Of course she does. Everyone should know about Deborah, shouldn't they? The Deborahs of this world need discussing. They need a constant airing – in her case, literally. Zoë needs to know. Forewarned is forearmed. And I'm sure Mr Bickerdyke here, who can get undressed very, very quickly if called upon to do so, might like to be warned about Deborah, too.

Jerome Look, come on, Corinna, why drag that up again . . .

Mervyn I think we might be in essence be straying away from the basic issues here . . . (*He beeps again.*) Ignore that. Ignore that! That is me, this time, that is definitely me.

Corinna (*confidentially, to Nan*) Never mind, Zoë. Later, when we're alone, darling, I'll tell you all about Deborah. (*She laughs.*)

Nan (*laughing*) You'll tell me all about Deborah, darling.

Corinna I think Zoë and I have a lot more in common than I thought.

Jerome I don't think Zoë has anything to say to you at all.

Corinna What's the matter? Frightened she might hear the truth?

Jerome Not at all.

Corinna That's a man's greatest nightmare, isn't it? All the women in his life getting together and talking about him. What's he like at breakfast, darling? What's he like in bed?

Nan He'll soon get the hang of it again, I'm sure.

Corinna blinks.

Corinna What did she say?

Jerome laughs loudly. Nan follows suit.

Jerome God, this girl's sense of humour is wicked sometimes. Wicked. Isn't it, precious?

Nan kisses him. Corinna is very puzzled.

Corinna (*staring at them both*) Yes . . .

Mervyn I think if I could hop, step and jump in again at this point. Just – looking at the time . . .

Corinna Listen, we can keep this very simple. The situation is this. Geain has reached an age now when I am more than happy for us both to share responsibility, Jerome. I am happy that she sees you. I am happy that she spends time with you.

Jerome You what?

Corinna My only –

Jerome You are saying this now, after – ?

Corinna My only –

Jerome After four years of – ?

Corinna May I please finish? My only misgiving has been the thought of Geain coming to see you here. The combination of you, the flat and the general state of this neighbourhood always seemed to me strong enough reason to prevent her coming. Well, the neighbourhood certainly hasn't improved but – thanks I suspect to Zoë, quite a lot else has. So I withdraw my objections. Geain may come and see you if she likes, whenever she likes.

Jerome Do you hear that, Mr Bickerdyke?

Mervyn Yes, indeed.

Jerome You are bearing witness to this?

Mervyn I am.

Jerome Well. That's that, isn't it?

Corinna Presumably. It's up to Geain. That's if Mr Bickerdyke has no objections?

Jerome You don't have objections?

Mervyn No, no.

Jerome There's no problem, is there?

Mervyn Well . . .

Jerome What?

Mervyn There is one aspect with which I'm not entirely happy, I have to confess. I mean, although the youngster has to come first, indeed her interests are of paramount importance – everyone, in a sense, needs to be considered. And I'm not altogether convinced that there aren't certain individuals – certain aspects of the existing – (*He beeps. In time, he goes on to 'answer'.*) – ignore that – please – ignore that – aspects of the existing status quo that could suffer – as the result of any subsequent modified arrangements – regarding the possible – alteration of the present – custodianship of the youngster. As of this present time.

    Corinna makes a loud snoring noise.

If you follow me.

Jerome Do I take it you are not happy for Geain to come here?

Mervyn Well . . .

Jerome You don't consider us suitable?

Mervyn It's difficult to put into words . . .

Jerome I'm her father.

Mervyn Oh, quite.

Jerome And Zoë loves children. She adores them. She was saying so only the other day. Tell them your feelings towards children.

A slight pause. Nan does not react.

(*remembering the key word*) Sweetheart.

Nan (*promptly*) I'd love to have children of my own. Wouldn't that be lovely to hear them rushing about the flat, laughing and yelling? With the right man – someone who'd share them – they'd be everything I ever wanted. I suppose you're either maternal or you aren't. I know which I am.

A silence.

Jerome (*moved*) Darling, thank you.

Nan Thank you, darling.

Mervyn (*rather moved*) Well, what can one say . . . ?

Corinna What indeed?

Mervyn I'll be honest with you, Mr Watkins. What I've experienced here this afternoon has been for me – as a married man myself – heart-warming. You and your – fiancée – Zoë – well – you can feel it when you walk in the door. You can almost sense the happiness.

Jerome There you are, then.

Mervyn It's just that I'm a little afraid of what might happen if we introduced Geain into this house. There is, on the one hand, the real hope that your own happiness could have a beneficial effect on the youngster –

Jerome It's bound to.

Mervyn Ah, but it has been known to happen, that because the couple were so contented, the introduction of the youngster actually upset the happy status quo. And the couple became unhappy as a result of having the youngster with them. Consequently, the youngster was no longer in a happy home but an unhappy one. Which naturally in turn made it, the youngster, feel guilty because it felt responsible for causing that unhappiness. Which had the knock-on effect, of course, of making the youngster unhappy, which won't do at all. Because, after all, the bottom line is the happiness of the youngster, is it or is it not, correct me if I'm wrong?

A pause. They stare at him, trying to work out what he's said.

Corinna Your job's a good deal more complicated than most people imagine, isn't it, Mr Bickerdyke?

Jerome You feel that Geain might upset me and Zoë?

Mervyn I'm saying she could. At her present stage of adolescence. Which is – complex.

Jerome And that, in turn, would upset Geain?

Mervyn It's possible.

Jerome Well, that's simple enough. If that happens I'll get rid of her.

Mervyn I beg your pardon?

Jerome I'll get rid of her.

Mervyn Get rid of Geain?

Jerome No, of course not. Not Geain. I'll get rid of Zoë. That's easy enough.

Mervyn (*stunned*) You'd get rid of her?

Jerome Yes. We'd – you know – split up. For the sake of the child.

Mervyn Just like that?

Corinna What does Zoë have to say about that?

Jerome Darling, you wouldn't mind us splitting up for the sake of the child?

Nan I wouldn't mind us splitting up for the sake of the child, darling.

Jerome There you are, you see, she doesn't mind at all.

Mervyn But that's what you did before.

Jerome What?

Mervyn You and your wife. That's what you did before. That's the root of the problem now. You can't do that again. Think of the youngster. We must think of the youngster, Mr Watkins.

Jerome Yes, that was with her mother. That was different. I mean, this is only with – only – with –

A pause.

Corinna Only some woman or other, he was going to say.

Jerome No.

Corinna Well, Zoë. You're taking this all very calmly,

dear. I hope you know what you're doing. Personally, I'd have punched your precious fiancé on the nose.

Nan kisses Jerome on the cheek.

Oh well, save your breath. Never mind, Zoë, if you're very good in this life, you might just come back in the next as a shoe-cleaning kit. You'll enjoy that.

Jerome There is no need to be offensive, Corinna. Just because the sight of two people completely and hopelessly in love distresses you, there's –

Corinna In love? Jerome, you are treating this woman like a doormat. How dare you? And Zoë, for heaven's sake, darling, stand up for yourself.

Nan stands up.

Nan Standing up, darling.

Jerome (*swiftly*) Darling, sit down.

Nan (*sitting*) Sitting down, darling.

Mervyn Listen, I must just be allowed to finish the point I started making . . . Which is, that this is all a big hypothetical if. Much more likely is that Geain will respond to the peaceful friendly ambience and the reverse will happen. The relationship between the three of you will take root and blossom . . .

Nan Oh, yes. Arkadina in Chekhov and Queen Margaret in *See How They Run*.

Mervyn I beg your pardon?

Corinna What?

Jerome She wants to go and study. Darling, you need to go and study.

Nan (*rising immediately*) I need to go and study, darling.

Nan goes off to the bedrooms.

Mervyn Do you think you may have offended her?

Corinna Impossible.

Mervyn I don't know, some people may not care to be referred to as shoe-cleaning equipment.

Corinna Oh, surely not in Zoë's case? Living with Jerome, that comes under the heading of a compliment.

Mervyn looks at his watch.

Mervyn They're rather late, aren't they? I think I might phone the car. Do you think that would be an idea? Make sure they're all right?

Corinna If you like.

Jerome Do you want to use the – (*indicating his phone*)?

Mervyn No, no. I'll use my other line. It's quite all right.

He moves off to the hall to speak in private.

Corinna Well. Congratulations, Jerome. I'm very, very, very pleased for you. I'm delighted. (*Pause.*) I'm so thrilled, you've no idea. (*Pause.*) No, really, I am. I'm being perfectly sincere. (*Pause.*) At least one of us has managed to . . . (*Pause.*) I'm really pleased. Honestly. You must be – so happy. (*Pause.*) You're very lucky, both of you. (*Pause.*) She's lovely and obviously wonderful for you and you're both very much in love. (*Pause.*) Who could ask for anything more?

Jerome I couldn't?

He smiles.

Corinna No.

A pause.

(*with sudden suppressed fury*) You smug bastard.

Mervyn returns from the hall.

Mervyn Sorry to interrupt . . . They're here. The car's just arrived. Apparently, they were –

He is cut short by the doorbell ringing. The face of a short-haired, dark-chinned hermaphrodite appears on the screen.

Mervyn Ah, I'll get it. I'll get it.

He goes out to the hall again.

Jerome No, don't open the door without . . . (*seeing what is on the screen*) No, don't open it. Don't let that thing in here.

On screen, Mervyn opens the door.

What's he doing? (*diving for his swordstick*) What's the idiot think he's doing? He's letting in every monster in the neighbourhood.

Corinna Jerome, dear. That is Geain.

Jerome What?

Geain enters the flat and closes the door. The screen blanks.

Corinna That's your daughter. That's Geain. Remember?

Jerome (*stunned*) Geain? That is Geain?

Geain enters. In the flesh, she looks if anything slightly more grotesque. She wears a not unfamiliar parody of male work clothes circa 1955. But hers are carried to some extreme. Heavy boots, cord trousers with a wide leather belt, padded rather incongruously at the crotch, old, faded shirt open at the neck to reveal the currently fashionable 'hairy vest' i.e. an undershirt knotted with a mass of supposed chest hair. The back of her jacket is studded with the words: SONS OF BITCHES. *Her hair is short, brushed straight back and oiled; her only make-up the blue-chinned, unshaven look.*

Geain (*cursorily*) 'llo.

She strides into the room, picks up a sandwich and sits, without ceremony or introduction. Jerome stares, thunderstruck. Her brusqueness, one suspects, also hides a shyness.

Corinna Here she is.

Geain (*scowling*) He.

Corinna Sorry, my mistake. He. You remember your – son Geain, don't you? This is your father, dear.

Geain (*nodding to Jerome*) 'llo.

Jerome manages to open and shut his mouth. Geain crams another sandwich into her mouth.

Mervyn (*with inappropriate avuncularity*) Did you manage to buy that game you were looking for, Geain?

Geain (*scowling*) No.

Mervyn Oh, why was that?

Geain (*muttering*) Daughters.

Mervyn What's that?

Geain Daughters.

Mervyn Tortoise?

Geain Daughters. Daughters of Darkness.

Mervyn Oh, those, yes. What about them?

Geain Wouldn't let me in.

Mervyn Wouldn't let you in? In where? In the shop?

Geain No.

Mervyn Why ever not?

Geain They hate us. We hate them.

Mervyn Oh, dear. That's not very friendly, is it?

Corinna They're great rivals apparently. Amazing as it may sound, the Sons of Bitches and the Daughters of Darknesses aren't speaking to each other at all.

Geain Rancid sows.

Corinna (*to Jerome*) Your son, you will observe, has joined the Male Dominance Movement – the Top Missionaries . . . whatever they're called.

Geain (*through her sandwich*) The Missionary Position.

Corinna Missionary Position.

A silence.

Well, I've no doubt you two will have lots to talk about. (*Pause.*) Talking of missionaries, shouldn't you call Zoë? She should meet Geain, surely?

Mervyn Oh, yes. Let's bring Zoë in.

Jerome (*still dazed, calling*) Darling!

Nan's voice (*from the bedroom*) Hallo, darling?

Jerome Darling, come in. My – my – Geain's arrived.

Nan (*off*) Right you are, darling. Just a tick.

Corinna Zoë is Dad's new friend, Geain. His fiancée.

Geain looks at Jerome scornfully. Jerome looks at Geain and gives a little despairing moan.

403

Geain Huh!

Nan enters from the bedroom.

Nan (*brightly, as she enters*) Hallo! Hallo! Hallo! Welcome! Welcome! Welcome! Sorry, I completely lost tra–

Corinna This is Geain, Zoë. Geain, say hallo to Zoë.

Geain stares at Nan. Nan stares at Geain. For various reasons, neither of them speaks.

Ah. (*softly*) Geain, at least say hallo.

Geain 'llo.

Jerome (*rather automatically*) Darling. This is Geain. Treasure.

Nan (*at once*) Well, who's this beautiful little girl, then? You must be Geain, mustn't you? Well, Geain, I'm Zoë. And we're going to be very, very good friends, aren't we? I hope we are. Now would you like to come into the kitchen with me and I'll give you a big glass of orange, how about that? Come on, then, come with Zoë . . .

Geain (*backing away from Nan's outstretched hand*) Get off. Get her off me.

Nan Off we go. I've got a big surprise for you out here, Geain.

Before anyone can stop them, Nan has dragged the protesting Geain off to the kitchen.

Corinna (*somewhat alarmed*) Geain won't drink orange juice, Jerome . . .

Jerome Hang on, I'll stop her, I'll . . .

He makes to follow them.

Mervyn (*quite forcefully, for him*) No, no, no, no, no.

Jerome stops.

Jerome What?

Mervyn Leave them together. Please. The very best thing that can happen. A chance for them to get to know each other.

Jerome Yes, but – she wasn't supposed to do all that – she –

Mervyn Please. Trust my judgement. I am trained in these matters.

Corinna She'll never get Geain to drink orange juice, I can tell you that.

Mervyn Then they will no doubt resolve matters between them. Geain will tell Zoë no, thank you, Zoë, I do not want orange juice, thank you very much indeed, I would like a glass of milk. Or somesuch.

Corinna Or somesuch.

Mervyn And Zoë will no doubt defer to Geain's request and give her what she wants –

Jerome Possibly.

Mervyn And that way a bond will be formed between them. We call that, in my line of work, a Self-Seeding Relationship.

There is a crash from the kitchen.

Nan (*off*) Oh, for goodness' sake, you extremely stupid old bat. Who put that there, then?

Jerome makes to go off again.

Jerome I'd better just go and –

Mervyn No, no, no. Please, please, Mr Watkins. Trust me.

Jerome It's just, you see, that Zoë isn't –

Mervyn No, I appreciate that. Zoë is not used to youngsters and she'll have to learn as she goes. No doubt she'll make mistakes. Being human, it would be extraordinary if she didn't.

Jerome It would.

Mervyn But what's happening out there is a mutual exploration process. Now, please. Leave them to explore each other. Let's all sit down, keep calm and allow nature to take its course.

They sit. A silence. A crash.

Corinna Jerome, she'll kill her. If you leave them together, she'll kill her.

Mervyn Oh, come now –

Corinna Well, we could at least listen to them, couldn't we? See they're all right? I take it the rooms are still wired for sound? Did you know, Mr Bickerdyke, he records everything? Be careful. When Geain and I lived here – every word, every breath we took was recorded and played back to us.

Jerome Nonsense.

Corinna It's true.

Jerome I never played half of it back to you.

Mervyn (*who has been listening more towards the kitchen*) They seem very quiet now. I'm sure things are going to be fine. We mustn't expect results straightaway but – it's a start.

Corinna I still don't think she should be left out there alone with her . . .

Jerome I don't know. Maybe it's all right. Zoë's – very gentle . . .

Corinna I'm talking about Geain. Nobody tells Geain what to drink. I've still got this bruise where she kicked me because I bought the wrong biscuits.

Jerome I hope she doesn't try and kick Zoë.

Corinna Yes, she's turned into a right little thug, your daughter. First suggestion she isn't going to get her own way, she punches and kicks. Good luck. That's all I can say. Maybe you'll have more success with your child than I have.

Another crash from the kitchen.

Jerome Let me get one thing clear. That – thing in there is no relation of mine – that transvestite truck driver . . .

Mervyn Mr Watkins –

Jerome (*with a cry*) What have you done with my little girl? I want my little girl. I've never seen that thing before. (*yelling at Corinna*) What is it? I don't want that. Take it away! Screw it back on the church roof where it belongs . . .

Mervyn Mr Watkins, will you please control yourself?

Jerome is silent.

Corinna It's all right, Mr Bickerdyke, I'm accustomed to these outbursts, believe me. In reply to your question, Jerome, I have done nothing – because there was nothing that I or anyone else could do. Geain does what Geain likes and stuff the rest of the world. I can't think who she – sorry he – inherits that particularly unpleasant side of his nature from, so we can only hazard a guess. But he – she – *it* does what it likes. *It* goes to school, *it* has friends, *it* wants to be like *its* friends. If its friends choose to dress up like that, I can't stop it. Because, as it explains to me, if it doesn't dress up like its friends then it won't have any friends any more. I have to admit that it's not a great deal of fun having a female male chauvinist kicking me all day, demanding to be waited on hand and foot and referring to me as a dozy cow. But looking at some of the alternatives it might have chosen, I've decided to grin and bear it. Now if you want to try and alter her, you're welcome to try. Go ahead. Please. Because I really do need help, Jerome. I can't do it alone. I really believed, after I left you, that I could cope with anything. I was wrong. I cannot cope with Geain as she is now. Maybe in a few years, when she's . . . There you are, I admit it. And I am shocked by my own inadequacy. I am even a little ashamed. It's made a trifle more bearable because I'm absolutely certain that nobody else, in these circumstances, could have coped any better than I did.

Mervyn (*gently*) I'm sure you've done everything that a single parent could, Corinna.

A brief silence.

It's very quiet out there, isn't it?

Before they can move, Nan comes back from the kitchen. She waits by the doorway.

Nan Here she is, Mummy. Here she is, Daddy.

Geain comes in slowly from the kitchen. She looks slightly dazed. Her face is now clean, almost gleaming. She has on a too-long nightdress. She carries a large frilly doll in her arms.

Jerome (*muttering*) Oh, my God . . .

Corinna (*stunned*) Geain!

Mervyn Well . . .

Nan And what are we going to sing, Geain?

Geain scowls.

Geain. (*prompting her*) 'Baa baa . . .'

Geain I'm not saying that . . .

Nan All together.
Baa baa black sheep, whither do you wander?
Four and twenty blackbirds baked on a tuffet – good –
The little dog laughed to see such fun
And said what a good boy am I. Woof! Moo! Well done.

*Nan claps. The others follow suit in a perplexed
manner.*

Geain (*not without admiration*) She's mad.

Mervyn That's a new one on me, certainly. (*He laughs.*)

Nan (*laughing, taking hold of Geain's hand*) Now we're
off to bed. Goodnight, everyone. Say goodnight.

Geain I'm not saying goodnight.

Nan (*dragging her away*) That's it.

Geain (*struggling vainly as they go*) I can't go to bed now,
you dumb woman . . .

They go off to the bedrooms. A cry from Geain.

Nan (*off*) Oh, for goodness sake, you extremely stupid
old bat. Who put that there, then?

They stare at each other.

Mervyn Well, I must say. In all my years, I've – What a
remarkable woman. Quite remarkable.

ALAN AYCKBOURN

Jerome is aware that Corinna is quite upset.

Jerome Well, it's – it's just part of her – basic – original – I mean it was there already in her, you see . . .

Mervyn As it is within all women, Mr Watkins. All women. (*A pause.*) Well, that's a problem solved.

Corinna Would you think it terribly rude of me, Mr Bickerdyke, if I were to ask you to leave us alone for a moment.

Mervyn Ah, well . . .

Corinna Actually, I don't really care if you do find it terribly rude of me. Would you go, anyway.

Mervyn (*springing up*) Yes, of course. I'll – I'll wait in the (*indicating the kitchen*).

Jerome The kitchen.

Mervyn I'll wait in there, shall I? I have to phone my – Yes. Excuse me. (*He takes a handful of sandwiches as he goes.*) Excuse me.

Mervyn goes to the kitchen. Corinna and Jerome are silent for a second.

Corinna All I want to say is – I think I'll leave now. Quietly. I'll leave Geain with you and Zoë. All right?

Jerome Ah.

Corinna Well, that's what you'd like, isn't it? That's what you wanted?

Jerome Yes.

Corinna I mean obviously she'll have to return to me – at some point – she has to go back to school for one thing. But she could stay here for a couple of weeks, anyway. See how it works out.

410

Jerome You're happy to do that? You think that's best?

Corinna Frankly, Jerome, I feel so demoralized I don't know what I think. All I actually feel like doing is crying. I mean, that woman's done more with that kid in five minutes than I managed in five years.

Jerome That's just her being a stranger, she –

Corinna I might have been able to cope with that, if Zoë'd at least been – terribly plain or – homely – or . . . I thought for one glorious moment she was actually very dim. But then, of course, it turns out she isn't. She's obviously very intelligent, shrewd, cool, sexy, wonderful with kids, a great actress, singer, dancer, terrific in bed – the only thing she lies about are her cakes – and it's bloody unfair, Jerome. (*She starts to cry.*)

Jerome Oh now, come on –

Corinna How can it be allowed to happen? After all you've done? All the rotten, traitorous, lousy, underhand things you've done to me. What right have you to somebody like that? You're a bastard, Jerome. You're barely human. What have you ever done in your life to deserve *anyone*?

Jerome Well, I can't answer that . . . I really can't.

Corinna There is no justice. That's all. None. Here's me – (*She sniffs.*) I haven't found anyone, do you know that? Nobody.

Jerome Ah, that's only because you have very high standards. Quite rightly . . .

Corinna I've got no standards at all. Not any more. I'll take anyone who's available. I'm a forty-year-old bank manager who sits crying in her office. What use is that to anybody? Do you know I gave a man a loan the other day solely on the grounds that I wanted to go to bed with him?

Jerome My God. And did you?

Corinna Of course I didn't. I found out he only borrowed the money so he could get married. I'm losing my judgement, I'm losing my confidence and then that bloody child comes home from school and kicks me because of a packet of biscuits. I can't cope any more. I just want to go somewhere and lie down.

Jerome stares at her, amazed.

(*amused, despite herself, by his expression*) There! I bet you never thought you'd hear me talking like this. (*Pause.*) How did she get Geain to *wash*? I never got her to wash. She stank to high heaven. Sweat is macho. Well. Tell Zoë to keep up the good work. I'll collect the exciting Mr Bickerdyke and slink away.

Jerome Yes. Well, you never know your luck, you may –

Corinna Don't you dare. Don't even suggest it. I have a fragment of pride left. Well, cheer up. You're not allowed to be miserable. You've got what you wanted, haven't you?

Jerome Yes.

Corinna As you usually do. (*Pause.*) I'll tell you something amusing, shall I? You know, half the reason I came here was to see how you felt about – felt about, you know, coming back.

Jerome Coming back?

Corinna Yes, I – well, when I thought you were still on your own here, I thought that we might all three get together. Have another go. But I didn't know about Zoë, of course. Now she's staked her claim, I don't think I could compete with that. Not the state I'm in at present. (*Pause.*)

Still, I thought that would amuse you. (*Pause. She rises.*)

Jerome (*slowly*) Just a second . . .

Corinna I'll call Mr Bickerdyke.

Jerome Wait . . .

Corinna I don't think there's much else to say, Jerome.

Jerome There's something I need to tell you. Please.

Corinna No, I don't want to hear about –

Jerome No, you see, things are not – altogether as they seem. The reason Zoë is here at all is because – I needed someone here – to impress you.

Corinna Well, she did, well done.

Jerome No, that's the only reason she's here, you see, so that you and Mr Bickerdyke – so you'd let Geain stay here. Because it looked OK.

Corinna What exactly are you saying? Are you saying that Zoë is only here for our benefit?

Jerome Yes.

Corinna She isn't here normally?

Jerome No.

Corinna Then who is she?

Jerome She's – she's an actress. She really is an actress. This is just a – short engagement. So to speak.

Corinna What did you do, hire her?

Jerome Right.

Corinna (*staring at him*) I see. I see. (*She is exercising a great effort of self-control.*)

Jerome (*watching her, apprehensively*) So that's OK, then, isn't it? I mean, now you don't have to be upset. Do you? You don't need to feel jealous of Zoë. Or – or inadequate. Or unattractive. She's just an actress – who – who looks good and can handle children. But she's nothing compared with you. I mean, if you'd only said you – you wanted us to – Well, that's great. You know, that's what I wanted? Isn't that amazing? That's exactly what I wanted. There we were, the two of us – both wanting the same thing – and . . . Isn't life sometimes little short of miraculous? (*Pause.*) Alleluiah!

Corinna (*icily*) I hope you're recording all of this, Jerome. You'll no doubt have such a good laugh playing it back to yourself later. (*calling*) Mr Bickerdyke.

Jerome What the hell's the matter, now?

Corinna Mr Bickerdyke!

Mervyn returns from the kichen. He is putting away his phone.

Mervyn Coming. Just talking to the wife. We're having a dinner party tonight. My big chief is coming. With her husband. My wife reckons my chief is after me for bigger things. I said to my wife, I don't care what she's after so long as it isn't my body. (*He laughs.*)

Corinna (*frostily*) We're just leaving, Mr Bickerdyke.

Mervyn When you're ready. All settled?

Jerome Leaving? I thought –

Corinna I'll just fetch Geain. She must get dressed. (*calling as she goes*) Geain!

Mervyn Geain! But I thought . . .

Corinna goes off towards the bedrooms.

What's happening? I thought Geain was staying.

Jerome Yes. Things seem to have . . . changed. Something seems to have caused Corinna to change her mind.

Mervyn Yes? Well – strictly between us, Mr Watkins – your ex-wife appears to me to be a woman operating under some considerable inner stress.

Jerome Yes?

Mervyn Not, if you'll pardon my humour, quite the woman you'd want to see handling your investments. (*He laughs.*)

Corinna returns.

Corinna Right. I've called her.

Mervyn What's caused the change of plan, may I inquire?

Corinna I'm afraid, Mr Bickerdyke, we've both been the victim of one of my husband's practical jokes.

Mervyn We have?

Corinna Zoë is not what she appears. She was merely rented by Jerome for the afternoon. She doesn't belong here and she doesn't live here.

Mervyn But why – ? (*to Jerome*) Why did you do that?

Corinna To deceive you, Mr Bickerdyke, and to make a fool of me. That's why.

Jerome That is not why I did it –

Corinna (*calling*) Geain! If we leave now, Jerome, you can send your actress home early. You may even get some of your money back. I presume she's rented by the hour.

Jerome I don't understand you. I thought you'd be pleased.

Corinna Delighted. Thank you so much.

Mervyn I don't follow this? I don't follow this at all.

Geain appears, still in her 'nightdress', holding Nan's hand. They stop in the doorway.

Corinna Come along, Geain, there's been a slight confusion, we're going home.

Jerome Just a second, just a second . . .

Mervyn Now, let me get this straight. Are we saying that this woman, that Zoë is not living here with you? She is not a permanent companion but someone you have rented . . . ?

Jerome I don't see that the terms on which she's staying here make the blindest bit of difference, anyway.

Mervyn No difference?

Jerome Either she's suitable or she isn't suitable. It doesn't make any difference whether I'm paying her.

Mervyn I hardly think that argument holds water –

Corinna Of course it doesn't. Don't waste your breath. Come on.

Mervyn I mean, you may as well say there's no difference between a legal wife and a prostitute – I don't think I can accept that argument . . .

Jerome Let me tell you that that – that woman (*waves his hand in Nan's direction*) – has more dignity, more sense of loyalty and responsibility than any other fifty women you can name put together . . .

Corinna You? What do you know about women . . . ?

Jerome (*to Mervyn*) Anyway, what's made you change your mind all of a sudden? You liked her well enough –

Mervyn Ah, yes, but this was before I'd heard . . .

Jerome Couldn't keep your eyes off her, could you? Ogling and leering at her, your mouth stuffed with cake, you grubby little berk . . .

Mervyn Now, now, now, now . . .

Corinna Will you stop this?

Mervyn If you think that a remark of that sort will do your case one ounce of good –

Jerome (*simultaneously*) If we're having to rely on decisions from people like you, matey, what's it matter anyway? The ship's already sinking.

Corinna (*loudly, silencing them*) Will you shut up, both of you!

A silence.

Thank you. There is no point in arguing over this. Geain, come along please, we are going home. (*Pause.*) Geain.

Geain No.

Corinna What?

Geain I don't want to go.

Corinna You don't –

Geain I'm staying here.

Jerome There you are. There you are, you see. Out of the mouths . . . You heard that, Mr Bickerdyke? My daughter chooses to stay here with me. Could that be clearer?

Geain Son.

Jerome What?

Corinna Son. At least get its sex right.

Jerome My son, then, has chosen to stay with its father. Its natural father. There is justice. Thank you, God, there is justice.

Corinna This you note, Mr Bickerdyke, from a man who a few minutes ago asked to have this transvestite truck driver screwed back on the church roof.

Jerome That was a joke. That was a joke – between men. Eh, Geain?

Corinna Geain, I appreciate that after four years of me, your father probably holds some small novelty appeal. But may I warn you, dear, that it wears very, very thin, very, very rapidly.

Jerome Don't listen to that, Geain. Ignore this woman's prattle.

Mervyn May I just – I'm going to have to bound in here, once again . . . Geain. I'm afraid there's no question of your staying here, dear . . .

Jerome Don't listen to him, either. He's an old woman.

Mervyn Please, Mr Watkins. So far as I can gather, Geain, that woman whose hand you are holding is someone your father rented – for the day. Zoë is an actress pretending to be a friend of your father's. But she does not belong here and she doesn't intend staying. She is not a woman, therefore, we consider suitable to look after you. Do you understand that, Geain?

Geain She's not a woman.

Mervyn What?

Geain I said she's not a woman.

Corinna What do you mean, she's not a woman . . .

Geain She's a machine.

418

Mervyn (*laughing*) Now, come along, Geain, that's rather baby talk for someone of your age, isn't it – ?

Geain She is. (*indicating Jerome*) Ask him.

Jerome Well, I'm sure your father isn't going to – He's certainly not going to – He won't . . . He's not . . .

> *He is looking to Jerome for a denial but tails off when he doesn't get one.*

Jerome Yes, Geain's right. She's a machine.

Corinna I have never heard such . . . They're both as mad as each other.

Geain (*lifting Nan's skirt to reveal her metal upper legs*) Look.

Corinna (*screaming*) Oh, dear God.

Mervyn (*with her*) Wah!

Corinna (*in a low voice*) What is it? What have you let near her . . .

Jerome It's only a – It's just a machine.

Corinna But I've never seen – Where did it come from?

Jerome Er – from the man down the hall, actually.

Corinna The man down the hall? What man down what hall? Get it away from her, Jerome.

Geain Him.

Corinna Him. Get it away from him.

Jerome She's only a machine. It's harmless.

Mervyn But how did you come by this machine, Mr Watkins? I mean, where did it come from originally? I presume you didn't make it yourself?

Jerome No. This man gave it to me and I just – patched it up, that's all. Got it working again –

Corinna Patched it up? You?

Jerome Yes.

Corinna You can't even mend the front door. Get it away from him.

Jerome She can – He can walk away from it if he wants to. It's perfectly safe.

Corinna Geain, walk away from it.

Geain I don't want to walk away from it.

Mervyn You still haven't answered my question. Where did this thing originate?

Jerome It – it originated in a factory – it was a prototype for a model that never went into full production. The firm went broke. There's no need to worry. That was actually designed to look after children. It's technically an automatic child-minder. So. Geain couldn't be safer. Could he?

Mervyn (*suspiciously*) What was the name of this thing?

Jerome Well, it's a a NAN 300F. You probably wouldn't have –

Mervyn Oh yes, I have. I have indeed. I know all about the NAN 300F, thank you very much.

Corinna What about them?

Mervyn My department had to deal with the whole business.

Corinna What business?

Jerome Nothing. There were a few teething troubles –

Corinna What sort?

Jerome Just teething troubles . . .

Mervyn Yes, I suppose you could term them that. If you call putting a baby in a microwave oven teething troubles –

Corinna It did what?

Jerome Not this one. This one didn't do that.

Mervyn One of them did, Mr Watkins, one of them did.

Corinna It put a baby – ?

Jerome That was entirely the mother's fault.

Mervyn The mother's?

Jerome It wasn't the machine's fault – the mother had her kitchen moved around and never told the machine. I mean, how can you expect a machine to know any better –

Mervyn I don't see how you can possibly take the side of a machine against a human being.

Jerome Against most human beings, very easily. If human beings behaved a bit less like human beings and a bit more like machines, we'd all be better off –

Mervyn That is the most extraordinary argument I have ever heard . . .

Corinna Look, would you mind? That thing, that baby-killer, is at present holding my son's hand. Will you please do something about it? Mr Bickerdyke?

Mervyn Yes, I'll – I'll . . . Right (*speaking to Nan, slowly and nervously*) Let go. Let go her. Go let!

There is no response from Nan.

Corinna Oh, for heaven's sake. (*approaching Nan determinedly*) Will you let go of my child's hand at once? (*Standing bravely eye to eye with Nan.*) Do you hear me?

Nan I know what you're after, dear, and you're not going to have him. If you want Jerome, the only way you're going to get him is over my dead body, you calculating little trollop.

Corinna (*stepping back*) Oh, dear God . . .

Nan You'd better watch your step, Mrs Danvers, or one of these nights you're going to wake up with your throat cut.

Corinna (*retreating*) What have you put in this thing, Jerome? Who have you got in there?

Jerome No, she must have mistaken you for –

Corinna I know who she mistook me for, thank you, I'm not a complete fool . . . But who does she imagine she is?

Jerome (*intrigued by this question*) I don't know, you know. I never really asked her.

Corinna Are you going to tell it to release our child?

Jerome Not unless our child wants to be released.

Corinna How can you let this happen? You heard what he said.

Mervyn It's all right. Leave this to me. I'll stop this. (*to Nan*) Come on. Or I may have to resort to force.

Jerome I wouldn't –

Mervyn (*approaching Nan*) Come on. You have no right to that child . . .

Jerome Be careful, she may think you're a child-molester.

Mervyn I'm certainly not a child-molester, how dare you? (*to Nan*) Come along . . .

Mervyn tries to pull Geain away from Nan. Nan grips Mervyn's face in the palm of her hand for a second. Then, with a seemingly effortless push, sends the man reeling back across the room. Mervyn trips and falls on to his back.

Geain (*admiringly*) Yeah!

Corinna Stop her!

Jerome Nan!

A loud intermittent whooping sound is heard as Mervyn's personal alarm system goes off.

Corinna What the hell's that?

Jerome It must be his alarm system.

Corinna Well, switch it off. Get him to switch it off. Geain, come along.

Geain No.

Corinna It's dangerous. Darling, you saw what it did to Mr Bickerdyke.

Geain Yeah!

Nan I saw what it did to Mr Bickerdyke, darling.

Corinna Oh, dear God. It's mad. It's a mad machine. Will somebody stop that noise?

Jerome I think he's unconscious.

Corinna Well, you do it . . .

Jerome I don't know if I can. I don't suppose it's designed to –

*Jerome starts to fumble around under the inert Mervyn's
shirt. He comes out with a handful of wire. He pulls it
hopefully. Under the next, he unravels several yards of
wire from somewhere within the recesses of Mervyn.*

Corinna Just do it. Now, come along, Jerome, how do I
get this machine away from Geain? Please.

Jerome Call it darling. You have to call it that. She's
programmed to respond to 'darling'.

Corinna Oh, yes? Well, don't count on it as a general
principle. (*approaching Nan*) Darling . . . Hallo. Darling.

Nan Hallo, darling.

Corinna Oh, this is ridiculous . . . Jerome, will you switch
that off –

Jerome (*his hands full of wire*) I'm trying to switch it off.

Corinna (*trying again with Nan*) Let go, darling. Geain,
please, sweetheart . . .

Nan (*promptly*) I'd love to have children of my own.
Wouldn't it be lovely to hear them rushing about the flat,
laughing and yelling? With the right man – someone
who'd share them – they'd be everything I ever wanted. I
suppose you're either maternal or you aren't. I know
which I am.

Corinna (*over this*) What is it talking about? Jerome, it's
gone completely berserk, it's off again . . .

Jerome It's OK. You just keep feeding it trigger words,
that's all –

Corinna What the hell are you talking about, 'trigger
words'?

*Jerome leaves Mervyn swathed in wire. He comes over to
help Corinna. Mervyn, at this moment, starts to recover.*

Jerome Look. You just have to do this, that's all. Darling.

Nan Yes, darling.

Jerome Darling, let go.

Nan Letting go, darling.

Nan immediately releases Geain's hand.

Geain (*promptly retaking Nan's hand*) No.

Corinna Geain, for goodness' sake . . .

Mervyn gets to his knees and reaches with difficulty down the back of his jacket. The alarm stops.

Mervyn It's all right, I'm all right, I . . . (*aware of the wire that emanates from him*) My God, what's all this? What have you done to me? I'm coming apart.

Corinna Oh, do be quiet.

Mervyn Look at this. What have you done?

Jerome I'm sorry, I was trying to switch you off.

Mervyn Well, thank you so much. You've successfully unravelled my Italian thermal singlet. Thank you so very much.

Corinna (*back to Nan*) Darling, let go. Darling, let go.

Nan does not respond.

Jerome, she's taking no notice of me.

Jerome No, that's odd.

Mervyn A hundred and forty-three pounds' worth of imported garment here.

Corinna Oh, do shut up about your precious vest.

Nan kisses her on the cheek. Corinna leaps back.

Get away! Get away!

Jerome Darling, let go.

Nan does not respond.

No, I think Geain's overridden her. It's a safety thing. She won't let go unless Geain lets go.

Corinna Then, Geain, let go.

Geain No.

Mervyn All right, I'll deal with this. I'm going downstairs and I'm going to fetch help. I'll bring our friends up from the car. They'll sort it out, don't you worry.

Mervyn goes off along the hall. In a moment, we see him go out of the flat on the video screen. He leaves the door open.

Corinna Well, what are we going to do? Eh?

Jerome There's nothing we can do. If she won't let go, she won't let go.

Corinna Geain, listen to me . . .

Geain I'm not letting go.

Corinna Why not?

Geain I don't want to.

Corinna But. That's a machine. You can't stay with a machine, can you?

Geain Why not?

Corinna Because – because it's a machine –

Geain Dad did.

Corinna Yes. Well, your father's – Your father's your father. But ordinary people . . . like us – we can't stay –

(*She gives up.*) Jerome, for God's sake, tell her.

Jerome (*unconvincingly*) Yes. Geain. You see, you can't stay with a machine, can you – ?

Geain Why not?

Jerome Because. Human beings are – better. They're far superior to machines because . . .

Geain Why . . .

Jerome Because human beings are . . . they're . . . (*He pauses.*)

Corinna (*impatiently*) For God's sake, Jerome! Tell her why they're better –

Jerome (*desperately*) I can't think of a reason! Not a single one! I think she's right.

Corinna She's not right. You are not right, Geain. And neither is he. Listen. In the past, your father and I, we have – we have both been selfish, we have been thoughtless and stupid and – human. But we have also been, in our time, warm and spontaneous and amusing and joyful and – loving. Which is something we can also be, because we are human. But which that machine can never be. You see?

Geain seems to be still waiting to be convinced.

What we are going to do now, the three of us – you, me and Jerome – we are going down to that car and we are driving home together. And we're all going to start again. All of us. As of now. Isn't that right, Jerome? Jerome?

Jerome Right now? This minute?

Corinna Yes.

Jerome What about all this gear, I can't just . . . ?

Corinna Jerome, get this straight. It is us – or your gear. It

427

is this thing – (*indicating Nan*) – or us. Decide.

   A brief pause.

Jerome Yes. OK.

Corinna (*irritably*) Well, which is it to be?

Jerome (*moving to her*) You. Of course, you.

Corinna All right. Then, that's it. Geain? Will you let go now? Are you coming with us?

Geain (*finally releasing Nan*) OK.

   She moves to Corinna and Jerome. The three embrace.

Corinna Thank God.

   Mervyn appears on the video screen hurrying back into the flat.

Right. Change your clothes, we'll get in the car.

Geain Yeah.

   She is about to go off to fetch her clothes from the kitchen when Mervyn rushes in.

Corinna It's all right . . .

Mervyn No, it is not all right. We are under siege.

Jerome What?

Mervyn Those Daughters – whatever they call themselves. They're swarming all over the place outside. Our two are only just managing to hold them off. We have to leave now.

Geain Rancid sows.

Corinna Oh, dear Lord. Geain, come as you are. You haven't got time to change now.

A clang as a missile hits one of the shutters.

Mervyn We do have to hurry.

Corinna Tell them we're coming, tell them we're on our way.

Mervyn Quick as you can.

Another missile.

Corinna Geain . . .

Geain Right. (*to Nan*) Cheerio then. (*to Jerome*) Can Zoë say goodbye to me?

Corinna Geain, do come on.

Geain I want Zoë to say goodbye to me.

Jerome Darling. Say goodbye to Geain.

Nan Goodbye, Geain dear. See you soon. See you very soon. (*She waves.*) Bye-bye. Bye-bye.

Geain Bye, Zoë. See you again.

Corinna No, darling, you won't be seeing her again, I'm afraid. Sorry about that. Goodbye.

Nan stops waving. More missiles hit the shutters.

All right. Jerome?

Jerome I'm coming, I'll just fetch a few . . .

Geain Come on, Dad.

Jerome Yes, I will. I promise. You go on.

Corinna They won't wait.

Corinna and Geain go out down the hall. We see them on the screen leaving the flat. The door remains open. The screen is left lit. Jerome goes off to the bedroom.

Nan is left alone. In a moment, she moves and sits in the chair. A silence. Then, the same technician's voice that we heard at the start emanates from somewhere within Nan. Her lips move vaguely in sync.

Voice NAN 300F, series four, model 99148622G for Gertie. Function now completed. System final closedown – in two minutes. Safety count commencing at sixty seconds.

Nan sits very still, swaying slightly as she sings softly to herself.

Nan (*sings*)
You're not my first love . . .
It would only be a lie if I pretended –
In the past there have been others
Who have slept between these covers
But I promise
Though you're far too late in life to be my first love,
You'll be my last love.
I swear to you, you're gonna be my last love . . .

As she sings, Jerome comes back with a hastily packed holdall. He gives Nan the merest of glances. Another missile hits the shutters. Jerome goes to the console. He seems to be deliberating what to take with him. He stands undecided. Corinna appears on the screen as she re-enters the flat. A moment later, she comes in from the hall.

Corinna Jerome, what are you doing?

Jerome Sorry, I was just –

Corinna They're swarming around out there. There's dozens of them. They're trying to get at Geain. I told her not to come dressed like that. Are you coming?

Jerome Listen, when you –

Corinna (*impatient*) What?

Jerome When you said all that about us – restarting – was that just to get Geain to leave or –

Corinna No, of course it wasn't. I wouldn't have said it for that.

Jerome You sure?

Corinna Yes.

Jerome You want me back with you?

Corinna Yes.

Jerome Why?

Corinna (*desperately, at the end of her tether*) Because we both love you, Jerome. God knows why, but we love you. Love, love, love! All right. Now, come on, please.

Jerome I will. I'm coming. Go ahead. Tell them I'm on my way.

He kisses her.

Go on. Don't let them leave.

Corinna Be quick.

Corinna goes out. We see her leave once more on the screen. Jerome grabs up a tape, the one of Geain. He goes out after her.

Voice (*from Nan*) Safety count commencing. Sixty – fifty-nine – fifty-eight – fifty-seven – fifty-six – fifty-five . . .

As the count continues, the Voice slowly gets quieter and quieter until only her lips are moving. Jerome appears on the screen at the front door. He seems about to leave, changes his mind and comes back into the flat, this time closing the front door. Nan's count continues.

So does the sound of missiles striking the shutters with increasing regularity. Jerome returns and goes to the console. He stops the recording machine and winds it back.

Jerome's recorded voice . . . about us – restarting – was that just to persuade Geain to leave or –

Corinna's recorded voice No, of cours–

Jerome spools forward again. He replays.

. . . both love you, Jerome. God knows why, but we love you. Love, love, love! All ri–

Jerome plays around with the recording some more. Nan continues in silence, her mouth barely moving.

Love! Love! Love! . . .

Jerome (*like a man who has had a vision*) My God!

He rushes round the room uncovering the rest of the technical equipment that, till now, has remained unseen. Nearly everything in the room, it transpires, is actually part of Jerome's recording and sampling gear, including the coffee table. As he does this, a fresh series of furious clangs are heard on the shutters outside. These he all but ignores. While he does this, Nan's countdown reaches zero and she shuts down. Quietly and with very little sign. She lifts one hand slightly and then lets it drop. A final wave. Her head slumps and she goes limp. Jerome begins to work feverishly now, treating the original sound of Corinna's cry of 'love', sampling and synthesizing. A whole complex, interminable process, dramatically condensed into stage seconds. Jerome starts to play. At first improvising, then slowly growing in confidence as he goes, the texture ever thickening, building in volume. A great chorus of varying 'love's – all stemming from Corinna's orginal. This is his 'love'

432

*composition. He plays for perhaps three or four
minutes. During Jerome's playing the doorbell must
have rung unheard because the screen is filled with the
faces of Corinna, Geain and Mervyn all silently shouting
at the video camera outside to be readmitted. This is
swiftly interrupted by the image of Lupus appearing on
the screen – apparently the phone has rung, too. Jerome
fails to notice any of it. Lupus is on some sort of
hospital trolley – evidently on his way for surgery. He is
swathed in bandages and is only barely recognizable.
But his spirit, beneath all that, seems reasonably
unimpaired. He waves his arms, talking animatedly, if
inaudibly. He shows Jerome his one unbandaged thumb
in a thumbs-up sign, as always reassuring his friend not
to worry about him. Lupus is slowly wheeled away
from the camera, up the corridor. This image is cross-
cut with increasing speed as Corinna's, Geain's and
Mervyn's images momentarily override the incoming
video call. Finally, a nurse's hand switches off the
hospital picture. On screen, at the front door, Corinna
and company take a final look behind them and rush
away. Rita, the Daughter of Darkness, yelling inaudible
obscenities, comes racing up the hall brandishing an
iron bar. Noticing the camera in passing, she pauses to
smash it. The screen goes dark. Jerome, oblivious, plays
on like a man possessed. Finally, with a great flourish,
he finishes. A silence. He stands, triumphant.*

Jerome (*jubilant and breathless*) That's it! That's *it*!

*A silence. A missile, thrown from outside, clangs against
the shutters. Jerome does not react.*

(*already feeling rather anti-climactic*) That's it. (*He looks
around him and sits.*) Yeah! (*Pause.*) That's it, then.

*He sits all alone. And realizes how alone he is. As the
missiles continue to clang – curtain.*

MAN OF THE MOMENT

Characters

Vic Parks
Trudy, *his wife*
Cindy, aged seven, *their daughter*
Sharon Giffin, *their children's nanny*
Ruy, *their Spanish gardener*
Marta, Ruy's wife, *their Spanish maid*
Kenny Collins, *Vic's manager*
Jill Rillington
Douglas Beechey
Ashley Barnes, *a TV floor manager*
plus
seven actors (six non-speaking)

Setting: The patio/pool area of Vic's and Trudy's
Mediterranean villa.
Time: One day, recently.

Man of the Moment was first performed in Scarborough at the Stephen Joseph Theatre in the Round on 10 August 1988. The cast was as follows:

Jill Rillington Lynette Edwards
Trudy Lesley Meade
Kenny Collins Simon Chandler
Ruy Daniel Collings
Douglas Beechey Jon Strickland
Vic Parks Peter Laird
Cindy Lisa Bailey *or*
                Charlotte Kershaw
Sharon Giffin Shirley-Anne Selby
Marta Doreen Andrew
Ashley Barnes Peter Forbes
David Adam Godley

Directed by Alan Ayckbourn
Designed by Michael Holt

It was subsequently performed at the Globe Theatre,
London, on 14 February 1990. The cast was as follows:

Jill Rillington Samantha Bond
Trudy Diane Bull
Kenny Collins Simon Chandler
Ruy Daniel Collings
Douglas Beechey Michael Gambon
Vic Parks Peter Bowles
Cindy Joanna Relf *or*
            Diana Endsor
Sharon Giffin Shirley-Anne Selby
Marta Doreen Andrew
Ashley Barnes Terence Booth
David Paul Stewart

Directed by Alan Ayckbourn
Designed by Roger Glossop

Act One

The paved patio/pool area of a modern, moderate-sized
(three-bedroomed) villa in a Spanish-speaking area of the
Mediterranean. At one side, a glimpse of the villa itself.
White stucco walls and wooden shutters. The edge of the
living area – tiled floor with rugs – perhaps the end of
what promises to be a very long drinks bar. Large, open
sliding doors leading out from the living area on to a
shaded area. Here, a table and chairs to seat about four.
Moving away from the house further, a step down to a
slightly sunken sunbathing area. Here, two or three sun
loungers and a low table. At the other side, steps up again
to the back gate of the villa, which in turn leads to a
carport and the rough road.

   Also visible, the raised, angled corner of the swimming
pool (deep end). It is possible to walk around the pool,
either along the deep end to reach the diving board
(unseen) or along the poolside to reach the shallow end.
One or two shrubs in tubs. Perhaps a toy left lying about,
betraying the presence of young children.

   At the start, though, none of this is visible. Just a light
on **Jill Rillington** who sits on the patio in a chair beside the
table, angled out facing away from the house. **Jill** is in her
early thirties and looking good – certainly at first glance.
Every inch the assured, charming TV reporter/presenter.

   She is at present doing a piece to camera, though we
won't guess this immediately. The film crew are out of
sight and remain so throughout. Sometimes we will hear
their distant voices calling to **Jill** but their words are
impossible to decipher.

Jill (*to camera*) Hallo. I'm Jill Rillington. In this edition of *Their Paths Crossed*, we tell a story that started seventeen years ago in the slow and sneet of a Surrey Novem . . . Oh, piss! Keep rolling. We'll go again. Snow and sleet. Snow and sleet . . . (*slowly*) Snow – and – sleet . . . Here we go. Snow and sleet. Hallo. I'm Rill Jillington . . . My God, I don't believe this – Right, straight in – keep turning. Hallo. I'm Jill Rillington. In this edition of *Their Paths Crossed*, we tell a story that started seventeen years ago in the snow and sleet of a Surrey November morning and finishes – (*She gestures. As she does so, the lights spread out to include the whole area, rather as if the camera had pulled back to include her surroundings. We see she is wearing a discreet radio mic attached to her blouse. On the table beside her is a cardboard folder containing research material, press clippings and interview notes.*) – here. In the brilliant sunshine of a glorious Mediterranean summer. It's a story which has – fittingly perhaps – almost a fairy-tale ring to it. A tale with a hero and a villain – even a damsel in distress. But this is no child's fable, it is a true story. This is the real world where nothing is as it seems. This is the real world where heroes are easily forgotten; this is the real world where the villains may, themselves, become heroes. And as for distressed damsels – well, are they in reality ever truly rescued? I'll leave you, the viewer, to judge for yourself . . . (*She pauses for a moment, looking towards the camera.*) And – cut! OK?

A shout of assent from the crew.

Did you get the wide? (*gesturing*) The wide?

Crew replies.

Good. Did you get this whole area? (*gesturing and yelling*) This whole area?

A yell from one of the crew.

What? (*She notices her radio mic.*) Oh, yes. Sorry, Dan. Didn't mean to burst your eardrums. Sorry, my love. (*She consults her watch. She makes to yell again then thinks better of it.*) George – (*quietly*) Sorry, love. Dan, can you tell George to set up the arrival shot. For the arrival. Can he do that? Where we talked about? On the bend? So we see this man's taxi coming up the hill and their first meeting at the front door? OK? George knows where. I'll be with you in a sec. Thank you, love. I'll unplug. Save your batteries.

> *She unplugs her mic from its transmitter in her pocket and tucks away the lead. As she is doing this, **Trudy** comes out from the house rather tentatively. She is only a few years older than Jill but looks rather more. Possibly due to an over-eagerness to please her husband Vic, Trudy has attempted to retain the look of someone ten years younger; an image presumably with which he originally fell in love. She has taken rather more care than usual this morning as the TV cameras are about.*

Trudy Sorry. Is it all right for me – ?

Jill Yes, we've finished. It's quite all right.

Trudy Would you all care for coffee? A cup of coffee?

Jill Well, I'd love one. I think the crew are probably OK. They seem to have brought their own – refreshments.

Trudy Sure?

Jill No, it's probably best to let them get on. We need to set up for this new shot. I want to catch Mr Beechey actually arriving here straight from his hotel . . .

Trudy Yes, yes, yes . . .

Jill And hopefully his first meeting with your husband . . .

Trudy Yes, yes. I don't know if Vic's . . .

Jill Is he still not back?

Trudy Well, he should be. He said he would be. (*moving to the gate*) Kenny was going to see if he could . . . Just a minute, I'll . . . (*calling to someone*) Kenny, is he coming? Can you see them? No?

Jill No?

Trudy No, I'm sorry. He only took the children down to the beach. With Sharon. She's their nanny. You can usually see them on the beach down there . . . He did promise he'd be here . . .

Jill (*rather coolly*) Yes, he did.

Trudy It's not like him to do this. I'll make the coffee. It may have just slipped his mind. (*smiling*) Once he gets with the kids . . .

Trudy hurries back into the house.

Jill (*smiling*) Yes. (*Sourly, looking at her watch again.*) Bugger him.

She is gathering up her folder from the table as **Kenny** *comes through the back gate. Late twenties or early thirties. He is one of the new breed of young manager/ agents with a cool, laid-back, slightly public school, unflappable exterior which just serves to conceal any insecurity beneath.*

Kenny No. No sign.

Jill Well, where is he?

Kenny Digging on the beach. Burying the kids. Bonking the nanny. I don't know.

Jill But he knew about this. He knew . . .

Kenny Oh, yes, he knew all right.

Jill I mean you knew it, Kenny, we talked about it last night . . .

Kenny I know, he definitely knew . . .

Jill He knew I wanted to catch their first meeting . . .

Kenny I know, I know . . .

Jill I needed that on camera. He knew that.

Kenny I know, he knew. He said you'd said it to him, I know . . .

Jill I said it to him. You know I did.

Kenny I know. He knew, all right, he knew . . .

Jill Then why the hell isn't he here if he knew?

Kenny I don't know. (*Pause.*) You know Vic.

Jill Yes.

Kenny You can't tell him.

Jill I don't see what makes him so special.

Kenny He's a star, darling. A star. Isn't he? (*Pause.*) He won't let you down. Don't worry.

Jill There's no point in saying that. He just has.

Kenny You can film it later. The meeting. You can mock it up later.

Jill I doubt it.

Kenny Why not? Vic can do that. He's a pro. He's used to that. He did a programme once. Visiting sick kids in hospital. He was 140 miles away in a London studio. No one ever knew. Except the kids he was meant to be visiting. He can do that sort of thing. Piece of cake.

445

Jill I'm sure Vic could. I'm not so sure about Mr Beechey.

Kenny No?

Jill No.

Kenny Not your television natural, I take it?

Jill He's about as lively as a sheet of laminated chipboard. I've just spent four days interviewing Mr Beechey. In his home town of Purley. I think I've got about twenty seconds of usable material. And those are the shots of Purley.

Kenny Not a talker?

Jill Oh, he talks. It's just he never says anything. You know, when I first started out with the BBC as a radio interviewer, I went on this course and they warned us that one day we'd all of us find ourselves interviewing the uninterviewable. I thought, after ten years, I'd managed to escape. And then along comes Mr Beechey. (*musing*) It's not that he won't talk. You can usually cope with that. We all get that. Then you can generally coax them round. Eventually. Or you say something so blatantly incorrect about them, they're forced to contradict you in self-defence. But this man, he's deadly. The point is, there's absolutely nothing you can say to him that he doesn't agree with. He smothers you with approval. It's like interviewing a fire blanket.

Kenny You normally only meet people like that during general elections, don't you? What about Mrs Beechey? Any joy with her?

Jill She spent the four days we were there hiding in the boxroom. I never got to speak to her at all. All I'm hoping is, once he's here – far away from the bright lights of Purley – he might open up.

Kenny (*wandering to the gate to look*) A little sunshine. Does wonders.

Jill Is Vic coming?

Kenny Can't see him.

Jill Listen, Kenny, I hope he's taking this seriously . . .

Kenny Of course. You know Vic. He's a pro . . .

Jill I mean, this may just be another tacky little interview as far as he's concerned . . .

Kenny He's never said that –

Jill . . . a jokey programme which only merits an eighth of his attention . . .

Kenny Whoever said that – ?

Jill . . . but for me this is important. It may not seem much to you, but if this works out – then I have their firm provisional promise of the other seven slots. That is eight in all . . .

Kenny (*duly impressed*) Eight, heavens!

Jill Plus – plus – wait for it! Plus another pencilled second series of eight in the New Year.

Kenny Sixteen, goodness . . .

Jill Right. Sixteen. Of my own series. Seventy per cent film – thirty per cent studio – me – nobody else – me alone –

Kenny (*humouring her along*) That's some doing. These days.

Jill Oh, I know a lot of people are sitting back there waiting for me to fall flat on my arse. Colin and Martin thing. Clare. She certainly is. And that Richard – whatsit. They are all dying for that to happen . . . Well, I've got

447

this far and no one is going to trip me up now. I've fought for this chance – just watch me go . . .

Kenny I will. I will . . .

Jill Not Mr Beechey, not you, not Vic, not that damp, septic tank of a film crew I've been landed with – and I know who saddled me with them, thank you very much, Mrs McIver, I'll settle you when I get back home, madam, see if I don't – God, is this mic still on? No . . . Oh, relief . . . Kenny, if the choice is this or making ten-minute promo videos of eager fringe companies from Stockport for the British Council, I know which I want to do. Just remember Vic owes me, Kenny. He owes me one. I helped him. Remember that. (*pointing to herself*) This kid from BBC Radio Bristol got that whole splendid career of his started. Remember that.

Kenny All right, all right.

Jill Just remember.

Kenny All right. Easy.

Pause. Jill simmers.

We love you. Promise. We're all mad about you.

Jill (*muttering*) I don't want love, I just want basic co-operation, all right?

Kenny (*moving back to the gate*) Relax.

Jill (*looking at her watch again*) He should be here. Why isn't he here? Neither of them are here. This is all I need.

Kenny It's only one minute past.

Jill By the time they get here, that film crew will want a break. I've never met anything like them. Every time they change film they have a union meeting. And it's no use trying to do anything after lunch, because they're all totally legless. There's that much camera shake, you'd think we were filming on the top of Mount Etna . . .

Kenny (*still at the gate*) There's a car in the distance just starting up the hill.

Jill Is it Vic?

Kenny No, it's not the jeep. It looks like a taxi from here. Probably your Mr Beechey.

Jill Right. Well, we can film him arriving, anyway. Get his reactions. If he has any. Keep a look out for Vic. (*as she goes*) You're his agent, get him here.

Kenny His manager . . .

Jill hurries out through the garden gate.

Jill (*calling*) George! Come on, get a move on. He's coming! Come on, come on!

As Jill goes, Trudy comes out from the house with a tray of coffee things.

Trudy Is something happening?

Kenny I think Mr Beechey's arrived.

Trudy (*without enthusiasm*) Oh. Good.

Kenny What's the matter? Nervous?

Trudy Not at all.

Kenny It was years ago. You weren't even around.

Trudy You know perfectly well how I feel about all this.

Kenny All right.

Trudy I blame you. You talked him into it. This programme.

Kenny When have I ever talked Vic into anything? When

has anyone? Come on. Don't blame me. Be honest. Have *you*? Have you ever talked him into anything?

Trudy doesn't reply.

(*his point proved*) Well, then.

Trudy He said he'd be back by now. He's forgotten. I bet that's what's happened. He always forgets what he doesn't choose to remember.

Kenny Sharon might have reminded him.

Trudy (*with ill-concealed dislike*) Well, I think telling the time's a bit beyond Sharon. I'd better fetch another cup. (*She makes to leave.*)

Kenny Haven't you got anyone to help you today?

Trudy How do you mean?

Kenny You know. To make the coffee? Fetch things out?

Trudy Oh, yes. Marta's here. Only by the time I've explained it to her, it's quicker to do it myself. I mean, she can speak quite good English. I know she can. She always understands Vic. It's just me. She doesn't seem to understand me at all. It's probably the way I talk, I don't know . . .

> *Trudy goes back into the house. Kenny wanders to the pool. He stoops and tests the water temperature with his hand. As he is doing this,* **Ruy,** *a man in his fifties, comes through the back gate with a pool rake. He ignores Kenny, as he ignores everyone, except on those rare occasions when Vic speaks to him.*

Kenny Good morning to you.

> *Ruy totally ignores him. He starts to rake the surface of the pool. This activity soon takes him out of view.*

(*sarcastically, in response to Ruy's lack of response*)
Thank you. And the same to you. Lovely chatting to you.
Now, you must excuse me interrupting but I have to get
on. Not at all. And the same to you.

> *Trudy enters from the house.*

Trudy (*talking to someone following behind her*) We're
just about to have coffee out here. If you'd care to join
us . . .

> *Trudy is followed by **Douglas Beechey**, a man in his
> early forties. He is, as Jill has hinted, quite staggeringly
> unimpressive on first acquaintance. He is, though, as
> with many of nature's creatures, compensated for his
> apparent total lack of aggression by an almost complete
> invulnerability to attack by others. His clothes are quite
> unsuited to the climate.*

Douglas (*as he approaches*) Isn't this glorious? Isn't this
simply glorious . . . (*stopping in the doorway to survey the
patio and pool*) Oh, now. This is glorious.

Trudy (*unsure how to react*) Thank you. May I introduce
(*indicating Kenny*) – have you met my husband's manager?

Kenny (*stepping towards them*) How do you do?

Trudy This is Kenneth Collins. Mr Beechey.

Douglas Douglas Beechey. How do you do?

Kenny Kenny Collins. Good to meet you.

> *They shake hands.*

Douglas Isn't this glorious? Isn't this just glorious? May I
– (*He indicates the terrace.*)

Trudy (*waving him in*) Of course.

Douglas (*exploring the area*) Oh. Oh. Oh. Oh. (*admiring* *the view from the garden gate*) Oh. (*investigating the pool*) Oh. Look at this pool. Doesn't that look inviting?

Trudy You're welcome to have a swim, any time.

Douglas No, I don't swim.

Trudy No?

Douglas No, no. Me and water, I'm afraid, we've never seen eye to eye. (*calling to the unseen Ruy*) Hallo. Good morning to you.

Trudy I was just fetching another cup. Excuse me.

Douglas Of course. May I help at all . . . ?

Trudy No, no. Wait there.

Trudy goes back into the house.

Douglas Well, I must say. Who could ask for anything more, eh?

Kenny Yes.

Douglas Glorious. Quite glorious. (*indicating in Ruy's direction*) Who's that? Is he one of the family?

Kenny No, that's the gardener.

Douglas (*impressed*) Oh. The gardener. I see.

Kenny Right.

Douglas Very impressive. (*looking around*) All you need now is a garden, eh? (*He laughs.*)

Kenny Well, I think he cleans the pool and – odd jobs, you know –

Douglas Oh, yes, I'm sure. I was only joking. I expect this paving would need weeding to start with. I should imagine. I suppose they get weeds here, don't they? Same as we do?

Kenny I would imagine so.

Douglas (*calling to Ruy*) Excuse me, I say . . . Do you get weeds? I say! Do you have weeds here?

Kenny I don't think he speaks much English.

Douglas Oh. (*calling*) *Gracias!* (*to Kenny*) That's the only bit of Spanish I know.

Kenny Pretty impressive.

Douglas I definitely don't know the Spanish for weed killer, that's for certain. (*breathing in the air*) Glorious! (*Slight pause.*)

Kenny Good flight?

Douglas Pardon?

Kenny Good flight? Out here? On the aeroplane? Did you have a good one?

Douglas Oh, glorious. I was with a very jolly crowd from Dagenham. Singing their heads off, all the way over.

Kenny Oh, yes?

Douglas When they weren't playing practical jokes on the crew, that was. You had to laugh.

Kenny Sounds fun.

Douglas Couple of them dressed up as air hostesses. Couple of the men. Then it turned out we were all staying in the same hotel. So . . .

Kenny That OK? The hotel?

Douglas Very clean. And the windows open. That's all I ever ask for in a hotel.

Kenny (*slightly baffled*) Really?

Douglas I need air to sleep, you see. Not that I stay in them very often. Oh, I'm savouring every minute of this, I can tell you. Free trip. Free meals. Free hotel. VIP treatment. And appearing on the television. You don't get that every day, do you?

Kenny You certainly don't.

Douglas Make the most of it, I say.

Kenny I should.

Douglas I see they were all out there to greet my arrival. The film crew. I got to know them all quite well. While they were sitting in our front room for four days. Good to see them again. All out there. Filming away. And dear old Jill, waving her arms about as usual. She doesn't half go at them sometimes. Mind you, they take it all in very good part. They're a very pleasant bunch. Very easy-going, I've found. Well, let's put it this way, we certainly had a few good laughs while they were in Purley. (*He has moved back to stand by the garden gate.*) That'll be the Mediterranean Sea? Down there? Right?

Kenny The bit covered in water. Where the land stops.

Douglas (*surveying the view thoughtfully*) The Med, eh? Well, well. That's something else I can tell people I've seen.

Trudy returns with the extra cup.

Trudy Here we are.

Douglas Well, I can't say I'm not a tinge green, Mrs Parks. I must say, this is just perfection.

Trudy Yes, we're very – lucky.

Kenny (*anxious to correct any wrong impression*) Mind you, you didn't get it for nothing, did you? You've earned it.

Douglas (*anxious to do the same*) Oh, yes.

Trudy Well, Vic earned it.

Kenny You both have.

Trudy (*smiling, unconvinced*) It's nice of you to say so.

Douglas Behind every successful man, don't they say?

Trudy I'm afraid my husband's still on the beach with the children. He should be back shortly.

Douglas Oh, how many children have you?

Trudy Two. Coffee, Mr Beechey?

Douglas Thank you. Do call me Douglas, won't you? Milk and three sugars, thank you.

Trudy Kenny?

Kenny Please. Usual. Black, no sugar.

Douglas And how old are the children, Trudy – may I call you Trudy?

Trudy Cindy is seven and Timmy is just five.

Douglas Lovely. One of each, then?

Trudy Yes.

Douglas They must love it out here.

Trudy Oh, yes, they do. (*offering him coffee*) Mr Beechey.

Douglas Thank you. Douglas. Please. Call me Douglas.

Slight pause, Kenny is served coffee.

Kenny Thanks. Do you have children, Mr – Douglas?

Douglas No. No. (*A slight pause as if he might be going to say something else.*) No.

Kenny Ah.

Douglas My wife was – Well, we made a joint decision not to have any. We decided we weren't ideal parent material. Either of us.

Kenny It's a pity your wife couldn't come with you.

Douglas Oh, no. Nerys is not a traveller.

Kenny No?

Douglas I'm afraid this sort of trip would be quite beyond her.

Kenny Oh. What a shame.

Pause.

Trudy She's – She's all right, is she? I mean, she's not ill, your wife?

Douglas Oh, no. She's very chirpy.

Kenny Oh, grand.

Douglas At present. She has her ups and downs, of course.

Trudy Don't we all?

Kenny Absolutely.

Pause.

Trudy You'll appreciate that I'm Vic's second wife. I wasn't around when – when all that happened – I mean, Vic and I, we've only been married eight years.

Douglas Yes, I did read he'd remarried. I read all about your romance. In his book.

Trudy (*not pleased*) Did you?

Douglas Sounded very romantic. Is that how it actually

456

was? Did he really abduct you from the middle of a public car park in the back of a transit van?

Trudy (*reluctantly*) Well, sort of, yes . . .

Kenny Mind you, Trudy was standing around for some time waiting to be abducted, weren't you?

Douglas laughs. Another pause.

Trudy No, what I'm saying is that – all that happened – all that – between you – happened while Vic was married to Donna, you see. I was not around then. I didn't even know him. I was married to somebody else as well, as it happens. Only that didn't work out.

Douglas That would be your previous marriage to the dental mechanic?

Trudy Yes . . .

Douglas Oh, dear . . .

Trudy (*faintly irritated*) No, what I'm saying is, I had nothing to do with that part of Vic's life. If they want to know about that – for this programme – then they'll have to ask Donna. Providing they can sober her up. By the time I met Vic that was all in the past. I wasn't a part of it and I don't really want to know about it. We're all different people now. At least I hope we are. And I have to say that I don't agree with this programme anyway. I don't honestly think they should be doing it. I'm sorry. I've said it to Vic and I've said it to her. That Jill Rillington. And now I'm saying it to you. I'm sorry. I think it's unnecessary. And hurtful. I think it's raking over old ground and opening old wounds. I'm not at all surprised your wife isn't here. If I were her, I certainly wouldn't be here. Not after what she – Still. As I say, I'm an outsider. I wasn't even around when it happened. And what Vic does is his own affair. But I am his wife and I think I might have

457

been consulted. I'm also the mother of his children – though you wouldn't think so sometimes, would you? (*She is suddenly on the verge of crying.*) Excuse me. I just have to fetch some – things . . .

> *Trudy hurries into the house. Douglas rises, amazed. Kenny remains seated.*

Kenny (*calling calmly after her*) Trudy . . . love . . . (*Silence.*) She'll be all right.

Douglas Oh, dear. I had no idea she felt . . . I mean, I wouldn't . . .

Kenny She'll be fine. Don't worry. Things are just a bit (*he gestures*) – you know . . .

Douglas How do you mean?

Kenny Between them. Her and Vic.

Douglas Oh . . .

Kenny Just at the moment. Temporarily. Nothing at all, really. Vic's a bit of a lad sometimes. I mean, I've known them both for ages. They're terrific people. Both of them. I should know. It was me who introduced them.

Douglas Did you really? That wasn't in the book.

Kenny Vic was just – getting going, you know, after – after his leave of absence – and he took me on – initially as his agent – and later on, as he got in greater demand, I became his personal manager. I got him his first weekly TV slot – regional, mind you – sort of local *Crimewatch/Police Five* sort of thing, you know – scare the old ladies off to bed type of show – and Trudy was a friend of the producer's secretary or somesuch. And. Romance, romance.

Douglas I hope this programme hasn't created a tension between them.

Kenny No, no, no . . . Why on earth should it? Nice plug for Vic. Nice holiday for you – as you say – all expenses paid. Who's it hurting? I mean, your wife didn't object, did she? And she has far more reason to than Trudy, hasn't she? But your wife's presumably perfectly happy for you to be here?

Douglas Well, Nerys had initial objections, I have to say. And she certainly didn't want to be any part of it herself. Although Jill Rillington did try very hard to persuade her to be interviewed. But Nerys said if I wanted to do it and Vic Parks wanted to do it, then who was she . . . I mean, the way Jill described the programme to me, I think it's a very interesting idea, don't you? What's happened to us all since. Since . . .

Kenny Oh, you bet . . .

Douglas Take Vic, for instance. He has had the most amazing career, hasn't he? Considering.

Kenny Oh, incredible . . .

Douglas I mean, from what he was then – to what he is now. He's an example to us all, isn't he? . . .

Kenny He is.

Douglas A remarkable man. You have to admire him. What he's done. Particularly for the young people. And all that from nothing.

Kenny Less than that really.

Douglas Absolutely.

Slight pause.

Kenny I suppose quite a lot must have happened to you, as well? In, what is it, seventeen years? You must have seen some changes in your own life.

Douglas One or two. (*He reflects.*) Not many really. I married Nerys, of course. And I changed my job. Well, I could hardly have continued at the bank.

Kenny Memories too painful, were they?

Douglas No, no. But people used to come in just to stare at me, you know. While we were trying to conduct bank business. And Mr Marsh – that was my manager at the time – he's retired now to Bournemouth – he felt my presence was not conducive to normal, satisfactory banking practices and he offered to request a transfer for me to another district. But I couldn't in all conscience leave Purley – I was born and bred there, you see – so I left the bank altogether. And then, hey presto, I was lucky enough to land a job straightaway with a local firm of double-glazing consultants, and I've been book-keeping for them ever since. Not an earth-shattering tale, perhaps, but one with a happy ending none the less.

Kenny And a success story, too. In its own way.

Douglas True. True. Nerys and I are both happy, anyway. That's the main thing.

Kenny And you've both got your health and strength.

Douglas And we've both got our health and strength, precisely. Well, Nerys is sometimes . . . But it's mostly in her mind. I've told her she looks fine. She really does. Her face is fine.

Kenny Why, she's not – is she – still disfigured, is she?

Douglas Oh, no, no, no. All there is – if you look very carefully, she's got the faintest traces of scar tissue, just around here (*he indicates the side of his face*) – but you really couldn't tell, I promise. He did a marvellous job, that surgeon. One of the best of his day, he was – he's dead now, alas. Died last year –

Kenny Oh, sad . . .

Douglas But if she wears the make-up, it's undetectable. No one could tell.

Kenny Fine, then . . .

Douglas The trouble is, Nerys won't always trouble with the make-up. She can't always be bothered. So then she goes out to the shops and people start staring at her – or she imagines they're staring at her anyway – I don't honestly think, myself, they bother to give her a second look, if you want the truth, still . . . Then she comes home upset and she won't go out of the house for months on end. I've said to her, Nerys, if you'd only wear the make-up, you wouldn't have all this upset, would you?

Kenny A lot of women wear make-up.

Douglas They do. I've told her that.

Kenny Most women wear make-up.

Douglas Yes. I mean, this is a special make-up, it has to be said. It's slightly thicker than normal. But it's the same principle. It's like I imagine they must wear on the television. Like dancers must wear. I expect.

Kenny Right.

Douglas I mean, if she was a man, I'd have understood her reluctance . . .

Kenny Oh, yes. If you were a man you wouldn't necessarily want to go strolling about in make-up, would you?

Douglas Not in Purley you wouldn't, certainly. But a woman.

Jill comes on through the garden gate. She is evidently angry.

461

Jill Sod them. They are useless. They are worse than useless.

Douglas (*rising*) Hallo, Jill . . .

Jill (*grimly*) Hallo, Mr Beechey. We may have to ask you to arrive all over again. We were just a little slow catching you first time around . . .

Douglas Right-oh, Jill. Just say the word. (*to Kenny*) I'm getting rather expert at this filming. She had me walking in and out of our kitchen, must have been thirty-five times one day. (*laughingly to Jill*) It was about that, wasn't it?

Jill (*unamused*) At least thirty-five. Is this coffee?

Kenny Help yourself. Trudy's just – just . . . doing something or other.

Jill helps herself to coffee.

Douglas I did a very good sprint round the local park for you, though, didn't I? We got that in one take, didn't we? I'm looking forward to seeing that. I ran for miles, Kenneth, you've no idea. Nearly killed me. Go on, the crew kept shouting, keep going. (*He laughs.*) I'm looking forward to that.

Jill Well, we may have to leave that bit out, Mr Beechey –

Douglas Oh, dear.

Jill We've got so much wonderful stuff already.

Douglas The crew will be disappointed. It was their idea, wasn't it?

Jill Yes. (*beaming at him with her best professional smile*) Anyway. You're here. That's the main thing. What are your first impressions then, Mr Beechey? Of this place?

Kenny Glorious.

Jill (*irritably*) What?

Douglas Quite right. Glorious. I couldn't have put it better myself. I must say, I've always heard tell of the dazzling world of show business, but this is the first time I've ever experienced it.

Jill You wouldn't mind it yourself?

Douglas I certainly wouldn't.

Jill How do you feel about someone like, say, Vic having it?

Douglas Lucky him, that's what I say.

Jill You don't feel it's wrong that he should have something like this and you don't?

Douglas I'm sorry, I don't quite follow, how do you mean? Is that a socialist question . . . ?

Kenny What are you trying to get him to say, Jilly?

Douglas Because I'm not a socialist. Actually, I'm not quite sure what I am just at present. The past few years I have been consciously withholding my vote –

Jill So you don't feel just a little bit jealous?

Douglas Certainly not.

Jill Not the teeniest bit?

Douglas No.

Jill Honestly?

Kenny Jill, the man's just said, he's not jealous –

Douglas (*cheerfully*) Oh, don't worry. She's always going on at me like this . . .

Jill I'm sorry, I simply cannot believe that after what

happened Mr Beechey can sit here among all this – wealth
– these spoils of the good life –

Kenny Come on, Jilly, it's one poky, run-of-the-mill villa in
the middle of hundreds – it's no big deal –

Jill Maybe not to you or Vic or me it isn't. But to someone
like Mr Beechey, it's beyond his wildest dreams . . .

Kenny What are you talking about? This place is littered
with people like Mr Beechey –

Douglas Do call me Douglas, please . . .

Kenny The place is populated by Mr Beecheys. You can
barely move for Beecheys, don't talk nonsense.

Jill (*angrily indicating Douglas*) If you had seen – if you
had seen, by contrast, the dingy little house this man is
forced to live in. On the edge of a roaring main trunk road
– rooms the size of this table – fading wallpaper . . . worn
carpets . . . God! (*She shudders.*) Sorry, Mr Beechey,
but . . .

Douglas (*without offence*) We're really both quite fond of
it, actually.

Jill (*calming down*) Just don't try and kid me he wouldn't
prefer this if he were given a choice . . .

Kenny And all I'm saying is, don't hold this place up as
some fantastic dream palace. It's a perfectly ordinary
holiday shack. A lot of people have one. Most people have
one. If they've bothered to save up . . .

Slight pause.

Douglas Mind you, I think we've got used to that house
over the years. You don't notice the little drawbacks quite
so much after a while. I must be honest, we have meant to
do something about that hall carpet for some years. But

it's getting a good match with the stairs, you see. That's the problem. They don't really make that mauve any more. It means I have to keep bringing the samples home with me – because, of course, Nerys can't face walking into Debenhams, certainly not on a Saturday morning.

A silence.

Kenny The man is just not the jealous type, Jill, forget it.

Jill (*with ill-concealed annoyance*) So you have no feelings at all about this place, Mr Beechey? Like you appear not to have feelings about anything very much?

Douglas Oh, I have feelings, Jill, I most certainly do. Very deep feelings. But I sincerely hope that envy is not one of them. Because envy in my book is a deadly sin and as a practising Christian, that is something I try to avoid.

Jill Super. I'm glad to hear it. Well, perhaps you ought to tell me something you do feel strongly about and we'll try and include that in the programme.

Kenny Jill, come on . . .

Jill Illegal parking on double yellow lines? Any good? Dogs fouling footpaths? Free double glazing for senior citizens?

Douglas (*thoughtfully*) I suppose evil, really.

Jill Evil?

Douglas Yes. I feel strongly about that.

Jill That's it? Just evil?

Douglas Yes. Only, it's often hard to recognize. But there's a lot of it about, you know.

A silence. Suddenly, there in the garden gateway stands **Vic Parks**. *A powerful man in his late forties. He has just*

*come from the beach and is wearing shorts, sports shirt
and canvas beach shoes. Holding shyly on to his hand is
his elder child* **Cindy,** *a pretty little girl of seven. The
others don't immediately see him.*

Vic Good morning. Don't we say good morning, then?

*Jill and Douglas rise. Kenny follows suit, rather more
slowly.*

Jill (*delightedly*) Vic . . .

Douglas (*obediently*) Good morning . . .

Kenny (*with them*) About time . . .

Vic (*gently*) Cindy, you get changed and then you take
Timmy up the other end of the pool, all right? And look
after him, OK?

Cindy runs off again.

(*shouting after her*) And do what Sharon says. You listen
to Sharon, all right?

Jill (*embracing him*) Hallo, Vic.

Vic Hallo, how's my girl?

Jill Grateful you've decided to turn up.

Vic Well, where are the cameras, then? Where're the
cameras? I thought this place would be a mass of people.
Cameras, sound men, extra lighting rigs . . . Look at it, I
ask you. Bugger all. I make my special entrance. Get
dressed up specially . . .

Jill I sent them off to do the mute shots. They'll be back in
an hour –

Vic They'd better be. I came all the way up from the
beach for this – (*to Douglas*) How do you do, Vic Parks.
You'll be –

466

Jill This is Douglas Beechey –

Douglas Hallo. Great to meet you. I'm a real fan –

Vic Well, that's very nice to hear. (*to Jill*) Listen, you'll get the kids in somewhere, won't you? Just one shot, eh?

Jill Oh, sure . . .

Vic Only I promised Timmy and Cindy they'd be on the telly, you see . . .

Jill I was hoping you would let us use them . . .

Vic Just one shot. (*to Douglas*) Have you got kids?

Douglas No, no. But I watch your programme. I watch *Ask Vic* every Tuesday –

Vic (*to Kenny*) Now, isn't that interesting? Here's another example . . .

Ruy, who has finished raking the swimming pool, has entered and is crossing to the back gate.

Morning, Ruy, lad –

Ruy (*cheerily animated*) Hallo, good morning, Mr Vic!

Vic (*to Jill and Douglas*) You know, they did a survey as to what categories of kids make up the viewing sample for *Ask Vic* and they actually found that – 15 per cent, wasn't it?

Kenny Thirteen and a half –

Vic Nearly 15 per cent of our viewers were adults over the age of twenty-one –

Kenny Age of eighteen –

Vic Isn't that incredible?

Douglas Incredible.

Vic No, you think about it for a minute. That's a big percentage, that is, 15 per cent.

Douglas Amazing.

Vic Whereas my evening show – *The Vic Parks Show* – that is exclusively adult. Well, point oh-one per cent kids, or something. So there's no cross spill the other way. Which I find very interesting.

Kenny It is on at eleven o'clock at night, of course –

Vic No. Even so.

Douglas Yes, it's a bit late for me, that one –

Vic What, early riser, are you? (*Claps him on the back.*) Nothing like it. We were down there at what, six thirty this morning. Magic. Best time to be on a beach. First thing in the morning. Virgin sand, sun coming up, not too hot, clear blue sea . . . Now, have you all got what you want? Drink? Food? Anything? Where's Trudy? Isn't she looking after you? I told her to look after you. (*calling into the house*) Trudy! Where is she?

Kenny Trudy's just –

Sharon Giffin *has entered from the garden gate. A girl of about nineteen. Overweight and sadly graceless. She is at present in a sulk. She carries a couple of baskets with towels, toys, etc., which presumably they've brought back from the beach. She is wearing a wetsuit top under her beach robe.*

Vic Sharon, find Trudy. Tell her to come out here.

Sharon (*flatly*) Yes, Mr Parks.

Douglas (*to Sharon*) Hallo, I'm Douglas.

Sharon (*all but ignoring him*) Hallo.

Sharon goes into the house.

Jill We're being looked after fine, Vic. You don't have to worry about us –

Vic No, I can't stand guests being left on their own. That's terrible. I can't stand that. (*feeling the coffee pot*) This is cold and all. (*yelling*) Marta! Marta! Sitting here drinking cold coffee. What the hell's going on here? Marta! Come out here. Sit down. Go on. Sit down.

They sit. **Marta,** *a Spanish woman in her fifties, enters in a hurry from the house. Normally dark and brooding but, as with her husband Ruy, in the presence of Vic she is effusive and charming.*

Marta Yes, Mr Vic?

Vic Marta, coffee. More coffee. Hot. More cups. Clean. Quickly. All right?

Marta (*taking the tray from the table*) More coffee, more cups.

Vic Hot coffee. Understand?

Marta Hot coffee.

Vic Hot not cold.

Marta (*hurring away*) Hot not cold. Yes, Mr Vic.

Marta goes. Vic sits at last, like someone about to hold court. Douglas is holding his old coffee cup. The occasional child's shout is heard from the direction of the swimming pool.

Vic Now then – that's sorted that out . . . (*seeing the children*) Look at those two. Look at those kids.

Douglas (*smiling appreciatively*) Ah . . .

Vic You got kids, have you?

Douglas Er – no . . .

Vic Have some. You don't know what you're missing. (*indicating Douglas's cup*) Leave that, she's fetching some more –

Douglas puts his cup down again, obediently.

(*indicating Kenny*) I'm always telling him that. Kenny. He should have some.

Kenny (*uneasily*) Well, it's tricky . . .

Jill Kenny's gay, Vic. He doesn't want kids.

Vic Why not? What obstacle's that? These days? Being a poof?

Kenny Quite a bit actually. Anyway, I hate kids, I loathe the sight of them.

Vic (*to Jill*) You should have some, too.

Jill No, thanks. I'll enjoy other people's kids. Much nicer.

Vic (*only just joking*) It's unnatural not to. Every woman who can should have kids. Like every man who can should grow a beard. Everything you can do you ought to do. Before you die. That's what we're here for. Right?

Jill Tell you what, I'll grow my armpits and you have the baby, OK?

Vic (*mock disgusted*) Dear, oh, dear. Right. What's the plan? (*to Jill*) You're going to make us two into telly stars, are you?

He winks at Douglas. Douglas laughs appreciatively.

Jill I thought the best way to go about this, Vic – with your approval, of course – is this morning, as soon as the boys come back, I'll pick up one or two mute shots here. But perhaps we could spend now, we three, just briefly talking about what we want to talk about. And then this afternoon – (*She hesitates as Vic rises and moves towards the house.*) This after–

Vic Carry on, Jill. Carry on, I'm listening . . .

Jill (*having to shout rather as Vic disappears*) This afternoon, I could start by talking with the two of you, just to contrast how you've both fared over seventeen years –

Vic (*off, calling*) Trudy! Trudy! (*calling back to Jill*) Seventeen years, yes, I'm listening . . .

Jill (*battling on*) And perhaps – I don't want to dwell on it too much – perhaps just recalling the last meeting between you both.

Vic (*off*) Where are my bloody cigars?

Trudy (*off*) They're in the drawer, there.

Vic (*off*) They are not in the drawer.

Trudy (*off*) Well, they were there.

Vic (*off*) Look at that. Look. Is that in the drawer? Is that what's meant by in the drawer?

Trudy (*off*) I know where they are, just a minute . . .

Vic (*off*) Well, bring them out here. We're trying to talk out here. Come on out. (*Vic re-enters from the house.*) Sorry, Jilly, sorry. I apologize. Carry on. (*Jill opens her mouth to do so.*) No, sorry, excuse me – before you do, let me say – Doug – Duggie – can I call you Doug?

Douglas (*delighted*) Yes, of course –

Vic Doug – this girl – discovered me. Can you believe that? This little kid – ankle socks – how old were you, then? Seventeen, something like that –

Jill (*rather coyly*) I was older than that . . .

Kenny Twenty-three, you were twenty-three when you met Vic –

Jill Something like that.

Vic This girl – she was – what? You were a local radio interviewer, weren't you?

Jill Right.

Vic I'd just – like, come out, you know – and she's doing this programme about – what was it? *Old Lags' Hour* or something, wasn't it?

Vic winks at Douglas. Douglas laughs appreciatively. The whole of the following gets related rather for his benefit.

No, seriously, it was a programme called – let me see *Facing Things* – right?

Kenny *Facing Up*, it was called.

Jill *Facing Up*.

Vic *Facing Up*, he's right –

Jill About long-term prisoners coming to terms –

Vic With the outside world . . .

Jill And this man, his first time on radio –

Vic The very first time I'd ever been on, this is –

Jill By the time we'd finished I'd got enough tape for about twenty-five programmes . . .

Vic And then when I'm leaving – you left out the best bit – just when I'm leaving, wasn't it?

Jill Oh, yes, right – and then just as he's leaving – leaving the studio – I'm absolutely exhausted by now, mind you – and he turns to me and he says –

Vic (*laughing*) I said to her, what about my book then?

Jill He says, you never asked me about my book.

Jill, Vic and Kenny laugh. Douglas joins in, though it's clear he doesn't know what they're all laughing about.

He's only written a bloody book as well . . .

Vic *My Life* by Vic Parks. Written during Her Majesty's Pleasure – and on Her Majesty's stationery.

Kenny (*to Douglas*) His biography.

Douglas Oh, yes . . .

Kenny The first one, that was –

Vic The authorized version. It was a shocker, wasn't it?

Kenny Not the one you've read –

Vic No, that's the second one he must have read.

Kenny That was *Life as a Straight Man.*

Vic That only came out a year ago.

Kenny Eighteen months –

Douglas It seemed to be very popular at the library. There was quite a waiting list at the Purley Branch –

Vic Five months at number one . . . Can't be bad.

Douglas And you wrote that yourself? I mean, that was actually yourself writing, was it?

Vic Er, more or less. More or less. They were mostly my words. That's fair to say, isn't it?

Kenny That's no lie.

Vic There was just – someone else putting them in the right order for me.

Kenny A little bit of help from John.

Vic A little bit of help from John. Bless him. How is he, by the way?

Kenny Much better.

Vic Good. Good. Give him my love.

Trudy comes out with a box of cigars and some matches.

Trudy Here you are.

Vic Ta. Sit down, sit down.

Trudy No, I –

Vic Sit down. We're just remembering my first book. Did you ever read that?

Trudy (*sitting, rather reluctantly*) No, I never read that one.

Vic (*to Jill*) It was a shocker, wasn't it? I don't know how I had the nerve to show it –

Jill Don't knock it, now. That started you off, that book.

Vic No, that was you, my darling. You started me off.

Kenny She recognized star quality . . .

Vic It was no thanks to that bloody book. I tried that, you know, with – must have been twenty-five publishers –

Jill But it was you reading that book that started your career. I mean, if some producer hadn't heard you reading it on *Pick of the Week*, you'd never have got on *Start the Week*. And if you hadn't done *Start the Week* they'd never have asked you to do *Stop the Week*, would they?

474

Kenny Or *Any Questions* . . .

Vic (*modestly*) True.

Kenny Or *The Book Programme.* Or *Did you See* . . . ?

Vic True, true . . .

Kenny And the rest is history . . .

Jill Absolutely true.

> *Pause, whilst they all consider Vic's mercurial rise to fame. Marta comes out with a tray of fresh coffee and five cups. Trudy pours coffee during the next. Marta hovers behind her. The sound of the children's shouts from the far end of the pool.*

Vic (*shouting to them*) Be careful now. Be careful, Cindy. Now, don't push him.

Trudy Are they all right?

Vic They're all right.

Trudy Where's Sharon? Shouldn't she be with them?

Vic She's getting changed, I think.

Trudy She should be with them . . .

Vic They're all right. Don't fuss. I'm keeping an eye on them. (*to Douglas*) You got kids, did you say?

Douglas No . . .

Vic You like them, though?

Douglas Oh, yes . . .

Vic Look at them. Look at those two . . . I love kids. Do you know what I'd do to people who hurt kids?

Douglas No.

Vic I'd sit them, naked, astride barbed wire . . .

Douglas (*wincing slightly*) Ah . . .

Trudy (*irritated by Marta's presence behind her*) Thank you, Marta, I can manage, thank you.

Vic No, let her serve round. She's waiting to serve round, Trudy . . .

Trudy I can serve round.

Vic No, let her. That's her job. That's what she's paid for. We're paying her to serve round. (*to Marta*) Go on. Serve round, you silly cow. Serve them round.

Marta (*a flashing smile*) Yes, Mr Vic.

Vic We're paying her. We might as well use the bloody woman. Like buying a light bulb and sitting in the dark otherwise, isn't it?

Vic winks at Douglas. Douglas laughs rather more weakly. Trudy has poured out all the coffee and, during the next, Marta circulates with the tray, allowing the guests to serve themselves with cream and sugar.

Anyway. (*to Jill*) You still haven't told us, sweetheart, have you, what your grand plan of campaign is. We await your plan.

Jill Well, I was trying to –

Vic (*about to light a cigar*) Cigar, anyone? Cigar?

They decline.

Sorry, excuse me, carry on.

Jill I thought that the three of us could do an initial three-handed interview this afternoon. Out here, if that's OK –

Vic What? You, me and him, you mean?

Jill Right.

Vic Right. Carry on.

Jill I'd like to use that to discuss, principally, how both your lives have changed over seventeen years –

Vic How long have you got? (*He laughs.*)

Jill Well, it'll have to be in general terms . . .

Vic It'll need to be . . .

Trudy Excuse me, but why are you going back seventeen years? I mean, if you're talking about Vic's career, that only started eight years ago.

Vic It started the day I met you, my love . . .

   Vic winks at Douglas again.

Trudy (*unamused*) No, I mean it. Why are you wanting to go back seventeen years? I don't see any reason to.

Jill Because – (*as if talking to a child*) That's the point of the programme, Trudy. That's the name of the series, *Their Paths Crossed*. And seventeen years ago, that's when their paths crossed. These two. Douglas and Vic.

Trudy Yes, I know. I just don't see why you have to go back through all that again. All that business in the bank – the trial –

Jill We're not. Not really –

Vic We are certainly not. Let's get that clear.

Trudy (*clearly upset*) I don't see any point in dragging all that up again. We've got the kids growing up. A new life. Why do you want to talk about it, for heaven's sake . . . ?

Vic (*sharply to her*) Trudy! Listen, we're not going to talk about it, all right? (*Pause.*) Look, I think, actually, Trudy,

in this instance, is right. We don't need to go back
seventeen years, do we?

Trudy No, we don't.

Vic It's pointless. I mean, I was inside for the first nine, so
what's the point?

Trudy There's no point.

Jill But seventeen years ago is when you met Mr Beechey.
That's when your paths crossed. As a result of which, his
life changed, your life changed.

Vic His life might have done. Mine didn't. I just went
back to prison. That was nothing new to me then, I can
tell you . . .

Jill Well, it certainly changed Mr Beechey's life –

Vic Well, do a programme about him, then. I don't mind.

Jill No, listen –

Kenny Vic, I think what Jill's saying is that that's the point
of the programme. I mean, unless you do trace back to
when you both met –

Vic No. Bugger it. I don't want to go back that far.
Trudy's right. What's the point?

Trudy No point at all.

Vic Anyway, it's all in my book. If you want it, it's all
there in the book.

Trudy It wouldn't have been in that, either, if I'd had my
way.

Jill (*trying to control her anger*) Well, terrific. (*Pause.*)
You're not prepared to talk about the bank raid at all,
then?

Vic Sorry, no. It's been done to death.

Jill Not like this it hasn't. (*Pause. Jill can see her programme disappearing.*) Not even in general detail?

Vic What do you mean, in general detail?

Jill I mean, just a general description of what happened. In very general terms. Look, I do appreciate that it isn't easy for either of you –

No one speaks.

I don't intend to go into any great lurid details. I was just planning to have both your voices speaking over a simple reconstruction – using posed actors in still pictures – I must stress that – I'm using stills, not even live action – I don't want anything sensational – God forbid – it's not a sensational slot, it can't be, it's scheduled for eight o'clock. That's all there would be. Just your voices over still pictures. Telling it as you remembered it. (*She stops and looks at them, awaiting response.*) I mean, none of what I'm saying is exactly new, you know. I did say all this to you, Kenneth. Originally. Months ago. Last November. Didn't I?

Kenny (*vaguely*) Yes. I know, it's just . . . Obviously, if Vic feels . . . (*He tails off.*)

Vic (*indicating Douglas*) Does he want to talk about this? You want all this dragged up again, Doug?

Douglas Well . . . I can see both points of view, really –

Jill Listen, the bulk of the programme, 99.999 per cent of it – I promise – is about what happened afterwards. About how you became a TV personality with an umpteen-million viewing figure –

Kenny Nine million.

Vic (*to Kenny*) Are we down to nine? Since when are we down to nine?

Kenny Only for last week.

Vic Why?

Kenny Motor show.

Vic Oh.

Jill (*sensing a victory*) I think one of the fascinating things is the way both your careers have reversed, in a sense. I mean, seventeen years ago, Mr Beechey here was a national hero. Just looking at these press cuttings . . . (*She opens her folder.*) One newspaper actually started the Beechey Awards – given annually to anyone having a go at criminals. Isn't that right?

Douglas Yes, they did. I presented them myself the first year. At the Grosvenor House. A very splendid do.

Jill (*rifling through the cuttings*) 'Get that Beechey spirit, Britain' . . . 'We will fight them on the Beecheys' . . . 'Beechey's the boy for us'. (*examining a press photograph*) Who are all these women with you, incidentally?

Douglas Do you know, I never really found out. They just turned up in a coach one morning. With the photographer. We all got very chilly, I recall. Especially them.

Vic (*examining the cutting*) Dear, oh dear. (*showing it to Trudy*) Look at that . . . Disgraceful. (*He tuts with mock horror.*)

Jill But, looking at all these press cuttings, I wonder who'd remember you now?

Douglas Oh, no one at all, I shouldn't think.

Jill So heroes do get forgotten?

Douglas I think ones like me do.

Kenny (*studying one of the cuttings*) How long did they keep up these Beechey Awards?

Douglas Oh, three years. Then the paper went on to something else. Raising money for the Olympic Games, I think.

Jill Rather sad, don't you think?

Vic No, that's life. Human nature. I mean, for the public, it's on to the next, isn't it? Has to be. Only natural.

Jill Only this particular hero was eventually to be replaced by the very man he so gallantly risked his life having a go at in the first place. A man who had fired a shotgun into an innocent girl's face –

Trudy Listen, if we're going to start on that –

Vic (*sharply*) Trudy, sit down . . .

Trudy sits. Silence.

(*quietly*) Now that is an oversimplified statement and out of order, Jill. And you know it. Now, I'm prepared to do your interview – I've said I would, so I will – I'm prepared to do all I can to help you with your programme – but not if we're going to have semi-libellous statements chucked about the place, all right?

Jill I don't see your objections. Everybody knows you shot her. As you say, it's in your book. So what's the mystery?

Trudy Because we're trying to forget it –

Jill If he's trying to forget it, why is he making money writing books about it?

Kenny No, that's totally unfair –

Vic Ten per cent of all my royalties from that book are going to recognized children's charities –

Jill (*riding over this*) Why's he got a kids' programme on television and a chat show at weekends?

Kenny Because, put at its simplest, Vic has a personality which the public at large warm to and want to watch –

Jill They watch him because he used to be a bank robber. That's why they watch him.

Kenny That's total and complete bollocks – excuse me – none of the kids who watch Vic have the faintest idea what he used to be –

Jill Yes, they have –

Kenny They weren't even born –

Jill Yes, they have because he tells them. Listen to me, kids, I went down the wrong street once and believe me, tangling with the law is strictly for mugs –

Vic Now, hold on. Hold on. Be fair –

Kenny Do you realize the number of kids this man has kept out of prison . . . ?

Jill I've no doubt he has –

Kenny There have been surveys done amongst underprivileged kids –

Jill I'm sure. I'm not saying Vic isn't doing a wonderful job. He is. Of course he is. All I'm saying is – all I'm saying – (*She hesitates.*)

Trudy (*coolly*) What exactly are you saying? Exactly?

Jill All I'm saying is – isn't it ironic that the hero is forgotten? And the villain has now become the hero. That's all. And isn't that a reflection of our time?

Trudy Fascinating.

Jill And whilst we're saying it, isn't it even more tragic that the person who lost most in all this – the victim herself – no one spares a thought for her at all. Except Douglas, of course.

Trudy (*muttering*) I knew we'd get round to this . . .

Vic If you think I didn't spend nine years of my life thinking about that girl, then you don't know me – that's all I can say. I have woken in the night – (*to Trudy*) I still do occasionally – don't I? In a sweat, wringing wet, still remembering it. So don't you come at me with that one. I paid –

Trudy Vic –

Vic No, let me finish – I paid the full penalty as prescribed by the law for what I did. In full. Fourteen years less remission – nine years. And that to me has to mean a debt paid in full. Otherwise what more can a man do? Eh? Go on blaming himself? What's the point of that?

Trudy No point.

Vic None. He has got to get up and do the very best with that which God has granted him to make amends with and try and put something back in the world, in the brief time left to him. And that is what, hand on heart, I have tried to do. Bear me out, Kenny, is that not what I have tried to do . . . ?

Kenny Absolutely, Vic.

Vic Right. (*to Jill*) Jill, there is no use in going back over the past where no one is going to benefit. It's not going to help me. (*indicating Douglas*) It's not going to help him. And it's certainly not going to help that poor bloody bitch who was injured – sorry, she's your wife, mate, I shouldn't refer to her like that . . . It's not going to help her either . . .

Trudy Not in the least.

Kenny Absolutely not.

Pause.

Vic I mean, you talk about villains, you talk about heroes. But what is that? It's very often a value judgement made by society, which has no basis in fact whatsoever. I mean, has it?

Jill I don't know. You tell me.

Vic Well, I'm telling you. It hasn't. I mean, take that instance. I'm cast as the villain, right? Because it just so happens that on that particular occasion it was me who happened to be the one who walked into the bank with a shotgun with the intention of robbing it. Another day, another time, another set of circumstances, it could have been someone else, couldn't it? Could have been you. Could have been him. Now, I'm not pretending that what I did was a right course of action – But. But, let's add these factors. I had no intention at any stage of using that firearm. It was on my previous record for all to see that I never used a firearm, I never condoned the use of firearms. I detest firearms. Even now – Well, we did a programme on firearms the other day, didn't we, Kenny? Kenny here will vouch for me, I couldn't even bring myself to pick one up, could I? And if you will care to check, and it is on record from sworn witnesses at the trial, the very first words I said when the three of us first came through those bank doors, my first words were: 'All right. Don't get excited and nobody'll get injured.' (*to Douglas*) You were there. Did I not say those exact words?

Douglas Nobody'll get hurt. Don't get excited and nobody'll get hurt, you said . . .

Vic There you are. Would I have said that if I'd come in there to shoot somebody?

Jill But the gun was loaded –

Vic Well, yes, it was loaded. What's the point of carrying an empty gun?

Jill So you knew you might use it?

Vic (*sharply*) I've said I had no intention of using it, all right? Is my word not good enough?

   A pause.

Douglas The safety catch was off, though.

Vic (*irritably*) What?

Douglas I said, the safety catch was off. I remember the police saying so at the time.

Vic Well, of course it was. Look, come on, be fair. You cannot walk into a bank with a gun and expect people to take you seriously if you've still got the safety on, can you?

Jill Why not?

Vic (*angrily*) Because people aren't going to take much notice of you for a kick off, are they? All they're going to say is, this geezer's an idiot, he's wandering round with his safety on . . .

Jill Most people would never know the difference, would they? I wouldn't know if a safety catch was on or off.

Vic Maybe you wouldn't. But some people would, that's all I'm saying . . .

Jill You mean other bank robbers?

Vic Look, there's plenty of people besides bank robbers who use shotguns, you know. I mean, a lot of people use shotguns. People working in the bank, they probably use shotguns –

Jill What, in the bank?

Vic At the weekend. They probably use shotguns.

Jill Do you use one?

Douglas No, I never use shotguns.

Vic Not him. I'm not talking about him. I mean, the managers. As a matter of fact, I think my manager shoots. (*to Kenny*) David shoots, doesn't he? David?

Kenny No, I think he water-skis.

Vic No. Well, there are some. Take my word for it. Anyway, the point I am making is, responsible as I may have been – and I've never denied that – for carrying a gun into that place (*indicating Douglas*), if this one hadn't come at me – if this six-and-a-half-stone boy-scout bank clerk hadn't come charging at me from the length of the bank – I would never have fired –

Jill You're not saying it was Mr Beechey's fault, are you?

Vic No. I'm not saying that. But if he hadn't been a hero, if he hadn't grabbed me, the gun would never have gone off accidentally and this girl would never have got hurt. I mean, as it was, he was clinging on – I was shouting – 'Be careful, it'll go off, it'll go off' – and I could see, you know, this girl was in the firing line –

Jill She was the one you'd been holding as a hostage?

Vic Yes, originally. But I'd released her in order to wrestle with him. As soon as I appreciated the danger, I let her go. I could see, though, as he and I were struggling, that the gun was twisting round towards her – (*to Douglas*) You had your back to her, so you couldn't have seen – and I was trying, you know, to pull it back away from her – and then, before I can do anything to stop it, bang – Right in the side of her face. It was a miracle, with the gun that close, she didn't lose an eye. A miracle. I thank God for that, at least.

A respectful pause.

Douglas She did lose her ear, though.

Vic Well, yes. Still. An ear's not the same as eye, is it?

Kenny I suppose she could grow her hair . . .

Douglas Yes, she did.

Vic She's all right now, then, is she?

Douglas Oh, yes. She's pretty chirpy. Has her ups and downs, of course.

Trudy Like most of us.

Vic Lovely girl.

Douglas Yes, she was.

Kenny Lucky man.

Douglas Yes, she was beautiful.

Jill She still is. From what I saw of her, anyway.

Vic She's not in the film?

Jill No.

Douglas I think she'd have found it difficult –

Vic Oh, yes.

Jill And, anyway, as I keep saying, this programme is really about you two. Not her at all. I don't want it to be

487

macabre or morbid or cause a lot of unnecessary pain – I mean, frankly, I'm not into that sort of programme, I'm sorry. I mean, I know some people make careers out of it, we've all seen them, they love to have the camera lingering over people crying and obviously in terrible distress, but I'm sorry, I find that simply gratuitous and tasteless. That's not what I'm here to do. And if that means I'm into old-fashioned programme values, then you'll have to forgive me.

Vic Hear! Hear! You and me both, baby. (*Pause.*) So is that it, then? Are we excused? Only I think I fancy a swim.

Trudy Just a minute. Have you agreed to talk about the robbery or not?

Jill Only very, very, very briefly. I need to a little, just to establish the programme.

Trudy Well, it had better be briefly.

Vic It'll be brief, don't worry. It's old news, anyway. Who's interested? (*indicating Douglas*) He doesn't want it dragged up, I don't want it dragged up. His wife certainly doesn't. So that's the end of it. You fancy a swim, Doug?

Douglas Er, no . . .

Vic Before we have a drink . . .

Douglas No, me and water, I'm afraid, I –

Trudy (*in sudden alarm*) Timmy! (*Trudy rushes off to the far end of the swimming pool.*) Cindy, hold on to him!

   Vic moves towards the pool after Trudy.

Jill (*seeing what's happening*) Oh, my God.

Vic Have you got him?

Trudy (*off*) You naughty boy. Don't ever do that again.

(*calling*) Yes, he's all right. My God, he nearly went in. (*to Timmy*) Now, I told you before . . .

Jill, Kenny and Douglas have risen to watch.

Kenny That was a close thing.

Jill He's all right, though.

Douglas Could have been nasty –

Sharon appears from the house. She has changed into her swimsuit. She stops to watch the commotion.

Sharon What's happening?

Jill Timmy nearly fell in. Weren't you supposed to be keeping an eye on them?

Sharon I just went to change – (*calling*) Is he all right?

Vic turns from the pool and looks at Sharon.

Vic (*beckoning Sharon*) Hey, come here.

Sharon What?

Vic Here. Come here.

Sharon crosses obediently over to him. Vic speaks to her quietly, but not so quietly that the others cannot hear him.

Where the bloody hell have you been, eh?

Sharon Pardon, Mr Parks . . .

Vic (*very close to her*) My kid was practically drowned, and where were you? Eh?

Sharon (*frightened*) I was changing, Mr Parks . . .

Vic Changing? I see. You were changing while my child was nearly drowning. That's your idea of looking after them, is it? Is it?

Sharon (*with a reflex smile due to pure nervousness*) No.

Vic I hope you're not laughing about this, girl, because I'm not. Are you laughing? It's a joke to you, is it? Is it a joke?

Sharon can't reply. She shakes her head.

Do you hear what I'm saying to you? I'm asking you, do you think it's a joke? Do you?

Jill Vic . . .

Vic I'm waiting to hear from you. Do you think it's a joke?

Sharon No, Mr Parks.

Vic Good. I'm delighted to hear that. Because if you had done, you'd have been on the next plane straight out of here, all right? Straight back to Macclesfield, all right?

Sharon Yes, Mr Parks.

Vic And in the meantime, did you not come equipped with a uniform? Eh?

Sharon Sorry?

Vic I said, did you not have a uniform when you arrived here?

Sharon Yes, Mr Parks.

Vic Then, in future, when you are on duty will you kindly wear it, as you're supposed to do.

Sharon Yes, Mr Parks.

Vic Is that understood?

Sharon Yes, Mr Parks.

Vic Then get upstairs and get changed. You look disgusting dressed like that, anyway.

Sharon rushes off, starting to cry as she goes. Vic glares after her.

Bloody girl. Do you know how much we're paying for her? ·

Jill It's all right, Vic, the kids are fine. Look, they're playing again. They soon forget.

Vic All right then. Time for a swim. (*calling to the other end of the pool*) Look out, you two. Here comes a crocodile . . .

Vic goes off to the end of the pool, throwing aside his shirt as he goes. In a second, we hear the diving board vibrate and then a splash as he dives in.

Jill Well, I suppose I'd better go and find my film crew. Wake them up.

Douglas Well. I'm ready when you are, Jill.

Jill (*drily*) Thank you, Mr Beechey. That's most reassuring.

She goes out through the garden gate. Throughout the next, Vic will occasionally appear at this end of the pool. He is evidently swimming length after length. Douglas and Kenny watch him idly. Vic turns and swims away.

Kenny (*at length*) You know, there's only one thing about that story of Vic's – I mean, it's not the first time I've heard it, naturally – but I've always wondered, why on earth did you do such a bean-brained thing like that? I mean, running straight at a man who's armed with a loaded shotgun? What on earth made you do it?

Douglas Do you know, I've often asked myself that and I haven't the faintest idea.

Kenny Do you make a habit of that sort of thing? Sudden reckless gestures? I mean, do you mountaineer, jump out of aeroplanes? Things like that?

Douglas No. Certainly not.

Kenny Extraordinary. I don't know about making you a hero. You were lucky not to have been locked up as a lunatic.

Vic appears momentarily at this end of the pool. He turns and swims back out of view.

Douglas Well, funnily enough, that's exactly what the police said to me at the time. They called it a very foolhardy, reckless gesture.

Kenny They still made a hero of you.

Douglas I don't think the police did that. That was the press. They said I'd captured the general public's imagination.

Kenny No problem. That's about as easy to capture as a dead chicken in a meat safe. Gallant bank clerk risks life to save fiancée?

Douglas So the story went. Actually, Nerys wasn't even my fiancée. Not at the time.

Kenny No? I always understood she was.

Douglas No, she was actually engaged to someone else when it happened, but – after the – accident – he – her fiancé – broke it off. And this reporter said it would be an altogether better story if he could say that Nerys and I were engaged. And I said it would probably be all right. And he said, well, when she'd regained consciousness, if subsequently we both went off the idea and decided to split up again, that would make another good story.

Vic appears briefly again.

Kenny Ah. (*He considers this.*) I see. Well, I think I'll have a dip. Expose the alabaster limbs. Just go and root out some trunks. You're not swimming?

Douglas No. If it's all the same.

Kenny It's all the same to me, chum.

Kenny saunters into the house. As he does so, he passes Marta, who comes out of the house and starts, unsmilingly, to clear the coffee things.

Douglas Very nice cup of coffee. Thank you. *Gracias.*

Marta ignores him. Douglas wanders around and explores the place a little. The children's shouts are heard, happy again. The distant splash of water. A plane flies over, Douglas shields his eyes and watches it pass. Vic appears once more.

Vic (*as he turns, spluttering*) 'S great. You want to try it.

He swims away. Trudy returns from the far end of the pool.

Trudy (*calling to the children*) You stay that end. Stay up that end, do you hear? Keep an eye on them, won't you, Vic?

Vic's spluttered reply is heard.

(*to Douglas*) Sure you don't want a swim?

Douglas No, I –

Trudy It's lovely and warm . . .

Douglas No, I – always look a little foolish in the water.

Trudy Oh, I'm sure you look fine . . . You should see me. These days. I'm no bathing beauty . . .

Douglas (*gallantly*) Oh, come now . . .

Trudy Nobody'll see you. Not here.

Douglas It's very peaceful. Quite a contrast. When I left first thing this morning it was pouring with rain.

Trudy Ah . . .

Douglas Forty-three degrees.

Trudy Yes?

Douglas Fahrenheit.

Trudy Yes.

Douglas I can never work out the other one, I'm afraid.

Trudy No?

Douglas That's a terrible admission for someone working in double glazing.

He laughs. Trudy smiles. Vic appears briefly in the pool again. They watch him.

He's a good swimmer, Vic.

Trudy Yes, he's very good. Mind you, he can do most things. Once he sets his mind to them. I've always said if Vic can't do something, then it's probably only because he doesn't want to do it in the first place.

She pauses as Sharon comes out of the house. She is now dressed in her nursemaid's uniform – a little incongruously considering the temperature.

Why on earth are you dressed up like that, Sharon? It's sweltering.

Sharon (*sulkily*) Mr Parks said I had to.

Trudy Really? Oh, well. If Mr Parks told you to . . .

494

Sharon (*aloof*) Excuse me, please.

She marches off towards the pool. Trudy stares at her sourly.

Douglas He certainly tore her off a strip just now, your husband.

Trudy Did he?

Douglas I wouldn't have cared to have been on the receiving end of that.

Trudy Don't worry. It always looks worse than it is.

Douglas Does he do that a lot, then?

Trudy Oh, yes. Quite a lot. It's not quite as it appears.

Vic appears again briefly.

Vic often shouts at women.

Douglas (*laughing uncertainly*) I hope not at you.

Trudy He's like a lot of men I've met. They don't quite know what to do with a woman when they've got her, so they shout at her.

Douglas I don't think I've ever shouted at Nerys . . .

Trudy No, well, you're probably different. Perhaps you're one of those men who do know what to do with a woman once you've got her . . .

Douglas (*laughing self-consciously*) I don't – quite know what to say to that. (*He laughs again.*) I hope I do. (*He laughs.*) I've got a pretty fair idea, yes. (*Pause. Suddenly feeling the heat*) It's going to be a scorcher, isn't it? A real scorcher.

Trudy Would you like to take your jacket off?

Douglas Er . . .

Trudy And your – pullover. You must be very hot.

Douglas Well, I think, with your permission – the jacket, thank you . . .

He removes his jacket. Trudy takes it from him and hangs it on a chair. As this is happening, Vic appears again briefly.

Thank you.

Trudy I'm sorry, I really am.

Douglas Sorry?

Trudy I mean, it must be obvious that I didn't want you to come here – I didn't want to meet you and I didn't want Vic to meet you again. I still don't know why he agreed to it. I suppose Jill must have . . . If you'd brought your wife with you – I don't know what I'd have done. Probably run away, I think.

Douglas There would have been no need for that, I'm sure.

Trudy I think you're amazing, I really do. When you think of what happened to her – and to you – and then you willingly come here and see us with – all this – Amazing. (*She laughs. Pause.*) Of course, being only human, it keeps occurring to me that maybe you want something from us. And maybe you haven't yet said what it is.

Douglas Is that how I appear to be?

Trudy No, you don't. Not at all. But one can't help wondering, none the less. Being only human. (*Pause.*) I don't know if there is anything we can do. I can do. Anything we can give you. Or offer you. But if there is . . . I mean it. Anything. Take it. Please. Take it.

She looks at Douglas. He looks at her.

Douglas (*gently*) No. Really. There's nothing you have that I could possibly take. Thank you all the same.

Trudy nods and goes into the house. Douglas looks about him once more. Then sits on a sun lounger. Cindy, the child, runs on from the pool. She is in her swimming costume and her wet feet leave a trail across the patio. She has a very soggy bunch of wild grasses and weeds. A child's bouquet. She stands in front of Douglas and holds them out to him.

Are these for me?

Cindy nods.

(*taking the offering from her*) Thank you very much. How lovely . . .

Cindy rushes away to the pool again.

(*as she disappears*) Thank you.

Douglas stands holding the bouquet. He looks around him. Then at the bouquet. The sound of splashing and Vic now playing with the happy children at the other end of the pool. Douglas continues to stand looking around. There is an expression on his face that could just be the start of a growing envy. Jill, quite suddenly and purposefully, walks out from the house, into the centre of the patio.

Jill (*shouting to the invisible film crew*) And cut.

The voices from the pool and the splashing stop abruptly.

Thank you. Thank you, Douglas.

Douglas Was that all right?

Jill Perfect. Thank you. (*to the crew*) Keep that set up, we've just got time to do their first meeting before lunch.

Shouts from the crew.

Yes, we can. We've got nearly fifteen minutes. Douglas, I want to do yours and Vic's meeting first, all right?

Douglas (*putting down his bouquet*) Right-oh, yes.

Jill is arranging three of the upright chairs into a loose semicircular 'interview' set-up. Douglas puts on his jacket again. A distant call from the crew.

Jill (*in response*) Why not?

Distant technical explanation.

Well, too bloody bad . . . Dan, I'm replugging now. This will be a mute sequence. It's just so I can talk to you. All right?

As she fiddles to reconnect her radio mic, Vic enters from the house. He has now changed and is spruced up for TV – a casual, manly image: blazer, lightweight tropical trousers, sunglasses and just the right number of shirt buttons undone.

Vic What's going on?

Jill I just want to do the first meeting with Mr Beechey, Vic – if you don't mind . . . The one we didn't get earlier.

Vic Nearly lunchtime, isn't it?

Jill No, we've got (*consulting her watch*) – twelve and a half minutes – I literally just want the two of you meeting, OK? Very simple. All in long. No sound. If I can get the establishing shot now, then we'll start the interviews after lunch. Douglas, my love . . .

Douglas Hallo.

Jill OK. Listen, I want you simply to come in through that gate – like this – (*she demonstrates*) OK?

498

Douglas (*watching her intently*) Yes. I came in the other way, originally. When I arrived. Does that matter?

Jill Not in the least.

Vic This is television. It's all fiction, son. All fiction. (*He winks at Douglas.*)

Jill (*slightly coolly*) Not all of it. But in this case it doesn't matter. (*demonstrating*) Now, I want you to walk to the middle of the patio – like this – stop – look around you – never seen anywhere like it in your life – gasp, gasp – and then we'll see Vic coming out from the house to greet you. OK?

Douglas Yes, yes . . .

Vic You want me from the house?

Jill Please.

Vic As soon as he stops?

Jill Yes. I can talk you through it. It'll be with voice-over this, eventually. I just want you both to meet, apparently start talking for a second or two, and then I'll come out and join you – and we'll sit – here – (*She indicates the three chairs, then into her mic.*) Are you getting all this, Dan? I hope you are, and can you relay it to George? Douglas, can you sit this side – here? (*She indicates one of the side chairs.*)

Douglas There. Right.

Jill And Vic, you'll sit here. OK?

Vic OK.

Jill Then I can be between you. All right, shall we have a quick run first? Can you both take your places. Douglas, just outside the gate.

Douglas hurries back to wait outside the gate, ever co-operative. Vic strolls back into the house in a rather more leisurely manner.

(*into her mic*) Dan, will you tell George we'll do it once so he can look at it. OK?

She looks in the crew's direction. A shout from them.

OK, this is just a rehearsal and – action. Thank you, Douglas. (*She steps back into the house doorway.*) Douglas . . . Come on, please . . .

Douglas sticks his head round the gate.

Douglas All right?

Jill Yes, come on. Come on. Keep walking in . . .

Douglas walks in through the gate. He has a lot of trouble walking to order. His arms and legs are rather uncoordinated.

Come on in further, Douglas. And try not to look at the camera if you can help it . . .

Douglas (*trying not to move his lips*) Sorry.

Jill Relax, try and relax. Douglas. Act normally . . .

Douglas Yes, I'm trying to act normally . . .

Jill Now, look around you . . . you haven't seen this place before, have you?

Douglas No.

Jill Look around then. Take it all in.

Douglas (*looking round, still speaking like an unsuccessful ventriloquist*) Yes, I'm taking it in, yes . . .

Jill Well, look a bit amazed – look a little awed by it all –

Douglas tries to look awed.

More. More. Isn't it an amazing place, Douglas? You've never seen anything like it in your life . . .

Douglas tries to look more awed.

Talk if you want to. You can talk if you feel like it . . .

Douglas (*looking around*) Sorry. There doesn't seem to be anyone here to talk to –

Jill (*muttering, despairingly*) Oh, Jesus . . . Thank you, and cue Vic . . .

Vic strides out from the house, hand extended.

Vic (*to Douglas, genially*) Hallo . . .

Douglas (*equally genial, shaking Vic's hand*) Oh, hallo, there.

Vic Hallo.

Douglas Hallo.

Pause.

Vic (*laughing*) That's about all I have to say to you.

Jill Keep talking, please. Just a bit more.

Vic You must be the man come to deliver the coal?

Douglas Pardon? (*getting the joke*) Oh, yes. Right. I've got it in the van out there.

Vic Oh, good. You sold your handcart, I take it?

Douglas Yes, oh, yes. I sold my handcart. Got fifty pesetas for it.

He laughs at his own inventiveness. Jill emerges from the doorway to join them both.

Jill Yes, OK, something like that. And then I'll say, hallo, sorry to interrupt – this might be quite a strange feeling for you both, meeting after – what is it – seventeen years?

Douglas Yes, seventeen.

Vic Is it seventeen? Good gracious me.

Jill And then I'll say something else and then I'll suggest we all sit down, shall we? (*She indicates the three chairs.*)

Vic What a charming idea!

Douglas Why not? Take the weight off the feet after my long journey. Phew!

Vic Good flight was it? Anyone fall out?

Douglas Wonderful flight. British Airways. You can't beat them. Not for flying.

> *Vic has sat down in his designated seat. Douglas, carried away by the improvised conversation, has seated himself in the middle chair.*

Jill (*irritated by all this badinage*) No, Douglas. Douglas . . .

Vic I think you're meant to be in that one, Mr Coalman.

Jill This one, please . . . That's mine.

Douglas Oh, I am sorry. I beg your pardon. Carried away. I really enjoy filming, you know. I didn't think I would. I think I could even enjoy it as a career.

> *Douglas sits in his correct seat, as he speaks. Jill sits in hers.*

Jill OK. Then as soon as we're settled here, I'll cut. And we'll pick it up after lunch for close-ups in these same positions, OK?

Douglas Yes, yes . . . That sounds a good plan.

Jill All right, Dan? That work all right for George?

A distant shout.

What?

The shout is repeated.

Yes, I know, I told him that. (*to Douglas*) They're saying, can you try not to notice the camera?

Douglas Yes, I'm sorry, I'm sorry . . .

Vic Try and defocus your eyes, that's the tip – otherwise it's very difficult not to look at it – The camera's like a magnet, you know what I mean . . . ?

Douglas Yes, yes, thank you . . .

Vic Defocus . . . That's what I do. That's the way to do it.

Douglas Thank you very much, I'll try that.

Jill (*who has been looking off towards the camera crew*) OK. Here we go for real this time. Places again, please. We're very short of time.

Vic goes back into the house. Douglas starts for the gate but is called back by Jill.

Douglas –

Douglas Yes, Jill.

Jill Just – when you meet Vic this time . . . I don't think you want to be – what shall I say – quite so overjoyed to see him . . .

Douglas Oh, no, no, that was just . . .

Jill I mean, here's a man you haven't seen for seventeen years and the last time you saw him he was firing a shotgun into the face of the woman you loved – so . . .

Douglas Yes, I see . . .

Jill I mean, it just looks odd – if you greet him like a long-lost brother. I think – you know – just a little wariness and a sense that perhaps you haven't *quite* forgiven and forgotten – I mean, I know maybe you have – but it would certainly look more natural – to the average viewer . . . Do you follow?

Douglas Yes. Yes. No, it was only . . .

A yell from the crew.

Jill (*in response to this*) Yes, OK, OK. We have to get on. We've got five minutes. Can you try and give me all that?

Douglas Yes, I'll try. I'll try.

Jill Bless you. Thank you, Douglas . . . Thank you very, very deeply.

Douglas goes off through the gate.

All right, everyone. (*into her mic*) Tell George to yell as soon as he's rolling . . . (*A pause.*) Stand by, everyone. One take. That's all we've got.

Slight pause. A distant shout.

OK. And – action! (*as she retreats right into the house this time*) Thank you, Douglas.

A slight pause. Douglas enters through the gate. His eyes are defocused, so he is tending to peer around a little myopically, his eyes screwed up.

(*muttering*) What the hell's he doing, he looks like Mr Magoo . . . (*calling*) That's lovely, Douglas. Keep going. Try and look up a little. Look around the place as you come in . . . Oh, no!

*Ruy has entered by the pool with a hosepipe in his
hand. He stops by the edge and watches the
proceedings. An ironic cheer from the crew, who are
evidently well away.*

All right. Keep rolling. Keep rolling. Keep going, Douglas.
(*hissing to Ruy*) Back! Back! Piss off!

Ruy appears not to notice her.

(*into her mic*) Dan! Dan! Can you hear me? Don't let that
man wander into shot. Someone get that sodding gardener
out of shot. (*calling*) Super, Douglas. Perfect. Now, stop
there and look around you. Just don't look at the
gardener, he's not really there.

*Someone, unseen, flicks the other end of Ruy's hosepipe
to try to attract his attention. Ruy fails to notice, so
engrossed is he in watching Douglas, who is staring
about him myopically.*

Come on, Douglas, give us a bit of surprise. (*hissing
angrily into her mic again*) Will somebody get rid of that
bloody gardener . . .

*Douglas tries to look surprised. Ruy's hosepipe twitches
again, rather more violently. He gives it a passing glance
but continues to hold on to it, watching intently.*

Come on, Douglas, real amazement now – (*furiously into
mic*) Get that half-wit out of shot! All the amazement you
can muster now, Douglas.

*Douglas is staring about him open-mouthed. As he
looks at Ruy, who is standing looking at Douglas,
equally fascinated, someone gives the hosepipe a really
fierce tug. Ruy is pulled off his feet, overbalances and
with a cry falls backwards into the pool. Douglas looks
genuinely alarmed.*

Douglas What happened?

Jill All right! Ignore that. He'll be OK. Carry on. We're desperately short of time. Cue Vic. Thank you, Vic.

Vic comes out of the house, genially, as before.

Vic Hallo . . .

Jill Remember, suspicious of him, Douglas – suspicious.

Douglas (*suspiciously*) Hallo, who are you?

Ruy (*bobbing up in the swimming pool*) Help!

Douglas turns to see if Ruy is all right.

Jill Douglas, keep looking at Vic. Remember who he is.

Douglas Yes, sorry.

Vic Did you have a good flight?

Douglas (*suspiciously*) What do you mean by that exactly?

Ruy (*coming up again*) Help! Mr Vic!

Douglas (*turning again*) Is he all right?

Vic (*genially, still*) No, I think he's drowning . . .

Jill Keep chatting, I need more chat. Don't worry about the gardener, he's not in shot. Keep chatting together. Vic, point out the garden to Douglas . . .

Vic (*obeying her*) Well, now. This is the patio . . .

Douglas Oh, yes . . .

Vic You may have noticed it as you walked over it. And that's our swimming pool over there . . .

Douglas Lovely . . .

Jill Super, that's super, chaps . . .

Ruy (*coming up again*) Help!

Vic And that's our gardener over there, coming up for the third time . . .

Jill Keep talking, Douglas. Come on. Time is against us.

Douglas (*worried*) Can he swim, do you think?

Vic I shouldn't imagine so. Not in those boots.

Douglas Good Lord . . .

Ruy Help! Please! Mr Vic!

Jill moves out to join them as before.

Jill Hallo there, gentlemen, sorry to interrupt –

Ruy Help!

Jill Vic, Douglas, this must be quite a strange feeling for both of you meeting after – what is it – seventeen years?

Vic Certainly is.

Douglas I think we ought to do something.

Ruy (*spluttering*) Aaarrgghh!

Douglas I really think he's drowning, you know . . .

Jill Douglas, how does it feel meeting after all this time?

Douglas (*distracted by Ruy*) What? Oh, very nice, thank you very much. (*He smiles.*)

Jill (*fiercely*) Don't smile. (*pleasantly again*) Well, perhaps we should all sit down, should we?

Vic Good idea.

Douglas Why not?

Ruy Aaarrgghh!

They all go to sit. Douglas, distracted, again threatens to sit in the wrong chair.

Jill This chair, Douglas, this one, please.

Douglas Sorry.

Jill And chat, chat, chat, chat, chat . . .

Vic Chat, chat, chat . . .

Jill (*getting up again*) And that's it. Super. Thank you both.

Ruy (*spitting out water*) Ooooorrrggghh!

Jill moves towards where the crew are and talks into her mic.

Jill Dan, can you ask George if he managed to keep off that idiot? Did he manage to keep the gardener out of shot . . . ? Ask him.

Vic moves to Ruy and starts to pull him, exhausted, from the water.

Vic Come on, you'll be all right. Come on, old lad.

Douglas stands watching, amazed.

You get off home and have your dinner. You'll feel better then . . . You mustn't interrupt the filming, you know.

Ruy (*weakly*) No. Thank you, Mr Vic, thank you. Sorry. Sorry.

Vic There you go . . .

Ruy (*staggering off along the poolside*) Sorry, Mr Vic . . .

Vic OK. Don't worry about it, old son.

Ruy exits gasping and panting. A shout from the crew.

Jill What? He did? Oh, terrific. (*to Vic and Douglas*)

That's fine. George apparently managed to pan off the gardener and still keep the full patio in frame, so we're OK. That's great. Lunchtime, is it?

Vic One minute past one.

Jill Pretty good going.

Vic Want a drink first?

Jill looks doubtful.

Come on, just a little one.

Jill Well, a little one perhaps . . .

Vic (*to Douglas*) Doug?

Douglas Mmm?

Vic Coming in for lunch?

Douglas (*still a little dazed*) Oh, yes. Thank you. Yes.

They all move towards the house. Douglas stops to pick up his bouquet on the way.

Jill (*as they go*) God, you know, I had this dreadful fear that that man was going to be in shot through the entire sequence. I mean, the thought of having to set the whole thing up again after lunch . . .

Vic steps aside to let Jill, then Douglas enter. Shouts are heard from the crew.

Vic (*returning to make out what they're saying*) What's that?

More shouts. Douglas and Jill come out again.

Jill What are they saying?

Vic Apparently you didn't say cut. They just want to know if you'd finished the shot.

Jill Well, obviously I've finished. Idiots. (*shouting*) Of course I've finished. (*loudly*) Cut!

A sudden blackout.

Act Two

Later that same afternoon. At the start, as before, there is just a light on Jill who sits on the patio doing a piece to camera. The film crew, as always, are out of sight.

Jill It became increasingly clear that the quiet, law-abiding, undemanding Douglas Beechey we had met and spoken to in Purley a few days before was a very different creature from the man who had arrived here at the Parks' villa earlier that day. Here was a person who, at last, seemed to have discovered a long-lost purpose. As each of his senses, in turn, took in the unfamiliar – the sweet perfume of luxury, the rich, clean vista of good living, the comfortable, self-confident murmur of opulence – his manner grew ever more watchful – increasingly thoughtful. Were these merely the signs of a man finally coming to terms with his lot? A man at last accepting that most unacceptable of truths – that life *is* unjust? Or was there a darker, more dangerous emotion starting to emerge from this hitherto undemonstrative man. Was this an anger, an envy, even a dim forgotten desire for revenge . . . ? (*She pauses, dramatically.*)

As Jill has spoken the lights have slowly widened, as before.

Cut. (*She rises and talks to the crew.*) That OK?

A shouted reply.

Yes, thank you very much. I meant technically OK, Dan – I can do without the editorial, thank you. Can we set up in the study now, please? We'll just do Vic's interview, then that's it for today, all right? (*waving them round*) Go through the front. Through the front door, it'll be easier. I'll see you there.

Jill gathers up her folder from the table. She flicks through it to find her questions for Vic. Kenny wanders out with a drink in his hand.

Kenny (*watching her*) Are you thinking of doing your interview with Vic fairly soon?

Jill Yes. They're just setting it up . . .

Kenny You'd better get a move on. The rate he's pouring it down himself, he won't be able to string two words together . . .

Jill God, I asked him to go easy –

Kenny Oh, yes? I'll tell him you're nearly ready. In the study?

Jill I'll be right there. He is forty-seven, isn't he?

Kenny Forty-seven, yes. Forty-eight next May.

Jill (*scribbling this on to her notes*) Does he mind it being mentioned?

Kenny He never has done.

Jill If I get Vic done now, then tomorrow morning I can spend with Mr Beechey and that leaves me the rest of the day clear – till our flight, to do general shots of the island . . . Should be all right. Always providing I can get Mr Beechey to say anything remotely interesting . . .

Kenny He tries his best, I think.

Jill It was a complete waste of time just now with the three of us. It was all Vic talking. Beechey never said a word –

Kenny Well, Vic's an expert, isn't he? I mean, he's done hundreds of these things. How many's Douglas done?

Jill I gave him his chance. Douglas, what do *you* think? Douglas, what do *you* say to that? You heard me. Nothing. Not a usable syllable. (*excitedly*) I tell you, Kenny, somehow or other – if I'm going to make any sort of programme – I have got to find a way to prise that man open. Get to the heart of him. I know, you see, I know that under all that suburban – blandness – that dreary flock-wallpaper personality of his – there is a real person there. There is pain – there is disappointment – there is a burning resentment – hopefully even hatred, who knows.

Kenny Really? Are you sure?

Jill There has to be. Please God there is.

Kenny He seems pretty well-balanced to me.

Jill There has to be. Or the man wouldn't be human.

Douglas comes out of the house. He has again removed his jacket.

(*switching her tone with accustomed ease*) Mr Beechey, I was just saying – I want to save you till tomorrow morning. All right? When you're fresh.

Douglas Just to suit you, Jill. I'll fit in with you. I must say though, after that lunch – not to mention that wine – I think you might be wiser to let me sleep it off. What a host, eh? What a host Vic is. It seems like every day is Christmas Day in this house.

Jill Don't you drink, normally?

Douglas Oh, Nerys and I are not averse to the odd glass of mother's ruin. But not quite in this quantity. (*He laughs.*)

Kenny I'll – er . . . see if Vic's ready.

Jill Thanks.

Kenny goes back into the house.

Douglas So we'll all be flying home tomorrow, eh?

Jill That's right.

Douglas Maybe we'll be on the same flight.

Jill No. I think we're going a little later than you. We've got the odd bit of filming to do tomorrow afternoon.

Douglas All go, eh?

Jill Well . . . (*She appears to be considering saying something.*)

Douglas Then what do you do?

Jill Er – then we have a look at what we've got – And edit. And then we cut it together using any additional studio sequences we decide to include – using actors – what we call reconstructed action . . .

Douglas Actors playing us?

Jill Probably . . .

Douglas Fascinating. Make sure you get a good-looking one for me, won't you? (*He laughs.*)

Jill (*smiling wearily*) And then I link the whole thing together, live, on the day . . .

Douglas Live. Goodness.

Jill Well, recorded live. In front of a studio audience, anyway.

Douglas What about that, then? All that work just for one programme. People just don't realize, do they?

A slight pause. When Jill speaks, it is in her most simple, honest tone. As of one who really is asking for his help.

Jill Douglas . . . ?

Douglas Yes?

Jill May I ask you something? Do you think – do you feel that I've been asking you the right questions?

Douglas How do you mean?

Jill Well, let me try and explain. Usually, someone like me, a professional interviewer – well, we try as best we can to get at what we hope is the truth, the core of the person we're interviewing. We ask them what we hope are the right questions and then, hopefully, they respond. Which in turn leads us to ask further questions and slowly we arrive at what we, the interviewer, wants to hear; and, more important, hopefully what you, the interviewee, wants to say. Now, I don't feel in our case that I've really got at the truth of you. Do you see? I haven't – I don't feel I've allowed you, yet, to say what you really, truthfully want to say. Now that is not a fault in you, Douglas. That, I'm ashamed to admit, is a fault in me, the interviewer. And I know, I should be able to cope with that. That's my job. That's what I was trained to do. But in our case, yours and mine, it's just not working. I admit it. And it's very unprofessional of me – but I'm actually appealing to you directly for help.

Douglas (*perturbed*) I see. I see. I thought we'd been getting on rather well.

Jill Douglas, be honest. I have done nothing more than scratch the surface of you. Be honest. Have I?

Douglas Er . . .

Jill Some people (*she clicks her fingers*) – you know. No problem. It's all there for the picking – open-cast mining. But I have to say it, in your case, you're a very, very, deep shaft indeed, Douglas. Too deep for me.

Douglas Well, how extraordinary. I've never thought of myself as that . . . You may be right. Maybe you just haven't been asking the correct questions.

Jill Take you and Nerys, for instance.

Douglas Yes?

Jill I mean, you've never really talked about your relationship with her. Are you happy together, for instance?

Douglas Yes.

Jill Truly happy?

Douglas Yes.

Jill No problems?

Douglas No. Not really. I can't think of any, offhand.

Jill Despite the fact that she can't face leaving the house?

Douglas Well, that's true, yes. But we've both learnt to live with that, you see . . .

Jill Doesn't it upset her?

Douglas No. She doesn't seem to mind. She doesn't want to go anywhere.

Jill Doesn't she get lonely?

Douglas No. She's never said so.

Jill What, all alone in that little house? Every day, while you're out at work?

Douglas She isn't all alone. People come to visit her.

Jill Who do?

Douglas Friends, relations . . .

Jill She has friends?

Douglas Dozens of them. They're always dropping in to see her. There are two of them staying there now.

Jill Women?

Douglas Yes, of course, women . . . And possibly her uncle Reg, if he can take the day off from the pet shop.

Jill But surely, Douglas . . . Douglas, there must be more in life for you both than just sitting together day after day in that damp little house . . . ?

Douglas No, it's not damp. That's one of the good things about it . . .

Jill But coming here – seeing all this – the pool, the villa, the sunshine . . . Wouldn't you like this for Nerys, at least? Even if not for yourself? Doesn't she deserve it after what she went through? Wouldn't you both adore to have all this, in your heart of hearts?

Douglas Frankly, no, I'm sorry, we wouldn't. Neither of us swims, Nerys is allergic to sunlight and, personally, I can't get on with Spanish food, not at all.

Jill (*growing desperate*) Well, somewhere else. Italy?

Douglas No.

Jill Greece? Sweden?

Douglas No, no. Not attracted, sorry. Despite their standard of living, they always look a rather glum sort of people, don't you think? They certainly do on television.

Jill Well, you can't always go by everything – (*She checks herself.*) Possibly.

Douglas You know, I have to say this, you're making me

feel rather guilty, Jill. I'm sorry if I'm being a disappointment. I'd have thought, though, that with all that misery you seem to meet up with in your job every day, a happy, contented couple might make a nice change for once. Wouldn't you have thought?

Jill (*in exasperation*) Sorry, Douglas, no. They wouldn't. Not at all. Happy, contented couples – happy, contented, middle-aged couples especially – do not make exciting films, they do not make watchable plays or readable books. Nobody wants to hear about them. Nobody's interested in them. Nobody even wants to look at paintings of them. And they certainly don't want to sit down and watch them on television. Happy, contented people are box-office death, Douglas. Because they generally come over as excruciatingly boring. They come over as smug and self-satisfied and superior and they drive the rest of us up the bloody wall and we really don't want to know about them. Not at all. All right?

A pause. Douglas considers this calmly, seemingly unoffended.

Douglas (*quietly*) How sad. That's all I can say. How very sad.

Jill (*realizing that she has been very rude, even by her standards*) I'm sorry.

Douglas No . . .

Jill If you and Nerys really are that rare and precious thing, a blissfully happy married couple, who am I to come between you . . . ? (*gathering up her things*) Well, I must see how my crew are getting on . . .

Douglas Good luck.

Jill goes to leave but turns back again, just before she does so.

Jill (*incredulously*) No, I'm sorry, I can't believe it. You are both *completely* happy?

Douglas (*worriedly*) Yes, I think we are. I was trying to think . . .

Jill Excuse me, but – sexually, as well?

Douglas (*blankly*) Sexually?

Jill Sexually, you know. Sex? Long winter evenings? And so on?

Douglas Well, no, we don't – No.

Jill You don't?

Douglas No.

Jill You mean you don't sleep together?

Douglas Yes, we sleep together, we just don't – No.

Jill Ever?

Douglas No. Not for some little while.

Jill What do you mean by some little while?

Douglas Er – probably about fifteen years, probably.

Jill (*stunned*) Fifteen years.

Douglas Yes, I should think – I should think about that, yes.

Jill (*appalled*) My God, how have you both managed . . . ?

Douglas Oh, I don't think it's ever been a problem –

Jill Fifteen years? I don't believe it. *Fifteen years?* (*Pause.*) You're joking. Fifteen *years*? Did you never try to talk to anyone about it?

Douglas No, we never felt the need. Anyway, I don't think anyone would be very interested. We – you know – we tried it for a couple of years when we first got married and – neither of us – found much to it, really – rather overrated, really – so we gave it up . . .

Jill Sorry. I have to sit down. (*She does so.*)

Douglas You all right?

Jill (*laughing weakly*) Yes. I couldn't include this in a programme, they wouldn't believe it . . .

Douglas Oh, I don't know. It's not that uncommon, you know. Nerys's Uncle Reg told me he'd never tried it at all and he's never missed it . . .

Jill Maybe it's genetic. (*Slight pause.*) *Fifteen years?* And you have never had it? Do you realize, Douglas, there are some of us, many of us, most of us, who spend all our waking hours thinking about having it and at night, if we're not having it, we dream about having it? We spend most of our lives trying to work out how we can get someone to have it with us and then, once we've had it, how we can get rid of the person we're having it with, so we can have it with somebody else? And you've never even bothered to have it . . . I don't believe it. And Nerys feels the same? She doesn't miss it either?

Douglas She's never said she has.

Jill What about children? Did she never want children?

Douglas (*quickly*) No. Never. She –

Jill What?

Douglas She never did. (*Pause.*) I think that maybe as a result of – her accident . . . she felt unable to cope with the responsibility of children.

Jill And you?

Douglas Oh, I quite understood why. I appreciated her decision.

Jill But would you have liked children, if she'd been willing?

Douglas Possibly.

Jill You'd have liked them? In other circumstances?

Douglas (*cautiously*) Yes . . .

Jill If, for instance, she hadn't been injured, you'd both probably have had them?

Douglas (*uncomfortably*) Er – who can say? Possibly.

Jill (*seeing some light at last*) Yes. Right. (*moving into the house once more, briskly*) We might talk further about children tomorrow, Douglas. In our interview. All right?

Douglas (*unhappily*) Yes. Yes, if you like.

Jill goes into the house. She seems rather triumphant. Douglas wanders out towards the pool. He is thoughtful. It is mid-afternoon, and very hot. Ruy comes through the garden gate with a block of rough stone, one of several such journeys he will make during the next.

Hallo.

Ruy, as always, doesn't even acknowledge Douglas's presence.

Dried off, I hope? (*He laughs.*)

A bird sings. A plane drones overhead. Douglas looks up again. Vic comes out on to the terrace, followed by Kenny. Vic has apparently had a bit to drink.

Kenny She says they're nearly ready.

Vic Well, they know where I am if they want me, don't they? It's too hot to sit in there.

He sits in the shade. Kenny does likewise.

(*calling to Douglas*) Get sunstroke if you stand around out there too long, mate.

Douglas (*turning*) Pardon?

Vic I said, be careful in the sun. If you're not used to it.

Douglas Oh, yes. Thank you. (*returns to the terrace and sits with them*) I thought you'd be doing your interview.

Kenny They're not quite ready.

Douglas Oh.

Pause.

Do you think ours went all right? Our interview?

Vic (*without enthusiasm*) It was all right.

Douglas You were wonderful. Never stuck for an answer.

Vic Well . . .

Kenny He's done it before. Once or twice.

Douglas Yes, I'm afraid that showed, so far as I was concerned. I'm afraid she floored me once or twice. I was completely speechless. She said she'd be able to cut them out, though. My hesitations. Ah.

Marta has come from the house with a freshly opened bottle of wine and some glasses on a tray. She places them beside Vic. During the next, Ruy returns empty-handed from the swimming pool and goes out through the gate.

Marta Mr Vic . . .

Vic Thank you, Marta. Is my wife coming out here, then?

Marta Mrs Parks is doing washing up, Mr Vic.

Vic Why is she doing the washing up?

Marta I don't know, Mr Vic . . .

Vic You should be doing the bloody washing up, not her. That's what you're paid for.

Marta I don't know, Mr Vic . . .

Vic You do the washing up, all right? Tell her to come out here.

Marta (*going back inside*) Yes, Mr Vic . . .

Vic pours himself a glass of wine.

Vic I don't know . . . (*holding up the bottle rather belatedly*) Anybody?

Douglas No, thank you.

Kenny (*gently*) Go steady, Vic.

Vic (*mimicking*) Go steady. You sound like my auntie, you great fruit . . . (*He drinks.*) No, I'll tell you something about interviews and being interviewed. The first thing you've got to remember is that, generally speaking, if you are the one being interviewed and feeling nervous, then the person interviewing you – nine times out of ten – he's even more nervous than you are. Because if it all goes wrong, if you cock the whole thing up, all you stand to do is make a fool of yourself – whereas for him – well, it's his job on the line, isn't it? Know what I mean?

Ruy returns through the gate with another piece of stone. He exits round the swimming pool.

Douglas Yes, I see. That hadn't occurred to me, I must say.

Kenny (*who has been watching Ruy*) What's he doing there?

Vic Ruy? He's building a bench – a little stone seat, the other end of the swimming pool . . .

Douglas Clever.

Vic Well, he's really a stone mason. But he's had a spot of bother with the local law . . . No, the other thing you've got to remember about an interview is that, normally, whoever's interviewing you will know less about what you're talking about than you do. Because nine times out of ten, he'll be talking to you about you – which makes you the resident expert, doesn't it? As far as you're concerned, it's a home game. He'll be nervous just coming down the tunnel, even before he's started. You see, there's an art to being interviewed. First, you've got to be able to use an interview to your own advantage. I mean, after all, what is an interview? This guy is more often than not trying to get you to say one thing – usually incriminating. And you, on the other hand, are wanting to say something of your own, entirely different to what he wants you to say. So it's a battle to the death, isn't it? If you're being interviewed, you have to turn it around, see? You say things like – that's a very good question, John, and I'd like to answer it if I may – with a question of my own. That always throws them, because they can't bear getting questions back at them. Because they're not usually geared for answers. Only for questions. Because they're interviewers, see, and not meant to have opinions. So they can't answer, anyway. But when they don't, that makes them look furtive. And when he does get a question in, if you don't like the one he's asked you, then give him an answer to another one . . . And when he interrupts you –

which he will do, once he realizes that you're giving him the wrong answer, you say to him, I really must be allowed to answer this question in my own way, John, please. And look a bit hurt whilst you're saying it. 'Cause that'll make him look a pushy bastard, too. And another tip, if you're giving an answer and you do happen to know the answer and don't mind giving it to him, talk as fast as you can while still making sense, but don't whatever you do leave pauses. Because they're looking for pauses, see, to edit you about and change your meaning. That's when they put in those nodding bits, you've seen them, when the bloke's nodding his head for dear life about bugger all and sitting in a different room. But if you don't pause, they can't get in to edit, can they? And if they can't edit you, they've either got to leave the interview out altogether, which means they haven't got a programme, which is generally disaster time, or they have to put in what you said in its entirety and not some version of what some monkey would have liked you to have said if he'd got the chance to edit you. And if you're in full flow and you do run out and you do have to stop, stop suddenly. Just like that. (*Quick pause.*) OK? Because that throws him as well. Because nine out of ten, if it's a long answer you've been giving him, he won't be listening, anyway. He'll either be looking at his notes or at the floor manager, or wondering how long's this bleeder going on for? And if none of that works and you're really up against it, have a choking fit, throw yourself on the floor, knock the mic over and call for water. That usually does the trick.

A pause. Douglas digests this.

Douglas There's a lot more to it than you imagine, isn't there?

Kenny True, very true.

Ruy crosses back to the garden gate, empty-handed

525

again. They watch him. Vic pours himself another glass of wine. Sharon comes out of the house and walks through the men. She is still in her uniform and is evidently very hot. Her face is lobster-coloured and she is moving slowly and heavily. She ignores them as she passes through and heads towards the swimming pool. But there is something self-conscious in her walk that tells us she is aware of their eyes on her. She stoops to pick up one of the children's toys.

Douglas (*as she does this*) Yes, but I think for the layman, such as myself, it's probably better just to answer the –

Vic (*watching Sharon*) Dear, oh dear, oh dear . . .

Douglas Pardon?

Vic Just look at the ass on that girl . . .

Kenny (*less enthusiastically*) Yes.

Vic Look at it. Acres of it, isn't there?

Sharon goes off round the side of the swimming pool.

(*watching her go*) Dear, oh dear . . . (*to Douglas, who has been rather embarrassed*) Sorry, Doug, you were saying . . . Sorry, I interrupted you.

Douglas (*who has forgotten what he was saying*) No, I was – no, I was just saying, put like you were putting it, it all seems a bit like a game, doesn't it?

Vic What?

Douglas Interviews. On television.

Vic Well, they are. Most of them. That shock you, does it?

Douglas No. Only occasionally, you know, people might genuinely be trying to say something, mightn't they? That they felt deeply about?

Kenny laughs drily. Ruy returns with another block of stone.

I wouldn't like to think it was all just nothing more than a game.

Vic (*pouring himself another glass of wine*) We all play games, don't we? One way or the other? We all do it.

Douglas Do you think so?

Vic Like – right now – I'm wondering what yours might be . . .

Douglas (*startled*) What?

Vic No, seriously. I'm very, very curious. What are you after, sunshine? Smiling away there. What are you after?

Kenny Vic . . .

Vic Well, don't tell me he came out here just to tell me what a nice man I am. What a lovely place I've got. Don't tell me he came all this way for that, because, frankly, I don't believe him.

Kenny He came to do the programme, Vic . . .

Vic Don't kid me. The programme? You mean to tell me he did all this for a programme? Just so he could see himself on the telly? I don't believe it . . .

Douglas I'm sorry, but I did . . .

Vic Well, I'm sorry, but I don't believe you.

Douglas I did. (*Slight pause.*) Well, and to – (*He checks himself.*)

Vic What? And to what?

Douglas And to – see you.

Vic To see me?

Douglas Yes.

Vic I shouldn't have thought you'd have wanted to see me again, would you?

Douglas Well, when Jill first wrote to us, I must say I didn't, no. But in the end – after Nerys and I had both talked about it – we decided I had to, really.

Vic Why?

Douglas You – you're – This might sound peculiar, but . . . Because you're still there. In our dreams, you see. After seventeen years. We still both dream about you. We wake up occasionally. In the night. Nerys has this terrible fear – it's quite ridiculous, I've told her – that one night you're going to break in downstairs and come up to get her. I've said to her, it's ridiculous – I mean, there you are on the telly twice a week or something, helping the kids or telling the old folk to mind how they go – I said, he's not going to want to break in here, Nerys – Not after seventeen years, is he? Still. You can't always control your imagination, can you? No matter how hard you try. So, don't take this wrong, but I was hoping this – meeting – might help to exorcize you. If you follow me. I told you it would sound peculiar.

> *A silence. Kenny looks at Vic a little apprehensively. Suddenly Vic laughs. He laughs loud and long. The wine helps. Ruy returns during this and goes out through the garden gate.*

Vic Well, I . . . (*He wipes his eyes.*) Well, I've been called a . . . I've been called a lot of things . . . (*controlling himself a little*) Look. Listen, Doug. I promise. I promise – you tell Nerys – tell her I'll never break in through her front window, all right? Tell her she's perfectly safe. I mean, I've been called a lot of things. (*to Kenny*) That's wonderful. Isn't that wonderful?

Sharon returns from the swimming pool. Walking slowly, as before, she carries an armful of the children's toys.

Hey, Sharon . . .

Sharon (*stopping*) Yes, Mr Parks?

Vic Where're Timmy and Cindy?

Sharon They're having their tea in the kitchen with Marta, Mr Parks.

Vic Sit down, then.

Sharon I've got to go and –

Vic Sit down.

Sharon Yes, Mr Parks.

Sharon sits, still holding on to the toys. She is obviously hotter than ever and slightly breathless.

Vic Get your breath back.

Sharon Thank you . . .

Vic Look at her. Puffing like a grampus, aren't you?

Sharon Yes, Mr Parks.

Vic Sweat running off you. (*to the others*) Look at her. Have you ever seen anyone sweating like that? It's dripping off her. I bet it's running off you underneath there, isn't it, eh? Eh?

Sharon doesn't reply.

Running down your arms? Trickling down your legs? If there's one thing I hate, it's to see a woman sweating like that. It's bad enough on a man, it's obscene on a woman, don't you agree?

Sharon sits unhappily. Ruy crosses with another block of stone.

I'll tell you something, Sharon. Do you know why you're sitting there, sweating like that? Do you know the reason why you're sat there like a great bowl of pork dripping? Do you want to know the reason? Because you are overweight, girl. You are fat. Let's face it, Sharon, you are a fat girl, aren't you? A big, fat girl.

Douglas Oh, I don't think that's fair, she's just . . .

Vic Here, let her tell you something, just a second. Sharon . . .

Sharon Yes, Mr Parks . . .

Vic Shall we tell them why you're so fat? Shall we? Shall we tell them your secret? It's because you are greedy, isn't it, Sharon? You eat too much. You are a guts. Aren't you? You're a glutton. Eh?

Sharon Yes, Mr Parks.

Vic Tell them what you ate on your last birthday, Sharon. Tell them. This girl, she told me that last year on her birthday, she sat on her own, in her flat in wherever it was – Macclesfield –

Sharon Huddersfield . . .

Vic Huddersfield. She sat there all on her own, singing happy birthday to me and she ate . . . What did you eat, Sharon? Tell them what you ate, go on.

Sharon (*muttering*) Twelve rum babas.

Vic Come on, say it louder . . .

Sharon (*loudly*) Twelve rum babas, Mr Parks.

Vic Twelve rum babas. Can you imagine that? Turns you

over, doesn't it? Still, we're working on you, aren't we, Sharon? We're slowly melting you down, aren't we?

Sharon Yes, Mr Parks . . .

Vic Getting her fit. Giving her some exercise. Working it off her. What were you learning this morning then? What was I teaching you this morning, Sharon?

Sharon Scuba diving, Mr Parks.

Vic Scuba diving. She enjoyed that – didn't you?

Sharon Yes.

Vic You should have seen her in her big black rubber suit flailing about in the water there, first thing. Like a big shiny, beached, humpbacked whale, weren't you . . .

Sharon suddenly starts to cry very quietly.

Douglas Look, I'm sorry, this is very, very cruel and unnecessary and I really don't think you should go on tormenting this girl simply because –

Vic You mind your own business –

Douglas (*undaunted*) – simply because she's a shade overweight and obviously very self-conscious about it, anyway. It is cruel and it is hurtful and it is –

Vic (*suddenly yelling at him*) I said, mind your own bloody business!

A silence. Sharon gets up and runs into the house. She passes Trudy who is coming out. Trudy looks at the men and appears to sum up the scene. Ruy crosses again, empty-handed.

(*to Douglas, softly*) I hope I don't have to remind you again that you are a guest in this house. And the way I choose to treat my staff is entirely my concern. OK?

Douglas is silent. Kenny clears his throat.

Kenny They should be about set up for that interview, I should think . . .

Trudy They were nearly ready, yes.

Vic I've been waiting here. Patiently. Plenty of things I could have been getting on with, too.

Trudy (*brightly*) I wondered if you wanted to take up my offer and stroll down to the beach, Douglas? While they're doing their interview?

Douglas Oh, lovely, yes. Thank you very much.

Vic (*sourly*) Yes, you take him down the beach, good idea.

Trudy (*faintly sarcastic*) Oh, dear. You haven't been disagreeing with my husband, have you? I hope not.

Douglas No, I –

Trudy You mustn't do that, you know. He only likes people who agree with him all the time. It's one of his little whims.

Vic What are you talking about?

Trudy It comes of being surrounded by people who nod at him all day at work. He prefers us all to nod at home, too . . .

Vic (*innocently*) What did I do, eh? What am I meant to have done, now?

Kenny (*laughing*) Can't imagine.

Trudy He surrounds himself with these little nodding animals. It's like the back shelf of a car in our house. We all do it.

Vic Bloody rubbish.

Trudy Yes, quite right, dear. Nod, nod.

Vic What a load of rubbish. (*to Kenny*) Isn't it? A load of rubbish?

Kenny (*nodding*) Oh, yes.

Trudy (*to Douglas*) It's about a mile's walk down there. Do you mind?

Douglas No, I'd like a walk.

Vic Take the jeep.

Trudy No, we want a walk.

Vic Be quicker in the jeep . . .

Trudy No, we want to walk. It's healthier . . .

Vic Healthier? What are you talking about, healthier?

Trudy Healthier. Walking.

Vic All right then, walk if you want to walk. I think everyone around here is just trying to wind me up, for some reason . . .

> *Ruy has entered with another block of stone.*

(*yelling jovially*) That's it, Ruy, lad. Get stuck in there, boy.

Ruy (*beaming, despite the exertion*) Yes, Mr Vic. You bet.

> *Ruy goes out.*

Trudy What's he building now? Not another garden seat?

Vic Why not?

Trudy Because he keeps building them and then you tell him to pull them down again.

Vic Because they were in wrong place, that's why.

Trudy Well, I hope this one's in the right place.

Vic I'll tell you that when he's built it.

Jill comes out from the house.

Jill Vic, Kenny – I'm most dreadfully sorry to have kept you waiting. Believe it or not, we are now finally ready to go when you are.

Vic Hooray –

Jill First, we had glare from the window, so we moved round and then we couldn't get back far enough for the two shot . . .

Vic (*rising, impatiently*) Come on. Let's get it over with . . .

Vic goes inside, taking his glass with him. He passes Marta, who comes out to clear the tray and remaining glasses.

Jill Kenny, you'll want to sit in, of course . . .

Kenny Well, I'd better. Just in case he says something your lawyers will regret later –

Jill (*laughing*) Oh, hardly. Surely not.

Kenny He's been known to. On occasions . . .

Kenny goes into the house. Jill is about to follow but lingers to watch Trudy and Douglas. Trudy has moved off the patio to look at what Ruy is building. Douglas has moved to join her. Marta, in due course, follows Kenny into the house.

Trudy (*turning to Douglas, smiling*) Well, shall we go?

Douglas (*smiling back*) Ready when you are.

Trudy and Douglas go out through the gate. Jill watches them go. The lights close down on to her, like a smooth, zooming close up.

Jill (*solemnly, to camera*) After seventeen long years, the strands were finally being drawn together – individual threads in a tapestry shaped over the years by the hands of countless separate participants – none of whom perhaps, individually, was consciously aware of the final picture which was slowly and inevitably being woven around them. And that picture? No less a portrait than the face of human tragedy . . . (*She pauses.*) (*calling*) I may need to do that bit again later, George . . . (*yelling back to them as she goes inside*) Sorry. Cut!

The lights change abruptly on her shout. It is suddenly a moonlit evening. Patches of shadow. Cicadas chirping. Very romantic. Perhaps marred slightly by some very syrupy country and western music emanating distantly from the hi-fi somewhere in the house. Pause.
    In a moment, Trudy and Douglas come through the gate. They have evidently just returned from their walk.

Douglas I'm afraid we've taken rather longer than we should have done.

Trudy No, we've only been a couple of hours. It gets dark much quicker out here. You get used to it after a bit. (*Looking towards the house.*) It doesn't sound as if anyone's missed us particularly, does it?

Douglas They can't still be filming, surely?

Trudy (*looking back through the gate*) The crew must have gone back to the hotel. Their van's gone, anyway. And her hire car. She's gone too. Thank God.

Douglas Ah, well. My turn tomorrow. In the hot seat.

Trudy Are you looking forward to it?

Douglas (*uncertain*) Well . . .

Trudy I wouldn't be, I must say.

Douglas I think the problem is that – well, what Jill would really like is a bit of conflict. She was saying to me at lunch that a good programme has got to have a bit of conflict. It needs conflict, otherwise people tend to switch off, apparently. Mind you, I don't. There's nothing I like better than a programme with no conflict in it at all. Nerys is the same. But obviously we're in a minority there. Everyone else seems to prefer to see people beating each other's brains out. Extraordinary. So, to create a bit of conflict, I think Jill would really like me to say a lot of things I don't particularly care to say. That's the trouble.

Trudy Like what?

Douglas makes to move on towards the house.

(*stopping him*) No, stay here a minute . . . Like what? What does she want you to say?

Douglas Oh . . .

Trudy No, you must tell me. I need to know. We must talk, you see. Mustn't we? It's been a lovely walk but we haven't really talked, have we? And we need to. We do, you know. And it has to be you and me. You can never talk to Vic, not about something he doesn't want to talk about, anyway. Nobody can. I mean, I'd have talked to your wife if she'd been here. But she isn't. And she obviously doesn't want to meet us or have anything to do with us, which is perfectly understandable. So it has to be us two, you see. Doesn't it? (*Pause.*) I mean, I need to know how you feel. How you really feel. You're very good at covering up, but . . . (*Pause.*) Do you see why I need to know? You must see. I have to know if you've forgiven us, you understand?

Douglas Us?

Trudy Yes. I'm a part of Vic. I married him, knowing

what he'd done to another human being. To another woman. And I had his children knowing that. I took on all of him. What do they say these days? (*smiling faintly*) A wife should be responsible for her husband's debts. (*Pause.*) So. I need to know.

Douglas I think, quite honestly, what's past is past, isn't it?

Trudy You really don't bear any resentment for what he did? To you? To your wife? The woman you were in love with? Didn't it matter? It's like it never mattered to you at all.

Douglas Oh, it mattered. Then. Of course it did. Only – Well, it wasn't as straightforward as that. It never is. Let me try and – explain, then. It's difficult. (*Pause.*) Working with me in this bank – I was twenty-four – twenty-five at the time – working with me, alongside me – was the most beautiful woman I have ever seen in my life, anywhere. Before or since. Her name was Nerys Mills and she was a stunner. And I was – besotted. That's the only word for it. Some days I couldn't look at her at all. My hands would shake and my voice used to crack and go falsetto when I spoke and I'd feel sick in my stomach, and one day I actually started crying without any warning at all. Right in the middle of serving a customer. In the end, I had to pretend I got hay fever. And that was very inconvenient, because then I had to remember to keep having it and take nose drops and things, otherwise people would begin to wonder what was really wrong with me. Anyway, needless to say – Nerys didn't take a blind bit of notice of me. No, that's not exactly true. She was generally very nice and polite, but, so far as romance went, I think I was definitely at the bottom of the reserves as far as she was concerned. She was actually unofficially engaged to this other man – (*darkly*) I forget his name now. I never forget names but I've forgotten his.

Trudy Did he work in the bank as well?

Douglas No, no. He was a salesman. A double-glazing salesman, actually. There's an amusing story to that, I'll come back to that. Anyway, I sat there and – longed for her – day after day – month after month – fantasized about her a little – nothing unpleasant, you know . . .

Trudy No, no . . .

Douglas And some mornings she'd have a chat with me between customers. And then the sun would shine all day, you know . . . (*He smiles.*)

Trudy (*smiling*) Yes . . .

Douglas And other mornings, she'd come in like thunder – something obviously had gone wrong the night before with her and old double-glazing . . . And then, of course, you never got a smile . . .

Trudy (*sadly*) Ah . . .

Douglas And as time went by, I marked her off in my own personal ledger in the desirable but unattainable column, along with the Silver Cloud and the offer to keep wicket for Kent – and I was just resigning myself to life without her and seriously considering whether the Royal Army Pay Corps might have a vacancy somewhere – when the bank raid occurred. And that did change everything. There's no doubt about it. I don't know why I did what I did. Your husband was right, it was madness. It just seemed the only thing to do at the time, that's all. There was this stranger in a balaclava threatening the woman that I cared more than my own life for . . . I couldn't help myself, you see?

Trudy (*engrossed*) No. I see. I see.

Douglas Afterwards, I went to see her a lot in hospital. Partly through guilt. Only partly. But, you see, if I hadn't run at Vic like that, she might never have – Not that she's ever blamed me. She's never once, ever – Never. Anyway, I went to see her, as soon as they'd let us in to visit. I imagined there'd be so many blokes round the bed she'd never even see me, anyway. And there were, to start with. I was just there waving my bunch of daffodils at her from the back of the crowd. And then slowly they all drifted away. Over the weeks. Stopped coming to see her.

Trudy How rotten. Aren't people rotten, sometimes?

Douglas Yes, I thought that at first. Then I realized later, of course. She'd been sending them all away. Subconsciously. A beautiful woman like she'd been, she couldn't bear to be seen like – that. She couldn't stand it. I mean, she wasn't vain. Not really. But if you're used all your life to people taking pleasure in looking at you, then it must be very hurtful when they suddenly start instinctively looking away from you. You couldn't blame people, altogether. She did look a terrible mess for a time.

Trudy But you didn't? Look away from her?

Douglas Well, I think I probably did, yes. As I say, it was only natural early on. But, you see, if I looked away from her, it didn't matter quite so much. Because she'd never valued my opinion of her anyway. So it never worried her. And there I was, with her all to myself. Visiting every day. Jollying her up. And over the weeks we got very friendly.

Trudy And did she fall in love with you?

Douglas I don't know.

Trudy But did she never say to you . . .?

Douglas No. And I didn't ask her. It didn't matter. She liked me. And more important, she needed me. That's what mattered. And I loved her. (*He smiles.*) I was going to tell you, you know, when I'd left the bank, I applied for my present job with this double-glazing company. I thought it might – you know – increase my standing with her. Since she seemed to have a liking for double-glazing men. Ridiculous. We laughed about that later. I never regretted it, though. They're a grand bunch. Anyway, she came out. And we married quietly. And we got a joint mortgage on number fifty-three and we've lived there ever since. With never a cross word, I'm happy to report. (*Pause.*) So what do I say? Yes, I do – I hate Vic because of what he did to the most beautiful woman in the world? Or, thank you very much, Vic, for being instrumental in arranging for me to marry the unattainable girl of my dreams? Difficult to know which to say, isn't it? (*Pause.*) All right. I know you might well say, what about her? What about poor old Nerys? Being forced to settle for minor league when she was naturally first division. Well, all I can say is, without prejudice, and I am not a swearing person, you appreciate – but that man she was engaged to originally – old double-glazing the first – he was a complete – pillock. He really was. He treated Nerys like – well, there were times when – not just me, you understand . . . We all could have done – in that bank. Including Mr Marsh. This man – he treated her as only a handsome man can treat a beautiful woman. If you know what I mean.

Trudy Yes. I do. I think I do.

They listen to the music for a moment.

Douglas (*cheerfully*) Well, that's – that's my life. Sorry if I bored you. (*Pause.*) This is very pleasant music, isn't it? Country and western? Am I right?

Trudy (*weakly*) Yes. Vic likes it. We used to . . . When we were . . . (*Her voice tails away.*)

Douglas waits for her to finish the sentence. She doesn't. She is evidently in some distress. She rocks about. She looks at Douglas. Suddenly and unexpectedly, she kisses him on the mouth. Then pulls away and avoids his look. He, after taking a second to recover, avoids her in turn. They sit, pretending it hasn't happened.

Douglas (*at length*) Yes, I'm very partial to country and western music. They always manage to come up with a good tune, don't they?

Trudy (*in a little voice*) I'm sorry. (*then, pulling herself together*) There's nothing we can do for you, then? Vic and I? Nothing?

Douglas Do?

Trudy Well, to help in any way . . . Money or . . .

Douglas (*rather embarrassed*) Oh, no.

Trudy (*equally embarrassed*) Sorry. I didn't mean to –

Douglas No, no . . .

Trudy It's just so rare to meet someone who doesn't want something from us these days . . . I suppose that's called being successful. Or is because it's us who are offering? Is that why you're saying you don't want anything?

Douglas No, it's not that. I just don't think there is anything. Thank you very much. Well, I think I must away down the hill to my own hotel. They'll be serving dinner soon . . .

Trudy You're welcome to stop and have supper with us if you –

Douglas No, that's very kind of you, but you'll see quite enough of me again tomorrow.

Trudy Well, wait there a second, I'll fetch the keys and run you back –

Douglas No, please.

Trudy It's no trouble –

Douglas I'd rather walk, I really would. Really. I don't get the chance to walk around islands that much.

Trudy (*reluctantly*) Well . . .

Douglas Thank you for all your hospitality today. You've been very kind. You really have. (*He starts to move back towards the gate.*) Straight down the hill, I take it?

Trudy Yes. Only when you get to the fork that leads to the sea – the one we took – go right instead of left.

Douglas Simple enough. Well. See you tomorrow, Trudy.

Trudy Goodnight, Douglas.

Douglas (*turning in the gateway*) Er . . . (*smiling*) There's one thing I wouldn't have minded, I suppose. Not that you could have given it to me. But since you mentioned wanting things . . .

Trudy What's that? Anything we –

Douglas No, I was just thinking. I was a hero, I suppose, for all of a year. People wrote to me. Sent for my photograph. Asked my advice. Listened to what I had to say. I think it would have been nice to have been a hero for a bit longer . . .

Trudy You still are –

Douglas . . . silly. I'd probably never have missed it, only . . .

Trudy – to people like Nerys you are. And I bet there are others who still remember . . .

Douglas No, I think I'm best remembered now as the idiot who tackled an armed robber and nearly got someone's head blown off in the process. I think you ended up with the hero, Trudy, not poor old Nerys. You stick with him. You stick with Vic. If you're looking for heroes. See you in the morning.

 Douglas goes out through the gate. Trudy stares after him.

Trudy (*faintly*) Yes . . .

 She gets up to go into the house. Then decides that, if she's going to cry, she'd better cry out here. She sits down again in the shadows. She hugs herself and starts to weep quietly and privately.
 In a little while, there is a faint slapping sound from the direction of the swimming pool. Trudy becomes aware of this and stops crying to listen. Sharon appears, walking along the side of the swimming pool towards the deep end. She has on her black wetsuit, rubber helmet and flippers. She carries a weighted diving belt. She is also crying. In fact, she is in a desperate, heartbroken state. She stops at the end of the swimming pool, a tragi-comic, fat, black, rubber-clad figure.
 Trudy watches her, astonished. Sharon, unaware she is being watched, looks towards the house and starts to fasten the diving belt about her waist.

(*cautiously*) Sharon? Sharon . . . What are you doing there?

Sharon (*between sobs*) Mrs Parks . . .

Trudy What are you doing, Sharon?

Sharon I'm going to kill myself, Mrs Parks.

Trudy (*moving to her, alarmed*) You are going to what?

Sharon I'm sorry, Mrs Parks. I love him so much, and he doesn't care about me at all.

Trudy Sharon . . .

Sharon (*as in one breath*) He just says I'm fat and I've got to get thin and I've tried to get thin but I can't get thin whatever I do because when he says he doesn't love me I just keep eating because I'm so unhappy you see and then when I eat then I just get fatter you see and then he doesn't love me . . . and I love him so much, Mrs Parks, and I'm ever so sorry . . .

Trudy Yes . . . I'm sorry, Sharon . . . I know how it is, believe me I do . . .

Sharon No, you don't – you can't . . .

Trudy Yes, I do. I promise, Sharon, I do . . .

Sharon Nobody knows –

During the next, the music from the house stops as the record comes to an end.

Trudy Sharon, it's a passing thing, I promise. It's something we all go through. Most of us, God help us. It'll pass . . .

Sharon No, it won't pass. I've loved Vic for years . . .

Trudy Years? What do you mean, years? You've only been with us two months . . .

Sharon I seen him on the telly. I used to watch him on the telly and I used to write to him on *Ask Vic* and he used to write back to me, he did, I promise . . .

Trudy Sharon, he gets thousands of letters a week. He doesn't even read them, let alone write back . . .

Sharon He did, he wrote to me and it was in his writing. And he used to tell us on the telly if we had problems how to deal with them and not to worry and then when I got this job working for him I just thought it was going to be

544

so wonderful and he's just been horrible to me . . . I don't know what I've done . . . What have I done wrong, Mrs Parks?

During the next, Vic comes out of the house and listens, unnoticed.

Trudy (*fiercely*) The only thing you did wrong, Sharon . . . the one and only thing you ever did wrong was to love him in the first place . . . Because he is not a man to love, Sharon, I promise you. Not if you can possibly avoid it. I speak as one who has tried for eight years, Sharon, to keep loving him. While that bastard has abused me and ignored me and taken me for granted – while he has been screwing his way round Television Centre and half of ITV – I have looked after his kids and his house and his bloody, bad-tempered old mother in Beckenham . . . And I have tried to keep loving him . . . I swear to God I have tried. And if you are honestly clinging on to life in the hope of getting one tiny scrap of care or consideration back from that self-centred, selfish – scum bucket – then all I can say is, you'd better jump in there now, Sharon, and cut your losses.

Sharon, understandably, is a little bemused by this outburst. She stands indecisively. Vic steps out further on to the patio. Both women see him for the first time.

Vic Well, well. You know what they say. You never hear good about yourself, do you?

Trudy Tell her, Vic. Talk to the girl, for God's sake.

Vic Tell her what?

Trudy I just caught her trying to drown herself . . .

Vic (*amused*) What?

Trudy Vic, talk to her . . .

Vic What do you want to drown yourself for, Sharon?

Trudy What do you think . . . ?

Vic I have no idea. I have no idea why this great big girl should want to drown herself . . .

Sharon sobs and finishes fastening her belt.

Trudy Vic . . .

Vic Why? Just tell me?

Trudy Because of what you've said to her. Done to her.

Vic What?

Trudy Whatever you said – whatever you did. I don't know. I don't want to know . . .

Vic I've never laid a finger on her, have I? Sharon, tell her, I've never laid a finger on you . . . Have I? Eh?

Sharon (*unhappily*) No, Mr Parks . . .

Vic There you are. No. She confirms that . . .

Trudy (*shouting*) You know bloody well what you've done to her, Vic, now do something about it . . .

Vic Right, that's it, forget it. I am not being shouted at. Let her jump . . .

He turns to move into the house. Sharon prepares to jump into the pool.

Trudy (*yelling*) Vic . . .

Vic (*furiously*) Let the stupid cow drown herself, what do I care? Go on. Jump, jump, jump then . . .

Sharon jumps into the pool. Weighted down by her diver's belt, she sinks rapidly under the dark water and vanishes in a trail of bubbles.

Trudy (*screaming*) SHARON!

Vic (*surprised Sharon has done it*) Bloody hell!

  Vic moves towards the pool.

Trudy Vic, get her out. Dive in and get her out, for God's sake . . .

Vic I'm not diving in there. Not in these clothes.

Trudy Vic, the girl is drowning.

Vic She's not drowning. She can stay under for hours. She's built like a bathyscope . . .

Trudy Are you going in to get her, or not?

Vic You dive in.

Trudy I can't get her out, she's far too big for me, she's enormous, Vic . . .

Vic We could sprinkle rum babas on the surface, that'll bring her up . . .

Trudy You bastard . . . (*desperately*) Oh, dear God. (*running to the gate and yelling*) Douglas! Douglas! He's gone . . .

Vic (*peering into the pool, meanwhile*) Sharon! I can see you down there, Sharon.

Trudy (*running to the house and calling*) Kenny! Kenny, come out here, please!

Vic Kenny went down to the shop – we were running out of vino . . .

Trudy If she dies, Vic. If that girl dies . . .

Vic Nobody would miss her except the national union of bakers . . .

Trudy (*running at him in fury*) You . . . God, I hate you! I really so hate you! (*She attacks him with both her fists.*)

Vic (*amused and fending her off easily*) Hey, hey, hey!

Trudy (*beating at him*) I'd so love to . . . hurt you . . . like you . . . hurt . . . other people, sometimes . . .

She lands a blow that Vic doesn't care for. He takes her a little more seriously.

Vic Oi! Now, Trudy! That's enough. You've had your fun . . .

He starts to pinion her arms to protect himself. Trudy continues to fight and Vic is forced to turn her away from him and grab her neck in the crook of his arm in a traditional headhold whilst pinioning her arms with his other hand. Trudy is finally incapacitated. She remains there, exhausted and infuriated by her impotence against his superior strength.

Barely have they finished struggling when Douglas runs back into the garden through the gate. He is halfway to the house before he sees Vic and Trudy.

Douglas (*as he enters*) What's the problem? I – (*He stops and stares at them in amazement.*)

Trudy (*weakly, choking in Vic's grip*) Douglas . . . please!

Vic (*calmly*) Now, it's all right. Don't get excited and nobody'll get hurt, all right?

Douglas reacts like a charger on hearing the bugle call. He gives a sudden wild yell of fury and rushes at Vic head down.

Douglas Aaaaarrrrgggghhhh!

Vic (*startled*) Jesus!

Vic pushes Trudy to one side in order to defend himself – not for the first time in his life – from Douglas's sudden wild onslaught. Douglas catches Vic in the

midriff. Trudy screams. Vic grunts with pain, winded.
Both men lose their balance. Vic topples into the pool.
Douglas is left kneeling on the edge, slightly winded
himself.

Trudy Douglas? Are you all right?

Douglas Yes, I . . . I'm . . . I'm sorry, I . . . Where's Vic?

Trudy He's in the . . .

As she starts to speak, Vic's hand grips the edge of the
pool. He hauls himself up. He looks very dangerous.

Vic (*breathless*) Right. There is about to be some serious
damage done. I can tell you . . . (*pointing at Douglas and*
Trudy in turn) To you. And to you. All right?

Douglas and Trudy draw back, nervously. Vic seems
about to climb out of the pool.
  Suddenly the waters part and a large black shape,
barely recognizable as Sharon, breaks surface and seizes
hold of Vic around the neck from behind.

As soon as I've . . . Uurrgghhh!

He is dragged under the water by Sharon's sheer weight.

Douglas (*genuinely alarmed*) Oh, my goodness, what is it,
a whale?

Trudy No, it's Sharon . . .

There is a great deal of frenzied threshing about under
the water. Rather like an old Johnny Weissmuller film.
Trudy and Douglas watch, unable to do much else.

Trudy (*during this, vainly*) Sharon . . . Vic . . .

Douglas (*likewise*) Vic . . . Sharon . . .

The waters finally still. Sharon comes up for air and
props herself against the side of the pool, breathlessly

and strangely happy. Trudy and Douglas approach her cautiously.

Trudy Sharon . . . ?

Douglas Sharon . . . ?

Trudy Are you all right?

Sharon (*gathering enough breath to speak*) Yes, thank you, Mrs Parks . . .

Douglas (*trying to calm her desperate breathing*) Easy. Easy now . . .

Trudy (*A sudden thought*) Sharon, where is Mr Parks?

Sharon (*apologetically*) I'm standing on him, Mrs Parks.

Trudy and Douglas react with alarm.

Douglas Sharon, for goodness' sake . . .

Trudy (*with Douglas*) For God's sake, get off him . . .

Together, they start to haul Sharon out of the water.

Sharon (*as they do so*) I'm very sorry, Mrs Parks . . .

Trudy All right, Sharon, all right. Out you come now.

They land her on the poolside like a large, beached mammal. Vic floats to the surface. Unconscious or worse. Sharon lies panting while Trudy and Douglas pull Vic from the water.

(*to Douglas*) Turn him over, we must get the water out of him . . .

Douglas Right.

They turn Vic over.

Sharon (*as they do so*) Can I give him the kiss of life, Mrs Parks . . . ?

Trudy No, you can't, Sharon. Stay there, please.

She and Douglas try to work on Vic rather ineffectually.

I don't know what you do. I think you have to pump his ribs somehow . . .

Douglas I'm afraid I don't really have much of an idea . . . Me and water, you know . . .

Sharon (*heaving herself up*) Here, let me . . .

Trudy No, Sharon, I'd rather you . . .

Sharon It's all right, Mrs Parks, I've got my life-saver's medal.

Trudy (*rather surprised*) You have?

Sharon In the Huddersfield baths. Here, let me . . .

Sharon takes over from Trudy and Douglas. She sits astride Vic and pumps away vigorously. Trudy and Douglas watch her anxiously.

Trudy Anything . . . ?

Sharon No, I don't think he's . . . He's not responding.

Trudy Oh, God.

Sharon Hang on.

She rolls Vic over and tries the kiss of life a couple of times. There is no response.

Trudy (*anxiously*) No?

Sharon No. I'm sorry, Mrs Parks, I . . . (*starting to cry as the realization finally hits her*) I'm sorry, I'm ever so sorry . . . (*She kneels weeping again. A silence.*)

Trudy I don't know what we're going to do. I don't know.

Silence.

What are we going to do?

Douglas I suppose we'll have to report it. To the police, won't we?

Trudy If we report it, we'll have to tell them everything. We'll have to tell them it was Sharon. We can't have Sharon blamed for this . . .

Sharon (*tearfully*) I didn't mean to, Mrs Parks . . .

Trudy (*comforting her*) It's all right, Sharon, it's all right. (*She considers.*) OK, I'll tell you what we're going to do. We're all going to have to tell the same story, all right? Douglas?

Douglas Yes?

Trudy Sharon? Are you listening to me?

Sharon Yes, Mrs Parks.

Trudy We're going to have to say this. Vic was very drunk – that's true, anyway – and he came out here on his own and must have decided to take a swim. And, Sharon, you were upstairs and you heard the splash and you rushed downstairs and called for help – only Kenny wasn't in –

Douglas What about the couple? You know, the Spanish couple? Do they live in?

Trudy Yes, but they'll be watching television, they'd never have heard . . . And then you came out here, Sharon, you see . . . ?

Sharon Yes . . .

Trudy And you found Mr Parks floating unconscious in the water –

Douglas In all his clothes?

Trudy Yes. Good point. We'd better take some of those off him . . .

Sharon (*starting at once*) Right . . .

Trudy No, let me finish. And then you dived in, Sharon –

Sharon Was I wearing my wetsuit?

Trudy No. Well done. You'd better take that off, too.

Sharon What, now?

Trudy Yes.

Sharon (*softly*) I've got nothing underneath, Mrs Parks.

Trudy (*angrily*) Sharon, we are talking about murder. If you are going to worry about being done for indecent exposure . . .

Sharon (*starting*) Yes, Mrs Parks . . . (*She begins to unfasten her belt.*)

Trudy No, let me finish first. And then, finally, Douglas and I came back from our walk in time to find you trying to revive Vic. But to no avail. How does that sound?

Sharon Brilliant.

Trudy (*to Douglas*) All right?

Douglas (*obviously unhappy*) Yes. I don't see an alternative, really, but –

Trudy (*taking this as agreement*) Sharon, strip off. Douglas, help me with Vic . . . Quick as you can, everyone.

The three work in silence, concentrating on their tasks. Sharon takes off her belt, then her hood and flippers. Douglas and Trudy start to undress Vic with difficulty, removing his jacket, shirt, shoes and socks. As they are doing this, they are unaware of the audience that starts

553

to assemble. Through the back gate, Kenny enters. He has the jeep keys, having just returned from the shops. He carries a couple of loose bottles of wine. Behind him comes Ruy, who carries the bulk of their purchase, namely a full case of wine. They stop and watch the proceedings with horrified fascination. Soon after, Marta comes out from the house with a tray, looking for stray dirty glasses. She stops, likewise, to watch suspiciously. Sharon is about to do the final lap of her striptease and remove her wetsuit. She is on the point of doing this when she becomes aware of their audience. She freezes, open-mouthed, staring. Trudy and Douglas take a second or so longer to realize. They are on the point of removing Vic's trousers.

(*to Douglas*) Right. You pull off his trousers, while I hold him . . .

Douglas (*struggling*) Yes.

It is a difficult operation.

Trudy God, he's a weight . . . Sharon, can you help us?

They struggle again.

Douglas Hang on.

Trudy He's so . . . He's so . . . Sharon, don't just stand there – please – come and . . .

Trudy finally becomes aware of why Sharon has frozen. Douglas is the last to notice. They stand up, guiltily.

Kenny What the hell is going on?

Silence, Vic, released, flops over, very obviously dead.

What have you done to him? What have you done to Vic?

Trudy (*feebly*) We were just . . . We were just . . . undressing him.

Kenny What's happened? He looks dead. Is he dead?

Trudy (*softly*) Yes, he's dead.

Marta (*crossing herself, whispering*) Mr Vic!

Ruy (*likewise, crossing the carton of wine*) Mr Vic!

Kenny (*softly*) Jesus . . . I think I'm going to have to phone the police, aren't I?

Douglas Yes, I think you are . . .

Sharon whimpers.

Trudy No!

Kenny How did it happen, Trudy? I need to know.

Trudy Well . . .

Sharon Well . . .

Douglas (*stepping forward unexpectedly*) It's all right, leave it to me. (*to Trudy and Sharon*) I'm sorry. There's no other way. There's only one thing worth telling and that's the truth.

Kenny Quite right. It's my experience, in cases like this, that there's absolutely nothing like the truth. Absolutely – nothing like it at all.

Before Douglas can start to explain, **Ashley Barnes,** *a TV floor manager complete with two-way radio, steps on to the floor, appearing unexpectedly and as from nowhere. The lights close down to a small area round him, momentarily.*

Ashley (*with great authority*) Sorry, everyone. We need to stop for just a second. Sorry. Bear with us, we won't be two seconds. (*listening to instructions from his earpiece*) Mmm . . . yes . . . mmm . . . hmm-mmm . . . yes . . . OK . . . I see . . . yes . . .

While Ashley listens, the general lighting returns. The actors playing Vic, Douglas, Trudy, Sharon, Kenny, Ruy and Marta have left the stage to be replaced by their counterpart 'TV' actors, who are to be used to mime out scripted events. This switch should have occurred as swiftly and unobtrusively as possible. Although none of the replacement performers concerned are particularly miscast (it is sufficient that they are different), there have been one or two cosmetic improvements. The new Sharon is slim and really quite attractive in her shapely wetsuit. She has shed the helmet and has her hair tied back. Vic is possibly glamorized a little, too, in an anti-hero sort of way. He's certainly less drunk. Ruy and Marta are a shade more 'Spanish'. All the clothing – apart from Sharon's – is similar but not identical to their original counterparts. The ensuing action is as silent as possible, leaving Jill's voice to serve as a 'voice-over' to it.

(*having received final instructions*) OK. I'm afraid we have to go back just to Sharon jumping in the pool.

The actors immediately start to move.

My apologies, everyone, this is purely for cameras. Many apologies. We'll go when you're ready, everyone . . . (*to the audience*) Do bear with us once again, ladies and gentlemen. I'm afraid these things do happen. I crave your patience.

The replacement Vic goes off into the house, gathering up his wet clothes as he goes. Replacement Marta precedes him. Replacement Sharon goes off along the pool taking her discarded gear with her. The other replacements go off, Trudy and Douglas following Ruy and Kenny out through the gate. As this happens, the real Jill comes on from the house. She is in her smart presenter's outfit. She stands on the patio, waiting. She carries a clipboard. She is in her most tense, unsmiling, professional mood at present.

Sorry, Jill. We'll need to go from the top of that final sequence again.

Jill The final sequence?

Ashley From where she jumps in.

Jill OK.

She consults her clipboard. The lighting changes slightly. Although the general area stays lit, there is a bright 'special' on Jill.

Ashley (*listening to a final instruction from his earpiece*) OK? Thank you, Jill. (*yelling*) Quiet studio, please. (*to Jill*) In your own time, Jill, whenever you're ready.

He moves back as he speaks. As Ashley goes off, Jill hesitates a second, then moves up a couple of gears in order to do her piece to camera.

Jill And so to the final events of that tragic night. The crew and I had finished for the day and had gone back to our hotel to have dinner. For a description of what followed we must rely, therefore, on the testimonies of first Sharon, the nanny, then Douglas and Trudy, and finally Vic's manager, Kenneth Collins. Piecing together these various eyewitness accounts, the following is almost certainly a true picture of what occurred.

As Jill speaks, the previous scene is enacted again. If the facts are different, then so are the performers.

Trudy, in the company of Douglas Beechey, had decided to take a stroll to the beach. Kenneth Collins had walked with Ruy, the gardener, to the local store to buy extra provisions. And whilst Marta, the maid, was preparing supper in the kitchen, Vic sat in the living room relaxing and listening to some of his favourite country and western music.

She pauses for a second to allow the strains of pre-recorded background country and western music to filter from the direction of the house. This is not the same as previously heard, probably more romantic. It plays gently under the rest of Jill's speech, accompanying the action that follows. The replacement Sharon enters during the next and stands gazing into the pool and slowly fastening on her diving belt.

Unknown to any of them, it was at this stage that the children's nanny, Sharon Giffin, decided that her life was no longer worth living. She resolved to kill herself. Perhaps the eventual realization that her secret, undeclared passion for Vic Parks could never be reciprocated, combined with a totally naïve misinterpretation of the kindness he had shown to her whilst she worked there, proved too much for this simple, semi-literate girl from Macclesfield. It was her good fortune, even as she fastened on her weighted scuba diver's belt and prepared to jump, that Vic happened to catch sight of her through the open windows. Realizing at once her intention, he rushed out to try and stop her –

The replacement Vic runs out of the house and stops for a minute staring at Sharon.

But he was too late to stop her jumping –

Vic yells silently at Sharon, who jumps into the pool. Vic starts to run to the pool, shedding his shirt and trousers as he does so. He leaps into the pool after her.

What happened next is unclear. Trudy and Douglas arrived back from their walk in time to see two figures struggling in the water in the darkness.

Replacement Douglas and replacement Trudy have

entered and hurried at once to the swimming pool,
where they haul Sharon from the water, during the next,
and bring her round.

Sharon, herself, has only the dimmest memory of being hauled from the water in a semi-conscious state. At first, both rescuers concentrated on reviving her, assuming that Vic himself – a strong swimmer and in good physical condition – had no need of assistance. By the time they realized all was not well, it was already too late. In his violent struggle with the desperate, frenzied girl, Vic Parks had received a glancing blow, sufficient to knock him unconscious and allow his lungs to fill with water.

Replacements Trudy and Douglas, under the last, re-
enact the sudden realization that Vic is still in the water.
They locate his body and start to pull him from the
pool. As they do so, replacements Kenny and Ruy
appear in the gateway. Ruy carries a box of groceries.
Replacement Marta appears in the house doorway. She
is wiping her hands on a kitchen towel and has evidently
been preparing food.

Despite frantic and repeated efforts, they were too late to save him. When the others returned to the villa, they found themselves little more than powerless spectators, forced to witness the final act of a needless tragedy. That night marked not only the end of a life but the end of a living legend.

During this, Sharon sits exhausted, Trudy and Douglas
make efforts to save Vic. Marta, Kenny and Ruy stand
watching anxiously. Finally, Douglas looks up from
Vic's body and shakes his head. Marta, Kenny and Ruy
move in slowly and incredulously. They kneel with the
others around the body, forming a moving and well-
grouped tableau which then freezes while Jill concludes
her speech.

How best to sum up Vic Parks? A man whose life, ironically, ended as violently as it had started. But in between how to describe him? Hero or villain? Latter-day saint or merely late-twentieth-century showman? The arguments will continue. Perhaps his best epitaph is a piece of advice given spontaneously to a young viewer to whom he said: 'Don't complain to me that people kick you when you're down. It's your own fault for lying there, isn't it?'

She sits in the chair in which she started the play. The music fades out or finishes gently. The lights, from now on, close down on Jill. The others remain frozen and are all but lost in the gloom. By the end of the next, Ashley has reappeared at the edge of the set. Jill's manner now lightens from the solemn/reverent to the fireside/jokey level for her final wind up.

Sad to say, that's the last of *Their Paths Crossed*. If you enjoyed this short series but think that four wasn't *quite* enough, tell you what – why not drop them a line up there and let them know? Them. You know the ones I mean. As for me, I'm off to pastures new but I hope we'll meet again soon. Next week at this time – and quite coincidentally – the start of *The Very Best of Vic* – a series of twelve special programmes featuring selected highlights from his recent series. And don't forget, too, you Vic Parks devotees who happen to be in the London area next month, I'll be co-presenting what's planned to be the first of the Annual Midland Bank Vic Parks Awards for Youth – founded, of course, in memory of the man himself. That's at the Royal Albert Hall on Saturday the 18th. There's still a few seats left. So do try to get along if you can. Remember, it's all in a very good cause. Oh, and incidentally, there's a fabulous country and western line up, too. But in the meantime, that's all from me, Jill Rillington. Bye for now. And mind how you go, won't you? Bye.

Jill smiles into the camera and holds her expression for a second or so. Ashley steps forward into the middle.

Ashley Thank you, everyone. Just hold it a minute, please. We're waiting for clearance.

He waits. Patiently listening to his earpiece.

Jill (*sweetly, to the audience*) They just have to check that last bit through. See if we've managed to get it right this time. Won't be a second.

A pause. We wait. The actor playing replacement Vic is now sitting up and whistling quietly to himself. The others wait patiently.

Actor (*the actor playing replacement Ruy*) Jill . . . Jill!

Jill Hallo?

Actor I don't know if you noticed, but the second time I came on a tidge later at the end there. I hope that was OK.

Jill (*rather impatiently, the man is obviously a pain*) I'm sure that was fine, David . . .

Actor I mean, I could do it again if they want it . . .

Jill It was fine. I don't think they were on you, then, anyway.

Actor (*faintly disappointed*) Oh, right. Fair enough.

Ashley is getting instructions through his earpiece.

Ashley (*speaking to the gallery*) Yep . . . yeah . . . yep . . . Great, grand, thank you. Thank you, Jill, thank you very much, everyone. They're very happy with that. Thank you.

The actors leave by the various exits.

Jill (*as she goes, cheerily to the audience*) Bye.

Ashley (*briskly and brightly, it is a well-oiled routine*)

Right. Ladies and gentlemen, just before you leave – I know you're all dying to get home. One last little request – I know, I've been making requests all evening, but this, I promise you, is my last request for just one vast burst of your really *warmest* applause. That I know only you can give me. We have yet, you see, to record one little further item. Which is, of course, our final credits sequence. That's when all those names of people you've never even *heard* of, doing jobs you don't even know what they *are*, this is when their names go *racing* across your screen while you're busy putting the cat out and couldn't care less anyway. Well, fair enough, but they've got to be there and, more important, one of the names is mine, so when you see that go through – my name is Ashley Barnes, by the way – watch out for it – Ashley Barnes – special loud applause for that, then I get more money, right . . . Seriously, as much *warm* applause as you can give us. Let's tell the people at home what a really good time you've had and then who knows, perhaps they'll believe they've had a good one, too. And we'll get a second series after all. All right? So on my signal – we'll be going with the final music . . . In just a few seconds. (*Slight pause.*) I hope. (*Pause.*) Yes, here we go. (*He stands. He smiles at the audience. He gets the countdown from the gallery. He holds up his hand and counts down with his fingers, mouthing silently with this*) Five . . . four . . . three . . . two . . .

> *He starts the applause. The final credit music plays under this. The curtain call is taken. The actors leave the stage. The music stops.*

Thank you all very much indeed. Goodnight. Get home safely now. (*as he moves away from the floor*) Thank you very much, studio.

> *The stage lights snap off to be replaced with the house lights.*